The Broadcast
Century and Beyond

The Broadcast Century and Beyond

FIFTH EDITION

Robert L. Hilliard and Michael C. Keith

Focal Press
Taylor & Francis Group

NEW YORK AND LONDON

First published 2001
This edition published 2010 by Focal Press
70 Blanchard Road, Suite 402, Burlington, MA 01803

Simultaneously published in the UK by Focal Press
2 Park Square, Milton Park, Abingdon, Oxon OX14 4RN

Focal Press is an imprint of the Taylor & Francis Group, an informa business

Library of Congress Cataloging-in-Publication Data
Hilliard, Robert L., 1925-
   The broadcast century and beyond / Robert L. Hilliard, Michael C. Keith. – 5th ed.
      p. cm.
   Includes bibliographical references and index.
   ISBN 978-0-240-81236-6 (pbk. : alk. paper) 1. Broadcasting–United States–History. I. Keith, Michael C.,
1945- II. Title.
   PN1990.6.U5H48 2010
   384.54'0973–dc22   2009053962

ISBN 13: 978-0-240-81236-6 (pbk)

To Christina: Helping others find a better life through philanthropy of the self.
To David: Using the arts and media for people and peace.

—Robert Hilliard

To Norman Corwin: Whose words soar highest in the broadcast century.
—Michael Keith

CONTENTS

Please visit the companion website: www.focalpress.com/9780240812366 to find additional online resources.

As we write this, more than a century has passed since words and music were first sent successfully through the air and more than three quarters of a century since pictures were added to the words and music.

During the past century and into this new one, broadcasting and its related new and emerging media means of distribution have been both praised and vilified. They have been deserving of both: praised when they have fulfilled their potential and obligation to society by providing unbiased and stimulating ideas, information, and entertainment that mark and contribute to the progress and growth of humanity, but vilified when the ideological biases of their owners and/or operators supersede their objective responsibility and inculcate in their audiences partisan support of or opposition to economic, political, social, or environmental problems or needs that suit the media owners' rather than the public's interests.

Because the media are the most powerful forces in the world for influencing the minds, emotions, and, frequently, even the actions of humankind, we continue to attempt, in each succeeding edition of *The Broadcast Century* since it was first published in 1992, to relate the development of broadcasting and media to the political, economic, and social world they both reflect and affect. We recognize that the media (in many countries, radio and television alone) have awesome power—and responsibility.

We are patriotic enough to believe in the democratic principles of our country—that they are designed to serve the many, not the few. We have both served our country beyond our everyday commitments to make our democracy work for everyone, one of us in the combat infantry in World War II and the other also in the army, during the Vietnam War.

We are unabashedly prejudiced in that we agree with the Congress of the United States in its establishment of the law of the land that the airwaves belong to the people. We believe that broadcasting has a responsibility to serve the public interest, convenience, and necessity, as stated in the Communications Act of 1934. We do not hesitate to note when government, the broadcast industry, advertisers, or pressure groups have attempted to usurp the people's right to uncensored news and the highest quality of entertainment, culture, education, information, and all the other format content of which the media are capable.

When broadcasting is used to manipulate and control the public—as, for example, it has been used in our electoral system to promote political candidates it favors and ignore those it does not favor and by promoting "sound bites" instead of substance, thus creating its chosen candidates as frontrunners and winners—we have tried to show it.

In the ending chapter of this edition of *The Broadcast Century*—not the last or final chapter, of course, in broadcasting's continuing history—the chronology of events and practices in the media reveals one of our major concerns: that the democratic principle that the airwaves belong to the people is rapidly being eroded. The removal of restrictions on media monopolies by both major political parties in the United States has facilitated and encouraged conglomeration and consolidation that serve the rich and powerful at the expense of the not so rich and powerful, including those who own and operate media outlets; writers, producers, directors, performers, and technicians who work in the media; and the vast viewing and listening public. We try to note such trends, whether or not we step on the toes of the rich and powerful.

We praise the media when they present unbiased coverage of events that affect the lives of all people—events relating to war, terrorism, the environment, the economy, education, poverty, and other areas vital to our 21st century existence. We criticize the media when their personal vested interests distort the information they present to the public, whether through false, incomplete, or omitted reports. We believe our democracy can only survive through open truth, and we note without hesitation where the media have reported as truth the lies of high government officials, distorted the facts and figures of a shrinking economy and increasing unemployment, omitted information known by the rest of the world about war and terror, and helped cover up information about who knew what and when about corruption. These actions are taken to protect others in and out of politics who are, like the media moguls, also rich and powerful.

When we believe the principles of democracy are being served by the media, we do not hesitate to praise, and when we believe they are not being served, we do not hesitate to criticize—whether the subject is a producer, a pauper, or a President.

We have tried to provide an easily readable work for the student and the public alike, one that deals with the key issues, events, and people in the history of radio, television, and the newer media. We do not pretend to the erudition of Erik Barnouw's trilogy on broadcasting, *A Tower in Babel, The Golden Web*, and *The Image Empire*, nor to the volume of data and information in Christopher Sterling and John Michael Kittross's *Stay Tuned*. In relating the history of the media to the world in which it has developed and continues to grow, in this edition we have attempted to strengthen the timelines that parallel key events in given years in broadcasting and media and in the world at large. We have also continued with our use of "retro-boxes," which provide first-hand accounts from people involved in the past and present of broadcast history. We would like to express our special thanks to Clifford Kobland for his excellent sidebars in this new edition. His formidable effort greatly enhances the pedagogical value of our publication.

We are grateful to those broadcast pioneers and current practitioners who generously offered advice, information, and commentary, and it is to them that we also dedicate this book.

ROBERT L. HILLIARD AND MICHAEL C. KEITH

Chapter ONE

In the Beginning . . .

Genesis to 1920

In these early moments of the 21st century, we tend to be surprised from time to time when we read a current news story about a "broadcast pioneer" or hear a radio interview or see a television program with one of the men or women who were involved at the very beginning of broadcasting. For most people—that is, anyone under 75 years of age—radio seems to have been around forever. For people not yet 40, the same seems to be true for television. Many of us are sometimes startled to learn that the not-too-old-looking gray-headed person we have seen in a TV interview or met in person is a television pioneer.

But when we consider that the first radio station in the United States was licensed by the federal government in 1921 and full commercial television operation was authorized in 1941, we realize that broadcasting is, indeed, a 20th-century phenomenon.

Like all new inventions, however, neither radio nor television blossomed full grown out of the ether. As many inventors have said, they "stand on the shoulders" of those who preceded them. Each new discovery is based, either directly or indirectly, on previous work in a similar area of endeavor. Samuel F. B. Morse's wire telegraph in 1835 led to Alexander Graham Bell's wire telephone in 1875, which, in turn, set the stage for Guglielmo Marconi's wireless, or radio, telegraph in 1895. The next logical step was a wireless telephone.

No one knows for certain when the first human voice was communicated over the airwaves, but the predecessor of modern radio is frequently attributed to Reginald A. Fessenden's work in 1906, with an acknowledgment to Nathan B. Stubblefield's experimental transmissions as early as 1892. Finally, it took Lee de Forest's 1906 invention of the audion, a tube that could amplify the signal for distance broadcasting purposes, to make possible the development of radio as we know it today. De Forest is generally considered the "father" of American radio.

But even de Forest didn't do it alone. His successes were dependent on the earlier work of the American inventor Thomas Alva Edison and the English engineer Sir John A. Fleming, and on the efforts of dozens of other scientists—such as James Clerk Maxwell and Heinrich Hertz—before them. The groundwork for radio and television was laid in the 19th century.

DOI: 10.1016/B978-0-240-81236-6.00001-9

1794	**1835**	**1837**	**1844**	**1858**	**1864**
Claude Chappe develops the semaphore.	Samuel F. B. Morse invents the electromagnetic telegraph.	Philip Reis experiments with magnetism to generate sound emissions.	First telegraph circuit established between Baltimore and Washington.	Transatlantic telegraph cable links the United States with Europe.	James Clerk Maxwell theorizes the existence of electromagnetic waves.

Diffusion

Diffusion of innovations is a theory that deals with the how and why and the rate at which a new technology spreads. Of all the major communicative technologies, television was far and away the quickest to be adopted (that is, people actually purchasing the product); VCRs were the second fastest, while cable and the telephone have been among the slowest. Television was in over half of all U.S. households within some eight years of the generally accepted date of the birth of TV broadcasting. It took the VCR just a few years longer to reach that level. Radio was in half of U.S. homes some 12 years after the medium came of age in 1920. Once cable morphed from being simply a community television antenna into the form we know it today, it achieved majority penetration in about 20 years. Among the conditions that diffusion theory stipulates for adoption of a new technology include a cost assessment, its functionality and ease of use, and perhaps most important, hands-on demonstration. When Americans were able to share the enjoyment that their neighbors experienced from television, they immediately knew they wanted a set in their own home. Television had an advantage in that radio had created the form, conventions, and structure of an in-home commercial entertainment medium.

The Ancients to the 21st Century

There has always been a need for mass communication. When the first caveman or cavewoman danced the first dance, it was for the purpose of conveying an event, an idea, or a warning to a group of cave dwellers. Cave drawings, many of which are considered artistic, did not have "art for art's sake" as a purpose; they were meant to tell something to others. Distance communication to a group of people has been sought throughout history: fire and smoke signals, drums, sunlight reflection, musical instruments, gunfire. War has always been a progenitor of inventions for distance communication. The Argonauts conveyed messages from their ships by using different sail colors. Julius Caesar constructed high towers at intervals so that sentinels could shout messages along a route; some historians estimate that a communication passed along by this means could progress 150 miles in only a few hours.

The ancient Greeks developed a system of using flags to signal between ships. In medieval times, when gunpowder became a key ingredient of warfare, the number and frequency of cannon fire were translated into signals. When a town came under attack, the populace was warned through the ringing of bells. Trumpets were used as signals into the 20th century. The heliograph was used extensively for centuries, reflecting sunlight off a mirrored surface as far as seven miles.

1872	**1884**	**1887**	**1895**	**1897**	**1899**
Mahlon Loomis receives a patent for nonradiation wireless.	Paul Nipkow develops the mechanical scanning disk.	Heinrich Rudolf Hertz proves Maxwell's theory on the existence of radio waves.	Guglielmo Marconi sends and receives a radio signal.	Karl Ferdinand Braun produces a cathode ray oscilloscope.	Marconi sends a wireless signal across the English channel.

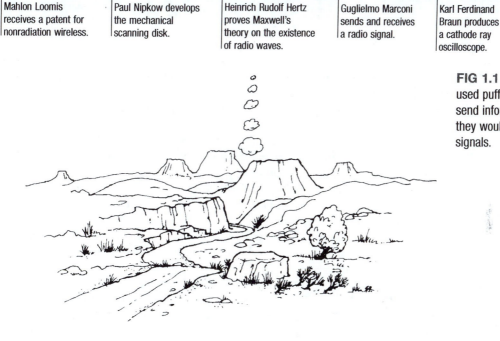

FIG 1.1 Native Americans used puffs of smoke to send information. Later they would use broadcast signals.

Native Americans used puffs of smoke during the day and torches and flaming arrows at night to send information. One of the most important preelectronic distance information systems was the semaphore, an ancient Roman device redeveloped by Claude Chappe in France in 1794; the French government erected towers five miles apart and placed huge cross arms at the top of each. The semaphore continued to be used even after the invention of the telegraph and telephone. In some parts of the world, carrier pigeons are still used as message carriers over long distances.

As early as 1267, the basic concept of using what we now know as electricity for conveying messages was suggested by the English philosopher Roger Bacon—who was promptly imprisoned for allegedly advocating "black magic." Three hundred years later, in Italy, Giovanni Battista della Porta was ridiculed after writing a book on "natural magic" in which he proposed that magnetism could be used to transmit information. It wasn't until the late 18th century that the notion of electricity as a useful tool was accepted, due to such inventions as the Leyden jar and to Benjamin Franklin's experiments with lightning. The late 18th and early 19th centuries saw seminal discoveries in the nature of electricity by physicists all over the world, including Michael Faraday in England, André Ampère in France, George Ohm in Germany, and Count Alessandro Volta in Italy. The last three names are immortalized as standard terms for electrical functions today.

Samuel F. B. Morse's invention of the electromagnetic telegraph in 1835 opened the door to the distance communications of today. It took six years of struggle and rejection, however, before a grant from Congress in 1841 to run a telegraph line between Washington, D.C., and Baltimore established the acceptance of the telegraph. Its success in conveying the results of the Democratic National Convention in 1844

The United States opens the door to China.	Movie "peep shows" become viewing rooms.	William McKinley retains the Presidency.	First Nobel Prizes are awarded.	President McKinley assassinated; Theodore Roosevelt succeeds him.

1900 **1901**

| The word *television* is first used, in France. | | Reginald Fessenden uses a spark generator to send human voice. | | Russian scientist, Constantin Perskyi, coins term television. |

enabled Morse to raise enough private funds to extend the telegraph to Philadelphia and New York, and within a few years telegraph systems had been constructed in other parts of the country. In 1861 Western Union built the first transcontinental telegraph line. During this same period, in 1842, Morse proved that distant signals could be sent underwater as well, and in 1866, after a number of unsuccessful tries, Cyrus W. Field established a transatlantic underwater cable between Europe and the United States, linked in Newfoundland.

The importance of these new techniques for distance communication was reflected in the U.S. government's assumption of regulatory powers. The Post Roads Act of 1866 authorized the postmaster general to fix rates annually for telegrams sent by the government. In 1887 the government authorized the Interstate Commerce Commission (ICC) to require telegraph companies to interconnect their lines for more extended public service.

The transmission of voice messages by wire—as differentiated from the "dit-dah" signals of the telegraph—did not come about until 1876, when Alexander Graham Bell was credited with the invention of the telephone when, on March 10, he uttered these famous words over a wire to an associate: "Mr. Watson, come here. I want to see you." The first regular telephone line was constructed in 1877, between Boston and Somerville, Massachusetts.

But even the great Bell stood on the shoulders of those who came before. Decades earlier, scientists such as G. G. Page, Charles Borseul, and Philip Reis were experimenting with the electromagnetic transmission of sound. In 1837, for example, Reis discovered that the magnetization and demagnetization of an iron bar could cause the emission of sounds. Some historians credit Reis with the initial development of the principle of the telephone. With the founding of the Bell Telephone Company in 1878 and the incorporation of the American Telephone and Telegraph Company (AT&T) in 1885, the growth of distance communication in the United States was assured.

Yet the telephone was not immediately praised or even accepted. Just as with later inventions, such as television, the telephone created nightmare visions of control of the masses and invasions of privacy. A cartoon in the *New York Daily Graphic* of March 15, 1877, for example, illustrated what the artist called the "terrors of the telephone" by showing a speaker at a telephone-like device mesmerizing masses of people listening simultaneously throughout the world. Of course, the opposite was also present: cartoons, articles, and even popular songs lauded the potential wonders of the telephone, including the distance dissemination to mass audiences of music, information, drama, and education, precisely what radio broadcasting was initially lauded for when it began. In fact, in 1881 a French engineer, Clément Ader, filed a patent for "Improvements of Telephone Equipment in Theaters" for the purpose of putting telephones on theater stages so that subscribers could hear the performances at home. Ader's Paris Opera Experiment was an example of wired broadcast transmission.

| Picasso's first Paris exhibit. | American Automobile Association founded. | Peasant uprisings in Russia. | Boston beats Pittsburgh in the first World Series. |

1902
1903

| Marconi sends a wireless signal across the Atlantic. | Fessenden develops a continuous-wave (electrolytic) detector. |

IN THE BEGINNING . . . .

Even before wired voice transmission came into use, scientists were seeking means of wireless transmission. In 1864 a Scottish physicist, James Clerk Maxwell, predicted the existence of radio waves—that is, waves on which communication signals could be carried, similar to the signals that could be carried over telegraph wires.

This area of study became known as *electromagnetic theory*. As early as 1872, a patent for nonradiation wireless was obtained in the United States by Mahlon Loomis, and in that same decade William Cookes developed the first cathode ray tube. But actual distance transmission still hadn't been invented. In 1887 theory turned into reality when a German physicist, Heinrich Rudolf Hertz, projected rapid variations of electric current into space in the form of radio waves, similar to those of light and heat. In 1892 he sent electric waves around an oscillating (regularly fluctuating) circuit. So important were Hertz's contributions that his name has been adopted as the measure of all radio frequencies.

Although aural transmission was still being perfected, even back in the 1880s scientists were experimenting with visual transmission potentials that 40 years later would turn into television. In 1880 a Frenchman, Maurice Lablance, developed the principle of *scanning*, in which an image is converted to electric signals by a line-by-line registration of its features. This principle would become the basis for video technology. A German scientist, Paul Nipkow, implemented this principle in 1884 by designing the first mechanical scanning disk. Before the end of the century, in 1897, the German physicist Karl Ferdinand Braun produced a cathode ray oscilloscope that could visually observe electric signals—but that would take a backseat to radio.

It is the Italian inventor Guglielmo Marconi who is credited with the first successful demonstration of the wireless, or radio, telegraph. In 1895 he sent and received a radio signal and in 1899 showed that it could be done at a distance, across the English Channel. Later that year Marconi came to the United States to report the America's Cup yacht race by wireless for the *New York Herald*; while in the States he formed the American Marconi Telegraph Company, which would later prove to be a key power in the establishment of radio stations. That same year, 1899, the U.S. Navy tried out wireless communication.

During the same period, an immigrant to the United States from Serbia, Nikola Tesla, invented the system of alternating current and experimented with various forms of wireless transmission. One of the world's greatest inventors in the last of the 19th century and in the early 20th century, he has been largely neglected by historians. In fact, Marconi received the Nobel Prize for an invention that appeared to be adapted directly from a prior Tesla invention. Eventually, in 1943, Tesla was legally recognized as the inventor of radio transmission, his early patents given precedence over Marconi's.

FIG 1.2 James Clerk Maxwell theorized the existence of electromagnetic waves. *Courtesy David Sarnoff Library.*

| Russians massacre Jews, Bulgarians massacre Moslems, Turks massacre Bulgarians. | The Wright brothers' first flight. | Department of Commerce and Labor established. | Roosevelt elected to full term as President. |

1904

Sir John A. Fleming invents the diode tube.

Radio broadcasting, however, was still some years off. As noted earlier, some attribute the first wireless transmission of a human voice to the inventor Nathan B. Stubblefield, who in 1892 spoke the words "Hello, Rainey" to an assistant a distance away in an experiment near the town of Murray, Kentucky. Yet the basis for AM radio is the electron tube, and it is generally assumed that at the time of Stubblefield's experiments it had not yet been invented, and that Stubblefield used both induction and conduction at very low frequencies. Although in 1883 Thomas Alva Edison had observed the emission of electrons from a heated surface, such as a tube's cathode, the discovery of the electron is credited to the British researcher Sir J. J. Thomson for a series of experiments he conducted in the 1890s. Nevertheless, further steps, specifically an electron tube and amplification, were necessary before the electron could be used for broadcasting. Sir John A. Fleming and Lee de Forest took those steps some years later. De Forest, noted earlier as the father of American radio, presaged the future as the 19th century came to an end. In 1899, in his doctoral dissertation at Yale University, de Forest wrote on the spread of the radio waves discovered in the preceding decade by Heinrich Hertz. It took yet another decade to enter the Broadcast Century.

FIG 1.3 Guglielmo Marconi was the first to successfully demonstrate the wireless telegraph. *Courtesy RCA.*

| St. Louis World's Fair. Lynching of Negroes in the United States increases. | Japan attacks Russia. | First U.S. film theater opens. | *Potemkin* mutiny as czar massacres protesters. | San Francisco earthquake. |

1905   **1906**

Lee de Forest creates the audion tube.

IN THE BEGINNING . . .

The First Decade, 1900–1909: The Wireless Arrives

The first decade of the 20th century saw a rapid advancement in the inventions, business organization, university experiments, and citizen interest required to make radio a reality. Several names—Fessenden, de Forest, Fleming, and Marconi—were principally responsible for the development of broadcast radio before the end of the decade.

At the same time that a Canadian, Reginald A. Fessenden—who was later to be credited with the first true radio broadcast—was working for the U.S. Weather Bureau to experiment with disseminating weather information by wireless, Marconi was setting up an experiment that would earn worldwide headlines and become a significant spur to further radio development. In 1901 Marconi and his assistant, George Kemp, listened to a telephone receiver on top of a hill in Saint John's, Newfoundland, and heard the Morse code signal of three dots, for the letter *S*, which was being transmitted from Cornwall, England, more than 2,000 miles away. That same year the U.S. Navy, influenced by Marconi's previous successes, replaced its visual signaling and homing pigeons with the wireless telegraph. Other U.S. government agencies, including the Army and the Department of Agriculture, conducted experimental operations with wireless.

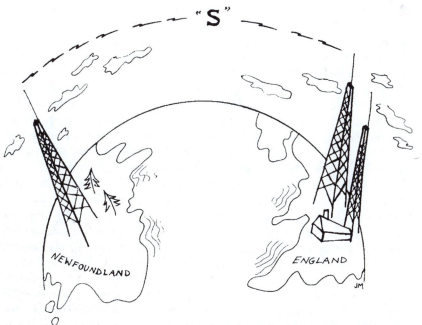

FIG 1.4 Marconi's wireless audio crosses the Atlantic in 1901.

Pure Food and Drug
Act enacted.

Captain Alfred Dreyfus
exonerated.

United Press news
agency formed.

1907

German Professor Alfred Korn
sends first pictures by telegraph.

Crystal detector for radio
circuits is developed.

Fessenden sends voice
and music over the
wireless.

FIG 1.5 John Ambrose Fleming, developer of the diode tube.

Ships of various nations adopted the wireless, and its success at protecting life and property became so widespread throughout the world that in 1903 an international conference was held in Berlin to discuss common distress-call signs for ships and to promote wireless communication between ship and shore—which was not yet in practice—as well as between ships. A few years later the international distress signal, SOS, was adopted and remains in use today.

The next goal was to transmit the human voice comparable distances over the wireless. Both de Forest and Fessenden were confident that it was possible to do so. In 1902 each established a communications business: Fessenden's National Electric Signaling Company and de Forest's Wireless Telegraph Company. Fessenden believed it was necessary to go beyond Marconi's basic approach, and instead of a wave interrupted with intermittent impositions, he advocated a continuous wave on which modulations would be superimposed. He had demonstrated in 1901 that it could be done, and in 1902 he developed an electrolytic detector. Two years later, in England, the engineer Sir John A. Fleming developed the glass-bulb detector, which was a simple electron tube, a diode, that was necessary to receive voice signals. But the diode couldn't amplify the electronic signals.

Other experimenters were engaged by the wireless. A professor at the University of Graz in Austria, Otto Nussbaumer, was doing almost the same thing as Fessenden and Fleming. He invented a detector circuit that peeled off the sound at the receiving end, enabling him to send sounds rather than just dots and dashes. Using an experimental transmitter, he yodeled an Austrian folk song that was heard in the next room, ostensibly the first "music" ever transmitted by wireless. But he, too, lacked the means for amplification necessary for true broadcasting.

De Forest took the next step. He added a third element, or grid, to the Fleming vacuum tube and in 1906 filed a patent for his tube, calling it the *audion*. This "triode" tube enabled the signal to be amplified, making possible distant voice transmission over the wireless, and ushered in the age of radio. The following year, de Forest formed the de Forest Radio Telephone Company, which began broadcasting in New York. An entry in his diary that year stated: "My present task is to distribute sweet melody broadcast over the city and sea so that in time even the marine far out across the silent waves may hear the music of his homeland."[1]

But Fessenden had already beaten de Forest to it. Thanks to a high-frequency alternator, on Christmas Eve in 1906 radio operators on ships in the Atlantic Ocean hundreds of miles off the U.S. coast heard something unprecedented on their earphone receivers: a person speaking, then a woman singing, then someone reading a poem, followed by a violin solo and verses from the Bible. Imagine the surprise of the

[1] Wireless transmissions were enhanced using a device called the *high-frequency arc* (also know as the *Poulsen arc*). The early experiments of de Forest and, to some extent, others were significantly aided by this innovation.

| Cubist art born. | Arturo Toscanini makes U.S. debut. | Ford's Model T makes its debut. | William Howard Taft elected President. |

1908

The word *television* is used for the first time in a scientific magazine.

De Forest broadcasts from the Eiffel Tower.

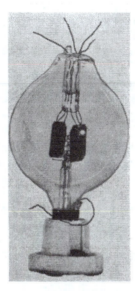

FIG 1.6 The de Forest audion tube made radio broadcasting possible.

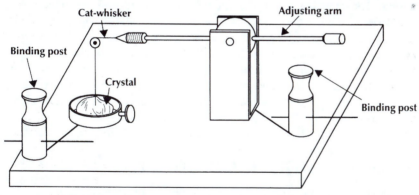

Cat-whisker

Adjusting arm

Binding post

Crystal

Binding post

FIG 1.7 Diagram showing the construction of a typical crystal detector of the 1920s.

wireless operators, accustomed as they were to the familiar click and clack of the telegraph, when they heard voices and music emanating from their receiving apparatus. Transmitting from Brant Rock, Massachusetts, Fessenden himself played the violin and read from the Bible. He ended by wishing his audience a Merry Christmas and promising to broadcast again on New Year's Eve. This was the first distance radio broadcast.

De Forest, however, ultimately got the most acclaim. Before the decade ended, he had established himself as the foremost practitioner of radio. In 1908 he and his wife, Nora Blatch, broadcast from the Eiffel Tower in Paris and were heard as far as

Admiral Robert Peary reaches the North Pole.

Louis Blériot makes first English channel airplane crossing.

NAACP founded.

Edison demonstrates first talking pictures.

1909

1910

Charles D. "Doc" Herrold launches the country's oldest station in San Jose, California.

The Wireless Ship Act of 1910 is the first legislation dealing with radio.

500 miles away using a high-frequency arc, not a vacuum tube. They returned to the United States as celebrities. Technically, reasons had been established for stations to begin surfacing around the country, although the apparatus of the medium had not yet fully evolved.

But distance broadcasting was not yet to be. First, where would the backing come from to set up stations, transmitters, and necessary equipment? It would be more than a dozen years before the concept of advertising would establish the economic base for broadcasting.

Second, what would be the purpose of a radio station except for experimental purposes? Who would listen? The general public had no receivers, although there was growing interest by citizens who began to seek transmissions from the experimental stations through homemade crystal detectors that had been developed in 1906. Three entities were most interested in radio: the pioneers, who wanted to see their inventions reach their ultimate potentials; physics, engineering, and other science departments in colleges and universities, which added the study of this new electronic phenomenon to their courses; and the maritime service, through which radio received its greatest boost in the early years of the next decade.

Two significant events occurred in 1909. First, a steamship, the SS *Republic*, sank after a collision at sea, but most of the people on board were saved with the help of the wireless. Second, Charles D. "Doc" Herrold, an engineer who had been involved in some of the early experiments with radio transmission, and his wife, Sybil, began broadcasting over a transmitter he had built in San Jose, California. Although some historians say that Herrold's station, ultimately called KQW, is the country's oldest, it did not broadcast to the general public on a regular schedule; that designation is acknowledged to belong to KDKA in Pittsburgh, which began doing so more than a decade later.

The Second Decade, 1910–1919: Toward the Radio Music Box

Few new inventions have taken as much time as radio to become exploited or made available to the general public. Despite the fact that by 1910 the technical development of radio was nearly advanced enough to warrant the establishment of stations nationwide, it didn't happen then. For one thing, the medium still lacked a fully developed vacuum tube. For another, many people continued to think of radio primarily for point-to-point information exchange, and general understanding of its value for broader purposes took a little more time. Perhaps the continuing preparation during this decade guaranteed radio's immediate success when regular broadcasting finally began in 1920. Throughout the decade, innovative applications of wireless voice distance transmission added more and more proof of radio's potential.

Carnegie Endowment for International Peace formed.	Amundsen reaches South Pole.	Marie Curie wins Nobel Prize.		

1911   **1912**

Radio amateurs build receivers.

Titanic sinking demonstrates importance of the wireless as hundreds are saved when distress signals are received by area ships.

It was de Forest who began the decade with the most dramatic demonstration. Building on Clément Ader's attempt at the Paris Opera almost 30 years before, de Forest hung a microphone over the stage of New York's Metropolitan Opera House, set up his arc transmitter backstage, and strung an antenna on the roof, using a long fishing pole as a mast. Because few individual members of the public had radio sets, de Forest put receivers in several public locations in New York. Although, as the

FIG 1.8 Radio pioneer Lee de Forest sends a message over his wireless apparatus, a radiotelephone.
Courtesy Smithsonian Institution.

Woodrow Wilson elected President.	Lenin and Stalin join forces.	Niels Bohr propounds atomic theory.

1913

Inspired in part by the dramatic role of the wireless during the *Titanic* disaster, Congress enacts the Radio Act of 1912.		Sybil Herrold becomes first female deejay.

New York Times reported, interference "kept the homeless song waves from finding themselves," the experiment was considered successful. Some people at various distances had heard parts of *Cavalleria Rusticana* and *Pagliacci* with the voices of Emmy Dustin and Enrico Caruso, the latter the greatest singer of the time and arguably of all time. This event further spurred the interest of budding engineers and amateurs in radio and whetted the public appetite for what could come.

Only two suppliers were making radio parts available, but nonprofessionals bought tubes, transmitters, and antennas and began sending out signals. Radio was an oddity—to some, equivalent to a circus sideshow—and in fact wireless demonstrations became sideshow attractions at fairgrounds. Department stores, as a means of attracting customers, had radio demonstrations. Radio was a toy, a hobby, and amateurs soon found that in some areas there were so many signals that they were interfering with one another.

Governments realized the significance of the new device and understood the value of wireless radio for health and safety. Its use in the maritime services had resulted in several international conferences to establish common practices, but because the United States had not yet become a signatory to the agreements of a second Berlin conference—held in London in 1906, following the first one in 1903—the international community withdrew an invitation for the United States to attend the third conference, scheduled for 1912. Congress then quickly enacted the Wireless Ship Act of 1910, the first legislation dealing with radio, which adopted the international regulations.

Two years later, the tragedy of the *Titanic* emphasized the importance of wireless radio. Although the luxury liner had received wireless warnings that icebergs were in its path, its radio operator refused to heed the warnings, telling the other operators to clear the air so that he could complete sending personal

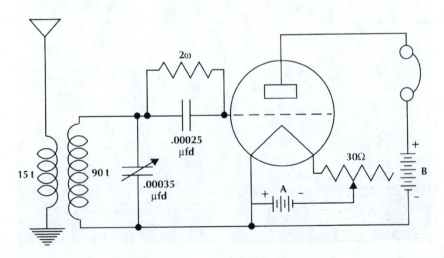

FIG 1.9 Diagram of a detector, serving as an element in a 1911 receiving set.

| U.S. income tax established. | Mahatma Gandhi's arrest and jailing—first of many. | World War I begins. Panama Canal opened. |

1914

| Edwin H. Armstrong develops the regenerative circuit. | Patent wars begin. |

messages from the ship's passengers to Europe and America. After the *Titanic* hit an iceberg and began to sink, SOS signals were sent; however, most operators on nearby ships had gone off watch, and only the *Carpathia* responded to the SOS and saved many lives.

The *Titanic* disaster proved once and for all the worth of wireless radio for safety purposes. As the now disputed legend has it, it also provided a young wireless operator at the Wanamaker Department Store in New York with the publicity and impetus to later mold American broadcasting into his vision. Legend has it that 21-year-old David Sarnoff picked up a signal that the *Titanic* had run into an iceberg and that he stayed on duty for 72 hours, informing authorities and passengers' families and friends of what was occurring. Although it is generally accepted that once Sarnoff learned of the disaster, he did stay at the Wanamaker store wireless for three days, there is some question as to when and how he heard of the sinking, inasmuch as it happened after the store had been closed for the day and took place more than 1,000 miles away, beyond the accepted range of radio signals at the time.

Nevertheless, Sarnoff was able to follow up on the publicity he received and became a pioneer and a leader in the growth of the new medium.

FIG 1.10 The wireless helps save lives and makes the front page. *Courtesy The New York Times.*

| Federal Trade Commission established. | Transcontinental telephone service begins. | Albert Einsten sets forth theory of relativity. | Germany sinks *Lusitania*. |

1915

| American Radio Relay League formed. | American Society of Composers, Authors, and Publishers (ASCAP) founded. |

On the governmental side, the Berlin International Radio Telegraphic Convention met in London that year, 1912, and enacted regulations to further wireless conformity and compatibility, including the assignment of call letters for radio stations and the establishment of radio regulations by each signatory country. To comply, the United States enacted the Radio Act of 1912, generally considered to be the forerunner of later regulatory acts—the Radio Act of 1927 and the Communications Act of 1934. Many consider it to be the first law in this country—the 1910 Wireless Ship Act notwithstanding—to regulate radio communications. The Radio Act of 1912 dealt with the character of emissions and the transmission of distress calls, set aside certain frequencies for government use, and established licensing of wireless stations and operators, placing implementation under the Secretary of Commerce and Labor. The act stated, in part,

> that a person, company or corporation within the jurisdiction of the United States shall not use or operate any apparatus for radio communication . . . except under and in accordance with a license . . . granted by the Secretary of Commerce and Labor . . . that every such license shall be in such form as the Secretary . . . shall determine and shall contain restrictions . . . that every such license shall be issued only to citizens of the United States . . . shall specify the ownership and location of the station . . . to enable its range to be estimated . . . shall state the purpose of the station . . . shall state the wavelength . . . authorized for use by the station for the prevention of interference and the hours for which the station is licensed to work.

The science and business of radio developed simultaneously. In 1913 a young radio amateur, Edwin H. Armstrong, developed a feedback, or regenerative, circuit that greatly increased amplification; he patented the circuit the following year. (Years later, Armstrong would become better known as the inventor of frequency modulation, or FM, radio.) At the same time, the infamous radio "patent wars" were beginning. In 1913 AT&T, seeking to establish a wireless monopoly, began to buy up some of de Forest's patents. In 1914 the Marconi Wireless Telegraph Company sued the De Forest Radio Telephone Company over rights to the audion tube. Elements of the device—incorporating discoveries by Edison, Fleming, and de Forest—were partly owned by both companies. A court decision in 1916 left neither of the then-principal litigants, Marconi and AT&T, in control of the audion. Even the new Armstrong regenerative circuit patent was challenged—by de Forest. Patent litigation served to tie up the development of radio for years.

Engineering achievements, however, moved on. In 1915 AT&T transmitted the human voice across the continent for the first time, using repeater stations between New York and San Francisco, generating sound waves through small equipment at

Italy declares war on Germany.

1916

| A powerful wireless alternator is designed by Ernest F. W. Alexanderson. | Theatre Guild, Neighborhood Playhouse, and Provincetown Players established. | ASCAP music licensing service is formed. | Voices broadcast across the Atlantic. |

each repeater site. That same year speech was sent across the ocean from Arlington, Virginia, to the Eiffel Tower in Paris. De Forest demonstrated radio at the San Francisco World's Fair, receiving broadcasts from "Doc" Herrold's station in San Jose, albeit a short distance in communication today but impressive at the time. At the General Electric Company, a scientist named Ernest F. W. Alexanderson perfected an alternator that considerably improved the quality and reach of the radio signal, and the Marconi Company, in an attempt to expand its dominant role in radio, immediately began negotiations for the purchase of Alexanderson alternators.

While all this was happening, a development in the music field indicated perhaps more than anything else the kind of growth and programming radio would have. Musicians and music publishers were becoming concerned about the use of music on the new experimental radio stations without compensation to the music's creators. Thus, they organized into the American Society of Composers, Authors, and Publishers (ASCAP) to protect their creative works. It was to counter ASCAP that the National Association of Broadcasters (NAB) was formed less than a decade later. Both organizations continue to play key roles in broadcasting today.

Professors and students in physics and engineering departments of colleges and universities broadcast informal programs as practical applications of their principal study, electronic theory. Their work took on a pragmatic approach: Who was interested in information that could be received over a radio set? The most significant broadcasts were from Midwestern universities to farmers, providing reports from time to time on weather conditions, crops, producer prices, Department of Agriculture advisories, and other things that an isolated farmer might otherwise have to wait days to learn. Such broadcasts grew throughout the decade, resulting in many of the regularly scheduled stations in the early 1920s being licensed to colleges and universities.

In 1916 de Forest further demonstrated the future of radio by broadcasting music and Presidential election returns from New York, spurring the public's increasing interest. Parenthetically, his election broadcast is most remembered because he misinterpreted the returns and declared Charles Evans Hughes, rather than Woodrow Wilson, the winner.

A memorandum purportedly discovered in the back of a desk at the National Broadcasting Company (NBC) 30 years later might have considerably speeded the development of radio had it not been allegedly pigeonholed by the officials of the Marconi Company. David Sarnoff, then the commercial manager for the American Marconi Company, wrote to his general manager, Edward J. Nally, that the company should market a "radio music box." He advocated the development of a plan that would make "radio a 'household utility' in the same sense as the piano or phonograph."

Margaret Sanger opens first
birth control clinic.

President Wilson
reelected.

David Sarnoff supposedly
writes the "radio music
box" memo.

De Forest broadcasts the
Presidential election returns.

The memorandum is a most accurate prognostication of what could have happened, and did happen, to radio. Some cynics have wondered why the memo remained unknown for so many years, even during Sarnoff's reign over the Radio Corporation of America (RCA) and NBC, before it was discovered.[2]

DAVID SARNOFF

CHAIRMAN OF THE BOARD, RCA

I have in mind a plan of development which would make radio a household utility. The idea is to bring music into the home by wireless. The receiver can be designed in the form of a simple "radio music box," placed on a table in the parlor or living room, and arranged for several different wavelengths which should be changeable with the throwing of a signal switch or the pressing of a single button. The same principle can be extended to numerous other fields, as for example, receiving lectures at home which would be perfectly audible. Also, events of national importance can be simultaneously announced and received. Baseball scores can be transmitted in the air. This proposition would be especially interesting to farmers and others living in outlying districts.

Sarnoff's "radio music box" memo, sent to the management of the American Marconi Company in 1916. Recently, some scholars have questioned the existence of this memo, suggesting that it was written years later to enhance Sarnoff's status in radio history.

FIG 1.11 An older Sarnoff as chairman of RCA.
Courtesy RCA.

[2] Recent scholars have concluded that the memo was likely composed long after radio had entered the home. Documents at the Smithsonian, according to Elliot Sivowitch, appear to support the existence of a 1916 radio music box demo by Sarnoff. The debate continues.

| Child Labor law passed. | United States enters war in Europe. | Russian Revolution. |

1917

All radio equipment is appropriated by the U.S. Navy due to World War I.

Sarnoff's Music Box Memo

While controversy still swirls over whether Sarnoff was so prophetic as to envision, in his 1916 "musicbox memo," how radio could become a viable medium, there may be some clues in the document that confirm the accuracy of the date. Sarnoff possessed an enormous ego and a tendency toward self-aggrandizement, qualities that served him well throughout his stewardship of RCA and NBC. Returning to the corporation following his Army service in WWII, during which he rose to the rank of general, he insisted that his underlings address him as "General" Sarnoff. Considering these traits, one would expect that if the memo was penned after radio had become a commercial success, Sarnoff would have constructed it to confirm his prescience. Yet the document contains some glaring errors that simply do not stack up when measured against Sarnoff's quest for self-glorification. For one, it grossly underestimates the speed in which the public would buy a radio, forecasting a 7% penetration into American homes when in reality it was in the 20% range by the mid-1920s. For another, it proposed the financing of broadcasting through receiver sales, an idea that had proved totally impractical very early on. If Sarnoff had indeed post-dated the memo, one would expect that he would have avoided such mistakes.

Not only did the patent wars continue to delay the full arrival of radio, but the war in Europe also intervened. When the United States entered World War I in 1917, all radio equipment, both commercial and amateur, was either sealed or appropriated by the U.S. Navy. From August 1, 1918, to July 31, 1919—even after the war was over— the government ordered federal control over telephone and telegraph communications as a war measure. In one sense, this action preempted the civilian development of radio; in another sense, scientists and engineers working for the government were able to have the resources and equipment to refine the technical aspects of radio. Interestingly enough, radio was not used by the armed forces for battle purposes as much as one might presume. It was tried out primarily for airplane-to-ground communications. On the home front, however, the government ensured the future of radio by establishing radio schools to train personnel for federal positions, and in 1917 it built three high-powered wireless transmitters designed to cover the South Pacific—at Pearl Harbor, Hawaii; at San Diego; and at Cavite in the Philippines. Another war occurrence resulted in a further significant step forward for radio. In 1918 the cutting of transatlantic cables by the German enemy limited messages between the United States and Europe. Utilizing the Alexanderson alternator to generate unprecedented high power, the United States was able to communicate with the American Expeditionary Forces and their allies through wireless telegraphy. The Alexanderson alternator helped President Wilson use radio to speed the peace process by enabling him to send, by Morse code directly from New Jersey to Europe, his famous "Fourteen Points."

| World War I ends. | World flu epidemic eventually kills 22 million. | Daylight Savings Time instituted. | Mussolini founds fascist organization in Italy. |

1918
1919

Armstrong invents the superheterodyne radio system.

After federal control expired in July 1919, private activity in radio resumed more strongly than ever. Although the navy attempted to retain permanent control over all radio use in the United States, Congress prevented it from doing so. Literally thousands of licenses were issued by the Secretary of Commerce for amateur and experimental radio stations.

The same names continued their leadership in the field, although it was clear that de Forest was being squeezed out by the Marconi Company and AT&T. Patent struggles and inventions continued apace. In 1918 Edwin Armstrong invented one of the most important wireless technological advancements, the superheterodyne system, and the British Marconi Company renewed its negotiations with General Electric (GE) to buy the Alexanderson alternator. This set the stage for the emergence, at the end of the decade, of media giants that for years to come would do battle to dominate radio.

The Department of the Navy and many members of Congress were concerned about the possible sale of the Alexanderson alternator, fearing that a foreign organization might then gain considerable control over U.S. communications facilities. At the government's urging, General Electric (GE) arranged through its chief attorney, Owen D. Young, to give British Marconi the rights to use the Alexanderson alternator in

FIG 1.12 This became RCA's world-famous trademark: "His Master's Voice."
Courtesy RCA.

Treaty of Versailles.	"Black Sox" baseball scandal.	Chicago race riots.

General Electric acquires the assets of the American Marconi Company.	RCA is formed by General Electric.	Vladimir Zworykin conducts television experiments at the Westinghouse Company.

Britain in exchange for GE's purchase of the American Marconi Company, thereby expanding GE's communication power, including ownership of a number of maritime and international stations. GE, however, was interested in manufacturing equipment, not operating stations, and it formed RCA to do the latter. GE officers Owen D. Young, Edward J. Nally, and—yes—David Sarnoff became, respectively, chairman of the board, president, and commercial manager of RCA. It wasn't long before RCA became a principal player in the new radio game, joining a patent pool with GE and AT&T to square off against another major player, Westinghouse.

By the end of the 1910 decade, there were some 20,000 or more amateur radio participants. Some 8,500 had licenses to operate their experimental sets, and they were poised to provide the talent for the new medium.

While the birth of modern radio was about to take place, work on a new medium, television, had already begun. One of its key participants, Vladimir Zworykin, arrived in the United States in 1919, having worked with an early television experimenter, Boris Rosing, at the Saint Petersburg Technological Institute in Russia. Within a year he would be working at Westinghouse, where he began some of the leading TV experiments in the United States.

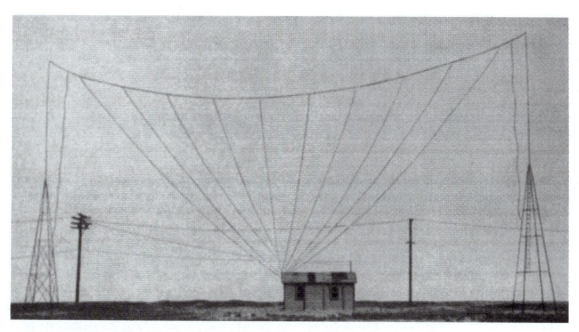

FIG 1.13 Wireless station and antenna site, circa 1919.
Courtesy Zenith.

FIG 1.14 Charles "Doc" Herrold.
Courtesy of Mike Adams.

Charles "Doc" Herrold of San Jose, California, is an obscure broadcasting pioneer whose most important work took place between 1912 and 1917. Although today most historians believe Herrold's claim that he was the first to broadcast radio entertainment and information for an audience on a regularly scheduled, preannounced basis, he is dismissed as a minor figure because he didn't have a long-lasting impact on the industry. Herrold can be compared to many of the modern-day Internet pioneers: an innovator with new, even revolutionary, ideas, but suffering from bad timing. Herrold arrived on the scene too soon.

The first evidence of Herrold's use of a crude radiotelephone to "broadcast" to an audience is found in his own 1910 published statement: "We have been giving wireless photograph concerts to amateur men in the Santa Clara Valley." Between 1912 and 1917 he operated a radio station, on the air every day, programming music and talk for an audience. That he accidentally stumbled onto what today we recognize as radio broadcasting may have evolved out of his role as the headmaster of a wireless trade school. Former students told of broadcasting the popular music of the day to an audience of friends and families, very much like college radio today.

Chapter TWO

The Roaring, '2Os

Promise, Chaos, and Controls

In 1920 radio finally came of age. On November 2 station 8XK in Pittsburgh (a special Conrad land station), later KDKA, broadcast the election returns of the Harding/Cox Presidential race and continued its broadcasting thereafter with regularly scheduled programs. Although KDKA is given credit for being the first station on the air to employ a regular schedule of programs, "Doc" Herrold's San Jose, California, station, ultimately called KQW, which started broadcasting in 1909, did provide a schedule in 1912 to amateurs who had built sets to listen, and music was being broadcast regularly from station 2ZK in New York in 1916. In Detroit William E. Scripps, publisher of the *Detroit News*, was conducting experimental broadcasting over station 8MK from his office months before KDKA started. At the University of Wisconsin, Professor Earle M. Terry, who had experimented with voice broadcasts using vacuum tubes during World War I, was by 1920 broadcasting weather forecasts every day. Although some historians credit the University of Wisconsin station, 9XM, which became WHA, with being the first station on the air, it was Terry himself who gave the credit to KDKA.

With so many stations doing earlier some of the things KDKA did in 1920, why is the Pittsburgh station now considered the first regularly scheduled broadcast facility? In part because it was the first one to reach the general public with continuing programming. The other stations reached mostly amateurs on an experimental basis. Before KDKA made its debut, it promoted the purchase of radio receivers among the public, and to be sure that at least some members of the public at large would hear its broadcast, the station's owner, the Westinghouse Electric and Manufacturing Company of Pittsburgh, bought receivers for some employees, executives, and their friends. In addition, Westinghouse arranged for two of Pittsburgh's leading newspapers, the *Post* and the *Sun*, to carry its program schedule. Although as few as 100 people might have heard the first broadcast, they were members of the general public as well as amateur experimenters and were scattered throughout Pennsylvania and even in the states of Ohio and West Virginia.

KDKA and the birth of broadcasting are synonymous with the name Dr. Frank Conrad, Westinghouse's assistant chief engineer, who for some years had been operating an experimental station, 8XK, out of his garage. During World War I his station

© 2010 Taylor & Francis. All rights reserved.
DOI: 10.1016/B978-0-240-81236-6.00002-0

Prohibition amendment passed.		Women vote for the first time in national elections.	

1920

Regularly scheduled programs are offered by KDKA.	AT&T joins cross-licensing pact with GE and RCA.

FIG 2.1 Site of many of Dr. Frank Conrad's early experiments that led to KDKA.
Courtesy Westinghouse.

tested military equipment built by Westinghouse. After the war he even began to inform other amateurs—his listeners—of broadcasts in advance. Conrad's work and the competition of the then media giants for control of radio resulted in the founding of KDKA.

Westinghouse's vice president, Harry P. Davis, had earlier that year established an agreement with the International Radio and Telegraph Company to try to compete with AT&T and the newly formed RCA and continued to buy as many patents as possible from Fessenden and Armstrong, including the latter's superheterodyne circuit, which greatly improved amplification.

To overpower other competitors and avoid a debilitating fight between themselves, AT&T and RCA joined forces and, with GE, signed a cross-licensing agreement for the patents they controlled. When a department store advertised "amateur wireless sets" for $10 in the *Pittsburgh Press*, citing Conrad's home-station broadcasts as an inducement, Westinghouse's Davis saw the opportunity for Westinghouse to enter broadcasting, enhance its image vis-à-vis its competition, and promote the marketing of the receivers it built. It had Conrad construct a more powerful transmitter than that of 8XK, which actually went on the air at the company's East Pittsburgh plant with test programs a week before its broadcast of the election results.

FIG 2.2 Conrad at the workbench of his station, KDKA.
Courtesy Westinghouse.

Because the experience at KDKA was duplicated to a greater or lesser degree by so many of the stations that followed it, it is worth noting several other aspects of KDKA's beginnings. Conrad, as announcer as well as operator of the station, began what other stations did later in attempting to determine whether anyone was actually listening to the programs. He asked, "Will any of you who are listening in please phone or write me at East Pittsburgh, Pennsylvania, telling me how the program is coming in. Thank you, Frank Conrad, station 8XK, signing off."

The new station played mostly music, principally that of live bands, whose members performed on the roof of the building because the acoustics were better. In bad weather, a tent was used. Finally, with the use of burlap and other materials to reduce reverberation, inside rooms were converted to studios. At some stations studios were very plain—literally broom closets; others soon became very ornate, resembling the music rooms of Victorian mansions. The number of each day's regularly scheduled broadcast hours grew monthly.

The post–World War I growth and power of the United States were reflected in and stimulated by radio. The prosperity and brashness of the Roaring Twenties, including the increasing domination of big business over the economy, gave importance to radio's live, national advertising potential. War had unified much of America

THE ROARING '20S

League of Nations established; U.S. Senate votes not to join.	Thompson machine gun patented.	Adolf Hitler begins to gather his forces.

Audience response sought by Dr. Frank Conrad.

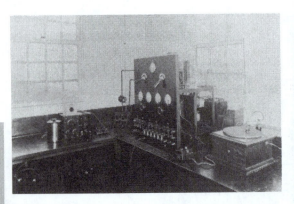 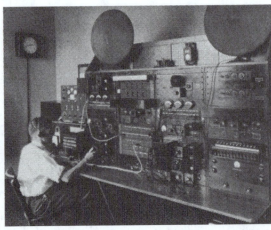

FIG 2.3 Early apparatus of two radio studios. *Courtesy Westinghouse and WTIC, Hartford, Connecticut.*

in terms of its own image and greatness and at the same time had introduced it to new ideas and attitudes from abroad. The United States as a whole emphasized the former, its own image, and rejected the latter, foreign ideas. Except for the increasing American role in, if not domination of, world trade, the United States isolated itself from much of the rest of the world and reveled in its own internal growth. The government's immediate postwar national xenophobia concerning "Bolsheviks"; the country's refusal to join the League of Nations; the national union-busting efforts, including police support of strikebreakers and "goons" and the framing and execution for murder of two radical labor activists, Sacco and Vanzetti, in Massachusetts; government efforts to stop the gangsterism that resulted from its Prohibition laws, even while many Americans romanticized the bootleggers; the public's blind eye to and even support of anti–civil rights and anti–civil liberties actions against ethnic and racial as well as political minorities; the first official entry of women as a group into the political process through electoral suffrage; the growing rivalry between urban and rural America, including the fear of big-city cultural domination; new American-born arts and culture, including the Jazz Age and the Harlem Renaissance; the solidification of the place of professional athletics in our culture; immigrants seeking the peace of isolation and "streets paved with gold"; people starving, but more people than ever before drinking champagne—all of this and more, the good and the bad, the joyful and the tragic, was the America of the Roaring Twenties. By and large it was a time of affluence and material possessions, the growth of a new economic middle class, new opportunities through mass production for unskilled and skilled workers, and a national devil-may-care euphoria. Radio fit perfectly into this heady postwar world, sometimes informing, sometimes educating, sometimes assuaging, and mostly entertaining, keeping people's minds on the happy days and off the troubles. Within a few years radio moved from a hobby to entertainment to a merchandising business.

24

Joan of Arc canonized.

Eugene O'Neill's *Emperor Jones* and *Beyond the Horizon* produced.

Westinghouse buys receiver patents from Edwin Armstrong.

Marconi opens Britain's first public broadcasting radio station.

FIG 2.4 The KDKA control room in 1920. Here the station's staff work the equipment for the Harding/Cox broadcast.
Courtesy Westinghouse.

1921

The first broadcast license granted by the Department of Commerce went to a Westinghouse station—but not KDKA. It went to WBZ, in Springfield, Massachusetts, on September 15, 1921. It wasn't until November 7 that KDKA officially got its license, the eighth one issued. Of the first nine stations licensed, four were owned by Westinghouse (KDKA; WBZ; WJZ, Newark, New Jersey; and KYW, Chicago) and only one each by RCA (WDY, Roselle Park, New Jersey) and the De Forest Radio Telephone and Telegraph Company (WJX, the Bronx, New York). By the end of the year more than 200 radio stations had been licensed.

Even though not the first licensed, KDKA lived up to its initial reputation by producing other kinds of "firsts." It carried the first remote church service broadcast, the first regular reporting of baseball scores, the first address by a national figure—Secretary of Commerce Herbert Hoover, on January 15—the first broadcast by a Congressional representative (Representative Alice Robertson, long before women were generally afforded such recognition), and the first time signals.

FIG 2.5 Less-than-extravagant accommodations: KDKA's rooftop studio shortly after the station's debut. *Courtesy Westinghouse.*

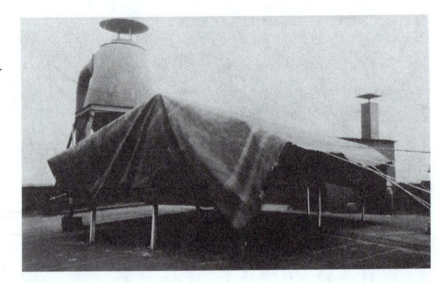

The broadcasting of sports events provided the greatest impetus for the purchase of radio sets—not unlike the phenomenon today that sees major sports events garnering the highest television ratings. This development was materially aided by the greater signal distance generated by the new 500-watt transmitters, which began to replace the 100-watt transmitters at key stations. The first broadcast of a championship fight, between heavyweights Jack Dempsey of the United States and Georges Carpentier of France, prompted the purchase of thousands of radios, as did the first broadcast of baseball's World Series, between the New York Yankees and the New York Giants, later in the year. It was estimated that perhaps 500,000 people heard each of these sporting events—an amazing figure, considering the limited number of sets in operation during only this second year of formal broadcasting. Thousands of people who couldn't care less about sports were converted to radio by a different event: being able to listen to the live broadcast of President Warren G. Harding's Armistice Day (now Veterans Day) address from the Arlington Cemetery Memorial.

Although RCA dominated the international wireless market, it continued to face stiff competition from Westinghouse for the domestic market. RCA's chairman, Owen D. Young, proposed that Westinghouse join its cross-licensing cartel. Westinghouse, seeing this as a possible opportunity to make headway in the international arena, accepted. Young also included the United Fruit Company, which, oddly enough, had significant patents on crystal detectors and loop antennas. Before the year was up,

WBZ is the first station licensed by the federal government.

Among KDKA's "firsts": broadcasts of remote church service, baseball scores, addresses by national figures, and time signals.

FIG 2.6 KDKA's first performance studio. *Courtesy Westinghouse.*

the RCA alliance controlled more than 2,000 key radio patents. David Sarnoff, who, as noted earlier, would become the key figure and power in the development of U.S. broadcasting, had become RCA's general manager. Young was impressed with Sarnoff's grasp of the medium's technical potential (it was Sarnoff who convinced Young of the value of using shortwave rather than longwave transmissions for better signal distance and quality) and its long-range economic potential (Sarnoff stressed radio's value as a lucrative merchandising device at the same time it served the entertainment and informational needs of the public).

The race was on to sell radio receivers and broadcasting components. In fact, many of the early stations were owned by the manufacturers of such equipment, using the station's programming to motivate people to buy sets; these purchases would in turn stimulate the construction of more stations. They also promoted their own products, frequently attaching the name of the product to whatever entertainment group they hired to perform on the station. Westinghouse itself produced a state-of-the-art set for $60—affordable for middle- and upper-income families but still very expensive for working people, whose typical pay was about a dollar a day. But other sets could be purchased for about $10. One way Westinghouse promoted its sets was to establish stations in cities where it had manufacturing plants.

First Miss America
contest.

First Armistice Day on
November 11.

A young Philo T. Farnsworth
conducts television
experiments.

Sports broadcasts inspire
receiver sales.

FIG 2.7 The first factory-
built radio receiver enters
the home in 1921.
Courtesy Westinghouse.

Not only were manufacturers who produced electronic equipment used in the construction of stations and receivers eager to sell their new products, but department stores set up stations in their stores to draw customers, and hotels did the same thing. The sound from phonograph records did not reproduce well over the air, so almost all music was performed live. Besides, the listening audiences didn't want to hear records; they had phonographs at home. They looked forward to hearing live, at home, some of the performers they previously could hear only by paying to go to nightclubs or vaudeville theaters.

All over the country, ads appeared for large and small companies that made radio equipment, such as the Crosley condenser and a variety of RCA products. Catalog companies, such as Montgomery Ward, heavily promoted the sale of radios and radio equipment. Even so, many people still constructed their own sets. The novelty of the new medium and the strong selling campaigns produced one of the heaviest demands for a new product in the country's history.

Radio sold not only equipment but education as well. The glamour of radio resulted in radio training schools springing up in various cities. The National Radio Institute of Washington, D.C., for example, ran full-page ads headlined "Do Amateurs Realize the Wireless Opportunities That Await Them?" The ads touted the potential

Albert Einstein wins Nobel Prize
for his theory of relativity.

Unknown soldier buried at
Arlington National Cemetery.

More than two dozen new
stations enter airwaves.

New 500-watt
transmitters provide
stronger radio signals.

for fame and fortune in the new field. Those who filled in and mailed a coupon received a "free book, *Wireless, the Opportunity of Today*."

Even as early as 1921 a new kind of entertainment talent began to emerge. Because the audiences were still relatively small, because the geographic coverage of a given station was limited, and because there was virtually no money to pay performers, well-known stars of vaudeville, nightclubs, the stage, and movies could not be drawn into radio. The first talents to become known—aside from a few new acts that worked cheap—were therefore the announcers, and even they tried to remain largely anonymous. Outside of managers and engineers who at first announced their stations' programs in the manner of Frank Conrad at KDKA, one of the first full-time announcers was KDKA's Harold W. Arlin, who was responsible for a number of firsts (such as announcing the first play-by-play sports broadcast). At WJZ in Newark, New Jersey, Thomas H. Cowan created a new designation for the announcer by establishing the practice of using initials rather than his name—"This is ACN" (for "This is Announcer Cowan, Newark"); this became the procedure at almost all stations for many years. New York area stations became the breaking-in ground in the early 1920s for the most famous announcers, including such people as Graham McNamee and Milton Cross, who remained at the stations for decades.

Aside from these developments in radio, in 1921 Philo T. Farnsworth, at the age of 15, was already experimenting with visual transmission concepts that would result in his becoming the "father of American television."

1922

The operational basis for U.S. broadcasting as it exists today was established in 1922 by one event: the first commercial. On August 28 a new AT&T station in New York City, WEAF, which became the NBC flagship station, carried a paid, 10-minute talk by an executive of the Queensboro Corporation extolling the virtues of buying an apartment in a new suburban development called Hawthorne Court—today a highly urbanized area. The station charged $50 for, as it was then called, the "toll-cast" presentation. Four more afternoon presentations were given, and one was made in the evening for $100. These first paid commercials resulted in the sale of apartments, and advertising as the support base for U.S. broadcasting was born. But it took time. Although WEAF received two more accounts—from Tidewater Oil and American Express—income was still insufficient to cover station expenses. What AT&T promoted at the beginning of 1922 as "commercial telephony" didn't begin to make real inroads until a year later. In fact, at a radio conference in Washington, D.C., called by Secretary of Commerce Herbert Hoover, the idea of advertising was discussed negatively, with Hoover stating that he felt "it is inconceivable that we should allow so great a possibility for service to be drowned in advertising chatter." Nevertheless, in 1923, after 14% of the stations operating in

Hitler's storm troopers
attack political opponents.

Picasso's *The Three Musicians* unveiled.

First broadcast of
championship fight inspires
receiver sales.

RCA alliance controls
2,000 key radio patents.

FIG 2.8 Commercial radio was launched at WEAF with this lengthy "toll-cast" designed to sell homes.

Vischer Randall

This afternoon the radio audience is to be addressed by Mr. Blackwell of the Queensboro Corporation, who through arrangements made by the Griffin Radio Service, Incorporated, will say a few words concerning Nathaniel Hawthorne and the desirability of fostering the helpful community spirit and the healthful, unconfined homelife that were Hawthorne's ideals. Ladies and gentlemen, Mr. Blackwell.

Mr. Blackwell

It is fifty-eight years since Nathaniel Hawthorne, the greatest of American fictionists, passed away. To honor his memory, the Queensboro Corporation, creator and operator of the tenant-owned system of apartment homes at Jackson Heights. New York City, has named the latest group of high-grade dwellings "Hawthorne Court."

I wish to thank those within the sound of my voice for the broadcasting opportunity afforded me to urge the vast radio audience to seek the recreation and daily comfort of the home removed from the congested part of the city, right at the boundaries of God's great outdoors, and within a few minutes by subway from the business section of Manhattan. This sort of residential environment strongly influenced Hawthorne, America's great writer of fiction. He analyzed with charming keenness the social spirit of those who had thus happily selected homes. and he painted the people inhabiting those homes with good-natured relish.

There should be more Hawthorne sermons preached about the utter inadequacy and the general hopelessness of the congested city home. The cry of the heart is for more living room, more chance to unfold, more opportunity to get near the Mother Earth, to play, to romp, to plant and dig.

Let me rejoin upon you as you value your health and your hopes and your home happiness, get away from the solid masses of brick, where the meagre opening admitting a slant of sunlight is mockingly called a light shaft, and where children grow up starved for a run over a patch of grass and the sight of a tree.

Apartments in congested parts of the city have proven failures. The word `neighbor` is an expression of peculiar irony—a daily joke . . . .

1922 had gone off the air due to a lack of funds and the remaining stations were desperate to find some way of meeting costs, advertising was again considered as the financial solution.

A principal problem was that the owners of the more than 200 stations that existed at the beginning of 1922 were supporting them for the purpose of either selling their own products (by the end of the year 40% of the stations were operated by manufacturers or sellers of radio receivers) or promoting their own services (such as churches, newspapers, and hotels). At the beginning of the year only a

Former President Taft becomes Chief Justice of Supreme Court.

Reader's Digest begins publication.

1922

British Broadcasting Company founded.

Commercial radio is launched at WEAF.

handful of stations were owned by newspapers; at the end of the year the number was 69. College stations at first didn't seem to worry about finances for survival, inasmuch as they were, as they are today, educational tools of their institutions and were supported as such. The first college station to be licensed, in 1922, was Emmanuel College in Michigan; by the end of the year, 74 colleges and universities had stations on the air.

People were buying radio receivers as fast as they could afford to and as quickly as the receivers were available for this new phenomenon. A lot of money for that time—$60 million—was spent for sets in 1922. The desire for receivers was so great that the demand by retail franchises outstripped the supply of sets. Drugstores, flower shops, clothing establishments, shoe stores, grocery stores, and even blacksmiths and undertakers sought radio-receiver franchises. About 200 distributors served some 15,000 retail outlets. As the agent for GE and Westinghouse products, RCA was at first the dominant force in the market with its receivers and loudspeakers, which acquired the names Radiola and Radiotron, and it tried to force distributors to carry its entire line of equipment. But as the number of manufacturers and the competition grew, each producer began to promote its own brand name and the performance qualities of its product; after a year or so, the public had a choice of many sets at competitive prices. People who couldn't afford brand-name receivers made their own crystal sets from kits—similar to the more sophisticated kits sold today by Radio Shack—or bought factory-made crystal sets for as little as $10 (a figure that was equivalent to two weeks' wages for many blue-collar workers).

Programming innovations spurred listener interest: a concert by the New York Philharmonic, President Calvin Coolidge's address to Congress, a "School of the Air" series, the first church services. The Secretary of Commerce prohibited a number of higher-powered major stations from playing recorded music, and the need for live talent grew. Stage celebrities began to appear on radio, notably through broadcasts of Broadway shows, such as *The Perfect Fool*, with Ed Wynn, and *Ziegfeld Follies of 1922*, with Will Rogers. Bertha Brainard, who became known as the "first lady of radio," began regular programs of theater reviews and information in 1922, and the "King of Jazz," Paul Whiteman, made his radio debut that year. The first dramatic series went on the air on GE's Schenectady, New York, station, WGY, and the first sound effects were used in *The Wolf*, a two-and-a-half-hour play on the same station.

Although the introduction of name talent boosted radio, it also created a problem. Most talent worked for free, seeking the publicity and exposure of the medium. Performers soon began to feel exploited, however, and frequently simply didn't show up for programs. In fact, some of the performing unions were so concerned about the lack of specified pay that they advised their members not to appear on radio shows.

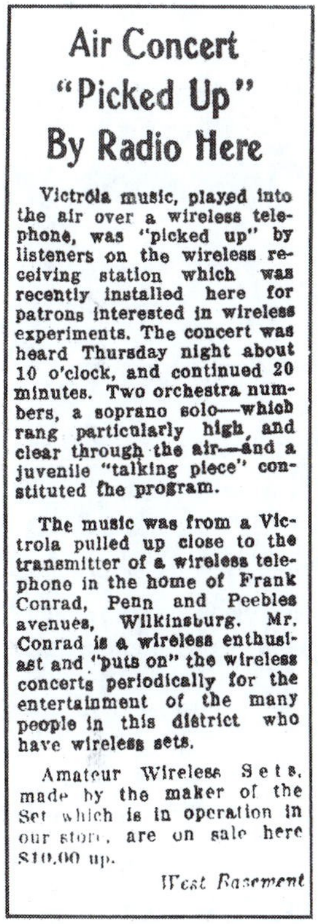

Air Concert "Picked Up" By Radio Here

Victrola music, played into the air over a wireless telephone, was "picked up" by listeners on the wireless receiving station which was recently installed here for patrons interested in wireless experiments. The concert was heard Thursday night about 10 o'clock, and continued 20 minutes. Two orchestra numbers, a soprano solo—which rang particularly high and clear through the air—and a juvenile "talking piece" constituted the program.

The music was from a Victrola pulled up close to the transmitter of a wireless telephone in the home of Frank Conrad, Penn and Peebles avenues, Wilkinsburg. Mr. Conrad is a wireless enthusiast and "puts on" the wireless concerts periodically for the entertainment of the many people in this district who have wireless sets.

Amateur Wireless Sets, made by the maker of the Set which is in operation in our store, are on sale here $10.00 up.

West Basement

FIG 2.9 In the early days, radio broadcasts consisted of news stories. Note the revealing information in this newspaper item. *Courtesy Westinghouse.*

Remote broadcasts added another new dimension. The first remote pickup of a football game, between Princeton and the University of Chicago from Stagg Field, Chicago, by AT&T station WEAF in New York, further advanced sales of receivers. Attempts to monopolize programming were as strong as attempts to control the technical aspects of radio. AT&T turned down non-AT&T stations' requests for use of AT&T long lines for remotes, and its competitors were forced to rely on the lower-quality Western Union lines, which were not designed for voice transmission.

Technical innovations, especially the demonstration in 1922 of the superheterodyne receiver by Edwin Armstrong, emphasized the increasing reach of radio. The first transatlantic broadcast took place on October 1 from London to WOR in New York. That same month saw a demonstration of high-power vacuum-tube transmission among New York, England, and Germany. Westinghouse's vice president, H. P. Davis,

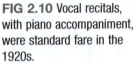

FIG 2.10 Vocal recitals, with piano accompaniment, were standard fare in the 1920s.
Courtesy WTIC.

Teapot Dome scandal
breaks.

Jimmy Doolittle crosses United
States by plane in one day.

Edwin Armstrong
demonstrates
superheterodyne
receiver.

First transatlantic
broadcast.

stated that there were no limitations to the potentials of interconnection, that "relays will permit one station to pass its message on to another, and we may easily expect to hear in an outlying farm in Maine some great artists singing into a microphone many thousands of miles away. A receiving set in every home, in every hotel room, in every schoolroom, in every hospital room . . . it is not so much a question of possibility, it is rather a question of how soon."

As radio grew, it found itself hindered by technical problems and the lack of government regulatory authority. For example, all radio stations broadcast on a frequency of 360 meters, except for government announcements and weather stations, which used 485 meters. With virtually all stations on the same frequency, interference was inevitable, and for a while radio tried to solve the problem by sharing days of the week and hours of the day. Although a new frequency of 400 meters was established for radio, only the more powerful stations—in wattage and finances, and with live programming—got this less congested frequency. In fact, in 1922 a number of stations started a voluntary "silent night" that lasted several years: On a designated evening, all local stations went off the air to allow the public to hear some of the higher-powered, distant stations, such as KDKA, which had star programming.

Frequency problems and unchecked licensing, whereby anyone who wanted to could get authorization to put a station on the air, prompted Secretary of Commerce Hoover to call the National Radio Conference mentioned earlier. Representatives of the leading radio manufacturers and station owners, such as RCA, AT&T, Westinghouse, and GE, were invited to attend, along with representatives of federal agencies and some key individuals from the technical and financial sides of the field. Congress turned down the conference's recommendation that the Secretary of Commerce be given authority to establish requirements for licensing, frequencies, and hours of operation. Some historians suggest that the reason was political, that certain members of Congress did not want to put such power into the hands of Hoover, who was considered a possible Republican candidate for President in 1924. (Hoover did run and was elected to the Presidency in 1928.)

The government was, however, forced to do something about station call letters. As the number of stations increased, the government began to run out of the three-letter call signs that had initially been assigned, so four-letter combinations began to be used. Many stations sought combinations that reflected the owner's name or initials or that promoted their programming or area. For example, of stations that were still on the air in the 1990s, WIOD (Miami) stands for "Wonderful Isle of Dreams," WTOP (Washington, D.C.) indicates "Top of the Dial," WNYC (New York) is the New York City municipal station, and WGCD (Chester, South Carolina) means "Wonderful Guernsey Center of Dixie." A few years later, in 1927, international agreements divided up call-letter prefixes geographically.

Radio prompted the growth of associated media industries as early as 1922, as it was to continue to do. Key radio publications containing mainly feature stories and

Benito Mussolini marches on Rome, establishes fascist government.	U.S.S.R. formed.

New frequency added for higher-power stations.	Newspapers invest in radio properties.

schedules were founded that year: *Radio World, Radio Dealer,* and *Radio Broadcast,* which later became the present-day *Broadcasting.* At the same time, not every citizen was enamored of the new medium. Like most new inventions, radio created fears, some reasonable and some unreasonable. One long-told story is that of the farmer who complained to the management of station WHAS in Louisville, Kentucky, that a flock of blackbirds was flying over his farm and one suddenly dropped out of the sky, dead. "Your radio wave must have struck it," the farmer insisted. "Suppose that radio wave had struck me?"

A noteworthy 1922 event reflected U.S. sociopolitical attitudes. According to the researcher Estelle Edmonston, this was the year that African-American involvement in the medium began. Edmonston states that Aubry Niles, Flouroy Miller, Noble Sissle and his orchestra, Juan Hernandez, Fran Silvera, and comedian Bert Williams were put on the air by N.T. Grantlund at WHN in New York. It would be many years, however, before African Americans would be given the opportunity to perform in broadcasting on a regular basis.

As the euphoria of the audio medium grew, so did the prospect of a visual medium. On June 11 *The New York Times* carried a photo of Pope Pius XI that had been transmitted, as the *Times* stated, through "a miracle of modern science." It was the first transatlantic radio photo.

1923

The success of remotes the year before naturally suggested the potential for interconnection, and the first "network"—or, as it was called then and is still called by many broadcasters and in many legal documents, "chain"—broadcast took place on January 4, 1923. WEAF sent a five-minute saxophone presentation over telephone wires to Boston's WNAC, broadcast simultaneously by both stations. (In October 1922, WJZ in Newark and WGY in Schenectady had simultaneously broadcast the World Series—but they were joined not by voice but by telegraph wire.) Throughout the year a number of stations interconnected for carriage of each other's programs, including the first permanent hookup, on July 1, between WEAF and WMAF (South Dartmouth, Massachusetts), for the latter station's carriage of WEAF programs. Interconnection experiments culminated in what many media historians consider the first true network, the connection by wire on December 6 of WEAF (New York), WJAR (Providence, Rhode Island), and WCAP (Washington, D.C.). Continued advances in the use of both wireless and wire for programming ranged from shortwave programs from the United States to England and from Los Angeles to Honolulu to short-range wire transmission of live entertainment from Gimbel's department store to WEAF in New York.

New programming and new personalities made their mark. The first play especially written and produced for radio was broadcast by WLW, Cincinnati.

Michigan's Emmanuel
College receives first
college station license.

$60 million spent on
radio sets.

Variety programs made media stars out of such vaudeville performers as Billy Jones and Ernie Hare, who set a standard for and opened the microphones to many similar comedy acts that would soon follow. Through his voice quality and verbal descriptions, Graham McNamee recreated the excitement and atmosphere of sports events so effectively that he would be the medium's premiere sports announcer for decades to come. In addition, H. V. Kaltenborn began the news commentaries that would make him famous into the age of television. But even in 1923, as today, music was the dominant programming on radio—only then it was mostly live, emanating from hotel ballrooms and specially built studios that were furnished to look like ballrooms or elegant music rooms, resulting in the phrase "potted palm music." There was, of course, classical music, too; in fact, the first sponsored program was one of classical music, the *Eveready Hour*, in 1923.

News had not yet made its mark. There were no radio news services. Some stations read or paraphrased the stories from their towns' daily newspapers. A few enterprising stations sent out staff to gather local stories. Some newspapers provided stations in their communities with news summaries to be read over the air. But mostly, news was largely ignored. The principal news broadcasts were Department of Agriculture and Weather Bureau reports to farm areas. A dramatic combination of radio news and public service was demonstrated in 1923 when radio helped locate the kidnapped son of the radio/TV inventor Ernst Alexanderson.

FIG 2.11 Radio quickly caught the imagination of the public, as demonstrated in this 1923 photo of a home crystal receiver and its young fans.
Courtesy Westinghouse.

THE ROARING '20S

1923

FIG 2.12 Some stars (such as Ethel Barrymore, at right in photo) began answering the call to the airwaves.
Courtesy Westinghouse.

RADIO BROADCASTING NEWS

Vol. 3   MARCH 31, 1923   No. 13

Ethel Barrymore in "The Laughing Lady", recently broadcasted from Station WJZ. Left to Right—Alice John, Katherine Emmet, Violet Kemble Cooper, and Ethel Barrymore.

Programming progressed, but it was not all positive. A portent of charlatan hucksters and televangelists of a later day, a Dr. John R. Brinkley started station KFKB in Milford, Kansas. The license was finally revoked some years later because of Brinkley's sales promotion of his own patent medicines and other dangerous or false drugs and even a "goat gland operation" for male sex rejuvenation.

Some of the most dramatic advances in programming came in the field of politics. The right-wing backlash following World War I had made the United States isolationist, the country even refusing to join the League of Nations, while much of the rest of

New era for labor as eight-hour workday forced on U.S. Steel.

USSR is formed.

First original radio play is offered by WLW.

The Eveready Hour is the first sponsored program.

ASCAP inspires creation of the National Association of Broadcasters.

the world was seeking continuing peace through international cooperation. On June 23 President Warren G. Harding made a speech about the World Court that was heard by an estimated 1 million-plus people—a remarkable number for that period and, according to some historians, the true beginning of a politician simultaneously reaching and influencing a huge segment of the public. Plans for a coast-to-coast hookup to follow up the success of Harding's speech were shelved because of Harding's death shortly afterward. Although radio carried the inauguration of the new President, Calvin Coolidge, coast to coast on a 21-station hookup, Coolidge refused to use the radio medium. No wonder; he spoke in flat, nasal, boring tones. But at the opening of Congress on December 23 (a first for radio), he allowed his speech to be carried by a seven-station network linked by AT&T from New York to Dallas. This resulted in another first: broadcasting making a politician look or sound more appealing than he or she really is. The microphone was placed close to Coolidge and emphasized the lower tones, giving his voice a power and resonance that it ordinarily didn't have. This gave him a new image of strength that, in the opinion of many, bolstered support for his isolationist views and for the United States' political detachment from many developments in Europe, including, later, the rise of Nazism.

FIG 2.13 An Aeriola Senior radio receiver. *Courtesy RCA.*

Former President Woodrow Wilson, increasingly ill and near death, was persuaded to make a speech on radio supporting U.S. participation in the League of Nations. For the preceding few years, since the end of his presidency in 1921, he had been largely ignored and virtually forgotten. But the day after his speech, some 20,000 people crowded the streets in front of his home in Washington, urging him to come out to talk to them and be cheered. The Coolidge and Wilson events were among the first examples of the power of the media to affect and even control politics.

As programming and technical proficiency grew, so did the problems that come from unregulated competition. Both RCA and AT&T believed that their patents had been infringed on. RCA was concerned that the thousands of entrepreneurs who were making radio sets with RCA tubes were illegally using processes that it controlled. AT&T claimed that any station using a transmitter not manufactured by its Western Electric subsidiary was violating its patent rights. AT&T offered the 600 or so stations it believed were in violation the option of (1) continuing to broadcast on their "illegal" transmitters in exchange for annual licensing fees or (2) going off the air. The conflict reached Congress, which asked the Federal Trade Commission (FTC) to investigate—the first serious investigation by the government of alleged monopoly practices in the media industry, something that would occur frequently in subsequent years, especially following the establishment of the Federal Radio Commission in 1927 and the Federal Communications Commission (FCC) in 1934.

Creative artists complained that radio stations were using their works without permission, usually without compensation. Most concerned was the American Society

German inflation rises; 4 million marks = US$1.	Hitler "Beer Garden Putsch" fails.

Vladimir Zworykin demonstrates the beginnings of a partly electronic television system; patents iconoscope tube.	President Coolidge's address to Congress is carried by seven-station hookup.

of Composers, Authors, and Publishers (ASCAP). The previous year, ASCAP had demanded royalties from radio stations that used the copyrighted music of its members. The stations countered that they were popularizing the music, resulting in increased sales of records and sheet music. In 1923 ASCAP negotiated an annual license fee of $500 with WEAF and, using this agreement as a base, sought similar agreements from other stations. When ASCAP won a court case upholding its legal rights, additional stations agreed to a fee (usually about $250 a year), but others simply stopped using ASCAP music. The music, however, was essential, and a number of stations met in Chicago and formed the National Association of Broadcasters (NAB) to fight ASCAP and try to work out a plan for free use of the music in exchange for promoting it. Ultimately, NAB and ASCAP negotiated an annual "statutory" fee for unlimited use of the music. NAB eventually became the broadcasters' principal trade association and lobbying organization in Washington, and today, seven decades later, the same two organizations meet every few years to negotiate a new music-use contract.

These and other problems, especially the increasingly crowded airwaves, prompted Secretary Hoover to call a second National Radio Conference. As a result of this conference, stations were divided into three groups. First were high-powered stations of 500 to 1,000 watts and between 300 and 545 meters on the radio dial. These stations were to serve wide areas with no interference; prohibited from using phonograph records, they were required to present live music. Second were stations with a maximum of 500 watts, operating between 222 and 300 meters—stations intended to serve a smaller area without interference. Third were low-powered stations, all on 360 meters and all required to share time to avoid interference; many of these stations, therefore, operated only during the day to avoid the interference caused by the sky wave reflection of the amplitude modulation (AM) signal over long distances after dusk.

The conference also discussed the need for an equitable distribution of frequencies and stations across the country. Further, it recommended that Congress pass a bill establishing a federal regulatory agency to facilitate the growth of radio; however, two more National Radio Conferences would be necessary before that would happen.

Once again, in 1923, as radio grew, so did the genesis of television. Facsimile, or wirephoto, experiments continued, and in Britain, John Logie Baird developed a mechanical scanning system by which he transmitted by wire a silhouette television picture about the same time that Charles Francis Jenkins, an American using a mechanical system he developed at AT&T, transmitted by wireless a picture of President Harding from Washington to Philadelphia. Significant in terms of the future of the visual medium, Vladimir Zworykin, continuing his experiments at Westinghouse, demonstrated the beginnings of a partly electronic television system.

Great Tokyo earthquake; Frank Lloyd
Wright-designed hotel survives.

Teapot Dome oil scandal
widens.

Mechanical scanning system
developed by Britain's John
Logie Baird.

Jenkins experiments with
wireless facsimile.

FIG 2.14 This balloon
was used as an airborne
antenna (and billboard) in
the 1920s.
Courtesy Westinghouse.

1924

The third National Radio Conference, in 1924, continued to try to solve the problem of chaos on the air. The major result was the expansion of frequencies allocated for radio broadcasting to 550–1,500 kilocycles (kc), with power up to 5,000 watts. Still, the interference continued and another conference was scheduled for 1925.

There were troubles on the business front for broadcasting as well. The FTC completed the report of its monopoly investigation begun the previous year and issued complaints against RCA and seven other companies, known as the "patent allies," for their alleged stifling of free competitive growth of the medium.

Some government officials were taking a more favorable attitude toward radio, however; Calvin Coolidge, who had looked askance at radio when he succeeded Harding as President following the latter's death in 1923, was now running for the Presidency on his own. He used a 26-station, coast-to-coast hookup to make a campaign speech. Other politicians jumped on the radio bandwagon, too, following radio's coverage of both the Republican and the Democratic National Conventions of 1924, coverage that stimulated heavy increases in the purchase of radio sets.

Gershwin's *Rhapsody in Blue* debuts.

Second radio conference held.

NAB formed to counter impact of ASCAP.

Hoover assigns needed frequency spectrum to three classes of stations.

FIG 2.15 President Coolidge and Secretary Hoover address a gathering of broadcasters at the White House for the third National Radio Conference, December 1924.

Radio was growing all right, and public support was increasing, but many stations were wondering how and where they would get the funding to stay on the air. The few attempts at advertising had not taken off as hoped, and there was no widespread commitment to use commercials as the financial base for the medium. What were the alternatives?

Secretary of Commerce Hoover wanted the radio manufacturing and sales industry to support the stations. In fact, at the third National Radio Conference, he said, "I believe that the quickest way to kill broadcasting would be to use it for direct advertising. The reader of the newspaper has an option whether he will read an ad or not, but if a speech by the President is to be used as the meat in a sandwich of two patent medicine advertisements there will be no radio left." David Sarnoff of RCA said radio should be financed through grants and endowments, as museums and libraries are. A GE official, Martin P. Rice, advocated what was later to become the dominant system of support in many countries throughout the world, the licensing of individual sets; he also suggested voluntary contributions from listeners. But none of these solutions was about to work in the United States, because the costs of personnel and equipment were much higher than any of these revenue alternatives—other than license fees for sets—were likely to offset. Within a year it had become clear that advertising was probably the only viable financing method.

Pop music favorites include "Barney Google," "Yes, We Have No Bananas."

Ten millionth Ford auto is produced.

1924

H. V. Kaltenborn begins radio commentary.

Third National Radio Conference calls for the establishment of the standard broadcast band between 550 and 1,500 kc.

FIG 2.16 A broadcast production at Chicago station KYW.
Courtesy Westinghouse.

THE ROARING '20S

Still, stations were stymied. AT&T's earlier agreements with stations, giving them permission to use its transmitters, included exclusive rights for AT&T to any advertising (or "toll broadcasting," as it was then called) on those stations. AT&T charged an additional fee when any station carried paid advertising, thus reducing the income the station earned from that advertising. The so-called Radio Group, headed by RCA, and the Telephone Group, headed by AT&T, were locked in a struggle over this issue and several others. The following year, 1925, the two groups agreed to binding arbitration to solve the dispute. The arbitrator found in favor of the Radio Group. Now both groups had to find common ground if radio were not to split apart entirely. Until they could agree—which they did the following year, 1926—advertising was not permitted. Even then, the kind of advertising that was done was what today is called institutional—the goodwill promotion of a company or of a product or a service but without specific details or "hard-sell" information on actual purchasing. It would be a few years more before the modern concept of commercials took full hold.

The number of listeners and potential customers grew. When Westinghouse brought Armstrong's superheterodyne receiver into the patents pool, RCA was able to produce a set with highly improved reception. It was, as one might expect, fairly expensive. An RCA competitor, Crosley, countered with a small $10 set; its one tube, however, could receive a signal of only up to 15 miles distance. The approximately half million sets in use in 1923 grew to more than 1.25 million in 1924, with the public spending about $139 million for new receivers that year.

41

Vladimir Lenin dies; Joseph Stalin becomes chief successor.	J. Edgar Hoover becomes director of FBI.

FTC reports on monopoly in broadcasting.	Some 1.25 million radio sets in use.

Even though broadcasting was still in its childhood, its remarkable growth in just a few years prompted the people's representatives in Congress to be concerned about possible future monopolization by private interests at the expense of the public interest. In fact, in 1924 Congress passed a bill that presaged the Radio Act of 1927 and the Communications Act of 1934, in which it asserted the government's authority to regulate radio and clearly stated that the "aether" (ether), or airwaves, belonged to the people.

1925

A fourth National Radio Conference tried again to solve radio's problems of overcrowded airwaves and interference. Although many recommendations were made, including extended license periods for stations, wartime radio powers for the President, and safeguards against censorship, the one concrete result was a freeze placed on the issuing of new licenses. The purpose of the freeze was to give broadcasters and the government a respite from dealing with increasing growth crises so as to be able to determine some workable solutions for the future. The Department of Commerce did, however, permit existing stations to be bought and sold. Hence, the practice of owning stations for the purpose not of providing programming in the public interest but of making a quick buck by reselling in a short time—similar to what happened in broadcasting under the deregulation of "trafficking" in the 1980s—began to invade the industry.

Congressman Wallace H. White, Jr., of Maine had introduced bills following previous National Radio Conferences that would give the Secretary of Commerce the power to regulate radio, but none was approved. He did so again after the fourth National Radio Conference in 1925; this bill, after a number of revisions, would be passed two years later as the Radio Act of 1927.

College stations continued to grow. More than 150 such stations were authorized by the Department of Commerce, with about 125 actually on the air. But attrition began to set in: 37 went off the air in 1925 alone.

As controversial issues, such as the Scopes trial, were broadcast by stations such as WLS, the public continued to buy sets almost as quickly as they could be manufactured. Some estimates put the sales of receivers in 1925 at as many as 2 million, and by the end of the year one out of every six homes in the United States had a radio set.

As professional radio grew, so did amateur radio. Many of the people who for years had experimented with the new medium at home continued to do so as a hobby, not making a transition into the new world of stations and the business of broadcasting. They found that the growth of formally programmed stations tended to restrict their use of radio to broadcast to one another. The American Radio Relay League had been established by these amateur, or, as we now call them, "ham," operators before World War I, and it was now expanding. In 1925 a conference was held with representatives from 23 countries, resulting in the formation of the International Radio Union to fight the regulations that were restricting the growth of amateur operators throughout the world.

FIG 2.17 "The aether belongs to the people. . . . " Popular microphones of the 1920s.
Courtesy Steele Collection.

FIG 2.18 Microphones were often concealed to reduce performers' anxiety. In this instance the microphone is disguised with a lamp shade. *Courtesy WTIC.*

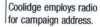

THE ROARING '20S

As music on radio expanded, both live and recorded, the phonograph and the vaudeville industries were beginning to feel the pinch. Many people stopped buying records because they could now hear the music free on radio. Many also saved vaudeville house admission fees by staying at home and hearing variety acts and bands free on their radios, much like what happened to local movie houses when television came into U.S. homes. Although vaudeville started a downward slide from which it never recovered, the reverse was true for the

THE ROARING '20S

1925

Coolidge delivers first Presidential radio address from White House.

Fourth National Radio Conference moves industry closer to important solutions concerning interference.

FIG 2.19 Interested spectators look on as New York station WRNY broadcasts.

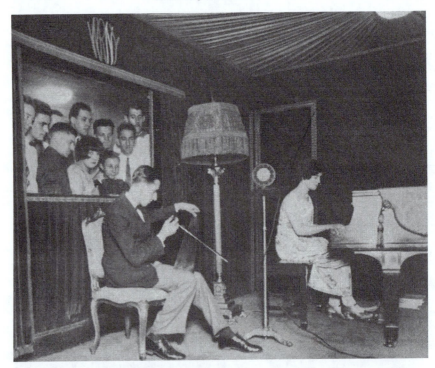

FIG 2.20 Conductor Walter Damrosch led the New York Symphony over the radio in 1925. This event marked the beginning of a long tradition of live classical music broadcasts. *Courtesy Anthony Slide.*

Ku Klux Klan marches on
Capitol.

World treaty outlaws
poison gas.

One out of every six
homes has a radio set.

International Radio
Union is formed.

record industry. Eventually, the promotion of records on radio resulted in greatly increased sales, and some record companies began to bribe programmers to play their records.

1926

A most significant event in 1926 established the concept and organization of network broadcasting that continues even today. At the urging of David Sarnoff to establish what he called a central broadcasting system, RCA (50% owner) joined with GE (30%) and Westinghouse (20%) to found a new entity, which they called the National Broadcasting Company (NBC). Leasing AT&T lines for hookup, RCA set up an initial network of 19 stations. For a flagship station, it bought AT&T's WEAF in New York for $1 million—a huge sum for those days. Ironically, the selling of WEAF was the beginning of the end of AT&T's venture in broadcasting, even though it later attempted to set up its own network. That NBC's bottom line was business, the same bottom line for broadcasting concerns today, was reflected in its choice of its first president, Merlin H. Aylesworth. Aylesworth had managed the National Electric Light Association and had business acumen but allegedly little knowledge of broadcasting; it was said that he didn't even own a radio set.

NBC started off its new network with a blockbuster—a huge special from the grand ballroom of the Waldorf-Astoria Hotel in New York, featuring leading orchestras, popular singers, and opera stars of the day, with an invited elite audience of some 1,000 people. It even carried remotes, including one from Kansas City featuring Will Rogers, the country's outstanding humorist. The program was carried by 25 stations nationally and heard by millions of people. So successful was NBC's concept that by the end of the year it had two networks: the NBC Red Network, with WEAF as the key station, and the NBC Blue Network, with another New York City station, WJZ, as the flagship.

Why Red and Blue? Perhaps the most authoritative explanation is that when NBC was drawing the paths of the two planned networks on a map of the United States, it used a red pencil for one and a blue pencil for the other. A later story is that to determine which programs originating in the same studio went to which network, one line taped onto the floor was colored red, the other blue. Yet another account has it that the wiring of one set of stations was wrapped in red while the other was covered in blue. NBC had a stronghold on national broadcasting—one it would retain, despite competition from new networks, for more than 15 years, until the federal government broke it up.

With the settlement of the AT&T Telephone Group versus RCA Radio Group fight, the NBC affiliates were able to carry advertising, and NBC began an aggressive campaign to seek sponsors for its shows. Not only did it sell time on its network programs, it purchased time on its local stations, slots it also sold to advertisers. Within a year

THE ROARING '20S

Chinese students killed by British in Shanghai protest.

First transatlantic phone call.

1926

Baird demonstrates first television pictures in London.

A U.S. district court rules that the Commerce Department does not have statutory power to prevent stations from interfering with one another.

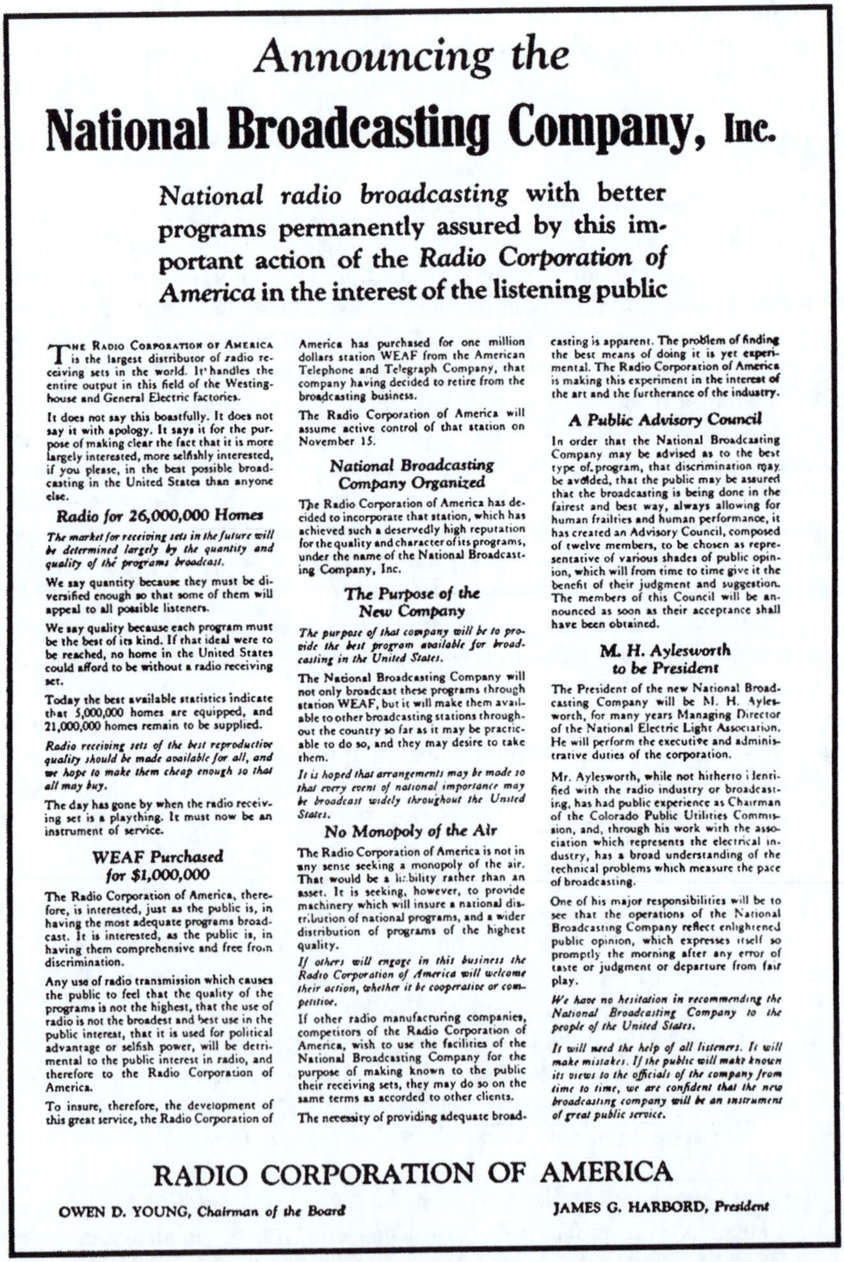

Announcing the

National Broadcasting Company, Inc.

National radio broadcasting with better programs permanently assured by this important action of the *Radio Corporation of America* in the interest of the listening public

THE RADIO CORPORATION OF AMERICA is the largest distributor of radio receiving sets in the world. It handles the entire output in this field of the Westinghouse and General Electric factories.

It does not say this boastfully. It does not say it with apology. It says it for the purpose of making clear the fact that it is more largely interested, more selfishly interested, if you please, in the best possible broadcasting in the United States than anyone else.

Radio for 26,000,000 Homes

The market for receiving sets in the future will be determined largely by the quantity and quality of the programs broadcast.

We say quantity because they must be diversified enough so that some of them will appeal to all possible listeners.

We say quality because each program must be the best of its kind. If that ideal were to be reached, no home in the United States could afford to be without a radio receiving set.

Today the best available statistics indicate that 5,000,000 homes are equipped, and 21,000,000 homes remain to be supplied.

Radio receiving sets of the best reproductive quality should be made available for all, and we hope to make them cheap enough so that all may buy.

The day has gone by when the radio receiving set is a plaything. It must now be an instrument of service.

WEAF Purchased for $1,000,000

The Radio Corporation of America, therefore, is interested, just as the public is, in having the most adequate programs broadcast. It is interested, as the public is, in having them comprehensive and free from discrimination.

Any use of radio transmission which causes the public to feel that the quality of the programs is not the broadest and best use in the public interest, that it is used for political advantage or selfish power, will be detrimental to the public interest in radio, and therefore to the Radio Corporation of America.

To insure, therefore, the development of this great service, the Radio Corporation of America has purchased for one million dollars station WEAF from the American Telephone and Telegraph Company, that company having decided to retire from the broadcasting business.

The Radio Corporation of America will assume active control of that station on November 15.

National Broadcasting Company Organized

The Radio Corporation of America has decided to incorporate that station, which has achieved such a deservedly high reputation for the quality and character of its programs, under the name of the National Broadcasting Company, Inc.

The Purpose of the New Company

The purpose of that company will be to provide the best program available for broadcasting in the United States.

The National Broadcasting Company will not only broadcast these programs through station WEAF, but it will make them available to other broadcasting stations throughout the country so far as it may be practicable to do so, and they may desire to take them.

It is hoped that arrangements may be made so that every event of national importance may be broadcast widely throughout the United States.

No Monopoly of the Air

The Radio Corporation of America is not in any sense seeking a monopoly of the air. That would be a liability rather than an asset. It is seeking, however, to provide machinery which will insure a national distribution of national programs, and a wider distribution of programs of the highest quality.

If others will engage in this business the Radio Corporation of America will welcome their action, whether it be cooperative or competitive.

If other radio manufacturing companies, competitors of the Radio Corporation of America, wish to use the facilities of the National Broadcasting Company for the purpose of making known to the public their receiving sets, they may do so on the same terms as accorded to other clients.

The necessity of providing adequate broadcasting is apparent. The problem of finding the best means of doing it is yet experimental. The Radio Corporation of America is making this experiment in the interest of the art and the furtherance of the industry.

A Public Advisory Council

In order that the National Broadcasting Company may be advised as to the best type of program, that discrimination may be avoided, that the public may be assured that the broadcasting is being done in the fairest and best way, always allowing for human frailties and human performance, it has created an Advisory Council, composed of twelve members, to be chosen as representative of various shades of public opinion, which will from time to time give it the benefit of their judgment and suggestion. The members of this Council will be announced as soon as their acceptance shall have been obtained.

M. H. Aylesworth to be President

The President of the new National Broadcasting Company will be M. H. Aylesworth, for many years Managing Director of the National Electric Light Association. He will perform the executive and administrative duties of the corporation.

Mr. Aylesworth, while not hitherto identified with the radio industry or broadcasting, has had public experience as Chairman of the Colorado Public Utilities Commission, and, through his work with the association which represents the electrical industry, has a broad understanding of the technical problems which measure the pace of broadcasting.

One of his major responsibilities will be to see that the operations of the National Broadcasting Company reflect enlightened public opinion, which expresses itself so promptly the morning after any error of taste or judgment or departure from fair play.

We have no hesitation in recommending the National Broadcasting Company to the people of the United States.

It will need the help of all listeners. It will make mistakes. If the public will make known its views to the officials of the company from time to time, we are confident that the new broadcasting company will be an instrument of great public service.

RADIO CORPORATION OF AMERICA

OWEN D. YOUNG, *Chairman of the Board*

JAMES G. HARBORD, *President*

FIG 2.21 Newspaper advertisement proclaiming establishment of the nation's first broadcast network.

RCA creates the National Broadcasting Company.

AT&T agrees to abandon broadcast station operation involvement.

FIG 2.22 A 1926 broadcast of a Brooklyn Dodgers baseball game by Graham McNamee.

THE ROARING '20S

the 60-second commercial was established, and it became the economic lifeblood for broadcasters throughout the country.

A U.S. district court decision in early 1926 provided impetus for Congress to do what the National Radio Conferences of the four previous years and the Secretary of Commerce had unsuccessfully pleaded with it to do: establish a government radio regulatory body. It did so the following year, as a solution to the district court ruling that the Commerce Department did not have the statutory authority to prevent the Zenith Corporation from putting its station on a frequency other than that assigned by the Secretary of Commerce. In other words, in the Zenith case the court said that the government did not have the authority to prevent any station from using any frequency and power, even if they interfered with other stations. With total chaos on the air now legally possible, Congress seemed to have little choice.

1927

On February 18 Congress passed the Radio Act of 1927, which was signed into law by President Coolidge on February 23. It was also called the Dill-White Act, after its two principal sponsors, Senator Clarence C. Dill and Representative Wallace H. White.

FIG 2.23 A British Marconi Company transmitting antenna, beaming wireless signals to the United States in 1926.

NBC launches aggressive campaign for sponsors.

The act established the first broadcasting regulatory body in the United States, the Federal Radio Commission (FRC), consisting of five commissioners.

The FRC was given regulatory authority over radio, including the issuance of licenses; the allocation of frequency bands to various classes of stations, including ship and air; the assignment of specific frequencies to individual stations; and the designation of station power. Under the act, it was also given authority to require each station to control its own programming and to show that it had funding before it could be licensed. The FRC could deny a license to an applicant that had been found guilty of forming a monopoly, and it could prohibit control by a telephone company over a radio station or by a radio station over a telephone company. It was given authority to develop regulations for broadcasting, including networks. In addition, the Secretary of Commerce was authorized to inspect radio stations, examine and license radio operators, and assign radio call signs.

The FRC established the AM band as 550–1,500 kc (later expanded to 1,600 kc and, in 1990, to 1,705 kc). There were a total of 96 frequencies, and 40 clear stations were set up in eight geographic zones. Power was raised, up to 25 kilowatts (kW), and later to 50 kW for one group of stations, with others in intermediate categories, certifying the actions taken by the Secretary of Commerce following the fourth National Radio Conference.

Two of the more significant aspects of the Radio Act were (1) the requirement that stations operate in the "public interest, convenience, or necessity" (inspired in large part by Hoover's insistence that radio realize its great potential as an instrument for the public good) and (2) the declaration that all existing licenses were null and void 60 days after approval of the act. Although Congress did not specifically define what it meant by "the public interest," "convenience," or "necessity"—and has not done so to this day—the statement established the base for later regulation that went far beyond technical supervision, which was the principal motivation for the Radio

FIG 2.24 The distribution of radio frequencies and power allocations as of June 1927.

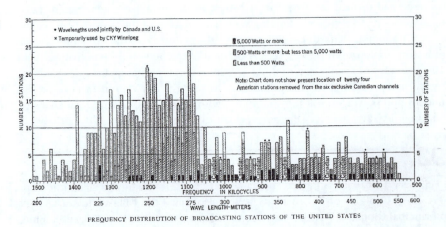

FREQUENCY DISTRIBUTION OF BROADCASTING STATIONS OF THE UNITED STATES

| First 16mm movie film produced by Kodak. | Gertrude Ederle is first woman to swim English Channel. |

1927

| Movement is made toward formation of radio regulatory commission. | Congress passes the Radio Act of 1927, creating the Federal Radio Commission. |

Act of 1927. The FRC did use its authority under that provision to take action in regard to certain program content that exploited or deceived the listener, such as religious charlatans intent on milking the public for donations, patent-medicine hucksters, and fortune tellers.

The voiding of existing licenses forced all stations that wanted to stay on the air to apply for new licenses. Most of them did reapply. But in setting up an orderly system of frequency and power assignments to solve the chaos, the FRC refused to renew the licenses of many stations and forced many others to less desirable frequencies. For the most part, the larger, more powerful, and more influential stations got the best frequencies. College stations, for example, were forced off the air by the dozens, many of them unable to get licenses and many more being assigned the worst frequencies, their former frequencies given to commercial stations. All in all, some 150 of the 732 stations on the air before the act was passed were forced to surrender their licenses.

Did the Radio Act of 1927 and the establishment of the FRC result in radio operating in the public interest? More than 40 years after passage of the act, one of its sponsors, former Senator Clarence Dill, was not so sure. In answer to a letter inquiring about the original Radio Act, he expressed concern that the FRC's successor, the FCC, was not protecting the public against commercialization of the airwaves and hoped the people would insist on use of frequencies for the "public interest" rather than for "private profiteers."

Rereading the Scarcity Principle

The legal doctrine known as the *scarcity principle* was premised on the assumption that unlike print, the airwaves were finite in terms of accommodating potential users and therefore the government had a role in regulating this limited space. Leading up to the 1927 Radio Act, chaos was rampant on the airwaves, resulting in interference with reception. The Federal Radio Commission felt that the sole cause of this issue was too many broadcasters. They pursued a policy that favored fewer, high-power stations operated by major corporate interests at the expense of many smaller, independent, noncommercial operators. In retrospect, if the FRC had really wanted to act in the public interest, it had other options to lessen interference rather than simply handing over broad swaths of the spectrum to fewer licensees. Among these options could have been reducing the 10khz separation between frequencies to allow for more stations to operate, at lower power, within the same bandwidth, which could have been accomplished by requiring operators to better calibrate their transmitters from "bleeding" over to another frequency, place stricter restrictions on maritime and amateur operators, and demand that manufacturers include, as a standard rather than extra cost feature, sets with precision tuners and that were better shielded from extraneous electromagnetic interference.

| Sacco and Vanzetti executed. | New York's Holland Tunnel opens. | "Lone Eagle" Charles Lindbergh flies solo across the Atlantic. |

United Independent Broadcasters is formed.

FIG 2.25 A radio audience questionnaire in the February 1927 issue of *Radio Broadcast* magazine.

TELL US WHAT YOU LIKE IN RADIO PROGRAMS

IF YOU have not already sent in your reply to the questionnaire, which was printed in the January RADIO BROADCAST, it is reprinted below. A large number of extremely interesting replies to our questions have already been received and the large mass of material is being tabulated as rapidly as possible.

Many correspondents suggested that space should have been allotted for a list of radio features that are distinctly unpopular with listeners. Expressions of that sort of opinion are always welcome to the conductor of this department. However, it was felt that there was a sufficiently wide range of subject covered in the present list.

While the names of readers of this magazine who are good enough to trouble to reply to these questions will be kept confidential, it will be of considerable assistance if those who reply to this questionnaire will include their name and address.

In replying to question four, please indicate definitely the title of a special part of an evening's broadcast, defining it by the title of the program. Some replies to this question merely indicated the call letters of a favorite station, which is, obviously, pretty indefinite.

The questions below are few, and some of them have the special virtue that they have never been asked before. Please use the space provided for your answers. Tear this sheet from the magazine, and if possible typewrite your replies. If the space provided is not sufficient, attach an additional sheet to this with your remarks. If you are interested in reading the replies—contribute some yourself. Address all questionnaires to

JOHN WALLACE,
RADIO BROADCAST,
Garden City, New York.

Please Answer These Questions

1. Do you listen to your radio evenings as you would to a regular show, or do you simply turn it on and use it as a background to other activities?

_____

_____

_____

(This question may seem silly, but we ask it because we have a growing suspicion that radio programs aren't as reverently listened to as the broadcasters suppose.)

2. Do you regularly tune-in on distant stations or do you regularly rely on your local stations?

_____

_____

_____

(They tell us that the DX hound is a fast-disappearing breed. Is he?)

3. If you had a hundred minutes to listen to all, or any part of the following broadcasts, how would you apportion your time? (Answer in spaces provided in the next column.)

Instrumental Music { Serious	_____	minutes
Light	_____	minutes
Popular	_____	minutes
Vocal Music	_____	minutes
Radio Play	_____	minutes
Speech	_____	minutes
Educational Lecture	_____	minutes
Miscellaneous Novelties	_____	minutes
TOTAL	100	minutes

(In answering this question, assume that each of the offerings is the best of its kind, say Coon-Sanders Nighthawks for the jazz, the New York Symphony for classical music, Ford and Glenn for the novelties, and so on.)

4. What are the six best broadcasts you have heard?

_____

_____

_____

_____

_____

_____

(We could refresh your memory with some notable broadcasts, but that might influence your choice. Anything is eligible, from an especially good dog fight broadcast, to a high-powered soprano solo, heard four years ago.)

Please answer these questions briefly and mail them at once to Mr. Wallace, at the editorial offices of RADIO BROADCAST, Garden City, New York. We prefer to have you write your replies on this page. The results of the questionnaire will be announced just as soon as it is possible to compile them.

FIG 2.26 Felix was TV's first image.
Courtesy David Sarnoff Library.

Meanwhile, broadcasters concentrated on what was in their own best interest. NBC's success prompted others to look at network possibilities. Early in 1927 the United Independent Broadcasters (UIB) association was formed, and although it signed on a number of affiliates it was unable to raise enough money to activate a

The Jazz Singer brings sound to movies.

UIB and the Columbia Phonograph Company unite forces to compete with NBC; renamed Columbia Broadcasting System (CBS) the following year.

Automobile radios are introduced.

Secretary of Commerce Hoover televised on a circuit from Washington, D.C., to New York.

THE ROARING '20S

real challenge to NBC. In fact, its financial condition was so shaky that AT&T wouldn't let it use AT&T interconnecting lines, for fear that UIB wouldn't be able to pay for them. The Columbia Phonograph Company was the chief rival of the Victor Phonograph Company, which was about to merge with RCA, the controller of NBC. Columbia decided to go into head-to-head competition with NBC by joining with UIB to form the Columbia Phonograph Broadcasting System, later to become the Columbia Broadcasting System (CBS) and NBC's principal network competition. With three networks in operation, there was no longer a need to clear the airwaves on a given night to receive large, live-performance stations, and the "silent night" practice was abandoned.

Sales of sets increased, as did the variety and impact of programming. RCA licensed several competitors, such as Crosley, Atwater Kent, Philco, and Zenith, to make sets under the so-called "patent-allies" patents in return for substantial royalty payments, thus increasing the availability of receivers. An estimated 15 million sets were in use in the United States, and in 1927 alone about $500 million worth of receivers were purchased. Although battery sets were still in use, especially in rural areas where there was no electricity, radios operating by electric power were increasing. However, one new use of battery-powered radios did arise in 1927: Automobile radios were introduced.

That year, people heard reporting of such events as Charles Lindbergh's return from Paris after making the first solo airplane flight over the Atlantic Ocean to become, arguably, the greatest U.S. hero of the century. This was the first time an event was covered by a number of announcers representing many stations.

Many companies sponsored programs bearing their names: *The Maxwell House Hour, The General Motors Family Party, The Eveready Hour,* and *The Sieberling Singers,* among others, all based around products still advertised today. Live concert music was a favorite and dominated NBC's schedule. Shows were live and had to be done correctly at air time. There was no way to record and play back programs with any degree of fidelity; besides, the government, the listeners, and the networks all promoted live programming.

So popular had radio become that newspapers were now beginning to worry seriously about competition. They were not so much concerned about radio news reports—radio had not yet developed its news broadcasts enough to compete seriously with the print press—as they were concerned that some of their advertisers were cutting back on their newspaper advertising and putting that money into radio advertising. In New York, for example, some newspapers that had carried radio program schedules for free now refused to print them unless they were paid to do so by the radio stations. These newspapers, however, began to lose readership to those newspapers that continued to carry radio schedules, and the boycott fizzled. But the competition grew, turned into resentment, and resulted in a press-versus-radio war a

FIG 2.27 The towers of one of the nation's earliest stations—WOW.

Composers with successful productions include Copland, Gershwin, Lehar, Milhaud, Rodgers, Kern, Shostakovich, Stravinsky, Weill.

Harlem Globetrotters founded.

Philo T. Farnsworth patents TV dissector tube.

AM band expanded by FRC.

few years later. The solution for some newspapers was to buy radio stations, and by the end of the year about 13% of the radio stations in the country were owned by newspapers.

Even as the still relatively new medium of radio was flexing its business and artistic muscles and moving from adolescence into maturity and power, an event occurred that would, in another quarter century, totally change the face of broadcasting in the United States.

The year before, in 1926, the English inventor John Logie Baird had given the first public demonstration of television, in London. Now it was the United States' turn. On April 7, 1927, in what was headlined in *The New York Times* the next day as America's first "test of television," Secretary of Commerce Hoover was televised on a circuit from Washington, D.C., to New York. Although the transmission was primitive by today's standards—a resolution of only 50 lines—Hoover could be seen and heard. *The New York Times* headline read, "FAR-OFF SPEAKERS SEEN AS WELL AS HEARD HERE IN A TEST OF TELEVISION." *The Times* described the event:

> Herbert Hoover made a speech in Washington yesterday afternoon. An audience in New York heard him and saw him. More than 200 miles of space intervening between the speaker and his audience was annihilated by the television apparatus developed by the Bell Laboratories of the American Telephone and Telegraph Company and demonstrated publicly for the first time yesterday. The apparatus shot images of Mr. Hoover by wire from Washington to New York at the rate of eighteen a second. These were thrown on a screen as motion pictures, while the loudspeaker reproduced the speech . . . . It was as if a photograph had suddenly come to life and begun to talk, smile, nod its head and look this way and that . . . . Next came . . . the first vaudeville act that ever went on the air as a talking picture . . . . The commercial future of television, if it has one, is thought to be largely in public entertainment—super-news reels flashed before audiences at the moment of occurrence, together with dramatic and musical acts shot on the ether waves in sound and picture at the instant they are taking place in the studio.

That same year another event took place that moved television even further along, from a mechanical to an electronic system. The American inventor Philo T. Farnsworth—who became known as the "father of American television"—applied for a patent for a dissector tube, which provided the base for electronic operation. He transmitted a television image with a resolution of 60 lines and experimented with a mechanism that could produce 100 lines. Prophetically, the image projected in his 60-line demonstration was a dollar sign ($). In 1990 Farnsworth's widow, Elma Farnsworth, commented on that 1927, first all-electronic transmission in terms of its influence on today's television: "He had the six basic patents used in every TV today. You take Farnsworth's patents out of your TV and you'd have a radio."

Babe Ruth hits record 60
home runs.

Rose Bowl game broadcast by NBC Blue.	Radio Act introduces concept of public interest, convenience, and necessity broadcasting.	Lindbergh's return from Paris is broadcast.

Belief in the prospective growth of the new medium was indicated with the founding of a new magazine dependent on television's fortunes, *Television.*

Today we have an excellent opportunity for Monday-morning quarterbacking by looking again at *The New York Times* story about the April 27 test of television. *The Times* was responsible, perhaps, for one of the great misprognostications of all time in one of the story's subheadlines. It said "COMMERCIAL USE IN DOUBT."

1928

It took a cigar company executive to rescue the Columbia Phonograph Broadcasting System (CPBS) from failure only a year after it was begun and to guarantee a competitive network system for America for at least the rest of the century. The Congress Cigar Company in Philadelphia, owned by William S. Paley's family, saw its sales zoom after it began advertising on the United–Columbia network. When CPBS began to falter, Paley bought a majority share for $300,000, became first its president and later its chairman, and led the renamed CBS until his retirement in 1983. To this day, only the name William Paley has rivaled that of David Sarnoff in debates as to who was the leading mogul in the history of U.S. broadcasting.

With these two resourceful and ambitious young men guiding the fortunes of the fledgling networks, the broadcast industry made quick advances. Stations increased, sets proliferated, and advertising grew. Broadcasting leapt forward as had the Roaring Twenties of speakeasies (illegal saloons operating during Prohibition), flappers (named for the loose clothing they wore), jazz, dance contests, and increased participation in sports. "Talkies" had invaded the movies; women were beginning to enter male-dominated fields, including aviation—Amelia Earhart made a transatlantic flight just a year after the solo barrier had been broken by Charles Lindbergh. It was a time of avant-garde art, music, literature, sex, and national machismo, from the popularization of artist Salvador Dali, writers Gertrude Stein and Ernest Hemingway, and composer George Gershwin to that of movie idols like Greta Garbo and Rudolph Valentino and hoodlums like Al Capone.

For those who were white and middle class, it was a decade of affluence, joy, daring, and abandon. The United States spent beyond its means, fueled by a "me generation" ensconced in materialism, incurring debts as though the money fountain would never run dry. The year 1928 would be the last full year of a carefree America before the stock market crash of 1929 and the subsequent Great Depression that plunged most of the country into gloom and poverty for more than a decade. But in 1928 programming, and especially its content, still reflected the nonchalant feeling of the country at the time: mostly music, increasing variety shows, some drama, a few feature programs oriented to the housewife, and not much news, education, or children's programming.

FIG 2.28 Will Rogers's radio broadcasts entertained millions during the medium's early days. *Photo by Lee Nadel.*

Republican Herbert Hoover elected President, defeating Democrat Al Smith, Socialist Norman Thomas, and Communist Eugene Z. Foster.

1928

Sales of radio sets increase dramatically.

CBS network purchased by William S. Paley.

Radio sales reach $750 million.

FIG 2.29 Opposition to proposal that broadcasters honor their public responsibility. This item appeared in the October 1928 issue of *Radio Digest*.

Programs a la Soviet

RADIO Commissioner Harold A. Lafount has proposed that every station making application for renewal of license shall submit a list of ten names of leading citizens of the community to act as an advisory board in arranging the station's programs. This board is to act without pay and to see that the station serves in the "public interest, convenience and necessity," according to the provisions of the Radio law. Mr. Lafount comes from the Pacific coast zone where people are more neighborly and help each other out without monetary consideration. The idea would not be at all practical east of the Mississippi. Imagine volunteer committees of ten telling the New York stations how to make up their programs!

In 1928, 677 broadcasting stations were on the air, and radio sales zoomed to $750 million, with about 8 million radios in use. The economic power of women was increasing, with programs and advertising beginning to reflect this fact. In addition, manufacturers were beginning to style radios as attractive pieces of furniture, promoting them not only as entertainment devices but as interior decor. More and more cars came equipped with radios or had them installed.

Advertising on radio was by now acceptable at most large corporations. The networks could reach some 60% of the population of the United States at a given time, interference was just about gone, and many companies saw sharp increases in sales after they advertised on radio. The manufacturers and distributors of radio sets were the largest advertisers on the medium. Although that's no longer the case, other leading advertisers in 1928—such as automobile, drug, and toiletries companies—continue to dominate today on both radio and television.

Advertisers used the advertising agencies that had been handling their print ads to handle their radio ads and supervise the programs they sponsored. The cost of sponsoring a complete program was comparatively lower than it is today. Advertising agencies literally prepared the entire package for a given advertiser. The agencies produced virtually all the sponsored shows on the networks—writing the scripts, hiring the performers, and designating the producers and directors. Because of their control over programs and commercials, ad agencies became the dominant power in radio and, later, in television. Their strength began to diminish in the 1960s, when the costs of production and commercial time for a given program became too burdensome for any one advertiser.

Ad agencies produce the majority of the sponsored shows on the networks.	Number of college-licensed stations dwindles.	First televised drama is aired by GE experimental station.

Though station owners and their stockholders were pleased with the growth of advertising, many of radio's pioneers, such as Edwin Armstrong, and political figures who had made it possible for radio to be established and to grow, such as Herbert Hoover, lamented the commercialization of a medium they believed should and would be used solely for entertainment, information, and education in the public interest.

The FRC apparently pleased enough of the industry, the public, and Congress to remain a while longer. The Radio Act of 1927 had established the FRC for just one year. In 1928 Congress renewed its mandate. In 1928 the FRC, following through on the frequency cleansing it had begun the year before, forced 83 stations off the air as it reallocated channels and licenses. The demise of the college-licensed educational stations continued, with 23 more closing their transmitters that year.

Television loomed larger on the horizon. Although the FRC did not encourage the growth of television, and the companies with large investments in radio did their best to keep the new medium from reaching a point where it could compete with their radio stations, experimental advances were made. The FRC granted an experimental license to RCA, and the GE experimental station in Schenectady, New York, began broadcasting on a limited but regular schedule, making history on September 11 with the telecast of the first television drama, *The Queen's Messenger*. The FRC acknowledged the future by assigning five channels for experimental television stations.

Managing the Radio Spectrum

To put into some context how a regulatory body handles the reality of a physical limit on the electromagnetic spectrum on which humans can hear radio sound (or watch a television picture), consider how radio is administered today. Currently there are close to 14,000 radio stations operating in the United States, squeezed into just 217 channels (100 of which are FM, the remainder AM). The entire spectrum is managed primarily by controlling operating hours, radiating power, and the height and location of transmitting towers. (The latter two effectively determine the range and direction of the signal.) Both AM and FM stations are divided into types that prescribe these conditions as well as the frequencies on which they can operate. On the AM side, a class of stations has been designated as clear channel, meaning that they effectively "own" their frequency for a large chunk of the nation, employ the most power, and use antennas that can be directed skyward at night and that—unlike FM, which requires line of sight to be received—can "bounce off" the atmosphere to increase their range. If you skim through the AM dial at night, you are likely to come across some station that is hundreds of miles from your location.

Kellogg-Briand Pact outlawing war signed by the United States.

FRC pulls plug on 83 stations in continued effort to cleanse airwaves.

Baird sends television signal across Atlantic.

First color TV demonstration.

The Davis Amendment

When Congress renewed the FRC's mandate in 1928, the legislation included an amendment by Tennessee Congressman Edwin Davis that called for equality of radio service to correct what many perceived as a geographic imbalance of broadcasting stations. Davis's amendment called for equal allocation of licenses, frequency bands, hours of operation, and radiating power. Heretofore, most of these perks had gone to the large population centers in the East and Midwest, leaving the more rural parts of the country with fewer stations, operating mostly at lower power. Davis felt that a powerful trust was dominating radio by favoring stations in heavily populated regions where advertisers could reach more people while ignoring the "public interest" of the sparsely settled areas in the South and Southwest. His amendment required the FRC to divide the country into five geographical zones and create a plan that would redistribute broadcasting facilities equally among them. The FRC designed an arrangement whereby each zone would have an equal number of clear, regional, and local channels. In this effort, Davis prevailed against strong opposition from both the radio trust and politicians from heavily populated regions. In the 1932 elections Davis lost to an opponent backed by big radio companies, and by 1936 the equalization amendment was repealed.

1929

Radio programming and the materialistic abandon of the Prohibition Era would roar together into the last year of the decade, the U.S. middle and upper classes mindless of the consequences. Music filled the airwaves: pop singers, pop instrumentalists, pop bands; serious music, too, from string quartets to symphony orchestras. Variety shows on radio increased as more and more stage and vaudeville stars began to test the waters of reaching more unseen people in one performance than they had played to in theaters throughout their careers.

Two types of radio drama made their debut: (1) the so-called "thriller" drama, somewhat equivalent to the horror and adventure TV programs of the last decades of the 20th century, and (2) serial drama, that is, continuing characters in a continuing story, a genre that expanded into many forms on radio, and later on TV, from day and evening soap operas to sitcoms to cop/cowboy/hospital clinic series. Their successes perhaps reflecting national attitudes of patronization, condescending tolerance, and insensitivity, the two series that made their network debuts in 1929 and continued for many years as U.S. favorites were both about ethnic minorities.

One of these shows, *The Rise of the Goldbergs*, was the continuing saga of an urban Jewish family. Although the characters and situations were stereotyped, they were treated gently and often with dignity. *The Rise of the Goldbergs* continued on radio and into television, ending only during the 1950s McCarthy era when the show's

Mickey Mouse makes film debut.

Automobile and drug companies among leading radio sponsors.

Networks reach 60% of U.S. population.

Congress renews FRC's term.

FIG 2.30 Presidential candidates take to the airways in 1928.

Amos 'n' Andy debuts
on NBC.

Cooperative Analysis of
Broadcasting established to
measure audience response to
network programming.

THE ROARING '20S

FIG 2.31 *Amos 'n' Andy* topped the list of popular network radio shows. The actors were white but put on "blackface" makeup. *Courtesy Anthony Slide.*

star, Gertrude Berg, protested the network's blacklisting of the program's male lead, Philip Loeb, and the program was dropped.

The other program that made its network debut in 1929 was *Amos 'n' Andy*, in which two white performers, Charles Correll and Freeman Gosden, portrayed the two black characters of the show's title. Although Amos and Andy were never shown as evil, they were presented in the racist stereotypes of the time: not very bright, inept schemers, somewhat lazy and shiftless, willing to bend the law if they could get away with it, generally irresponsible, and virtually illiterate. Despite many complaints, this program became the most popular radio show of its time—even a President of the United States allegedly ordered no appointments or meetings when *Amos 'n' Andy* was on the air—and perhaps the most popular of all time in any medium, with audience loyalty even exceeding that for the TV era's *Milton Berle Show* and *I Love Lucy*. *Amos 'n' Andy* later became a television series with black actors, but increased public concern about its racist implications ended the TV version's run in the mid-1950s.

Sponsors increasingly lent their names to the program titles. For example, in 1929 we could hear velvet-voiced announcers open programs by saying: "And now, the *Philco Hour*, with Leopold Stokowski conducting the Philadelphia Orchestra"..."the Chase and Sanborn Choral Orchestra"..."the Firestone Orchestra"..."*The General Motors Family Party*"..."*The RKO Hour*"..."*The Johnson and Johnson Program*, a musical melodrama"..."the Dutch Masters Minstrels"..."the A & P Gypsies Orchestra"..."the Cliquot Eskimos Orchestra"..."*The Old Gold Program*, with the Paul Whiteman Orchestra"..."*The Wrigley Revue*"..."the Lucky Strike Dance Orchestra"..."the Smith Brothers—Trade and Mark"..."the Stromberg Carlson Sextette"..."*The Empire Builders*—a thriller drama brought to you by the Great Northern Railroad." There were some news, public affairs, commentary, and even religious programs, but with few exceptions, they were all sustaining—that is, without paid advertising. Even back then, most of the public wanted the media to entertain,

FIG 2.32 Early network studios.

THE ROARING '20S

not stimulate, and radio was largely "chewing gum for the ears," just as much of television later became "chewing gum for the eyes."

With programming and advertising now inextricably entwined, how was the advertiser to know which programs to sponsor—which would most likely sell more of his or her product or service? In Cincinnati, Archibald M. Crossley established the Cooperative Analysis of Broadcasting to find out. Using principally morning-after phone surveys, Crossley estimated the percentages of radio homes that had listened to specified programs, and he made this information available to networks and stations for a fee. From that beginning, ratings evolved to their present-day dominance over television programs and radio formats. An interesting byproduct of Crossley's work was his finding that people listened to radio most between 7:00 and 11:00 P.M. He called this *prime time*. Seven decades later the same definition and breakdown of hours of prime time still apply.

Radio Becomes Commercialized with Little Public Discussion

When radio came along in the 1920s, few (apparently not even Sarnoff) thought it had any commercial potential, but by the time the networks formed, capitalists sensed the potential in selling large audiences to advertisers. These business interests dominated the newly formed Federal Radio Commission, which chose to turn over the scarce frequencies to large corporate networks without any public and little congressional deliberation. This is not to say that there wasn't any opposition to commercialization. Social conservatives, though supportive of free-market economics, were disturbed by the prospects of commercial interests taking control of programming that might distribute nontraditional Judeo-Christian values to the masses. Resistance also came from education, religious, civic, labor, women, and farm organizations, civil libertarians, scientists such as radio inventors Armstrong and de Forest, and future President Herbert Hoover, all of them presciently arguing that if private, profit-oriented interests controlled the medium, no amount of regulation or self-control could overcome the bias built into the resulting commercial system. They warned that commercial broadcasting would avoid provocative public issues while emphasizing whatever fare would attract the most advertisers. And because broadcasters and newspapers had a vested interest in a commercial radio system, very little notice of these issues reached the general public.

As commercialization increasingly dominated radio, many listeners and organization and governmental leaders increasingly expressed their concerns. In an effort to preempt the FRC from imposing programming and advertising standards on the industry, the NAB took the self-regulation approach and adopted a Code of Ethics. The code included recommendations that stations avoid broadcasting "fraudulent, deceptive, or indecent programs"; carry commercials only before 6:00 P.M.; and exclude false or harmful advertising. Compliance with the NAB code was voluntary;

FIG 2.33 Radio microphones follow President Hoover as he tosses out the first ball of the 1929 baseball season at Griffith Stadium in Washington, D.C. *Courtesy Artist's Proof, Alexandria, Virginia.*

many of its members subscribed to it, and some adhered to it. With changes over the years dictated by the growth of radio and the development of television, the NAB radio and television ethics codes lasted until they were dropped in the 1980s.

On October 29, 1929, one era came to an end and a new one began. On what was known as Black Tuesday, the stock market—the barometer of America's free-spending, live-for-today, 1920s philosophy—crashed. The stock market had been riding high, and not only the rich but even working people were investing in stocks, assuming that the sky ride would go on forever. As a result of the crash, businesses failed, many investors who lost everything committed suicide, and money and jobs dried up. It would get worse. At the end of 1929 more than 60% of the U.S. working population earned less than $2,000 a year; a few years later a family of four could live on $14 a week—if they could get that much. Fully 17% of Americans were out of work. People were literally starving and dying on the streets of urban areas and on the back roads of rural America. The free-spending, debt-incurring days had caught up with us, and it was time to pay the piper.

While the stock market crash ushered in the Great Depression, with millions of people descending into poverty and hundreds of thousands of businesses going under, radio boomed. Why? Because although tens of millions of Americans now could not afford the 10 cents for a movie show, they could be entertained for free on their home radios. Most of America became a captive radio audience.

Chapter THREE

The Terrible, '30s

Profit Amid Depression

In the 1930s, the number of radio sets in use continued to increase. In 1930 an estimated 40% of America's homes had radios. Considering the state of the economy, that was a large number. Listeners heard more and more vaudeville-type shows. As the Depression proved the beginning of the end for vaudeville theaters, or houses, as they were called, the performers tried to re-create their acts on radio, some successfully breaking into network radio and others settling for a job—any job—at a local station. Throughout this decade, many future entertainment stars got their start working for peanuts on small radio stations.

Successful network programs were given long-term renewals, establishing a star system that continues today. *Amos 'n' Andy*, for example, which had gone on the network only the year before, in 1929, contracted for five years, making its creators and stars, Charles Correll and Freeman Gosden, the highest-paid radio entertainers up to that time. As with other stars whose shows had one sponsor, their contract was with their sponsor, Pepsodent toothpaste, which in turn signed with NBC as the show's exclusive agent.

But perhaps the most significant event in programming was the introduction of regularly scheduled hard-news broadcasts on the NBC Blue Network with the reporter-commentator Lowell Thomas, who would remain a leading newscaster, first on radio, and then on television, for a half century. Another commentator who successfully used the power of the media to affect people's minds and emotions made his debut in 1930. Father Charles E. Coughlin exploited the airwaves for the next decade with a right-wing, anti-Semitic message of "social justice" that influenced millions of economically frustrated Americans. His audience was estimated to be as high as 45 million. One type of program, however, was at least temporarily restrained. In a landmark action, the FRC refused to renew the license of Kansas station KFKB, whose owner, Dr. John R. Brinkley, had used the station for medical charlatanism. As radio audiences in general grew, the Crossley research organization, established the previous year, began extensive ratings services.

Those who were concerned about the increasing demise of educational stations and who believed that radio should be principally an educational/informational medium formed two organizations to promote educational radio:

FIG 3.1 Publications such as this 1930 issue of *Radio News* kept radio enthusiasts well informed.

© 2010 Taylor & Francis. All rights reserved.
DOI: 10.1016/B978-0-240-81236-6.00003-2

THE TERRIBLE '30S

Pan Am established as the
nation's largest passenger airline.

Hoover signs controversial
tariff act.

1930

NBC begins regularly scheduled
hard-news broadcasts.

FIG 3.2 Father Coughlin's political preaching stirred a broad range of emotions and attracted large audiences.
Courtesy Anthony Slide.

(1) the National Committee on Education by Radio and (2) the National Advisory Council on Radio in Education. Their efforts were supported by an unlikely commercial ally, newspaper publishers, who were increasingly concerned with the draining off of newspaper advertising dollars into the entertainment programs of radio. CBS introduced its own educational program designed for the classroom, the American School of the Air.

One form of education through radio, although often lacking distinction, was that of programs for children, mostly on local stations. These shows consisted mostly of performers playing music for children and telling children's stories. A feature of many of these programs was the birthday greeting (usually sent in, of course, by a doting parent or grandparent). What a thrill for a child to wait expectantly by the radio on a birthday morning to hear his or her name announced on this magic medium for all the world to hear!

In a preview of the "media diversity" approach that would be taken by the FCC some years later, the U.S. government filed an antitrust suit against the longtime "patent allies" headed by RCA and including GE, AT&T, and Westinghouse. These companies' control of some 3,800 patents gave them almost monopolistic control of the production, transmission, and receiving equipment of radio—and of motion pictures and phonograph records as well—and put them in a position to impose their policies

Grant Wood's *American Gothic*
exhibited.

Organizations are formed to lobby
for educational programming.

Local stations develop children's
programs.

and beliefs on the content of the medium. While RCA was defending itself on this
front, it took a step on another that would result in its even greater growth as a radio
giant: David Sarnoff was appointed president of NBC.

On the technical side, Edwin Armstrong progressed with his idea for an FM
transmission system, determining that FM needed a wider bandwidth than AM to
avoid interference, and he applied for the first four patents that were to be the bases
for FM radio. AM wasn't worried about FM yet, however. But it did begin to worry
about TV, and CBS applied for a television license, not because it expected to begin
television programming in the near future but to protect its future interests and, as
the *New York Times* stated, "to be prepared for competition when radio is supplemented by visual broadcasting." Technical advances in television included a demonstration by NBC of what it called a Flying Spot Scanner, a refinement of the Nipkow
1884 disk, that separated images into transmittable segments. The NBC demonstration
used the cartoon character Felix the Cat as a subject on its 60-line transmission and,
although the picture was quite fuzzy, it was discernible.

Those less optimistic about television included the magazine *Radio World*, which
conceded that television was an interesting subject for experiment but still had a
long way to go: "The more the ordinary man discovers about the halting advance of
television, the more he is urged to be satisfied with radio as it is and to lay in his
radio supplies for the winter."

FIG 3.3 Expensive and
elegant cabinets housed
receivers so as to make
them a more integral part
of the parlor setting. This
1930s magazine
advertisement promotes
the popular RCA Radiola
62 cabinet model.

THE TERRIBLE '30S

Radios in Cars

Although automobile radios were available by 1927, it's hard to fathom
why anyone would've wanted one–when the engine was running you could
barely hear anything but static. The electrical energy generated by the motor
produced intolerable interference. (There were other obstacles that were
easier to overcome, such as making a radio small enough to fit yet sturdy
enough to take the abuse of rough roads.) The static problem was solved
by 1930 through a fortuitous meeting of Paul Galvin and Bill Lear. Galvin had
a company that manufactured battery eliminators, a product that allowed
battery-powered radios to operate on household current. Located in the same
Chicago building was Lear's radio parts business. The two united to solve the
problem and chose to demonstrate it at a radio manufacturers' gathering in
Atlantic City, but because they didn't have the fee for admission, they had to
display their product outside the convention hall. The success of a functional
car radio led to the formation of one of the communication technology giants,
Motorola. Lear became one of the legendary inventors of the last century with,
most notably, the Learjet, the first private jet aircraft, and the often ridiculed
eight-track audiotape player.

David Sarnoff is appointed president of NBC.

1931

Both the business and the programming of radio grew in 1931. There were more commercials, more giveaway contests, more gimmicks for selling products and services, and more promotional schemes for the stations themselves. As more money became available to hire name performers, more stars from the theater, concert halls, and nightclubs tried the new medium. Even Hollywood personalities, who by and large had snubbed radio, became aware of the medium's power to create and sustain national recognition.

Radio stations began using increasingly flexible portable equipment for what were called "stunts"—reporting live from caves, on mountainsides, even during parachute jumps. These first remotes were made possible by the assignment of shortwave frequencies by the FRC for short-distance use where wire facilities were not available.

While newspapers continued to battle the inroads of radio, one representative of the print medium joined the aural medium. *Time* magazine produced on CBS *The March of Time*, a weekly dramatization of the key news events of the previous seven days. The program caught on immediately, becoming a favorite much like *60 Minutes* has in more recent years. And the print medium spawned another electronic media magazine, one that was to become the most important journal of the business of broadcasting: *Broadcasting*. This industry publication provided the most comprehensive coverage of the radio medium (and later of TV and cable), especially in the areas of regulation, business, technology, and programming. The business of broadcasting was to take a huge jump in another direction, too: under way was the development of Rockefeller Center in New York City, which would become known as the home of Radio City, NBC's headquarters. But RCA was premature with an invention of one of its other divisions, the Victor Talking Machine Company. In 1931 Victor produced the first $33\frac{1}{3}$ plastic record; however, unsatisfactory quality, lack of record players, and poor marketing delayed its serious entry into the home until after World War II.

International programming increased. Foreign leaders who had been read about in newspapers and seen in movie newsreels that were sometimes weeks out of date were now heard live on radio. One of the great playwrights of all time, George Bernard Shaw; the Italian dictator Benito Mussolini; the Indian leader Mahatma Gandhi; and Pope Pius XI were among those who reached the American people from overseas by radio in 1931. The Pope's February 12 address on world peace was the occasion for a classic network goof. The speech was being carried by NBC's Blue Network. On NBC's Red Network at the same time was a remote light program, *The Shell Ship of Joy*. When the time came for the announcer, Cecil Underwood, to give the closing network announcement for *The Shell Ship of Joy*, he flipped the switch for the Blue instead of the Red Network and cut into the Pope's presentation with the words, "This past hour of fun and nonsense has come to you over KPO, San Francisco."

FIG 3.4 A 1931 Atwater Kent (superheterodyne) "cathedral" model table receiver.

Unemployment in United States reaches
16% as Depression deepens.

Time magazine sponsors
The March of Time on
CBS.

Victor experiments with 33⅓ rpm
plastic record.

The organizations that had been formed the year before to promote educational broadcasting found a champion in Representative Simeon D. Fess of Ohio, who unsuccessfully introduced a bill in Congress that would have reserved 15% of the radio frequencies for educational stations. Of the 129 educational stations that had been operating in 1925, only 51 were still on the air. It would be some years before such reservations were actually approved. In an unrelated action involving the government, AT&T, in an effort to extricate itself from the Justice Department's antitrust suit, withdrew from the patent-allies group.

Fifteen experimental television stations were on the air in 1931. But TV receivers were extremely expensive, and with the opposition of the radio-oriented networks it was not possible to subsidize the necessary programming to make the stations viable. Still, they hung on as best as they could, in anticipation of a rosy future. CBS was optimistic enough to begin TV broadcasting that year.

1932

The Great Depression had hit hard by 1932, and the principal escape for millions of homeless, hungry, and ill Americans—and for millions more on the edge of poverty—was radio. Losing oneself for a half hour, an hour, or an evening in jokes, laughter, and song was a welcome alternative to total despair. Tuning in to daytime dramas, in which the characters were sometimes worse off than listeners and had at least as many troubles, made life a bit more bearable. Comedians dominated radio. Eddie Cantor, star of musical comedy and vaudeville, topped the Crossley ratings with his weekly program in 1932. Another vaudevillian, Fred Allen, entered radio in 1932, offering a literate, dry sense of humor that kept his program on the air in the top 10 until it was outrated in its time slot by a quiz show, *Stop the Music*, in 1949. It was the beginning of the age of Jack Benny, Burns and Allen, Fibber McGee and Molly, Ed Wynn, Rudy Vallee, Al Jolson, and others who kept America laughing and singing for a few hours each week, not only through the Depression but for decades to come.

The national audience was now large enough to prompt advertisers to sponsor entertainment for targeted audiences; one such show that began its network run during the 1932–1933 season was the *National Barn Dance*. Another type of program that was to become highly popular, the morning talk show, also made its debut that season, *Don McNeill's Breakfast Club*.

Other types of programs increased, too: soap operas, drama, mysteries, Westerns, adventure, and crime. One of the most listened-to soap operas of the time was *One Man's Family*, which lasted for 28 years. Other new and growing program types included shows for women, with formats that emphasized cooking and beauty tips and that predominated until the women's movement in the 1970s prompted less sexist and more meaningful content in so-called "women's programs." Another successful

THE TERRIBLE '30S

format was radio's version of the gossip column, which made Walter Winchell a leading radio personality for many years.

Music continued to be the principal programming of radio, and an announcer at KFWB in Los Angeles introduced a new format that would become the standard for all radio pop music shows. Al Jarvis played records with commentary on his *Make Believe Ballroom,* a title and format that would be even more popularized a few years later when Martin Block did the same kind of show on WNEW in New York. Al Jarvis and Martin Block are generally considered the first radio disc jockeys, or deejays.

Radio news opened new vistas for radio journalists and for listeners. Live coverage of special events, such as the 1932 Republican and Democratic National Conventions, became commonplace. One of the most publicized crimes of the century, the kidnapping of the baby of America's most popular hero, Charles Lindbergh, spurred extensive radio coverage, one of the first national "media events." Radio carried not only news about the kidnapping but broadcast appeals to the kidnappers. Reporting the case daily to an eager public made the commentator Boake Carter one of the first media news stars. A few years later, in 1935, the same case—this time the execution of Bruno Hauptmann, who was convicted of kidnapping and murdering

FIG 3.5 Among the earliest radio performers who became stars of the medium were Ted Husing (left), Graham McNamee (center), and Milton Cross (right).

the Lindbergh baby—made a media star of another commentator, Gabriel Heatter, whose ad-libbing for almost an hour during a delay while reporting the execution held the rapt attention of millions of listeners.

As radio news grew, newspapers tried harder to muzzle this competition and pressured United Press (UP), a news service, to break its contract with CBS to provide 1932 election returns. The Associated Press (AP), UP's rival, agreed to provide election results to CBS and NBC free of charge. To counter this action, UP reversed itself on election night and offered its service, as did another competitor, the International News Service (INS). By the time the newspaper "extras" came out the next day, everyone with a radio set already knew what had happened. This was the beginning of the end of newspapers' dominance as news purveyors.

The business of radio took turns both toward and away from monopoly. The patent-allies split, RCA, GE, and Westinghouse separating by consent decree in order for the Department of Justice to drop its antitrust suit. That split gave stations more freedom. On the other hand, NBC became a wholly owned subsidiary of RCA, and William Paley, head of CBS, bought out the Paramount movie company's holdings in the company. These events gave RCA and CBS more control.

On the television front, NBC started broadcasting from its station in the Empire State Building, the world's tallest, constructed the previous year. In 1932, 38 experimental TV stations were on the air in the United States.

FIG 3.6 Lowell Thomas spent nearly a half century before the network microphone.

FIG 3.7 Hilmar Baukhage began his daily news broadcasts on NBC Blue in 1932. Later in the decade he would report from Europe on the rise of Hitler. *Courtesy Irving Fang.*

THE TERRIBLE '30S

Scottsboro Boys sentenced to death.

Fifteen experimental television stations are on the air.

RCA Radiola 80 receiver marketed.

FIG 3.8 H. V. Kaltenborn, the first radio commentator in the United States. *Courtesy Irving Fang.*

The Trigger of the Press-Radio War

It reads like a plot from a soap opera, but what sparked the decisive denouement of the Press–Radio War actually occurred, and the players were not some fictional characters but large corporate entities. During the early 1930s, as the Depression deepened, tensions rose among newspapers, the wire services, and radio. By 1932 the major newspaper cartel had persuaded the wire services not to furnish news reports to radio stations. Before the 1932 Presidential election, the United Press brokered a secret deal to provide CBS with the election night returns. But word of the deal leaked out, and under pressure from a council of newspaper owners who threatened to cancel their service, the UP voided the agreement. The Associated Press also heard of the deal, but not, so they claimed, of the cancellation and made its own arrangement to supply NBC with election night returns. And so, on election night, only NBC had the most up-to-date results while its major competitor, CBS, was left far behind. Now everyone was fuming—newspapers, of course; UP, which had sacrificed much needed revenue by breaking its contract with CBS; and CBS itself, which lost to NBC listeners who sought the latest results.

Comedians attract large audiences while music continues as radio's primary offering.

1933

While the stage was set for future war in Europe, a media war broke out in the United States when the newspapers finally took drastic action to curb the growth of radio and the siphoning off of its advertising revenue. In 1933 the "Press–Radio War," as it has been called, reached the fighting stage when the newspapers succeeded in convincing the three major news services—UP, INS, and AP—to continue offering their services only to those radio stations owned by newspaper members of the given wire service. Some years earlier, in 1928, the wire services had begun providing two reports daily to radio stations. The newspapers weren't too worried then, but by 1933 the networks and many stations were carrying daily 15-minute news reports. Most newspapers had already stopped printing radio schedules unless stations paid them to do so. The newspapers even convinced Congress to bar radio reporters from press galleries. CBS already had a large news department and set up its own news service. But the pressures were too great, and radio capitulated at the Biltmore Conference (named after the New York hotel in which it was held).

The two major networks, CBS and NBC, agreed to refrain from gathering their own news; they would carry not "hard news" but only commentary, which would be broadcast just twice daily in five-minute segments, unsponsored, and provided by the wire services through a Press-Radio Bureau, to be established the following year. Many independent stations and even affiliates rebelled at these restrictions, however, and began to set up their own news-gathering services. Only about half the stations subscribed to the Press-Radio Bureau. It was clear that the newspapers' strategy had not worked, and in less than a year the Biltmore agreement was undone. Although the wire services then began to provide full reports to radio again, radio realized the need for its own news-gathering services, with materials prepared specifically for radio delivery. Out of this need came the growth of network news operations, with CBS taking an early lead.

Radio news became more and more important to the American public. The new U.S. President, Franklin D. Roosevelt, inaugurated on March 4, 1933, began to take immediate, dramatic steps to cope with the economic disaster. On March 12, Roosevelt began the first of a series of radio talks to the nation that over the years would become known as FDR's "fireside chats." Roosevelt demonstrated the political power of radio; so effective were his fireside chats that for the first time the people felt they were in direct contact with their President, sharing problems and ideas and participating in the administration of their country. Roosevelt's use of radio, including some 28 (estimates vary) fireside chats during his tenure in the White House, was an important factor in his election to an unprecedented four terms.

The political power of radio was not limited to the United States. The dictator of Italy, Benito Mussolini, was using radio at least as effectively and was once quoted as saying that had it not been for radio, he would not have been able to gain the

THE TERRIBLE '30S

| MacArthur and Eisenhower lead army attack on "bonus march" war veterans in Washington. | Franklin D. Roosevelt elected President; says, "The only thing we have to fear is fear itself." |

Lindbergh kidnapping case becomes a major national media event.

FIG 3.9 FDR was a frequent presence on radio in the 1930s. *Courtesy David Sarnoff Library.*

control over the Italian people that he did. And in its last democratic election prior to the post–Berlin Wall unification of East and West Germany in 1990, Germany elected its Nazi party leader, Adolf Hitler, as its chancellor. Hitler also used the media with great effect. The rising tide of fascism in Europe and the actions of Germany's Hitler and Italy's Mussolini fed U.S. radio stations with news of increasing critical interest to the U.S. public. At the same time, the public wanted to escape from the realities that kept coming closer from over the horizon, and radio entertainment provided that escape.

Networks grew. NBC now owned 10 stations outright and was increasing its number of affiliates, as was CBS. Radio revenue decreased as the Depression deepened. Because people didn't have money to buy products, less advertising money was available—and anyway, why advertise if people had no money to buy? It was an oppressive circle. Nevertheless, radio was doing better financially than most other businesses in the country. Among other approaches, stations offered discounts to those sponsors who paid their bills within given time periods. During this time one advertising practice was established that still exists today: The Twentieth

Assassination attempt on
FDR fails.

1933

Patent allies—RCA, GE,
and Westinghouse—
break pact.

First car radios available.

Amendment—Prohibition—was repealed in 1933 and, although alcohol commercials were legal, CBS set a precedent by carrying only beer and wine ads and refusing those for hard liquor.

Programs and their stars became even more closely identified with the products that sponsored them. For example, Jack Benny's program "hello" during his longtime sponsorship by Jell-O dessert was "Jell-O again, this is Jack Benny." The year 1933 was a landmark programming year if only for one program that made its debut: *The Lone Ranger*. Not only did it become one of the favorite programs of all time, but it had tens of millions of people throughout the world humming and whistling classical music—its theme from Rossini's *William Tell Overture*.

The Biltmore Agreement

The settlement reached after two days of what was described as the "smoke and hate filled rooms in the Hotel Biltmore" that ended the Press–Radio War appeared to be a resounding victory for newspapers. The terms imposed severe restrictions on radio just as the nation was thirsting for news. The agreement stipulated that radio was to be limited to 30-word reports, sustaining (unsponsored) to be broadcast only twice a day, one after 9:30 A.M., the other after 9:00 P.M., times selected so as to ensure that these reports would air well after the morning and evening papers had been distributed. Radio could only cover items that were at least 12 hours old, with details supplied by the Press-Radio News Service, a newspaper-created entity. However, the agreement placed no restriction, save for the 12-hour embargo, on any form of news that was labeled "backgrounding" (news analysis) or commentary. A commentator could "interpret" events, offering context and meaning, something that listeners' desperately craved. And most significantly, backgrounding could be sponsored, obviously an enormous economic enticement for radio. Almost immediately, analysts flourished on the airwaves, and to demonstrate that these commentators were not reporting "news," they were usually budgeted under the station's Entertainment Division.

1934

The FCC, which continues to be the federal regulatory agency responsible for communications, was established in 1934. The Radio Act of 1927 did not give the FRC jurisdiction over telegraph and telephone carriers. Supervision of nonradio operations was divided among a number of federal offices, including the Post Office Department, the Interstate Commerce Commission, and the

THE TERRIBLE '30S

Prohibition repealed by
Congress.

FDR fights Depression with bank
holiday, National Recovery Act (NRA).

Newspapers, fearing
competition, cease wire
services to radio.

Department of State. In 1933 President Roosevelt directed an interagency committee to study the problem of government regulation of electronic communications. The committee recommended that a single agency be established to regulate all interstate and foreign communications by wire and radio, including broadcasting, telephone, and telegraph, with provisions for inclusion of newly developing media, such as television, that might fall into these categories. Congress thus enacted the Communications Act of 1934, which created the FCC. The FCC began operations on July 11, 1934, as an independent agency composed of seven commissioners appointed by the President with the advice and consent of the Senate.

Section I of the Communications Act of 1934 describes the purposes of the act in creating the FCC:

> regulating interstate and foreign commerce by wire and radio so as to make available . . . to all the people of the United States a rapid, efficient, nationwide, and worldwide wire and radio communication service . . . for the purpose of the national defense . . . promoting safety of life and property through the use of wire and radio communication . . . by centralizing authority [in the] Federal Communications Commission.

Various other sections and titles of the act dealt with the FCC's jurisdiction, definitions of the various services the FCC might regulate, FCC administrative procedures, and penalties for violations of the act. Over the years, the act has been amended many times, with a number of appendices added.

Whereas the industry had virtually begged for the Radio Act of 1927, now that it was a well-established, money-making business, it didn't like the idea of more extensive regulation. Led by its association, the National Association of Broadcasters (NAB), the industry generally opposed creation of the FCC, a new, more powerful federal communications office. Broadcasters were especially concerned with the FCC's renewal authority and the manner in which the Commission might require their compliance with the "public interest, convenience, or necessity" provision of the Communications Act.

More than 60% of the country's homes had radios in 1934, and radio sets could be found in more than 1.5 million automobiles. Some people even set up "radio rooms" in their homes; these persons were, of course, those who had large enough houses and money, not a very prevalent situation during the Terrible Thirties. But radio was so thoroughly established as a lifestyle necessity, even during the Depression, that the *New Republic* magazine wrote, "Radio is here! This is the art that encompasses all of the arts, the center of interest of the modern home, the culture font of today." Even members of the poorest household did with radio what is done with television today: At the beginning of each week, they looked at the radio schedule in a newspaper or magazine to decide what they should tune in to during the next seven days.

FIG 3.10 Car radios were becoming standard equipment in the 1930s, as this magazine advertisement shows.

One area that continued to get short shrift, however, was educational radio. The National Advisory Council on Radio in Education and the National Committee on Education by Radio were unsuccessful in gathering sufficient public or political support for an amendment to the Communications Act that would have reserved 25% of the frequencies for educational use. The Association of College and University Broadcasting Stations, a group that had been in existence since 1925, when many college stations were going on the air, reorganized itself into the National Association of Educational Broadcasters (NAEB). This organization eventually became the principal membership and lobbying group for educational radio and television and some years later was largely responsible for the Public Broadcasting Act of 1967. The NAEB continued in existence until 1981, when the strengths of the Corporation for Public Broadcasting (CPB), the Public Broadcasting Service (PBS), and National Public Radio (NPR) made NAEB's organizational approach and services no longer necessary.

LAYNE BEATY

FORMER NETWORK AGRICULTURAL REPORTER

It may be a coincidence that the first use of the term *broadcast* was agricultural, referring to the sowing of seeds. It is nonetheless fitting because in the early days of radio, when rural people lived in varying conditions of isolation, radio became a link to the outside world and a live-in companion for farmers and their families. Those first two radio stations, KDKA Pittsburgh and WHA Madison, emphasized such services. Stations justified the use of their assigned frequencies and power by their broadcasts of market prices, updated weather forecasts, information on better farming practices, government regulations, and commercials adapted for far-flung rural listeners. In my long career, those years spent broadcasting agricultural programs were undoubtedly the most rewarding in terms of public acceptance. My listeners

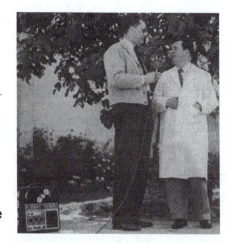

FIG 3.11 In 1947, when the United States was cooperating with Mexico to stop the spread of the costly hoof-and-mouth disease of livestock by killing and burying thousands of head of cattle in the quarantined areas of central Mexico, Layne Beaty, then the farm editor of WBAP in Fort Worth, Texas, went to the scene with his new wire recorder. Here he is pictured interviewing a top Mexican government veterinarian in Mexico City.
Courtesy Layne Beaty.

THE TERRIBLE '30S

| Hitler becomes chancellor of Germany following Reichstag fire. | Germany and Italy withdraw from League of Nations; United States still has not joined. | Midwest plagued by drought. |

1934

included not only country folk but urban professionals as well, and one network program (the old NBC *Farm and Home Hour*) drew mail regularly from the Wall Street area. On the air, I tried to be warm and friendly with some natural humor, not contrived, too corny, or suggestive—no inside jokes. I made as many personal appearances as possible, and this helped build listenership and goodwill for the station. Entertainment (music, etc.) and long features, early staples on farm programs before good roads and television, have disappeared, making way for shorter, more concise reports aimed at helping farmers and ranchers (and sponsors) turn a profit.

There was enough business for a fourth radio network, in addition to NBC's Blue and Red and CBS, and four stations (WGN, Chicago; WOR, Newark; WLW, Cincinnati; and WXYZ, Detroit) joined forces as the Quality Network to boost their individual advertising revenues, although without a centralized administration. This entity shortly became the Mutual Broadcasting System, which continues today, though it, unlike the other networks, did not add television to its operations. One of the network's stations, WLW, obtained special permission to operate with an experimental power of 500,000 watts in a bid to become, as it called itself, the "Nation's Station"—a phenomenon that didn't truly come to pass until decades later, with Ted Turner's nationwide distribution of his Atlanta television station, WTBS, on cable. WLW soon became a favorite station in much of the Midwest and in the evening in other parts of the country, with substantial income from regional and national advertising. This situation continued until 1939, when the FCC, under pressure from other stations to give them the same privilege, revoked WLW's 500 kW authorization except from 1:00 to 6:00 A.M., which had been its original hours under the experimental grant. In 1942, with restrictions on all communications due to the war, WLW was forced to go back to 50 kW full time, and this has remained the highest power for all AM stations since. (FM stations do not have this power limit.)

As audiences grew, so did advertising and, in turn, rating systems. A competitor to Crosley, Clark Hooper, made phone surveys of what the respondents were listening to at the time of the call and claimed that his method was more accurate than the Crosley next-day recall approach. Soon the Hooper ratings became dominant in the field.

The technical progress of both the old and the upcoming media continued. In 1933 Edwin Armstrong received patents he had filed as long as four years earlier for the frequency modulator limiter, the basis of FM radio, and in early 1934 he

Federal Communications
Commission is established.

Association of College and University
Broadcasting Stations spawns the
National Association of Educational
Broadcasters.

demonstrated FM for his old friend, NBC's David Sarnoff. Unfortunately for Armstrong and Sarnoff's friendship—and for FM—RCA and NBC were protective of AM growth and, if anything, preferred to promote TV rather than have a direct competitor like FM in the wings as the next new medium. After a year of experiments in the RCA quarters at the Empire State Building, Armstrong was told to leave. Although he gave a public demonstration of FM to the Institute of Radio Engineers in November 1934, and in 1935 the FCC allocated some channels to FM, these channels were largely unsuitable and in scattered places on the spectrum; FM would thus remain in abeyance for some years more. Another blow to Armstrong was the Supreme Court's 1934 decision awarding to Lee de Forest the rights to the regenerative, or feedback, circuit, the key to modern radio for which both had applied for patents in 1914. RCA had a licensing agreement with de Forest and backed him with its legal resources; however, it is now generally believed that Armstrong should have got the credit for the invention.

An interesting experiment that presaged the future was a 1934 demonstration of facsimile transmission through radio by its inventor, John V. L. Hogan. It was called a *radio pen reproducer*.

RADIO FACSIMILES—Above is the radio pen reproducer demonstrated by John V. L. Hogan, inventor, standing beside a table model radio receiver from which it operates. The 1-foot rule shows the relative heights. Shown also are samples of comic strips received on this reproducer during demonstration April 9 of transmitting and receiving apparatus ordered by WTMJ, Milwaukee.

A DEMONSTRATION of a new high speed facsimile radio system was given April 9 at the St. Moritz Hotel, New York, before members of the Radio Commission, radio engineers and representatives of the New York and technical press. The demonstration was presented by John V. L. Hogan, New York consulting engineer and inventor. It consisted of an hour's program during which a coordinated facsimile and sound program was received in the hotel from experimental stations W2XBB and W2XAR on the 1550 and 1594 kc. channels.

1935

Although still not close to the 99% penetration we know today, more than two out of every three homes had radios in 1935. Not only were the four national networks thriving, but some 20 regional networks were in operation. Independent stations were having a tough time competing with network affiliates, and more and more stations sought to affiliate, despite the long-term contracts and strong control demanded by the networks. As the economy began to show subtle signs of recovery, advertising grew, with ad agencies placing more than 75% of all radio commercials and concomitantly exercising even more power over programming.

Comedians continued as the public's favorite entertainers, with such performers as Jack Benny, Eddie Cantor, Ed Wynn, Burns and Allen, Joe Penner, and Fred Allen becoming household names. The year 1935 saw the debut on radio of a musical comedy performer who overcame his first negative impression of radio to become a star of it and, later, of television and movies for the remainder of the century—Bob Hope. The Big Band era was enhanced by radio, especially through such programs as *Your Hit Parade*, which featured the top songs of the week played and sung by top bands and singers; teenage (and even older) dance parties were planned around the Saturday-night broadcasts of *Your Hit Parade*. Another of the most popular shows of all time, one that continues to spawn imitators even today, moved from a local New York station to the NBC Red Network in 1935: *Major Bowes and His Original Amateur Hour*. The audience called or wrote in their votes for the best amateur performer of the night, urged on by Major Bowes: "The wheel of fortune spins, round

FIG 3.12 This article on the "fax machine" appeared in the April 15, 1934, issue of *Broadcasting* magazine. Popular application of fax technology was decades away.
Courtesy *Broadcasting*.

THE TERRIBLE '30S

Mutual Broadcasting
System becomes the
fourth network.

Lulu Belle

SHE IS THE BELLE OF THE
BARN DANCE

On Saturday Nights

The NATIONAL
BARN DANCE

Hear It Over
56 NBC STATIONS
COAST-TO-COAST

Over 40 Radio Artists including the Cumberland Ridge Runners, Maple City Four, Lulu Belle, Hoosier Hot Shots, Uncle Ezra, Tune Twisters, Arkansas Woodchopper, Hill Toppers, Henry Burr, and Verne, Lee, and Mary. A rollicking program of old time singing, dancing and homespun fun. Brought to you direct from WLS, Chicago, every Saturday night over

WJZ or KDKA
9:30 to 10:30 P.M., EST
Sponsored by ALKA SELTZER

Advertisement for a popular 1930s
network radio show.

FIG 3.13 Advertisement
for a popular 1930s
network radio show.

FIG 3.14 The list of
popular performers of
radio's golden age
included Bob Hope, Fibber
McGee and Molly (Jim and
Marion Jordan), and
Jimmy Durante.
Courtesy WTIC.

and round she goes, and where she stops nobody knows." Some of the greatest popular and classical stars in America got their start on the *Amateur Hour*, including, in its first year, a skinny kid from New Jersey named Frank Sinatra.

Children found radio a companion for all reasons, from rapt concentration to background sound for doing homework (although perhaps not so distracting for the latter as TV is today). In addition to preschool programs in the morning and early afternoon, networks and stations offered adventure stories beginning at 3:00 P.M., as soon as the school day ended, up to and past 6:00 P.M., the supper hour. Those old enough to remember the rush to the radio after school through the 1930s probably recall the musical themes, the commercials, and the announcers' introductions, as well as characters and plots of such shows as *Jack Armstrong—The All-American Boy*, *Dick Tracy*, *Little Orphan Annie*, *Buck Rogers—In the 25th Century*, *Chandu the Magician*, and *Bobby Benson*, as well as the perennial sound of "Hi-ho, Silver, awaaay" of *The Lone Ranger*. Programs generally reinforced, perhaps unintentionally, the racism of the country, rarely presenting racial minorities and, when they did so, mostly in stereotyped roles. The sexism one finds in some children's television shows today was present then: There were virtually no females in the radio adventure serials, except in secondary roles as helpmates to the male characters. And just as there is with television today, there was concern over the content of children's programs, principally violence. In fact, both CBS and NBC adopted guidelines designed to

The "Nation's Station," WLW, operates with 500,000 watts.

Armstrong demonstrates FM for Sarnoff.

Lee de Forest awarded rights to regenerative circuit.

FIG 3.15 Excerpt from a November 20, 1935, radio magazine showing the evening program schedule, top songs aired, and advertisement for a mystery feature.

7:00 p.m.
★ NBC—Amos 'n' Andy: WEAF KYW WCAE WRC WLW WTIC WFBR (sw-9.53)
★ CBS—Myrt & Marge, sketch: WABC WCAU WCAO WJAS WJSV (sw-11.83-9.59)
NBC—Easy Aces, sketch: WJZ KDKA WMAL WBZ WFIL WBAL (sw-11.87)
WDBJ—News
WIP—Uncle Wip's Roll Call
WOR—Star Lomax, Sports
WTAR—To be announced

7:15 p.m.
★ NBC—ALKA-SELTZER PRE-sents Uncle Ezra's Radio Sta-tion: WEAF WFBR WRC KYW WCAE (sw-9.53)
CBS—Imperial Hawaiian Band: WABC WCAO WJAS WJSV WCAU (sw-11.83-9.59)
NBC—Stamp Club; Capt. Tim Healy: WJZ WFIL KDKA WBAL WMAL WBZ (sw-11.87)
MBS—Lilac Time: WOR WLW
WDBJ—Talk on Beauty, Mrs. M. M. Caldwell
WIP—Little Theater of the Air
WTIC—Gordon, Dave and Bunny

7:30 p.m.
NBC—Our American Schools: WEAF WMAL WFBR KYW
CBS—Kate Smith, vocalist; Jack Miller's Orch.: WABC WJSV WCAO WJAS WCAU (sw-11.83-9.59)
NBC—Lum & Abner, sketch: WJZ WBZ WLW
Musical Moments; Vocalist and Orch.: WDBJ WCAE
KDKA—Lois Miller and Rosey Roswell
WBAL—News Parade
WFIL—Sunny Smile Club
WIP—Sylvan Herman's Orch.
WOR—Eddie Dooley's Football Forecast
WRC—Voice of Washington
WTAR—Fred Waring's Pennsyl-vanians
WTIC—Rhythm of the Day

7:45 p.m.
★ CBS—Boake Carter, News: WABC WCAU WJAS WJSV WCAO (sw-11.83-9.59)
NBC—Dangerous Paradise, sketch; Elsie Hitz and Nick Dawson: WJZ WBAL WMAL KDKA WLW WBZ (sw-11.87)
NBC—City Voices: WEAF WFBR
KYW—To be announced
WCAE—Around the Cracker Bar-rel
WDBJ—The Virginia Five
WFIL—Forty Fathom, skit
WIP—Mae Desmond
WOR—Rhythm Girls, vocal trio
WRC—Velvet Voices
/TIC—Frank and Flo

9:00 p.m.
★ NBC—Town Hall Tonight; Fred Allen, Portland Hoffa, Art Players, Amateurs; Peter Van Steeden's Orch.: WEAF WRC WLW WCAE WFBR KYW WTIC WTAR (sw-9.53)
★ CBS—Lily Pons, vocalist; Chorus; Andre Kostelanetz' Orch.: WABC WDBJ WJAS WCAU WCAO WJSV WPG (sw-6.12-6.06)
★ NBC—John Charles Thomas, baritone; Frank Tours' Or-chestra: WJZ WMAL WBZ WBAL KDKA WFIL (sw-11.87-6.14)
WIP—The Bronze Clock
WOR—Musical Moments; Solo-ist; Orchestra

9:15 p.m.
WIP—Amateur Hour
WOR—Heywood Broun, "Saying Things At Night"

9:30 p.m.
★ NBC—Twenty Thousand Years in Sing Sing; "Down to the Sea," drama; Warden Lawes: WJZ WBZ KDKA WMAL WBAL WFIL (sw-6.14)
CBS—Ray Noble's Orchestra; Babs and Her Brothers: WABC WHP WJAS WJSV WCAO WDBJ WCAU WPG (sw-6.12-6.06)
WCAU—Political Talk
WOR—Alfred Wallenstein's Sin-fonietta

10:00 p.m.
★ NBC—Cabin Revue; Starring Conrad Thibault, baritone; Frank Crumit, m.c.; Carol Deis, Virginia George, Lydia Summers, Eva Taylor, vocal-ists; Georgia Burke, dramatic actress; Chorus and Orchestra Direction Harry Salter: WEAF WTIC KYW WRC WCAE WFBR (sw-9.53)
CBS—On the Air with Lud Gluskin: WPG WJAS WDBJ WHP WCAO WCAU (sw-6.06)
NBC—To be announced: WJZ KDKA WBAL (sw-6.14)
CBS—Univ. Alumni Dinner: WABC (sw-6.12)
WBZ—Women's Press Club
WFIL—Musical Varieties
WIP—One Act Play
WJSV—Anton Godfrey
★ WLW—KEN-RAD PRESENTS Unsolved Mysteries
WMAL—Postillion
WOR—Husbands and Wives, Al-lie Lowe Miles and Sedley Brown
WTAR—Wrestling Matches

10:15 p.m.
WCAU—Republican Political Talk
WMAL—Board of Trade

11:15 p.m.
CBS—Ink Spots: WJZ WBAL WFIL
CBS—Abe Lyman's Orch.: WJAS WDBJ WHP
NBC—Leonard Keller's Orch.: WEAF WTIC KYW WTAR WFBR (sw-9.53)
KDKA—Dream Ship
WBZ—Joe Rines' Orch.
WCAE—Kav Kyser's Orch.
WCAU—Bert Block's Orch.
WLW—Los Amigos
WOR—Jack Denny's Orch.
WRC—Arthur Reilly

11:30 p.m.
NBC—(News, WEAF only); En-ric Madriguera's Orch.: WEAF WTIC KYW WCAE (sw-9.53)
CBS—Claude Hopkins' Orch.: WABC WHP WDBJ WJAS WCAO WJSV WPG
NBC—Luigi Romanelli's Orch.: WJZ WFIL WBAL WTAR WBZ WRVA
KDKA—Dance Orchestra
WCAU—Del Regis' Orch
WFBR—Husk O'Hare's B
WIP—Earl Denny's Orch.
WRC—Dance Orchestra

11:45 p.m.
NBC—Jesse Crawford, orga.: WEAF WTIC WFBR KYW WCAE (sw-9.53)
WCAU—Claude Hopkins' Orch. (CBS)
WJAS—Eddie Peyton's Orch
WLW—Tom Coakley's Orchestra
WOR—Jan Garber's Orchestra

12:00 Mid.
NBC—Leon Belasco's Orchestra: WEAF KYW
CBS—George Olsen's Orchestra: WABC WJAS WCAU WPG
NBC—Shandor, violinist; Harold Stern's Orch.: WJZ WBZ WFIL WMAL
KDKA—Dance Orchestra
WCAE—Buzzy Kountz' Orch.
WIP—Frank Juele's Orch.
WJSV—News
WLW—Ace Brizode's Orch
WRC—John Slaughter's Orch.

12:15 a.m.
WJSV—George Olsen's Orch. (CBS)
WOR—Veloz & Yolanda's Orch.

12:30 a.m.
NBC—Lights Out, mystery drama: WEAF WCAE WFBR KYW WRC
NBC—Chas. Dornberger's Orch.: WJZ KDKA WBZ WFIL (sw-6.14)
CBS—Phil Scott's Orchestra: WABC WCAU WJSV
WIP—Joe Frasetto's Orch.
WLW—Moon River
WOR—Dance Orchestra

End of Wednesday Prgms.

Hits of Week

SONG HITS PLAYED MOST OFTEN ON THE AIR

Song	Times
It Never Dawned On Me	30
Got a Feelin' You're Foolin'	27
Here's to Romance	25
On Treasure Island	22
Cheek to Cheek	19
Red Sails in the Sunset	17
Truckin'	15
24 Hours a Day	12
No Strings	11
In the Dark	10

BANDLEADERS' PICK OF OUTSTANDING HITS

Song	Points
I'd Rather Listen to Your Eyes	30
Cheek to Cheek	28
Lucky Star	25
I'm On a See-Saw	22
Everything Is Okey-Dokey	19
Oregon Trail	17
The Piccolino	15
I Found a Dream	13
Double Trouble	11
Isn't This a Lovely Day	10

reduce violence and promote such virtues as clean living, fair play, moral courage, and mutual respect. We know that radio, like television, has had a great impact on the thinking and behavior of youth. Many critics questioned how effectively the networks implemented their early policies regarding children's programming.

Although attempts were made to address the area of children's programming, radio news was beginning to move closer to legitimacy. In 1935 the UP began send-ing newspaper-style stories directly to broadcast stations. The following year UP took the next step: It created a totally separate wire service just for radio stations, with stories written especially for the audio, rather than the print, medium. Over at CBS, unbeknownst to anyone at that time, an era began as the reporter who would become broadcasting's most famous news and documentary personality joined the network. His name was Edward R. Murrow.

THE TERRIBLE '30S

Babe Ruth retires from baseball.	Social Security Act becomes law.

1935

Edwin Armstrong and RCA break alliance.

1936

As part of its reorientation of broadcast regulation, the FCC supported the repeal of the Davis Amendment to the Radio Act of 1927, which had provided for equal growth of radio stations in the various geographic sections of the country through allocations

FIG 3.16 High-definition television (HDTV) was on the minds of broadcast technologists from the start, as this 1935 magazine article shows.

RADIO NEWS FOR NOVEMBER, 1935   265

Demonstrates High-Definition *Television*

By Samuel Kaufman

TELEVISION! An economical receiver revealing large-sized images of live and filmed subjects! A row of dancing girls faithfully reproduced after transmission through the ether! An announcer discoursing and a cartoonist at work are viewed as well as heard on a home-type receiver!

A Special Demonstration

A Mickey Mouse cartoon with all of the famous rodent's capers clearly seen after transmission through the air! These were a few of the highlights of a special demonstration to the RADIO NEWS editorial staff at the Philadelphia laboratories of Farnsworth Television, Inc. The special tests were conducted by Philo T. Farnsworth, noted television inventor; A. H. Brolly, his chief engineer, and George Everson, secretary of the company, before the RADIO NEWS group, including Laurence M. Cockaday, editor, S. Gordon Taylor, managing editor, J. C. Meillon, Official Short-Wave Listening Post Observer for France, and the writer. The entire group was impressed with the clearness of images transmitted both through the air and over wires and reproduced on the convex end of a 9-inch diameter cathode-ray tube in a home-type set.

THE FARNSWORTH RECEIVER
Here is a complete receiver for home use, showing the cathode-ray tube screen at top and the high-fidelity speaker system in the lower grill. Tuning can be done by any person who knows how to tune a radio set.

Progress at the Philadelphia laboratories has gone ahead by leaps and bounds. The inventor said still greater refinements than those we viewed would shortly be applied. He is planning his own Philadelphia experimental station and expects it to be in operation at an early date.

"Television," Farnsworth declared, and his aides agreed, "has advanced to the point of having real entertainment value. We don't intend upsetting the radio industry but will make contributions to it. Interest in television throughout the world has grown tremendously in the last three or four months.

Need for Standardization

"Television has come through with some of the technical perfections but there are a few other things remaining to be ironed out in the art. For one thing, standardization should be done before commercialization. It is obvious that the Federal Communications Commission should apply the order. It is inevitable that all television groups would want it so, in order to clean up obstacles that are now apparent."

The Farnsworth transmitting and receiving systems depend entirely on the cathode-ray method. Two types of valves most in use at the Philadelphia

SCENES EASILY BROADCAST
The new Farnsworth system, the pick-up of which is shown at the left, easily transmits scenes such as this in which a number of characters are pictured with high definition.

Laboratories include a 15-inch diameter tube, yielding a 10 by 12 picture, and a 9-inch tube with a 6 by 7 image. Electro-magnetic focussing is employed exclusively, with the coils outside the tube.

Image size of 12 by 14 is considered ideal for home reception, but the Farnsworth technicians declare that, for home use, a small type high intensity, cathode-ray tube must be used in conjunction with optical projection. This method, they declared, has already been completed. (*Turn to page 308*)

PLANS TELEVISION TRANSMISSIONS AT AN EARLY DATE
This is Philo T. Farnsworth, who told the author that he intends to erect a television-radio transmitting station for experimental purposes in the near future to further demonstrate the practicability of his system for homes.

FIG 3.17 A radio receiver as end table. The idea was to enhance the utilitarian nature of the home living-room receiver.

Your Hit Parade joins NBC.

by zones and states. Now the FCC could license stations on the basis of population and demand, permitting the medium to grow as the marketplace required. The FCC also began what was to become the networks' and group station owners' greatest concern: inquiry into monopoly practices and, to start with, the ownership of more than one station in the same community.

While the politics between the government and the broadcasting industry were intensifying, so was the use of radio by politicians. "Sound bites" designed to convince citizens to vote on the basis of image rather than substance—the practice of television and radio in the United States during the 1980s and 1990s—had not yet been developed. But the importance of media in reaching the public was recognized sufficiently that more than $2 million—a large sum in the Depression-ridden 1930s—was spent on radio political campaigns in 1936. The Republican Party understood the impact of radio and combined entertainment and rhetoric in a program series entitled *Liberty at the Crossroads*, which presented issues from the Republican point of view through dramatic sketches.

Politics on radio created controversy. The Depression, having created millions more poor, prompted the organization of political movements designed to redress the imbalance of economic power and provide opportunities for the economically deprived and for racial and other minorities. The Communist Party of the United States reached a peak of membership and influence in the mid-1930s, and in 1936 its head, Earl Browder, made a speech on CBS. All hell broke loose. Right-wing organizations picketed and protested, a number of affiliates refused to carry the program, and the conservative Hearst press even called for the government to take over broadcasting, to prevent what the newspaper chain considered subversive use of the airways. They needn't have worried. The government didn't take over the radio system, and to this very day the broadcast media, operating as big business and dependent on advertising from big business, have rarely given airtime to controversial, especially left-wing, political opinions.

Right-wing radical opinion was carried, however, and so effective were some of its radio commentators that one of them, Father Coughlin—described earlier and considered by many an antidemocracy, profascist demagogue—became so popular through his use of radio that he was able to form a third political party for the 1936 Presidential election. As turmoil grew in Europe, radio carried increasing numbers of reports and programs from overseas, in fact doubling the number from the year before. Of great interest to many Americans was the coverage of the 1936 Olympic Games from Berlin.

The most important contribution to the art of the sound medium, though, was in another format. In 1936 CBS began its *Columbia Workshop* series, which introduced some of the finest writers and highest-quality experimental dramas and documentaries that broadcasting would ever know. Writers for the series included Norman Corwin, Archibald MacLeish, Stephen Vincent Benét, James Thurber, and Dorothy Parker.

FIG 3.18 Kate Smith was one of broadcasting's beloved entertainers.

THE TERRIBLE '30S

FIG 3.19 The popular CBS radio comedian Ed Wynn on *Texaco Star Theater* in 1936.

Vladimir Zworykin and Philo Farnsworth continued to improve television in the United States with their electronic scanning systems. The two inventors were locked in court battles to determine whose patent rights were paramount. RCA invested $1 million—a huge sum in the 1930s—in field tests of television. A coaxial cable for TV transmission was installed between New York and Philadelphia. In the meantime, however, England moved ahead, and in 1936, with the opening of a British Broadcasting Company (BBC) television studio in London, became the first country in the world to broadcast a regular TV schedule to the public.

1937

The Golden Age of Radio clearly had arrived by 1937. NBC and CBS competed for stage and movie stars to appear in their radio plays. One of the all-time classics, *The Fall of the City*, an allegory on the impending war in Europe, was broadcast on CBS. Its author, Archibald MacLeish, showed that radio could be a medium for poets. Arch Oboler's *Lights Out*, far more chilling than the already long-running *The Shadow*, made its debut on NBC. CBS hired a young producer-director-actor named Orson Welles to present the new *Mercury Theatre* series. Ultimately, hundreds of radio plays

FIG 3.20 After enjoying great popularity on radio, Jack Benny became a hit on television.

ARCHIBALD MACLEISH, HERMAN WOUK, AND IRWIN SHAW

Many literary figures who traditionally invested their talents in book rather than broadcast form supplemented their pre–World War II incomes with assignments in radio:

Radio could not have been more perfectly adapted to the poet's uses had he devised them himself.

—ARCHIBALD MACLEISH

I was a staff writer on the Fred Allen show. He set the style, he did much of the writing, and he was the final editor of what I and other writers contributed.

—HERMAN WOUK

Unfortunately, the only radio writing I did was soap operas, which I fear had little if any literary merit, and which I abandoned as soon as I got a contract to do my first play in New York. However, I do think that there was a rich tradition of writing in the area of radio drama.

—IRWIN SHAW

Jesse Owens sets Olympic records in Munich.

Germany and Italy aid Franco's insurgents in civil war in Spain.

Davis Amendment is repealed.

found their way into printed form and onto bookstore and library shelves around the country. In music, NBC established the NBC Symphony Orchestra, headed by the world-famed conductor Arturo Toscanini.

But not everything was peaceful in radio paradise. On *The Chase and Sanborn Hour* on NBC, the Hollywood sex symbol Mae West did what she was expected to: deliver her lines with sultry, sexual innuendo while playing the role of Eve in a sketch set in the Garden of Eden. So upset were some self-styled moral guardians of America that political pressure resulted in Mae West being blacklisted in radio for several years.

Broadcast news was given impetus by the accidental recording of the burning of the German dirigible, the *Hindenburg*, on its attempted landing at Lakehurst, New Jersey. Herb Morrison, a reporter for station WLS in Chicago, had brought a disc recording machine (there was no tape yet) to make a record of his report of the landing. There was no live coverage. Morrison's record, with his now famous words, "This is one of the worst catastrophes in the world" and, amid his sobs, "Oh, the humanity," was aired by all three networks the next day and prompted the increased use of recordings and live coverage at news events.

The networks were gearing up for the intensifying news events in Europe. CBS sent Ed Murrow there as a war correspondent. Although actual war had not yet broken out, Hitler's Germany was already on the march for more *lebensraum*.

THE TERRIBLE '30S

1936	
Top Radio Advertisers	Spent on Network Advertising
Procter and Gamble	$3,299,000
Standard Brands	2,275,000
Ford-Lincoln	2,251,000
Sterling Products	1,621,000
Colgate-Palmolive	1,556,000
American Tobacco Company	1,508,000
General Foods	1,472,000
American Home Products	1,447,000
Pepsodent	1,352,000
Campbell Soup	1,314,000

FIG 3.21 List of top radio advertisers during the 1930s.

Dust storms in Midwest,
floods in Northeast.

Innovative *Columbia Workshop* series airs on CBS.

Bruno Hauptmann electrocution in Lindbergh case is huge media (radio) event.

NEW YORK, MONDAY, OCTOBER 31, 1938.

Radio Listeners in Panic, Taking War Drama as Fact

Many Flee Homes to Escape 'Gas Raid From Mars'—Phone Calls Swamp Police at Broadcast of Wells Fantasy

A wave of mass hysteria seized thousands of radio listeners throughout the nation between 8:15 and 9:30 o'clock last night when a broadcast of a dramatization of H. G. Wells's fantasy, "The War of the Worlds," led thousands to believe that an interplanetary conflict had started with invading Martians spreading wide death and destruction in New Jersey and New York.

The broadcast, which disrupted households, interrupted religious services, created traffic jams and clogged communications systems, was made by Orson Welles, who as the radio character, "The Shadow," used to give "the creeps" to countless child listeners. This time at least a score of adults required medical treatment for shock and hysteria.

In Newark, in a single block at Heddon Terrace and Hawthorne Avenue, more than twenty families rushed out of their houses with wet handkerchiefs and towels over their faces to flee from what they believed was to be a gas raid. Some began moving household furniture.

Throughout New York families left their homes, some to flee to near-by parks. Thousands of persons called the police, newspapers

and radio stations here and in other cities of the United States and Canada seeking advice on protective measures against the raids.

The program was produced by Mr. Welles and the Mercury Theatre on the Air over station WABC and the Columbia Broadcasting System's coast-to-coast network, from 8 to 9 o'clock.

The radio play, as presented, was to simulate a regular radio program with a "break-in" for the material of the play. The radio listeners, apparently, missed or did not listen to the introduction, which was: "The Columbia Broadcasting System and its affiliated stations present Orson Welles and the Mercury Theatre on the Air in 'The War of the Worlds' by H. G. Wells."

They also failed to associate the program with the newspaper listing of the program, announced as "Today: 8:00-9:00—Play: H. G. Wells's 'War of the Worlds'". They ignored three additional announcements made during the broadcast emphasizing its fictional nature.

Mr. Welles opened the program with a description of the series of

Continued on Page Four

FIG 3.22 Newspaper account of audience reaction to the *Mercury Theatre of the Air* production of *The War of the Worlds*. *Courtesy* the New York Times.

As radio grew, with 80% of U.S. homes having at least one set and almost 5 million autos having radios, television moved closer to public realization. The FCC reserved a 6 megahertz (MHz) channel for television broadcasting. Philco was experimenting with a mobile unit in New York City and broadcast a 441-line image of a favorite comic strip character, Felix the Cat. Seventeen TV stations were in experimental operation throughout the country.

1938

What some historians consider the greatest event in media programming history occurred on Halloween eve, October 30, 1938. At 8:00 P.M. Eastern time, a CBS announcer began the weekly program by saying, "The Columbia Broadcasting System and its affiliated stations present Orson Welles and the *Mercury Theatre of the Air* in *The War of the Worlds*, by H. G. Wells." Three announcements during the program, produced by the then 21-year-old theatrical genius Orson Welles

FIG 3.23 This 1938 RCA type 44-B ribbon velocity microphone became the premier radio microphone. *Courtesy Steel Collection.*

FIG 3.24 KDKA's pre–World War II control center. *Courtesy Westinghouse.*

Edward VIII abdicates British throne for "woman I love."

Labor strikes grip U.S. industry.

1937

Nearly 8 million radio receivers sold.

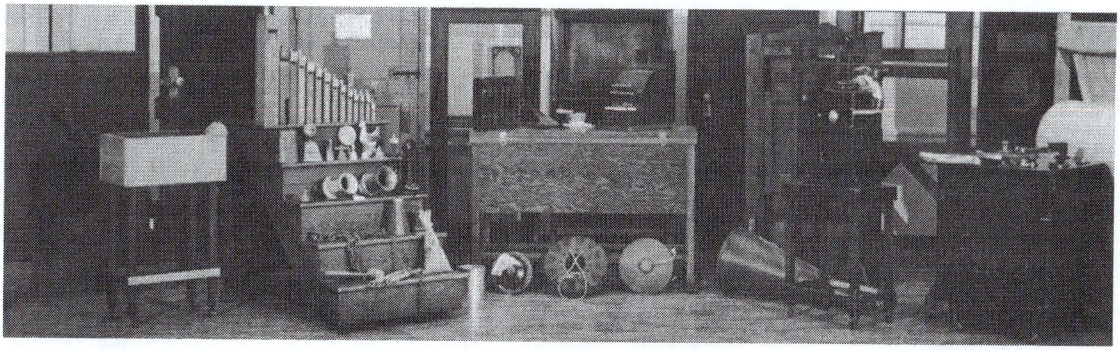

FIG 3.25 All manner of objects were assembled to create the sounds required for the production of radio scripts. *Courtesy WTIC.*

and a somewhat older theater guru, John Houseman, made it clear that it was a fictional drama. Welles's closing narration stated that "*The War of the Worlds* has no further significance than the holiday offering it was intended to be . . . the *Mercury Theatre's* own version of dressing up in a sheet and jumping out of a bush and saying 'boo.' . . . [I]f your doorbell rings and there's nobody there, that was no Martian—it's Halloween!" Nevertheless, the documentary nature of the presentation, with on-the-spot reporters describing the invasion from Mars, induced many listeners to think the Martian destruction of the earth was real. Tens of thousands of people panicked. Roads in areas of New Jersey and New York given as invasion sites in the play were clogged with fleeing people. Police and fire stations in the United States and Canada were deluged with calls from those seeking help and protection.

Why did so many people panic? Reports from Europe had for some time indicated the likelihood of a German invasion of neighboring countries. Only a month earlier, a meeting of key powers at Munich had avoided the immediate outbreak of war. Everyone knew it was coming as the consequence of print and broadcast coverage. The public psyche was set for an "invasion." So powerful was Welles's production that in subsequent years, when it was repeated in translation in other countries, it continued to result in panics and, in some instances, in riots and mob actions against stations by a public incensed that it had been fooled. Although rebroadcasts of *The War of the Worlds* in subsequent decades did not scare a more sophisticated America (nor did it frighten one of this book's authors, who heard the original when he was a youngster and, having read the Wells novel, accepted it as a good science fiction play), it remains one of radio's classics and continues to be used in broadcasting studies and classrooms. Yet in this opening decade of the 21st century, productions of *The War of the Worlds* are still banned in a number of countries throughout the world.

Newly established NBC Symphony
Orchestra is headed by maestro
Arturo Toscanini.

THE TERRIBLE '30S

A Social Scientist Looks at *The War of the Worlds*

The War of the Worlds is considered one of the most important broadcasts of all time. Serendipitously, scientists were presented a "natural experiment," an empirical, real-world examination of what is now called media effects. Before this time the most recognized study in this arena, even with its methodological flaws, was a collection of reports known as the Payne Fund Studies that explored the effects of movies. A more rigorous study by psychologist Hadley Cantril, begun almost immediately after the airing of *The War of the Worlds*, revealed a number of factors that correlated with believing this program was real. Cantril found that a majority of those influenced failed to make "reality checks" (checking other stations or the newspaper radio schedule), missed the opening disclaimer (there were four such announcements during the show, but by the time of the second one, at the bottom of the hour, panic had set in), were highly suggestible and tended to believe everything they heard, or held to a more literal reading of the Bible, trusting this was the prophetic end-time. But Cantril concluded that the most important factor was critical ability associated with education, since vastly fewer high school graduates and even fewer college grads believed it was a real alien invasion.

Though *The War of the Worlds* was fiction, the developing events in Europe were not, and shortwave broadcasts kept the American public informed. Networks began regular world news roundups. Ed Murrow covered Germany's annexation of Austria; another famed commentator, H. V. Kaltenborn, reported the attempts at the Munich meeting to avert war and also broadcast from the battlefields of the Spanish Civil War. In other programming, daytime soap operas, game shows, and audience participation programs gained in popularity, spurring increased advertising revenue. Although much broadcast music was on records, with music transcription services used by many stations, 64% of network programming was live. Writers and producers began to gain importance, and the person whom many critics regard as radio's foremost writer, Norman Corwin—still writing and teaching as this is written—joined CBS.

Even the FCC got into the act and warned broadcasters not to air programs that might delude or deceive the public, as some claimed *The War of the Worlds* did. In other actions designed to protect the public interest, the FCC began requiring annual station financial reports (a requirement that lasted until the deregulation period of the 1980s), adopted rules governing political broadcasts, and expanded its inquiry into multiple-ownership situations, specifically into network practices and their relation to and control over affiliates. This study of chain broadcasting was to have great impact on the structure of broadcasting.

Edwin Armstrong's invention looked like it was reaching fruition. He himself, having sold his extensive RCA stock, built his own FM station in Alpine, New Jersey—W2XMN, at 50 kW—which would go on the air the following year.

Hollywood sex symbol Mae West
heats passions during radio
broadcast, is banned from air.

Radio audience receives
an emotional account of
the *Hindenburg* disaster.

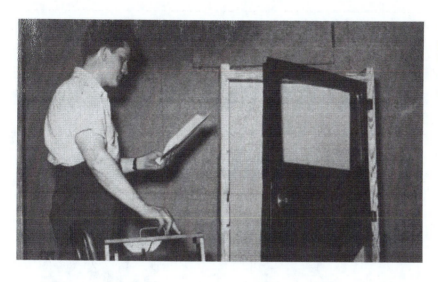

FIG 3.26 Sounds used in
programs were generated
live throughout radio's
early years.
Courtesy WTIC.

THE TERRIBLE '30S

The FCC reserved 25 FM channels in the 41–42 MHz band for noncommercial educational stations.

Television was gearing up for its public debut the following year, effecting a transfer from experimental to commercial operation. NBC continued to transmit from the Empire State Building, not only to the relatively few sets in homes but to TV receivers set up in public places; Germany and Russia were doing the same thing, also trying to catch up with the British. CBS opened the first of a number of TV studios in the building above Grand Central Station in New York City. One of this book's authors remembers rehearsing and performing in those studios well into the 1950s, by then overcrowded and lacking the facilities necessary for efficient production. Key programming in 1938 included the first telecast of a Broadway play, Rachel Crothers's *Susan and God*, and the first TV on-the-spot coverage of an unscheduled news event, when NBC's mobile unit, doing a nearby story, picked up a fire that broke out on Ward's Island. This latter happening had additional significance in that newspapers in various parts of the country carried the story with pictures they photographed right off the TV screen.

1939

Television made its public debut in New York at the 1939 World's Fair. On April 30, President Franklin D. Roosevelt officially opened the fair, with NBC televising the event to some 200 sets in about a 40-mile radius in the New York area and adjacent states. The timing, situation, and publicity marked this as the first public television broadcast, although, as we know, experimental stations had been offering programs to those who

FIG 3.27 This statue
honoring Philo T. Farnsworth
in the nation's capitol is
inscribed "Father of
Television."
Photo by Lee Nadel.

1938

The FCC reserves a 6 MHz channel for television broadcasting.

Some 64% of network programming is live.

had receivers for a dozen years. The FCC had not yet decided on a lineage standard and would not officially authorize limited commercial television broadcasting until the following year. But RCA's president, David Sarnoff, saw the World's Fair as an excellent promotional opportunity for the RCA-backed lineage standard of 441 lines/30 pictures per second and for RCA-manufactured TV sets, which were demonstrated in a "Hall of Television" in the RCA Building at the World's Fair.

FIG 3.28 Time marches on as one new electronic medium exerts an impact on another in this 1938 magazine advertisement.

Japan advances in China.	House Un-American Activities Committee (HUAC) established.	*Kristalnacht* in Germany heightens Nazi power.

	Radio's foremost writer, Norman Corwin, joins CBS.	FCC requires annual station financial reports, expands its inquiry into multiple ownership, and reserves 25 FM channels for noncommercial broadcasts.

ERIK BARNOUW

BROADCAST HISTORIAN/ WRITER

In 1939 Norman Corwin, a young CBS production man who had begun to impress management, was assigned to create, produce, and direct an Americana variety series to be titled *Pursuit of Happiness*, a CBS Sunday afternoon "public service" offering that was to include music, drama, comedy, and poetry. Corwin asked me to join him as writer-editor. I was to write the words for master-of-ceremonies Burgess Meredith, including his colloquies with guests. I was to have a budget for sketches by freelance writers. Since wars were in progress in various parts of the world, we decided on war and peace as a theme for one of the programs. For this I provided an opening from a Carl Sandburg poem, in which a little girl asks her father about war. He tells her that in wars, each side tries to kill as many of the other side as it can. The girl thinks about this a moment, then suggests:

GIRL: Sometime they'll give a war and nobody will come.

I received word from the executive producer, Davidson Taylor, that my script was fine except for the opening, which would not do. I was asked to devise a new one. When I went to ask why, he pointed out that it was a time of wars, in which the United States might conceivably become involved. If so, it would not be good if CBS were accused of promoting draft resistance.

I was taken aback. I respected Taylor, who was knowledgeable in the arts and took his work seriously. Had I committed an error of judgment? When I told Corwin about the discussion, he was furious and went at once to vice president William B. Lewis, who had commissioned him to create the series. Word came to restore my opening. I felt gratified. The incident was characteristic of Corwin, who also took his job seriously.

The episode still resonates for me. I believe many network executives would have acted as Taylor did. The industry's structure and tensions seem to condition people that way. They may be devoted to the Bill of Rights and cherish freedom of expression, but in troubled times they are ready, even eager, to walk in lockstep. They fall into line before a bugle has sounded. Yet in a democratic society, even

FIG 3.29 *Courtesy Erik Barnouw.*

| German *anschluss* of Austria. | Munich "peace in our time" conference. | German–Soviet pact. |

1939

War of the Worlds broadcast panics nation.

after war has begun, is there really any reason why a person should not be permitted to suggest that—as any child can see—war is stupid, wreaking problems worse than it is supposed to solve?

Religion and Radio

Religious freedom is one of the foundation stones of the United States. Hence the broadcasting of religious programs is a vital public service. First principle is that time devoted to religion is donated. The reason is obvious. To sell time would give an advantage to the religious organisation with the most funds available for such use.

In general, NBC relies for religious programs on the central or national agencies of the great religious faiths. Many other groups are also given time on the air on special occasions.

NBC serves religion in many ways. First, it serves the church, in the sense of its service to the chief faiths. Second, it serves individual listeners regardless of whether they are, or are not, members of any faith. Third, NBC religious programs further mutual respect and understanding by making it possible for adherents of one faith to hear the views of another. Yet no speaker ever attacks another faith, nor seeks to change the religious convictions of listeners. As a further service, radio brings to millions special religious events which previously were heard only by thousands.

Commenting on radio and religion a speaker recently said: "I can think of no greater benefit that can come to mankind at this time than the continued preaching of the need for understanding and tolerance among the different peoples, races and creeds of the world. If religion can carry that message to the hearts and to the minds of all the people throughout the world, radio will have justified itself a thousand times and more, for, after all, man's hope and aspiration for the last two thousand years has yet fully to be realised —Peace on earth, Good will to men."

FIG 3.30 Excerpts from a 1939 magazine advertisement promoting religious programming on radio. *Courtesy RCA.*

The broadcast industry supporters of the underdog got one of their few tastes of satisfaction in 1939. Vladimir Zworykin had developed the iconoscope and the kinescope, the tubes used in initial television transmission and reception, at RCA-NBC. Philo Farnsworth, who had developed a vital glass vacuum tube seal and the image dissector, had spurned an offer to work for RCA some years before and, during the ensuing years, had refused RCA's money and pressure to buy his patents. Farnsworth and Zworykin had filed similar patent applications. In 1939, an agreement was struck between Farnsworth and RCA for cross-licensing. For the first time, RCA did not control the patents it needed and had to pay royalties to someone else for the rights.

One of this book's authors remembers the landmark television broadcast at the World's Fair. Like others seeing this phenomenon for the first time, he recalls the magic and excitement of standing in line and appearing in front of a camera while a friend stood at a monitor a short distance away and shouted and waved in wonder to confirm that one could actually be seen as a living, moving image at another site. Alternating places with his friend, he got in the long line again and again to assure himself that somehow the sending of one's live image over the air wasn't some trick and really could be believed. The other author of this book remembers visiting New York City as a small child and marveling at seeing himself on a TV screen in a department store.

NBC began regular programming at that time, adding to its World's Fair coverage dramas, variety shows, sports, and special events. In May the first televised baseball game was presented. The *New York Times*, which in 1927 had reported the first test of television with the subheadline "COMMERCIAL USE IN DOUBT," now reported that baseball could not be successfully shown on television, stating, "Baseball is a thrill to the eye that cannot be . . . flashed through space."

Despite NBC's efforts, people weren't buying TV receivers in the way they had purchased radio sets almost two decades earlier. The cost of the RCA TV sets shown at the World's Fair ranged from $200 to $600, which was, at a minimum, one to two months' salary for a working person with a good job and as much as a year's pay for those scraping by. The millions out of work couldn't get money for food, much less for a luxury like television. But the potential was there, and by the end of the year eight manufacturers had produced some 5,000 TV sets.

Spurred by Edwin Armstrong, FM offered additional potential competition to AM, with 150 applications to the FCC for stations. Armstrong had demonstrated with his own FM station that his invention had several advantages over AM, including no static, comparable range with less power, and noninterference with other FM signals.

Franco becomes dictator of Spain.

Television has its public debut at the New York World's Fair.

First major league baseball game, Brooklyn Dodgers, televised.

BMI music licensing service formed.

The FCC barred educational stations from applying for AM frequencies, beginning the process that would result in almost all noncommercial or public radio stations licensed in the FM band. Today only some two dozen educational stations, most of them holdovers from the 1920s, are still broadcasting on AM.

The business of broadcasting found it necessary to both protect itself from a public that was beginning to be concerned with the impact of the media and to exert

DAVID BORST

COFOUNDER, INTERCOLLEGIATE BROADCASTING SYSTEM (IBS) —

The Intercollegiate Broadcasting System was founded in February 1940, when representatives from 13 colleges gathered at Brown University to plan the growth of campus-limited broadcasting at their schools. Ten of these colleges, Brown, Columbia, the University of Connecticut, Cornell, Holy Cross, Pembroke, Rhode Island State (now the University of Rhode Island), Saint Lawrence, Wesleyan, and Williams, are listed as charter members of IBS, although stations were in operation at only half of them. Dartmouth, Harvard, and the University of New Hampshire also sent representatives. To understand why this meeting was held, one must go back to the fall of 1936, when George Abraham and myself entered Brown. To enable his fellow students to hear his classical recordings and to permit two-way communication between rooms in his dormitory, George interconnected the output circuits of half a dozen radios in the building. The popularity of this novel scheme caught my attention, and I extended it to my dorm across the street, and even further. Before long a network of lines spread

over the Brown campus, linking dozens of dormitory rooms.

Serious programming was inaugurated the following year over the "Brown Network," and conversations were diverted to a second line paralleling the first. This second line was used to originate programs from points all over the campus, feeding into the main programming line at a central switching point. Approximately 100 radios were connected to receive the programs from the main program line. That's how college radio was launched.

Reprinted with permission from The Journal of College Radio, *a publication of the Intercollegiate Broadcasting System (IBS).*

FIG 3.32 Brown Network board meeting (1940) in George Abraham's dormitory room. George Abraham is in the center, and David Borst is on the far right.
Courtesy Dr. George Abraham.

FIG 3.31 Excerpts from a 1939 magazine advertisement promoting religious programming on radio.
Courtesy RCA.

THE TERRIBLE '30S

World War II begins.	House Un-American Activities Committee (HUAC) established.		Nylon stockings introduced.
	New NAB "Radio Code" is issued.	RCA signs television patent agreement with Philo T. Farnsworth.	HUAC expands "witch hunts."

FIG 3.33 David Sarnoff debuts TV at the 1939 World's Fair.
Courtesy David Sarnoff Library.

its own growing muscle for its own economic interests. The FCC issued a memo expressing concern with certain kinds of program practices, including lack of fairness in covering both sides of controversial issues, false or misleading advertising, frequent interruption of programs with commercials, excessive advertising, obscenity and profanity, racial and religious bigotry on the air, violence and torture on children's programs, promotion of liquor, and too much recorded music. To prevent the enactment of federal regulations regarding such programming, the NAB issued a "Radio Code" that set new standards of practice regarding children's programs; the number of commercial minutes allowed per hour in prime time; coverage of controversial issues principally in news and feature programs rather than in programs paid for by special interests (an action that, to some critics, meant keeping off the air any minority opinions); and fairness in news reporting. But compliance with the code was voluntary and had relatively little impact on actual broadcast practices. Radio stations, continuing their battle against paying music-use fees to ASCAP, decided to form their own music organization. Through the NAB, Broadcast Music, Inc. (BMI), was founded. Although BMI did acquire the rights to a fair amount of music, it was not able to replace ASCAP as the key provider, and the NAB-ASCAP contract negotiations continue today.

Chapter FOUR

The Furious '40s

War and Recovery— Full of Sound and Fury, Signifying . . . Transition to TV

The decade of the 1940s began with radios in more than 80% of U.S. households; 50 million-plus sets were in use. Advertising revenues for radio totaled $155 million in 1940. More and more newspapers solved the problem of competition by buying or constructing radio stations; in 1940 newspapers owned a third of the country's stations. FM continued to move forward, owing to the perseverance of Edwin Armstrong, and an FM broadcasters association was formed to lobby for additional spectrum space. The FCC established rules for FM radio, and by the end of the year dozens of new FM stations had been authorized. FM supporters touted the new sound, as *The New York Times* wrote, for its "golden tone, less noise, no interference" qualities. A number of stations used microwave interconnections to create FM networks. So impressive was the FM staticless signal that the FCC decided, in 1940, to authorize FM for television's sound. While this step would be a boon for TV, it would turn out to be a blow to FM. TV, not FM, was given priority as the new medium. The FCC authorized limited commercial TV operation, with the proviso that stations make clear to the public that they were still experimental. RCA, eager to sell its TV receivers to the public, was not about to adhere to the FCC dictum and advertised its sets on its NBC television station. So powerful was RCA that it even got the FCC to support its monochrome (black-and-white), 441-line, 30-frames-per-second system, even though Peter Goldmark, a CBS scientist, had already developed a workable color system using whirling discs.

Other technical advances anticipated the military needs of the upcoming years. Television was tried out in airplanes, and although miniaturization was still far off for TV, small radios were developed using dry batteries that could provide energy for vacuum tubes. Portable transmitters and receivers, including walkie-talkies, later became invaluable combat equipment.

News began to dominate programming, with more and more hours devoted to the war in Europe at the expense of light popular music and talk shows. CBS began to build up a corps of correspondents who would gain national respect and loyalty as the voices of the war: Ed Murrow's "London After Dark" nightly reports of the blitz; William L. Shirer's coverage of France's surrender to Germany at Compiégne; the voices of Howard K. Smith, Robert Trout, Eric Sevareid, and

© 2010 Taylor & Francis. All rights reserved.
DOI: 10.1016/B978-0-240-81236-6.00004-4

Peacetime military draft inaugurated.		Germany sweeps through Europe; Battle of Britain begins.

1940

FCC authorizes commercial FM broadcasting.	First TV commercial broadcast, for Bulova watches.

Charles Collingwood came into most American households during the next few years. The remarkable CBS team was orchestrated by CBS's chairman, William Paley, who told his European correspondent, Murrow, to hire the best reporters he could find, and Murrow did. Public interest in war news carried over into domestic politics, and television, to promote new audiences, for the first time broadcast the election returns as well as the Republican and Democratic National Conventions.

The public still wanted to be entertained, of course, and music would continue to be the most programmed radio format for the next few years—representing about 50% of the networks' schedules in 1940. But it encountered a roadblock. As a result of a lawsuit, a federal appeals court decided that records purchased by radio stations could be played without prior consent of the record company or the artists. Yet the statutory fee negotiated by ASCAP and NAB still remained, and in 1940 ASCAP raised its rates, believing that music played on radio harmed the sales of records and sheet music. ASCAP refused to renew many stations' contracts that expired at the end of 1940. Although the fledgling NAB-created BMI tried to take up the slack, ASCAP controlled the most desired music, and by the end of 1941 most stations had re-signed with ASCAP at compromise fees.

1941

The attack on Pearl Harbor on December 7, 1941, bringing the United States officially into World War II the following day, resulted in severe restrictions on radio and television's growth—and brought about some of radio's finest hours.

Beginning at 2:31 Eastern time that Sunday afternoon, December 7, 1941, the networks cut into their regularly scheduled programming to announce the Japanese bombing of the U.S. fleet at Pearl Harbor. Within hours, radio and even the relatively few television stations were broadcasting hastily assembled features and documentaries on Pearl Harbor, the Pacific area, and Japan. The next day, December 8, the largest radio audience to date—62 million people—heard President Roosevelt's "day that will live in infamy" declaration of war.

Aware of the value of electronic communications and equipment to the war effort, the U.S. government began a series of restrictions and controls that would continue throughout World War II and even into the postwar period. A number of factors prompted government action. One was the need for electronic parts by the military, resulting in the conversion of facilities that turned out radio and television parts for defense needs. Another was the matter of security. "The enemy is listening," "Loose lips sink ships," and similar slogans were taken seriously, and there was fear of spies using radio to convey or receive information that could help the enemy. Amateur stations were shut down to prevent such occurrences.

FIG 4.1 An older de Forest at work on television in the 1940s.

FDR elected to unprecedented third term.	Purchase price of an eight-room townhouse on New York's West Side: $2,600.

The Republican and Democratic National Conventions are broadcast.	ASCAP pressures broadcasters for higher fees.

A further goal of government action was to increase effective instant communication with our allies and to use the already proven propaganda power of radio to reach people in enemy countries. Shortwave international transmission was strengthened, including the development of a new "electrically steerable" antenna by NBC engineers. According to *The New York Times*, the antenna worked by "beaming the wave of a 50,000 watt international transmitter, its effective output is raised to something like 1,200,000 watts, and much greater signal strength results in the country over which the beam is aimed." In the following year, 1942, the government took over all private shortwave stations that could send a signal to foreign countries and put these stations' programming under the Office of War Information (OWI). Conversely, the government also set up a service to monitor foreign broadcasts, to intercept propaganda from the other side and any messages that might be used by subversive elements in the United States.

During the early part of 1941, before the United States' official entry into the war, the FCC took a number of actions affecting broadcasting. The commission's investigation into network monopoly practices begun in 1938 was completed with the issuance of a *Report on Chain Broadcasting*. This report was aimed at protecting individual affiliate stations from what the FCC felt was undue control by the networks. Among other things, it limited affiliate contracts to one-year renewable periods, permitted stations to use programs from other networks, prevented networks from interfering with station programming and scheduling prerogatives, and stopped networks from controlling affiliate stations' advertising rates for other than that network's programs. The report's most dramatic determination, however, was that NBC's ownership of two networks constituted an unacceptable monopoly. Both NBC and CBS were furious and attempted to convince Congress and the American public that the new FCC regulations would destroy broadcasting. They challenged the FCC in the courts. In 1943 the Supreme Court upheld the FCC, and NBC had to divest itself of one of its networks; it kept the Red and sold the Blue, which later became the American Broadcasting Company (ABC). Despite the networks' protests to the contrary, radio did survive, and years later, after television changed the structure and programming of radio, NBC, CBS, ABC, and the Mutual Broadcasting System (MBS), among others, were granted permission for multiple radio network operations to distribute different program formats. Only two months before issuing the 1941 *Report on Chain Broadcasting*, the FCC had announced that it was beginning an investigation into the newspaper ownership of stations, a study that would result in action in that area as well some years later. While proposing restrictions on some broadcast practices, the FCC loosened up in one significant area: License terms were extended from one to two years.

In April 1941 the FCC issued the first full commercial TV authorization after adopting the technical standard recommended by the National Television Systems Committee (NTSC) of 525 lines and 30 frames per second. This would turn out to

THE FURIOUS '40S

FCC issues first full commercial television authorization after adopting the NTSC 525-line standard.

Station license terms extended to two years.

FIG 4.2 As early as 1941, broadcasters saw the value of mobile television cameras. This DuMont field unit sports two cameras atop a three-quarter-ton truck.

be the poorest-quality television standard in the world, and in the 1990s it was one of the reasons for the pressure to adopt and implement a high-definition television (HDTV) standard to improve picture quality.[1] Both CBS and NBC converted from experimental to regular commercial TV broadcasting in July 1941, with about 15 hours of programming a week each.

The FCC also gave television new frequencies, replacing the previously used AM frequencies. It put FM on a new band, 42–50 MHz; television had channel space on some higher frequencies. FM and television had been fighting for the same desirable spectrum space, and the FCC's action prompted some FM advocates to suggest that the government was trying to hamper the growth of FM to protect AM. By the time the United States was in the war, there were some 40 FM stations on the air and about a half million FM receivers in use.

The FCC entered the area of program regulation in 1941 when, in deciding on a challenge brought by the Mayflower Broadcasting Company against the license

[1] The Smithsonian's Elliot Sivowitch reminds us today that in 1941 this standard was pretty good, considering that the British, who had the most active service, were using 405 lines. Sivowitch adds that engineers are not unanimous in their support and enthusiasm for HDTV. "It is not entirely what it purports to be," says Sivowitch.

Germany invades the U.S.S.R.

Report on Chain Broadcasting is issued by the FCC.	WNBT, the first commercial TV station, begins operating.	NBC and CBS convert to regular commercial television broadcasting.

renewal of a Boston station, it stated that broadcasters would not be permitted to editorialize—that is, a station could not use the airwaves to present the owner's particular points of view. The Mayflower decision set the stage for later rulings that would become known as the *Fairness Doctrine*, in which stations were permitted, even encouraged, to present controversial material but were required to present opposing viewpoints as well. Other kinds of programming were encouraged, especially those that aided the war effort. Immediately after Pearl Harbor, networks and stations began to plan and produce patriotic dramas, with characters and plots that were prodemocratic and antifascist.

In New York a young radio performer named Martin Block started a music show on WNEW in which he interspersed comments between records and gave the impression that people were listening to the bands and artists as they were actually performing. As earlier stated, this program, *The Make-Believe Ballroom*, would have a great influence on the development of radio's basic format, that of the disc jockey show.

1942

On one front, business as usual for broadcasting ceased in 1942; on another, it didn't. Radio stations that were on the air stayed on, and in fact, federal excess profits tax laws made it possible for them to keep pace with the rest of the economy and make money during the war. Radio became a necessity for Americans as an important and frequently on-the-spot source of news about the progress of the war. Virtually everyone had a family member or friend in the Armed Forces and avidly listened to daily news reports. In addition, the pressures and fears generated by the war—although U.S. civilians experienced none of the horrors and not even any of the deprivations of war, except for the shortage of some goods and services—and the long, arduous hours many civilians were putting in at war plants resulted in an increasing demand for escapist entertainment. Radio supplied it. In addition, the government understood the propaganda value of radio for boosting patriotism and morale, and radio admirably served that purpose, too.

On the negative side for broadcasting, the electronic and technical components of radio and of the fledgling television medium were needed for the war effort. Consequently, within a few months of the attack on Pearl Harbor, the government put a freeze on the construction of new stations, on the expansion of existing stations, and on the manufacture of radio and television receivers.

The United States' first year in the war was disastrous. The loss of the Philippines, the surrender and subsequent death march in the Bataan Peninsula, and the debilitating Coral Sea battle helped create depression and fear in the United States. This paranoia resulted in the U.S. government creating detention camps in which it concentrated more than 100,000 Japanese Americans, confiscating their homes, businesses, and personal property. By the end of 1942, however, the United States had

THE FURIOUS '40S

Japan attacks Pearl Harbor on December 7.	United States declares war against Japan.

FCC relocates FM to 42–50 MHz.	FCC rules against station editorialization.

begun to seriously challenge the Axis powers, beginning a series of Pacific island conquests with a victory at Midway Island and landing an invasion force in North Africa. These events raised national morale. Radio not only reported the news but was there while it was being made.

How was the United States going to handle its propaganda needs? In most other countries during wartime, the government took over the principal means of public information—newspapers, magazines, radio, and film. Because of newsprint shortages and the fact that there was a fair amount of illiteracy, in all countries radio was the principal day-by-day means of informing, stimulating, and persuading, with movies serving longer-range goals. Was a dictatorial takeover of the communication industries, or even of the radio medium alone, appropriate for a country that said it was fighting for democracy over fascism? The United States decided it was not. A lesser step was either to administer, or at least to oversee, the programming of radio, preparing the scripts and deciding on the productions and scheduling that would best serve the U.S. war effort. That step, too, was judged a bit drastic. The United States finally decided to seek radio's cooperation through voluntary means, perhaps with a little assistance and persuasion.

ARCH OBOLER

THE LATE ARCH OBOLER WAS ONE OF THE GOLDEN AGE'S PREEMINENT RADIO WRITERS _____

My plays were written for a very special medium—radio. Radio drama was a wonderful art form. First and foremost, a radio play is a collaboration; a marriage of elements—words, sound effects, music, actors, and the listener.

FIG 4.3 Arch Oboler's innovative radio plays entertained audiences throughout the turbulent 1940s. Here he directs *Lights Out*, WENR Chicago, 1935–1939.
Courtesy Havrilla Collection, Broadcast Pioneers Library.

Germany and Italy declare war on the United States.

Joe DiMaggio has 56-game hitting streak.

Martin Block's *The Make-Believe Ballroom* debuts—the forerunner to modern deejay programs.

President Roosevelt tells home audiences that the bombing of Pearl Harbor "will live in infamy."

The Office of War Information (OWI) was established in 1942 to handle this task. A highly respected radio news commentator, Elmer Davis, was named head of the OWI. Essentially, OWI prepared daily information bulletins on government aims and needs and sent them to networks and stations with the request that the producers, writers, directors, and performers attempt to incorporate the information and its purposes in their programs. The industry was happy to comply. OWI sometimes prepared scripts and even produced several programs on matters that were considered essential and offered them to the radio industry. For example, because cooking fat was needed for processing into the glycerin required for gunpowder, the government scheduled specific days on which housewives were asked to bring to collection stations the cans of cooking fat they had saved. This information was forwarded to radio producers, who then incorporated it into skits, discussion programs, and even the dialogue of characters on soap operas. As might be expected, more than one comedian felt compelled to remind housewives to "bring your fat cans" down to the collection depots.

Even music and variety programs joined in the patriotic effort. Such war songs as "Praise the Lord and Pass the Ammunition," "In Der Führer's Face," and "This Is the Army, Mr. Jones" were popular favorites throughout the war, and Irving Berlin's "God Bless America" became our unofficial second national anthem. Variety shows such as *The Army Hour* featured comments of fighting personnel, from privates to generals. Dramatic scripts and documentaries written and produced by the United States' best talents informed and inspired people in such program series as *This War* and *This Is Our Enemy*. Perhaps the program best known to troops overseas was *Command Performance*, a variety show featuring America's biggest stars. It was broadcast over all shortwave stations in an attempt to counter the anti-American propaganda on the radio programs of Tokyo Rose and Axis Sally, propaganda that affected the morale of many service personnel.

OWI also coordinated the release of all news announcements and decided on priorities for what should or should not be said over the air. For example, recruiting for the Armed Forces and the promotion of War Bond sales were high priorities, and stations were asked to voluntarily censor any information pertaining to troop movements, casualty lists, and rumors, as well as person-in-the-street interviews (lest some subversive element get onto the air something harmful to the war effort). Weather reports were censored, since enemy planes could use information about the weather to their advantage; even announcements of cancellations of athletic events were not attributed to the weather. An Office of Censorship issued a voluntary set of guidelines with which virtually all stations conscientiously complied. The NAB issued a guide to wartime broadcasting, listing in it a number of prohibitions, such as broadcasting information on war production, troop movements, scare headlines, commercials within news reports, sound effects that might be confused with air-raid sirens or other alarms, or any entertainment or commercial material that might be confused with important news bulletins. Though

THE FURIOUS '40S

1942

Because of the war, U.S.
government imposes
restrictions on electronic
communications.

Radio is the principal
source for news about
the war.

broadcasters took the war effort seriously, many were concerned that some of the censorship by the military was unnecessary and kept legitimate information from the public; one of the newspersons making public objection was Ed Murrow.

Advertising agencies and associations formed the Volunteer Advertising Council and lent their talents to writing and producing literally thousands of programs and spot announcements for the government, promoting everything from the salvage of scrap metal to writing V-Mail (single sheets that folded into their own envelopes and could be photographed in reduced form to save materials and space) to members of the Armed Forces overseas. Advertising blossomed during the war. A tax on excess profits, designed to reduce war profiteering, set a 90% levy on profits over and above what would reasonably be expected in normal times; an exemption was made for any such profits spent on advertising. Radio stations, ad agencies, and advertisers all benefited considerably from what was called "the 10-cent dollar"—that is, the amount it actually cost to get a dollar's worth of commercials. In 1942 radio set a new record of $255 million in gross billings.

Radio was considered so important that broadcasting was designated an essential industry and the Selective Service System set up deferments for certain radio personnel. Using its chain of shortwave and other stations in various countries of the world, the United States began the Voice of America (VOA), which very successfully produced programs carrying U.S. propaganda not only to enemy but to allied populations. A parallel system of radio stations, Armed Forces Radio (AFR)—which later became the Armed Forces Radio Network (AFRN) and in subsequent years the Armed Forces Radio and Television Network (AFRTN) and the Armed Forces Network (AFN)—was set up to reach U.S. personnel throughout the world. By the end of 1943, AFR operated 306 stations around the globe.

The bad news for the radio industry was that the Defense Communications Board ordered the cessation of the manufacture of all radio and television receivers and a freeze on the construction of new or the expansion of existing stations. Material and labor had to be invested in the war effort. More than 13 million radio sets had been sold in 1941; the total dropped to less than 4.5 million in 1942; and in 1943, with the war becoming more intense, only about 700,000 home sets were sold. The production of phonograph records was rolled back, too, because the shellac needed to make the discs was commandeered for war production. The government, however, did want stations that were on the air to stay, and these got priorities for maintenance and operating materials.

TV virtually ceased. For a while a few stations attempted to provide special programming, such as training for air-raid wardens and sports and variety programs for GIs in stateside hospitals where there were communal TV sets, but there was no economic base on which to continue. A major exception was the DuMont station in

Cocoanut Grove nightclub
fire kills 487 in Boston.

Office of War
Information created.

Voice of America
established.

Armed Forces Radio
begins serving U.S.
troops.

New York. It began broadcasting in 1942 and stayed on the air throughout the entire war, hoping to steal a march on the NBC and CBS TV stations, which went dark, and to become a challenging third TV network when the war ended. Ultimately, though, the power and resources of NBC and CBS won out, and a few years after the war the dreams for a DuMont television network ended.

World War II, like World War I, was responsible for the creation of new communication technologies for use by the Armed Forces—technologies that would immeasurably assist the growth of civilian communications once the war ended. For example, miniaturization of equipment for portability on the battlefield was a priority. One of this book's authors, who served as a combat infantry radio operator in Europe, remembers the relief of being able to exchange the large, heavy Signal Corps Radio (SCR-300) he carried on his back for the handheld walkie-talkie. Another key development was the attempt to facilitate the making, transmitting, and playing of audio recordings. U.S. and German scientists both were experimenting with a form of wire or tape to replace the bulky and breakable records. The United States used the wire recorder in 1943 but learned the following year that Germany had developed and was using the magnetic tape recorder—a much more advanced device that would later revolutionize the radio industry. The radio facsimile photo made advances, too, with U.S. and Russian engineers able to transmit aerial views of battlefields in less than 20 minutes from Moscow to the United States.

Not every development in broadcasting related to the war, however. The president of the American Federation of Musicians (AFM), James C. Petrillo, felt that the use of recordings on radio decreased the demand for live performances by his musicians. He asked stations to pay fees to AFM, similar to their payments to ASCAP. When they refused, he called a strike, forbidding AFM members to make any more recordings. The strike continued for two years.

1943

The FCC's monopoly rules and cross-ownership investigation resulted not only in the CBS–NBC lawsuit but in pressures on Congress from both the newspaper and the broadcast industries to stop FCC action. A Georgia congressman, Eugene E. Cox—who had been accused by the FCC of accepting illegal payments for representing a Georgia broadcaster before the FCC—convinced Congress to investigate the FCC. The court's upholding of the chain broadcasting rules and the forced sale by NBC of its Blue Network further fueled anger against the FCC. Cox chaired the committee that subpoenaed the records and personal finances of all FCC commissioners from 1937 on. Foreshadowing the McCarthy era a decade later, the Cox committee accused the FCC of being unpatriotic, of aiding subversives, of

THE FURIOUS '40S

Government places
freeze on the
manufacture of radio
receivers.

DuMont station in New
York begins telecasts that
last the duration of the war.

overstepping its authority, and of being corrupt. The results included an exposure of Cox's motives as well as the validity of some of the charges of corruption; the resignation of the FCC chairman, James L. Fly, the following year, 1944; and the withdrawal of two other commissioners. But the principal consequence from then on was to make the FCC more responsive and accommodating to the political power of Congress.

As the war escalated, so did the role of radio. The U.S. Army Air Corps joined the British Royal Air Force (RAF) in bombing Germany, the Allied invasion of Italy drove back the Axis powers and forced Italy to switch sides, the Germans were about to suffer a significant defeat at Stalingrad, and the U.S. forces in the Pacific were coming closer to Japan. Radio programs reflected the progress of the war, with some already beginning to deal with the requirements for peace and the postwar world. Even music enlisted—one program, entitled *Music at War*, raised morale by featuring songs of the various branches of the armed services. Situation comedies and comedy/ variety shows continued to be the most popular. With an uncharacteristic sensitivity, perhaps prompted by a growing understanding of the philosophy of the enemy, the U.S. government commissioned radio shows to heighten public perceptions of black (then called Negro) troops and of women in the Armed Forces. Such writers as Norman Corwin and William Robson produced series showing the heroism and abilities of blacks and women. Once the war was over, these kinds of programs, providing equal opportunity and countering bigotry, would not again be found to any extent in commercial broadcasting until the civil rights and women's liberation movements of the 1960s and 1970s, respectively.

Musicians' power was recognized in 1943 when certain recording and broadcasting companies began to pay fees directly to the AFM union. The strike called by Petrillo lasted another year, however, until the networks capitulated, too. Radio got a bonus from the FCC in 1943 when the commission extended the license periods for AM stations from two to three years.

Two important technical developments, one in the laboratory and the other in the courts, occurred in 1943. First, the use of radar was making it possible to detect enemy aircraft at far distances and to fly at night with significant reduction in the risk of collision or crash. *Broadcasting* magazine called radar the "wartime miracle of radio." Second, the Supreme Court issued a ruling in a case that stemmed from a controversy over who actually invented radio. Although Marconi had long since been given credit for developing its principles, an American engineer and physicist, Nikola Tesla, claimed that his notes and papers proved that he had in fact preceded Marconi in inventing the principles of radio. The Supreme Court upheld Tesla's claim—but too late for Tesla. Earlier in the year, bankrupt, depressed, alone, and unrecognized for what he felt was a great contribution to society, Tesla died. Today Tesla Societies are still trying to convince historians, the public, and the broadcast industry of Tesla's claim to fame as the true inventor of radio.

FIG 4.4 Old de Forest radio
equipment advertisement as
reproduced in a 1943
magazine.

United States puts Japanese American citizens in detention camps.	U.S. forces defeat Japan at Guadalcanal.	Wages and prices frozen as war measure.

1943

NBC is forced to sell one of its networks—the Blue Network, which later becomes ABC.

1944

The public continued to be hungry for news, especially as the tide of war turned in favor of the Allies and its end was almost in sight. D-Day signaled the invasion of Europe, and General Douglas MacArthur returned to the Philippines. The networks' percentage of program hours devoted to news had increased from about 7% in 1939 to about 20% in 1944. Shortwave transmitters carried battlefield reports from the Pacific, and information and entertainment from the United States to the Soviet Union. On-the-spot D-Day reports were described on wire recorders and as soon as feasible sent to relay stations in London for broadcast directly to the United States.

Music still dominated the domestic airwaves, accounting for about a third of the network's schedules; 75% of that was pop music by performers such as Frank Sinatra, Bing Crosby, and Glenn Miller. Drama comprised more than a fourth of NBC and CBS programming, with MBS devoting more than a third of its weekly hours to news and talk shows. After the war the volume of news would decrease, and drama, variety, comedy, music, and other entertainment programs would overwhelmingly dominate.

With the war still in progress, politics took on an even greater importance for the public. The largest radio audience up to that time, surpassing the previous records for President Roosevelt's Pearl Harbor address and for the reports on D-Day, listened to the November 7 election returns of Thomas E. Dewey's challenge to a Roosevelt bid for a fourth consecutive term; more than 50% of all radio homes in the country tuned in. The year 1944 solidified Clark Hooper's new ratings system; determined through random telephone calls, it replaced Crossley's as the principal method of radio audience measurement.

Media barons got a break in 1944. The FCC discontinued its cross-ownership study, and did not at that time go ahead with a ban on newspaper/radio station common ownership in the same community; it decided to rule on a case-by-case basis. The FCC also increased from three to five the number of TV stations a single entity could own. NBC and CBS made their AM programming available to the FM outlets of their AM affiliates at no cost and enticed more advertising by providing these additional outlets to sponsors at no additional charge.

The FCC began hearings in 1944 to determine what to do about frequency allocations for the expected growth of new and existing broadcast services following the war. One key issue was whether to continue the old, low-quality TV standards or to introduce new ones that had been developed during the war. The "old boys," an RCA-led coalition including NBC, GE, Philco, and DuMont, wanted to protect their already-huge investment by maintaining the old standards; the "new boys," a coalition led by CBS and including Westinghouse and Zenith, wanted their developing color system and higher definition in the ultra-high-frequency band to be given an opportunity in the marketplace. The old boys won. After extensive hearings, the FCC issued its decision the following year, 1945. The decision strengthened

FIG 4.5 Fred Allen became one of radio's foremost entertainers in the 1940s. His legendary radio feud with Jack Benny provided many laughs.

THE FURIOUS '40S

101

Porgy and Bess conquers Broadway.

The majority of radio programs reflect the war and its events.

FCC extends AM station license period to three years.

Supreme Court upholds Nikola Tesla's claim that he invented the principles of radio.

the existing very high-frequency (VHF) TV system, setting six channels in the 44–80 MHz band (the first of which was assigned for military purposes, later to be used for private radio); setting seven between 174 and 216 MHz; and moving FM from its previous 42–50 MHz spot to 88–108 MHz. Although this action gave FM considerably more channels—100, of which 20 were reserved for nonprofit educational licensees—Edwin Armstrong was furious. Not only had he lost the much more technically desirable lower frequencies, but the change made obsolete all of the almost 500,000 FM sets in use and all of the existing FM stations' transmitting equipment. More than one news story in June 1945 told how the FCC furthered television while hindering FM radio.

1945

FIG 4.6 Table-model receivers of the 1940s. Today, sets manufactured of Bakelite and Catalin plastic are expensive collector's items. They are characterized by vibrant colors, which increase their appeal.

On V-E Day, May 7, 1945, the war ended in Europe. Then, on August 6, the United States dropped the world's first atom bomb on Hiroshima, Japan; three days later another was dropped on Nagasaki, and Japan surrendered. Franklin D. Roosevelt did not live to see the end of the war. On April 12 he had died while resting in Warm Springs, Georgia. Radio carried the news of these momentous happenings throughout the world. One of this book's authors remembers the moment when he, along with other GIs in his company in Europe, heard the news of Roosevelt's death over AFR. Many of these battle-hardened veterans retreated to private places where they sat silently or cried, most of them having known no other President since their early childhoods, with FDR's fireside chats having created a closeness that made it seem as though the listener were a member of the President's own family.

Some months later in Germany, as editor of an occupation-force Army newspaper, the same author was able to redo the paper's format at the last minute because of an AFR midnight announcement of V-J Day, the end of the war in Japan—scooping all other Army newspapers, including *Stars and Stripes*. As did many other journalists, he quickly learned the power of radio to quickly disseminate news and information.

Other key reporting events in 1945 included the coverage of the charter meeting of the United Nations, with radio carrying the news to virtually every country in the world. What was to become one of the most famous broadcasts in radio history was Edward R. Murrow's April 15 radio account of the liberation of the German concentration camp at Buchenwald: "I pray you to believe what I have said . . . for most of it I have no words . . . murder has been done at Buchenwald." Murrow's broadcast made a profound impression on the American public. But although Murrow's sincerity was not doubted, some people were cynical. Why the pretense that this was new, they asked? The United States and the rest of the world had known about the extermination camps for years; they simply chose not to do anything about them.

With the war ended, radio writers and producers turned to serious drama as a way of creating their impressions of the lessons of the past and the hopes for the

War and Recovery—Full of Sound and Fury, Signifying . . . Transition to TV

Warsaw, Poland, ghetto uprising and massacre.	Italy surrenders to Allies.	D-Day: Allied forces storm Normandy beaches.

1944

The networks devote nearly 20% of their airtime to news coverage.

BRUCE MORROW

"COUSIN BRUCIE," LEGENDARY POP-ROCK RADIO PERFORMER _____

I believe I first realized the power of communications, especially broadcast communications, when I was about eight years old. I just finished school for the day and was merrily walking home. When I reached my block (New Yorkese for "street") I noticed that my mother and several of our neighbors were standing on our porch listening to a little brown box, and they were all weeping. My mom and all of those other strong Brooklyn women belonged in the kitchen preparing the evening repast for their families. What could have kept these loyal domestic stalwarts from their usual chores, I wondered. The little brown box was the

table-model Philco radio. This magical cube was telling these ladies that FDR had died and that the nation was in a state of mourning. I realized at that moment that anything so small that could cause such a big emotional reaction had to be magic, and I have always loved magic.

FIG 4.7 Bruce Morrow.
Courtesy Bruce Morrow.

FIG 4.8 Newspaper headline announcing victory in Europe—V-E Day.

THE FURIOUS '40S

| Paris is liberated. | Bandleader Glenn Miller lost in flight over English channel. | General Douglas MacArthur returns to Philippines. |

Radio covers Allied invasion of Europe.

future. In the latter part of 1945, the networks aired a number of classic dramatic programs. Perhaps the most outstanding radio play to capture the feeling as well as the substance of war and peace was Norman Corwin's *On a Note of Triumph*, aired on CBS, a production still used as a model for radio students and as a source of understanding for historians.

The business of broadcasting resumed. As the war was ending, the government reauthorized the manufacture of radio sets. But there wasn't much time to gear up again, and although only 500,000 radio sets were sold in 1945 (compared with about 13 million in prewar 1940), by the end of the year it was estimated that almost 89% of U.S. homes had radios. Radio advertising grew; one estimate indicates that 35% of all advertising dollars spent in 1945 went to radio. Competition increased, as the NBC Blue Network, which had been divested from NBC two years earlier and sold to Edward J. Noble, became ABC. The growth of news broadcasting and prestige during World War II prompted the development of public affairs programs following the war, and in 1945 *Meet the Press*, still running in the 2000s, made its debut on NBC.

Television moved more slowly. Of the dozen or so stations on the air when the United States entered the war, a few had already gone back on before the war ended, most of the others resumed as soon as the war was over, and a backlog of 150 applications for TV licenses sat at the FCC. TV sets were quite expensive and there wasn't that much to see. All stations were local, with regional networks still only in the developing stage. It would be years before television would be hooked up nationally.

The May and June FCC decisions that maintained the NTSC, RCA-backed monochrome standard and gave to television the frequencies previously assigned to FM, thus moving FM to less desirable space, also halted an area of growth that would not begin to reach its potential again for almost a half century. The band that had been used for facsimile experimentation in the 1930s and that by 1939 was used for the first home fax machines marketed by the Crosley Company in Cincinnati was the one given to FM. Although FM devotees were unhappy with the less desirable frequencies, facsimile advocates were devastated because facsimile operations ceased completely.

The euphoria in broadcasting was dampened once again by Petrillo's AFM. Petrillo ordered AFM musicians not to appear on television, stating that the AFM contract covered neither TV nor the simulcasting of AM and FM music. He wanted his union members to be given the jobs of "platter turners" (or disc jockeys, as they were later called) when a station did not employ a standby live orchestra or band to make up for playing recorded music. For several years AFM battled another union, the National Association of Broadcast Engineers and Technicians (NABET), for control of such studio personnel.

Technical advances helped the business and programming growth of broadcasting. Working to improve on its wire recorder and having discovered Germany's already developed magnetic tape recorder among captured German matériel in 1944, the United States was able to build its first tape recorder in 1945. RCA offered a significant technical advancement for television that year when it introduced the

| United Nations formed. | FDR wins fourth term. | Battle of the Bulge is the last gasp for Germany. |

Hooper ratings replace Crossley's as the principal method of radio measurement.

image-orthicon camera, which would replace the iconoscope camera, providing a higher-quality picture and reducing the need for excessively high levels of light. Although RCA was publicly negative about FM, having stopped its support of Edwin Armstrong and making him *persona non grata* at NBC, it was secretly developing its own FM system, applying for patents that were presumably technically different from Armstrong's.

1946

The public interest, convenience, or necessity aspects of broadcasting were brought to the fore by the FCC in 1946 with the issuance of its *Public Service Responsibilities of Broadcast Licensees.* Called the *Blue Book* because of its blue cover—and apocryphally because of its emotional effect on broadcast industry executives—it outlined station program responsibilities in the public interest and established the FCC's authority to see that stations lived up to those responsibilities. Among other things, the *Blue Book* set forth four categories of programming considered significant by the FCC: (1) sustaining programs, including those of networks; (2) local live shows; (3) discussions of public issues; and (4) advertising excesses, which the *Blue Book* sought to eliminate. Broadcasting cried "censorship," and the NAB claimed that the provisions of the *Blue Book* were unconstitutional, infringing on stations' First Amendment rights. The FCC countered that the *Blue Book* did not "promulgate new rules or regulations, but . . . codified the Commission's philosophy to help both licensees and regulators." Published amid a national euphoria of democratic feeling following the U.S. victory for the "people" over the "dictators" in World War II, the *Blue Book* received a positive response from government officials and citizen groups who put the interests of the public above those of industry. The *Blue Book* proved to be the base for continuing actions by the FCC during the next several decades— actions designed to result in programming that served the needs of the public through television and radio alike. The policies emanating from principles set forth in the *Blue Book*, including development of the Fairness Doctrine for the purpose of enabling all sides of controversial issues to be heard by the public, ceased 35 years later when the deregulatory, marketplace philosophy of the Ronald Reagan Presidency resulted in a reversal of the public interest mandate.

AM radio exploded. A postwar United States was eager for the good life, including entertainment, and radio provided it. The top performers in the country—singers, dramatic actors and actresses, comedy artists, even tap dancers—kept audiences in front of their radio sets night after night. The public was hooked on radio news, and in 1946 a whopping 63% of the people cited radio as their primary source of news. If newspapers were worried then, they had only worse days to look forward to. Radio continued as the principal source of news until television became the favored broadcast medium within a decade, and then the visual medium took over as the primary

THE FURIOUS '40S

105

| United Nations formed. | President Roosevelt dies; Harry Truman takes the helm. | Liberation of concentration camps reveals Holocaust horrors beyond belief. |

1945

| Thirty million homes have radios. | Radio carries news of FDR's death. |

news source. In fact, by the end of the 1980s the majority of the public said not only that they got most of their news from television but that they trusted television news even more than the news in their daily newspapers.

Both NBC and CBS capitalized on the postwar interest in news. CBS appointed Edward R. Murrow vice president for its news and public affairs operations, and Murrow immediately started a news documentary unit. That unit was first to become famous in radio and eventually to become even more famous in television, especially with the documentaries produced by Fred Friendly and Murrow himself. Students of broadcasting still study Murrow's *Who Killed Michael Farmer?* radio documentary and *Harvest of Shame* television documentary as seminal examples of how documentaries should be made. Even as early as the late 1940s, Ed Murrow began to display the "fire in the belly" that gave his documentaries not only a point of view but the strength and conviction to improve political and social conditions in the country. One new technological asset for news and documentaries was the audio tape recorder, which, in the next few years, would effect a profound change in news and public affairs and indeed in all production and programming.

With automobiles being produced again, the United States became a nation on wheels. Music dominated daytime radio as disc jockeys accompanied travelers along the highways. Announcers offered commentary and news to relieve the frustration and monotony of the increasing numbers of people who commuted to work by automobile. In 1946 the number of AM stations on the air grew from 1,004 to 1,520. By the end of the year, 35 million homes and 6 million automobiles had radios. Despite being set back by the FCC the previous year, FM began a slow regrowth, with 350,000 sets manufactured in 1946. Manufacturers, rashly optimistic, predicted that 20% of all sets manufactured the following year, 1947, would be FM. But it would be a number of years, following a slowdown and recession in FM growth, until that would actually happen. FM continued to be an orphan in the industry, and in 1946 the FM Broadcasters Association, for the previous seven years a part of the NAB, dissolved itself, stating that the NAB was unfairly promoting AM and TV over FM, and formed a new, separate organization.

Ham radio, banned during the war for security reasons, was permitted to operate again, using the full spectrum the amateurs had before the war. Before the end of the next year, 1947, however, the FCC forbade hams to use cryptography, as they had been able to do for many years, and instead required them to communicate in "plain language."

Dramatic developments took place on the TV front, too. New postwar sets went on sale, and the FCC received 600 applications for TV station licenses. Several television firsts occurred as the new medium attempted to capitalize on the excitement of live visual reporting, among them President Harry Truman's address to the new Congress as well as the opening of the United Nations Security Council. TV's growth potential was enhanced as both RCA and CBS began to release a number of their patents for licensing, including those relating to television sets and film equipment as well as radio

| Germany surrenders. | United States drops atom bombs on Hiroshima and Nagasaki. |

| Edward R. Murrow's broadcast of the liberation of Buchenwald concentration camp stuns nation. | Edward J. Noble launches the American Broadcasting Company (ABC) from NBC Blue purchase. |

FIG 4.9 The father of the Soviet atom bomb, physicist Peter Kapitza, is interviewed by CBS's Lee Bland (left) shortly after World War II. *Courtesy Lee Bland.*

receivers and transmitters and phonograph records. RCA unveiled a "large" TV—a 15 × 20-inch screen. Moving toward the same network structure as radio, television began to develop station connections. Coaxial cable was demonstrated, prompting *The New York Times* to state, "It will link nearly all the major cities of the country, and is expected eventually . . . to become the basis of a system over which television programs from any American city can be relayed to any other." The FCC authorized AT&T to build a Dallas–Los Angeles link as part of an eventual coast-to-coast cable hookup. NBC, much as it had done in the early days of radio, put together a network of four East Coast cities: New York; Philadelphia; Washington, D.C.; and Schenectady, New York.

CBS and NBC vied for the leadership in color television, both demonstrating their latest inventions. CBS's Peter Goldmark, who invented some of the most significant audio and video processes, developed ultra-high-frequency, high-quality sequential, or mechanical, scanning color TV; his invention was not, however, compatible with existing monochrome sets. RCA's color system was an all-electronic one and could be seen in black and white on existing black-and-white receivers but was of poorer visual quality. It was the FCC's responsibility to choose a color system for the country; it took the commission several years of waffling before it finally authorized a usable color TV system.

THE FURIOUS '40S

Japan surrenders.

Meet the Press debuts on NBC.

FM moved "upstairs" to 88–108 MHz.

United States builds its first magnetic tape recorder.

FIG 4.10 Recording an interview for Norman Corwin's *One World Flight* in 1946. Corwin is at the far right.
Courtesy Lee Bland.

The Controversy Over the FCC's 1946 *Blue Book*

In September 1945 FCC chairman Paul Porter commented that the radio channels belong to the American people and the people should make known what they want from those who hold a broadcast license. Porter's call drew a huge response. The war years had provided enormous profits for broadcasters as ad dollars flowed into radio with newsprint in short supply. To sell more time, stations canceled sustained public interest programs in favor of shows that would draw sponsors. Americans began to notice problems inherent with an advertising-supported radio system. In May 1946 the FCC released its *Blue Book*, which forced broadcasters to defend the commercial broadcasting system. Of all the items the FCC deemed were indicators of radio acting in the public interest, the one that troubled broadcasters the most was *commercial excess*. They were concerned with the ambiguity of the word *excess*. But they needn't have worried. At the bidding of the broadcast lobby, a Republican-controlled Congress pressured the FCC to back off, even having the House Un-American Activities Committee probe the Commission for alleged communist sympathies. Overall, the *Blue Book* resulted in a new consciousness of responsibility within the industry as major networks responded with some improvement in public interest programming.

Computer technology
unveiled.

Winston Churchill makes
"Iron Curtain" speech.

1947

Image-orthicon camera
introduced.

FCC introduces document called
the *Blue Book*, which outlines
broadcasters' public service
responsibilities.

LEE BLAND

FORMER NEWS WRITER, PRODUCER, AND DIRECTOR

Today, when recorders literally fit in your pocket, the cumbersome and temperamental wire recorder is hard to imagine. Ed Murrow once told me he booted several of them out the bomb bay door [of his plane] in World War II. But this primitive magnetic recorder was the only "portable" equipment available in early 1946, when Norman Corwin and I took off on his *One World Flight*. The machine itself weighed over 50 pounds and the spools of wire were about a pound each. It required 120-volt, 60-cycle current, so we carried along a converter, propelled by 12-volt storage batteries as a backstop in many countries with oddball voltages.

Fully charged batteries were almost nonexistent, particularly in places ravaged by war, like Poland. Hence the recorder often fought for its life, and speed changes resulted in Donald, Daffy, and Daisy Duck.

If nursing the machine along (and fighting grease which coated the wire) demanded constant TLC, our biggest problem on returning to New York four months later was yet to come: how to prepare the wire recordings for broadcast. After much consultation with CBS engineers, we decided to transfer every mile of wire—hundreds of hours—to instantaneous discs at Columbia Records. Simultaneously, we fed all of this to Ediphone at CBS, giving us a written transcript of every interview. The Ediphone

girls had a huge headache sorting through foreign language translations and Donald Ducks. As the transcripts became available, Mr. Corwin would select blocks of quotes, and I would isolate those passages and put them on discs for him. Off-speed recordings were corrected by Variac—[rheostat] control—and voices were filtered for greatest intelligibility and natural quality. When Mr. Corwin finalized each script in the 13-week series, we then fine-tuned each recorded excerpt in duplicate; the discs were cued in by two engineers simultaneously to protect against failure on the air. The dupes were never needed.

Despite inferior recording quality, Norman Corwin's *One World Flight* was an artistic and technical success, thanks to the support of many people in engineering. Incidentally, until Norman Corwin's *One World Flight*, CBS had a rigid rule against the use of recordings on the network. But Mr. Paley himself endorsed this project, so the ice was broken, and many other such documentaries followed—utilizing recordings by more advanced equipment, of course.

FIG 4.11 Lee Bland recording a program with composer Sergei Prokofiev in Moscow, June 1946.
Courtesy Lee Bland.

THE FURIOUS '40S

Nuremberg war crimes
trials take place.

Edward R. Murrow
implements documentary
unit at CBS.

Television development
accelerates.

Coaxial cable is
demonstrated.

1947

The Cold War mentality that was to destroy reputations and lives and bring the United States to the brink of fascism during the era called McCarthyism began its infiltration in 1947. The fear of Communism, much like the fear of Bolshevism that followed World War I, prompted similar right-wing assaults on constitutional freedoms.

For years the movie moguls had fought the development of unions and had particularly resented writers' attempts to get a share of the Hollywood pie. With the Cold War as an excuse, several studio heads invited the House Un-American Activities Committee (HUAC) to hold hearings in Hollywood on subversive activities, pointing specifically to a number of leaders of artists' unions, especially writers. Some studios felt that this way they could bust the unions and regain unchallenged control of all personnel and contractual arrangements. HUAC was eager to get as many headlines as it could, ostensibly in the interests of patriotic protection of its country. What better way than to investigate the most popular people in the country—movie and radio stars? "The Hollywood Ten"—producers, directors, and writers who were to be driven out of the industry or sent to prison—became a household phrase. That the headlines gave some HUAC members national reputations was presumably incidental. Although the "Red under the bed" hysteria started in the film capital, Hollywood, it soon spread to the radio and television capital, New York.

The director of the Federal Bureau of Investigation (FBI), J. Edgar Hoover, sent a report to the FCC suggesting that there was growing control of the broadcasting industry by Communist elements. The FBI began gathering secret files on anyone whose name it received, even anonymously, as suspect. Conservative radio personalities such as Walter Winchell fanned the flames with implied accusations of disloyalty on the part of those whose beliefs they disagreed with. Three former FBI agents started a newsletter called *Counterattack—The Newsletter of Facts on Communism*, in which they purported to counter the Red menace in broadcasting by listing the names of performers and others in radio and television who at one time or another might have been praised by, contributed to, or participated in an organization or event that the editors of *Counterattack* considered un-American. The "Red scare" grew into national paranoia and in the 1950s prompted a full-scale blacklist in film, television, and radio. (See actor John Randolph's personal account of blacklisting in the next chapter.)

Both AM and FM radio grew in 1947, with some 2 million FM receivers in use by the end of the year. But that was still only about one twentieth the number of AM sets and, although 238 FM stations were on the air and 680 more had construction permits, FM was still far behind the 1,298 AM stations in operation and the 497 additional ones authorized by the end of the year. Radio programming reached its peak with the same kinds of fare we now have on television, including a number of mystery and crime shows. As now, these shows had a full share of violence. In response to public criticism, NBC agreed not to broadcast such programs before 9:30 P.M., and other networks and stations soon followed suit. Self-censorship became a norm in

Dr. Benjamin Spock's book on baby care is published.	Telephone strike grips nation.

1947

Congressional proceedings televised for first time.	FBI director J. Edgar Hoover alleges Communist elements in broadcasting.

broadcasting, principally to preempt the possibility of even harsher restrictions by the FCC. But later on, when television violence drew high ratings, voluntary restraints on this kind of programming virtually disappeared.

Audiotape came of age in 1947. One of the consistently leading programs on radio in the 1940s was NBC's *Kraft Music Hall*, starring Bing Crosby, the most popular singer of the time. Crosby, though, did not like being tied down to the weekly chore of a live show, and the networks refused to permit recorded shows because of the inferior reproduction quality of the discs. Crosby quit after the 1944–1945 season and did not come back until the 1946 season, when ABC agreed to let him prerecord. The technical results were not good. For the 1947 season Crosby experimented with prerecording his shows on tape, which had been refined to reproduce with a fair degree of fidelity. By 1948 the value of audiotape was proved, and within a few years it became standard in the industry—although many programs continued to be done live.

Television was feeling the first surges of maturity, with CBS becoming the first network to contract to broadcast a major league baseball team's games—in this case, the Brooklyn Dodgers. Later in the year NBC broadcast the first televised World Series—the Dodgers against the New York Yankees, a lucky combination for NBC inasmuch as the largest audience for any of its stations was in the New York area. The first TV show especially designed for children, *Howdy Doody*, made its debut in 1947; it stayed on the air until 1960. Another children's show that began on a local station, in Chicago, and was later to move to network fame also started that year: *Kookla, Fran, and Ollie*. A pioneer anthology drama series, *The Kraft Television Theater*, began its long run on television.

Both NBC and CBS continued to demonstrate their respective color systems, and CBS petitioned the FCC to designate its system as the accepted one. The FCC said no. Another potential wave of the future for television was large-screen theater presentations, and RCA and Warner Brothers explored that possibility. It was not to come about for some years, and even then it was limited primarily to high-priced sports events, such as world championship boxing bouts. An important technical development was the invention of the zoom lens, or *zoomar*. Because videotape had not yet been invented, all programs were done live, and dollying in and out for close-ups and long shots was difficult in compact studios with limited space for cameras and with cables almost everywhere on the floor. The zoomar provided much greater artistic flexibility for directors and soon became a standard part of all TV cameras.

Shades of pay-TV! In 1947 Zenith developed what it called *Phonevision*, a system whereby the TV set is plugged into a telephone to receive scrambled TV signals, which are then decoded for a fee. Although Phonevision wasn't fully tested for another few years and did not indicate financial feasibility when it was, the increasing number of pay-TV programs in the 1990s suggests that Zenith knew what it was doing—but it was doing it almost a half century too early!

By the end of 1947, 12 television stations were licensed and 55 more had FCC permits to build.

THE FURIOUS '40S

111

Some 2 million FM
receivers in use.

NBC telecasts the World
Series.

FIG 4.12 Early
tape recorders like these
revolutionized
broadcasting.

Laugh Tracks

The much-maligned laugh track had its origins toward the end of radio's golden age. In 1947, Army veteran John Mullins, who had recovered embryonic audiotape recording equipment in occupied Germany following WWII, was invited to record an episode of radio's *Bing Crosby Show*. The crooner appreciated the idea of airing a show void of flubs, flaws, and weak performances, the bane of live radio broadcasts, so he soon recorded his rehearsals as well as the live audience reactions, which, because they were taped, could overrun scheduled time constraints, and then have the anemic parts edited out. He hired Mullin as his chief engineer; he proved not only to be a skillful tape editor but a potential producer, for when he sensed a performance lagging, he added recorded laughter. Crosby's producers greeted Mullin's inspiration with enthusiasm and shortly asked him to save laughter and applause snippets from successful programs that could be inserted when actual audience reaction was lifeless. The idea of a laugh track gained wider acceptance on radio as the medium's popularity waned and live studio audiences dwindled as well as on early television as more sitcoms and comedy/variety shows were filmed at movie studios that could not accommodate audiences.

Chuck Yeager breaks the sound barrier.		Taft-Hartley Act restricts labor's rights.
Harry S. Truman makes first televised Presidential address.	Howdy Doody and The Kraft Television Theater debut.	

1948

The first woman to serve on the FCC, Frieda Hennock, was appointed in 1948. Facing hostility from some colleagues and from most of the industry, she nevertheless was an effective force, standing her ground, sometimes stubbornly, to push for rule making in the public interest. Hennock was at the FCC during one of the most critical periods in its history: a time that included the "freeze" of 1948 through the *Sixth Report and Order* of 1952, which established the television and radio requirements that shaped the future of broadcasting and that have continued into the 21st century. One of her major contributions was an at times lonely fight to reserve noncommercial television channels for the exclusive use of educational institutions—what we today know as public television.

With the postwar explosion of new technologies, especially television, the FCC was faced with immediate problems of a shortage of TV frequencies, particularly in larger markets, where available TV channels were virtually all gone. Among other things, the FCC had to decide whether to allocate the most desirable audio frequencies to FM or to TV; it had to deal with potential TV interference that rivaled that of radio more than two decades earlier; it faced increasing demands for educational TV channels; and it had to determine which TV color system to choose for the country. There had been only 13 channels, all in the VHF band, available for domestic civilian use, and earlier in the year the FCC had taken Channel 1 away from such use and assigned it to nongovernment fixed and mobile services. The FCC's chairman, Wayne Coy, suggested that the commission look for additional frequency space for television use in the ultra-high-frequency (UHF) band. The FCC's earlier rulings on geographic distances between stations had resulted in insufficient mileage separation and, thus, in interference on co-channel stations. In addition, the demand for TV sets outstripped the supply, with major manufacturers, such as RCA, GE, and DuMont, trying to fill a half year's back orders. On September 29, 1948, the FCC put a six-month freeze on processing any new applications for TV stations. The six months stretched into more than three and a half years before the *Sixth Report and Order* finally resolved the issues (see coverage of the year 1952 in the next chapter). In 1947 the FCC also extended FM license periods to three years, banned censorship of political broadcasts by stations, and made it possible for many small and poor colleges to go into radio broadcasting by authorizing 10-watt stations. The 10-watters were later abolished at the beginning of reregulation introduced during President Jimmy Carter's administration.

TV stations that already had construction permits were allowed to build and go on the air during the years of the freeze—with more than 100 in operation nationwide by the time the freeze ended in 1952—but the freeze held back the rapid growth that was anticipated and gave radio a breather as the principal broadcasting medium. Although many top radio performers were lured to television, others remained in radio. But alternate forms of radio programming were already beginning

FIG 4.13 A 1948 advertisement for a "build your own TV" kit.

Zoomar (zoom) lens is invented.

All-black and All-Hispanic radio stations debut.

MARTIN HALPERIN

Former Armed Forces Radio Service and engineering pioneer _

I've been a sound recording engineer/mixer for over 45 years. Radio has always been my big love. From a very early age I wanted to be a part of that industry. Like many young people, I "worked" at the local radio station in my hometown while in high school—of course for no pay but just to be a part of it. Later I was a page at NBC in Hollywood while still in high school.

I met many people from the Armed Forces Radio Service while at the network. When I was drafted into the army I tried to get to AFRS after my basic training and was fortunate to do so. I spent 10 years there (part military and part civilian) as a recording engineer. At age 18 I was part of the military/civilian team that installed the first AFRS recording room in their building on Santa Monica Boulevard. We did not get our first tape machine (an Ampex 200) until about 1948, yet all the commercial programs sent overseas had to be edited. From the day the program was first aired in the United States until we sent a de-commercialized copy overseas, it took approximately six weeks. All commercials and reference to dates (the latter because of the time lapse for delivery) had to be deleted. How was that done without tape? Two 160-transcription disc copies were made for each program. A producer would listen to the program, note

the time where a commercial, date, etc., took place, and enter it on a log or cue sheet for the recording engineer. In playing back the discs, we would let one of the disc copies run up to the start of the item to be deleted and then segue to the second disc copy, which had been cued to start just past the end of the deleted section. If needed, music, applause, or laughter could be mixed in from a third turntable to make the segue seem natural. With these spots deleted, the programs were shorter than the original program, so I and E [information and education] spots were added as well as music to fill them out. This is a rather oversimplified description of the process. With the advent of tape splicing, this function became less of a chore. I should mention too that when we were first introduced to the tape recorder, we were more impressed by the fact that we could cut the tape to edit than we were by the audio quality. Prior to tape, when we made a mistake we had to start the recording over from the beginning.

FIG 4.14 Martin Halperin in the first Armed Forces Radio Service recording room, circa 1947, showing a 16-inch acetate disk to the announcer Del Sharbutt. *Courtesy Martin Halperin.*

to draw the biggest ratings as the traditional variety, comic, and drama shows made their transition to the visual medium. The quiz show—or, as it's now called, the audience participation or game show—became one of radio's most successful formats, with programs like *Stop the Music* and *Hit the Jackpot* among the favorites. Through a tax shelter plan, CBS gained an advantage over its rival networks. Working with MCA, the agency representing many of the country's star performers, CBS was able to lure Jack Benny, Edgar Bergen and Charlie McCarthy, Amos and Andy, Red Skelton, Burns and Allen, and other stars from NBC by setting up their programs under capital gains properties taxes rather than under earned income higher tax rates. In not too many more years these shows would leave radio and move to television—CBS television, of course. The 1948 talent raids continued into the following year. So successful was CBS's head, William S. Paley, in luring away top talent that Fred Allen announced on one of his 1949 NBC shows, "I'll be back next week, same time, same network. No other comedian can make that claim."

FIG 4.15 An early television test pattern. *Courtesy David Sarnoff Library.*

The TV stations on the air continued to draw larger and larger audiences, with concomitantly more advertising revenue and in turn more stars to draw even larger audiences and more advertising. *The Texaco Star Theater*, a comedy/variety show, was number one on television. Its star, Milton Berle, is credited with having been responsible for selling more TV sets than any other factor did in those early days, and with establishing the audience that made television successful. The nation stopped whatever it was doing to watch "Uncle Miltie" on Tuesday nights—just as it had done for years with the *Amos 'n' Andy* radio show. The comedian Danny Thomas, as a guest on one of Berle's shows, said, "Milton, you're responsible for the sale of more television sets in this country than any other person. I sold my set, my uncle sold his set. . . ."

A program that was to be a leader in the ratings for two decades made its debut in 1948. *Toast of the Town* featured as host a taciturn gossip columnist who, some critics said, was totally lacking in stage presence—Ed Sullivan. Sullivan was responsible for introducing many future performing stars on his vaudeville-type program. Subsequently called *The Ed Sullivan Show*, it featured in several episodes a swivel-hipped guitarist/singer from Tennessee named Elvis Presley, whose reputation required the cameras to stay focused above his waist during his entire TV debut (Presley appeared three times in the 1950s), and in another two appearances in 1964, four long-haired musicians from Liverpool, the Beatles. Another long-lasting program that made its first TV appearance in 1948 was *Ted Mack's Original Amateur Hour*, which for years on radio had been the top-rated *Major Bowes Original Amateur Hour*. One type of program popular then but rarely seen today, except on public television, was serious music. In 1948 the *NBC Symphony* program series was 10th on the TV ratings charts.

Politicians saw the value of television, just as they had with radio two decades earlier. Both the Republican and Democratic Parties held their national conventions in Philadelphia in 1948. Why? Because Philadelphia was on the coaxial cable linking New York to Washington, D.C., and was also connected by microwave relay to Baltimore. This constituted the largest network audience then available. Both candidates—the

THE FURIOUS '40S

DANIEL SCHORR

REPORTER/COMMENTATOR, NATIONAL PUBLIC RADIO _____

My first radio broadcast taught me my most important lesson about broadcasting. As newly appointed ABC stringer in the Netherlands in May 1948, I was booked for a live report on the morning news roundup. The story was big—the Congress of Europe, which brought together people like Churchill and Adenauer. Standing by in a little studio (with a squawky shortwave circuit) in Amsterdam, I was told by an ABC editor to listen to the ongoing program and to start my report when I heard myself introduced. Three times the editor warned me not to go one second over two minutes. When I had done my thing, I waited for comment, heard none, said several times "Hello, New York?" until an editor now busy with other things came back. "How was it?" I asked, rather anxiously. "Oh, fine," he said. "You got off in time."

FIG 4.16 Daniel Schorr.
Courtesy Daniel Schorr.

incumbent President, Harry S. Truman, and the Republican challenger, Thomas E. Dewey—made use of television. In fact, Truman deemphasized what had become a traditional reliance on newspapers and radio and instead combined a whistle-stop, stump-speech tour of the country with television appearances to win the election. Truman's inauguration on January 20, 1949, was the first to be televised. The four television networks—CBS, NBC, ABC, and DuMont—pooled their resources, as did the radio networks—NBC, CBS, ABC, and Mutual—to carry the ceremonies. Not only did tens of thousands of people buy sets for this event, but television receivers were installed for the first time in many schools so that students could see and discuss this milestone. *The New York Times* reported that more people saw this inauguration on television than had seen in person all the previous inaugurations put together. The network idea took hold, and regional networks were established, linking key cities in different areas of the country—for example, Cleveland, Chicago, Milwaukee, Detroit, St. Louis, and Buffalo as a Midwest network.

The two major networks, NBC and CBS, competed even beyond broadcasting—through their phonograph partners. RCA brought out a 45-rpm record and

Mahatma Gandhi assassinated.		Japanese war criminals hanged.

CBS launches successful talent raids, largely against NBC.		Ed Sullivan enters TV airwaves as host of *Toast of the Town.*

Columbia Records made a 33$\frac{1}{3}$-rpm long-playing (LP) record available for home use, leading to increased competition to persuade deejays, by then key elements in radio, to promote their products. Other inventions included demonstration of the transistor by Bell Laboratories and the kinescope method of recording pictures off the TV tube.

Edwin Armstrong was fed up. Not only had the FCC denied him the channels he felt were necessary for optimum FM growth, but RCA was using what he believed were his FM patents in television audio and in FM radio without paying him royalties.

FIG 4.17 Long-playing records, or LPs, not only provided better sound and more of it, they also required less room to store. Here inventor Peter Goldmark stands between stacks of old-fashioned 78s, holding his 33$\frac{1}{3}$ revolutionary disk. *Courtesy CBS.*

THE FURIOUS '40S

Milton Berle spurs TV
growth with *Texaco
Star Theater*.

Truman uses television to win
election; his inauguration is the
first to be televised.

Zenith, GE, and Westinghouse had all acknowledged the use of Armstrong's work and were paying him royalties. But not RCA; it wanted him to accept a one-time cash fee. Armstrong sued.

Meanwhile, *Counterattack* published the names of 192 organizations it claimed were Communist fronts, and it began to list the names of performers and others in broadcasting who it claimed were members of these organizations. In fact, only 73 of the organizations were on the attorney general's list of suspect groups, and most of those named were later removed. But the mud stuck.

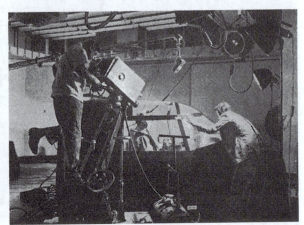

FIG 4.18 Late 1940s television production.

RCA introduces the 45-rpm record, and Columbia makes a 33⅓-rpm long-playing record available to consumers.	Bell Laboratory scientists invent the transistor.	*Counterattack* publishes a list of alleged Communist fronters.	The kinescope method of television recording is employed.

FREDERICK O'NEAL

THE LATE FREDERICK O'NEAL WAS PRESIDENT, COORDINATING COUNCIL FOR NEGRO PERFORMERS, ASSOCIATED ACTORS AND ARTISTS OF AMERICA, AND ACTORS EQUITY ASSOCIATION _____

During the late 1940s, we organized the Coordinating Council for Negro Performers. Our main purpose as performers was to secure employment of blacks in radio and television, as well as other forms of entertainment. More important, we wanted to change the impression of the viewing public to a more realistic image of blacks and others on the American scene. It was our feeling that television and radio were the greatest media of education and information in the world today. We approached the NAACP through the New York branch to discuss and act on this problem at their forthcoming convention in Atlantic City. Such activism on the part of that organization as well as others has been somewhat successful; we realize there is still much to be done.

FIG 4.19 Frederick O'Neal.
Courtesy Frederick O'Neal.

1949

A key FCC action that was to affect all programming in the future was its 1949 reversal of the Mayflower decision, in which it had forbidden stations to editorialize. Now stations could editorialize but were required to offer time for presentation of the other side of an issue. Coupled with court decisions and other FCC actions in the next few years and using the *Blue Book* as a cornerstone, the reversal of the Mayflower decision led to the development of the Fairness Doctrine. Under the Fairness Doctrine, stations were encouraged to present issues of controversy in their communities, and if they did so they could be later required to present all sides of a given issue. The Fairness Doctrine, attacked by many broadcasters as a restriction

1949

FCC reverses its stand on
prohibiting broadcast
editorials.

FCC issues document designed to
ensure a balanced presentation of
views. It would become known as
the Fairness Doctrine.

of their First Amendment rights and supported by many citizen groups as an extension of the general public's First Amendment rights, was in itself highly controversial, right up to the time of its abolition under the Reagan administration's 1980s deregulatory policy.

Home Ownership of Radio Receivers, 1922–1950

YEAR	SETS PER HOUSEHOLD
1922	0.02
1925	0.20
1930	0.40
1935	1.00
1940	1.50
1945*	1.50
1950	2.10

* Lack of increase owing to freeze on set
manufacturing during World War II.
SOURCE: U.S. BUREAU OF THE CENSUS.

The FCC continued to hold hearings and see color TV demonstrations—and continued to postpone its decision.

Although the hours of TV broadcasting were limited because of the scarcity of suitable material and because the advertising jackpot that was to permit the creation of such material had not yet arrived, TV's impact on radio nevertheless continued. Radio began to consider less expensive programming and to put on more quiz shows and music. Audience participation "giveaway" shows were popular—13 on ABC, 8 on CBS, and 7 on NBC. The FCC took a dim view of such programs and threatened nonrenewal of licenses for stations that carried them. It would be another decade before the real import of potential abuse was revealed in the quiz-show scandals that shook the entire broadcasting industry in the 1950s.

In addition, the fledgling networks were expanding. In January 1949, AT&T completed the cable connection of 14 cities in the East and Midwest.

Another highly successful radio show made its debut on television in 1949: *The Lone Ranger* rode right from radio into the video medium. And a new type of television program began with a 16-hour, $1.1 million cancer research fundraiser for the Damon Runyon Memorial Fund. Hosted by Milton Berle, Walter Winchell, Dean Martin, and Jerry Lewis, this was the first telethon.

Arthur Miller's *Death of a Salesman* wins Pulitzer Prize.

Television's impact on radio increases as talent from the latter leap to the new visual medium.

The telethon fundraiser is introduced.

The Academy of Television Arts and Sciences was created in 1949 for the purpose of honoring television shows and performers, similar to what the Academy of Motion Picture Arts and Sciences was doing with its annual Oscar awards. The television award was named Emmy after the image-orthicon camera tube, and in that first year it was presented for Los Angeles programs only. Early television fame was fleeting, however, for many artists. How many people have heard, much less remember, the name Shirley Dinsdale, the person voted the Outstanding Television Personality of 1949?

What did the Fairness Doctrine require?

The issue of reinstating the Fairness Doctrine surfaced when the Democrats took control of both the executive and legislative branches of federal government following the 2008 elections. Right-wing politicians and commentators, in response to offhand comments made by some Democratic legislators, fueled the subject. Early in his administration President Barack Obama's spokesperson stated that holding to his campaign promise, he was opposed to reinstatement, as did his nominee for FCC chairman. Conservatives, especially the vitriolic right-wing radio talkers that flood the AM dial, charged that the doctrine was an attempt to require broadcasters to give equal airtime for liberal counterpoints. But would it? Exactly what was this Fairness Doctrine? For one thing it never required *equal* airtime, something initially addressed in the 1927 Radio Act and intended to provide *equal opportunity* for qualified candidates for any public office. Equal airtime and the Fairness Doctrine are a commingled ruse invented by those who fill the airwaves with one-sided diatribes. The Fairness Doctrine primarily sought the *reasonable* opportunity for an airing of competing views on matters of public importance and was intended to encourage an open and robust debate. In practice, opposing viewpoints generally received about one sixth of the time given to the original perspective.

THE FURIOUS '40S

Communists defeat
Nationalists in China.

The first presentation of the
Emmy Award is made.

Television network links
increased in East and
Midwest.

First TV daytime soap opera,
These Are My Children, debuts
on Chicago NBC station.

FCC tightens its sta
lottery-type giveaw
shows.

FIG 4.20 A booklet
entitled *How to Watch TV*
advised viewers how to
avoid eye fatigue.
*Courtesy Smithsonian
Institution.*

Chapter FIVE

The Fearful '50s

Broadcasting and Blacklisting —A Decade of Shame

The Cold War that followed the "hot war" of 1939–1945 generated continuing audiences for media news, with the media exulting in their exacerbation of the confrontational atmosphere between the United States and the Soviet governments and people. The 1950s were a time when demagoguery and fear were rampant, both resulting from and engendering the rise of a U.S. Senator from Wisconsin, Joseph R. McCarthy, whose accusations alone mandated condemnation and ostracizing of thousands of Americans. The atmosphere of McCarthyism allowed labels such as "Commie," "Red," "pinko," "fellow traveler," and others to cause people's loss of jobs, expulsion from organizations, eviction from homes, incarceration, and, in some cases, suicide. No proof or trial was necessary. Guilt by accusation became the norm. So strong was McCarthy's power that even the World War II hero General Dwight D. Eisenhower, running for President, acquiesced to McCarthy's bidding in speeches and actions and, once he became President, was still not willing to stand up to McCarthy.

It was no wonder, then, in this national environment of fear, that the broadcasting networks capitulated to an organization named American Business Consultants, later called AWARE, that published in its newsletter, *Counterattack*, and in its 1950, 215-page report, *Red Channels*, the names of performers, writers, directors, and others in the communications field whose political views it considered "subversive." *Red Channels* was officially titled a "Report of Communist Influence in Radio and Television." Among the 151 persons listed therein were some of the outstanding artists of the time, ranging from Aaron Copland to Arthur Miller and Orson Welles.

After some initial protests by a few broadcast executives, broadcasting not only acquiesced but fully cooperated with the blacklisters. All the networks agreed to blacklist the people listed and to pay the blacklisters fees to check the names of all prospective talent on their programs. No proof of subversion was offered and none was required. *The New York Times* critic, Jack Gould, wrote that "*Red Channels* is the Bible up and down Madison Avenue." Hundreds of people's careers were ruined, and many others didn't work in their professions for many years solely because of the accusations or innuendos, most of them unproven and undocumented. Accusations accepted by broadcasting as proof of subversion included such things as having

© 2010 Taylor & Francis. All rights reserved.
DOI: 10.1016/B978-0-240-81236-6.00005-6

THE FEARFUL '50S

123

Senator Joe McCarthy launches anti-Communist crusade.		U.S. military action in Korea.

1950

Red Channels is published, listing alleged subversives in broadcasting.

opposed the fascist dictator Federico Franco during the Spanish Civil War, having aided refugees from Hitler, supporting repeal of poll taxes, contributing to the elimination of racial discrimination, advocating civil rights, and backing the improvement of relationships between the United States and the Soviet Union. Even some performers who supported blacklisting were blacklisted, not knowing why, unaware that because their names had become confused with or sounded like some others on the blacklist, the networks were afraid to hire them, too. The networks even submitted the names of child actors and actresses to the blacklisters to be checked for possible subversive activity.

JOHN RANDOLPH

TELEVISION, RADIO, FILM, AND TONY AWARD-WINNING STAGE ACTOR

FIG 5.1 John Randolph.
Courtesy John Randolph.

There was a dark phase in television from 1950 to 1965—when the Cold War had the world in its icy grip. The word *blacklist* came into our language with terrifying results in the communications industry. Hardest hit were the actors, writers, and directors. The networks and affiliates on every level crumbled under the pressure of self-appointed patriots, who wrapped themselves in the American flag. The union leadership in AFRA [American Federation of Radio Actors] and in SAG [Screen Actors Guild] collaborated with the witch-hunt hysteria that swept the land. TVA [Television Authority], the umbrella group that covered the new field of television, included SAG, AFTRA, and Actors Equity representatives. A special committee was elected by the membership at a TVA meeting to investigate blacklisting. It was to hold its meetings in closed sessions to protect witnesses. Before the hearings ended a majority of the committee found themselves blacklisted! Two famous directors of hit shows, who testified before that committee about "no-no" lists or "gray" lists that were used by their casting departments, were blacklisted within a week after they testified. The Secretary assigned by TVA leadership to keep minutes for a report to be given back to the membership was the conduit of the union leadership.

Networks agree to
blacklist those cited in
Red Channels.

CBS establishes the first
exclusively TV news post
in the nation's capital.

Artists who refused to sign the CBS loyalty oath and to testify were put on the list. Added to this list were actors who had been on still another list, which consisted of actors who forgot lines or who were considered troublemakers or whose names sounded like citizens who testified against state or federal investigative committees. This was the so-called "gray" list, which became a general blacklist and included suspected radicals, Communist or Socialist sympathizers, or members of any organization listed as subversive by the U.S. Attorney General.

Here's the way it worked on one level. All networks followed a general pattern when casting a show. For each character they would submit five to 10 names of performers to be cleared by former HUAC employees. Vincent Hartnett, who claimed to be an expert in this area, published a hate sheet called *Aware Incorporated* that was distributed to all agencies, officials, etc., in the business. He charged seven dollars a name (handling approximately 100 names a day) and then returned the network's submissions notated "acceptable," "questionable," or "politically unreliable." When David Susskind, who was producing *East Side/West Side*, questioned Mr. Hartnett about a nine-year-old child he needed on the show whose name came back marked "politically unreliable," Mr. Hartnett replied that [the child's] father had subscribed to the *Daily Worker*. David Susskind never submitted a list again.

In my own case, on an NBC live show (all major TV shows were live in 1951), I became a victim of a more sophisticated and brutal form of blacklisting. I had a good role opposite Anthony Quinn, and the show was to be aired the next day when Sidney Lumet, the director, was called "upstairs" by a vice

president, who told him to fire me immediately. He had been contacted by the Young and Rubicam Advertising agency and had been told that the sponsors of the show, Ammident Toothpaste, had been called by a Mr. Johnson of Syracuse (owner of three supermarkets), who said he would put signs on his store shelves that Ammident Toothpaste supports Communists like John Randolph. When Sidney Lumet explained that he could not replace me without cancelling the show, he was told that he could go ahead with the broadcast, but if he hired me again he was finished at that network. I worked, but it was the last time for years. Later, this story became the basis of an antiblacklist clause that was put into the Actors Equity contract—the first of its kind during the McCarthy era.

The damage to television was enormous. During the next 15 years over 400 actors' careers went down the tubes. Schools like the famous Neighborhood Playhouse, the Dramatic Workshop at the New School for Social Research, the Actor's Studio in New York, and the Actor's Lab in Hollywood were considered hotbeds of radicals, and their graduates were labeled as such. The beginning of the end for blacklisting came by 1965, when liberal and progressive slots were elected in all major unions. The death blow landed when a talk show personality named John Henry Faulk (elected president of AFRA in New York) got blacklisted, fought it for six years, and won a $3.5 million judgment suit against Vincent Hartnett and Johnson of Syracuse. Ironically, Mr. Johnson, who refused to appear in court, was found dead in a motel in the Bronx on the last day of the trial, just as John Henry Faulk's lawyer, Louis Nizer, had concluded his summation speech to the court.

THE FEARFUL '50S

Numerous firings of professors who refuse to sign "loyalty oath."

Zenith's Phonevision promotes pay TV.

Superman comes to TV.

The first artist officially blacklisted was Ireene Wicker, who hosted a children's program, *Let's Pretend*. Others blacklisted early on were dancer Paul Draper and harmonica virtuoso Larry Adler when a letter-writing campaign organized by a Red-hunting housewife urged the Ford Company to cancel an appearance by Draper and Adler on Ed Sullivan's Ford-sponsored *Toast of the Town*. Ford didn't cave in, but the incident so unnerved Sullivan that he cleared all future performers with the publishers of *Counterattack*, and Draper and Adler had to leave the United States for Europe in order to work again.

Another early blacklisted performer was the actress Jean Muir, who was fired from *The Aldrich Family* by its sponsor, General Foods, a few days before it made its transition from radio to television. Muir was listed as belonging to or supporting subversive organizations; one of her alleged "subversive" activities was signing a letter of congratulations to the famed Moscow Art Theater—the artistic inspiration for much of American theater—on its 50th anniversary. Philip Loeb, a regular on the long-running and highest-rated CBS series *The Goldbergs*, was listed and fired. When the program's star and writer for 25 years, Gertrude Berg, protested, the program was canceled. Berg's appeals to the presidents of CBS and NBC, William Paley and David Sarnoff, respectively, got nowhere. A few years later, barred from the industry to which he had devoted his life, Loeb committed suicide.

A Syracuse, New York, owner of supermarkets, Laurence Johnson, became a leading proponent of the blacklist, and through his status as an officer of the National Association of Supermarkets and through threats of boycotts of various products induced almost all the leading companies in the country to support the blacklist. Johnson promoted a lawyer by the name of Vincent Hartnett as an expert on Communism in broadcasting. Hartnett became a key clearance consultant; once he even refused to clear Santa Claus.

Should the FCC and federal government have acted to protect an individual's democratic political rights, as they did at a later date with equal opportunity laws and rules that prohibited broadcast stations from discriminating on the basis of race or gender? The FCC and the rest of the government in the 1950s—like the attitudes and behavior of most of the United States, business and public alike—were being held hostage by McCarthyism. Individually and collectively, government regulators, like the average citizen, were fearful of saying, much less doing, anything that would uphold traditional American freedoms but might cost them their jobs.

The blacklist ostensibly ended in 1962 when John Henry Faulk, a star performer blacklisted by CBS in 1956, finally won his multimillion-dollar lawsuit against AWARE and Laurence Johnson. It took years, however, before an unofficial blacklist disappeared, notwithstanding the networks' apologies for their actions. A "graylist" continued into the 1960s, and many performers, simply because they had been thrust into a position of being controversial, never worked again. CBS, despite its *mea culpas*, did not hire John Henry Faulk back—nor did any other network.

Why did broadcasters, networks, and stations give in to the blacklisters, and why might they well do it again? Not because they are political bigots or support totalitarian suppression of beliefs, but because the U.S. system of broadcasting is based on advertising support—and advertisers' decisions are dictated by their profit and loss statements. Advertisers disassociate themselves from anything—program content or performers—that potential customers in the audience might find too controversial and might prompt them to react negatively to the advertiser's message. Could a blacklist happen again? In the 1980s CBS dropped the *Lou Grant* show because some of its sponsors found its star, Ed Asner, to be politically controversial. Today, in the 1990s, many advertisers have withdrawn sponsorship of or demanded changes in program content that pressure groups find controversial, and networks have usually acquiesced. Even the outstanding public television station WGBH in Boston, coproducing a series for PBS in 1990 on the Korean War, changed important segments in the series following pressure from a conservative media lobbying group. Although public broadcasters are prohibited from carrying commercials, they frequently depend on corporate underwriters to fund their programs.

The Korean War, which began in 1950, offered broadcasting an opportunity to demonstrate its power to stimulate public debate and action—as broadcasting did 20 years later when it provided stark and candid coverage of the U.S. role in the war in Vietnam, quickening the public outrage that forced the United States to end its military actions in Southeast Asia. Yet in the 1950s even objective reporting was considered un-American by many. In 1950 Congress amended the Communications Act of 1934 to authorize the President to take over radio and television stations if deemed necessary for the national defense.

Political coverage otherwise began to mature on television, as it had done on radio in the previous decade. CBS established the first exclusively TV news post in Washington, D.C., assigning to it a former war correspondent and UP Moscow bureau chief, Walter Cronkite. The techniques of news reporting on TV still had a way to go, however. The networks continued to hire newsreel companies for filming their news material, and it would be a few years more before they would send out their own camera crews. News shows principally consisted of "talking heads"—that is, personalities sitting at desks and reading into the camera from scripts.

One of the political events in Washington, D.C., covered by television in 1950 and 1951 was the series of hearings of Tennessee Senator Estes Kefauver's committee investigating organized crime. Record numbers of people in the cities where the hearings were carried were captivated day after day by the TV camera's concentration on the hands of the star witness, Frank Costello, who objected to his face appearing on the screen. The close-ups on his hands revealed more about his feelings and attitudes than his verbal testimony did.

| Truman relieves MacArthur of command; old soldier doesn't quite "fade away." | Ronald Reagan stars in *Bedtime for Bonzo.* |

1951

| President Truman's address is televised in first coast-to-coast hookup. | TV catapults Tennessee Senator Kefauver to prominence during hearings on crime. |

RALPH EDWARDS

TV HOST AND PRODUCER

A live television show that was unrehearsed, spontaneous, surprised an unsuspecting subject, and continued with nonprofessionals instead of actors presented many challenges.

The fourth year of *This Is Your Life* brought us a situation that the media had

FIG 5.2 Ralph Edwards on the set of *This Is Your Life.*
Courtesy Ralph Edwards Productions.

wondered about for all of those four years: What would you do if your subject didn't show up? I found out—the hard way.

We had planned the "life" of Darlene Miller, a farm girl from Dubuque, Iowa, who had kept her brothers and sisters together after the death of their parents, overcoming many odds, including polio.

Airtime arrived and there was no Darlene Miller. Our spies told us that she was delayed by an accident on the Arroya Seco between Pasadena and the NBC Studios. What to do? This was "live" TV. We had to go on. We had no standby show and would not have been permitted to use a transcription in any event. We did the normal opening, and I went on stage, book in hand, and explained exactly what had happened: Our leading lady just wasn't there! Then I continued to do the show without Darlene. I told it through her brothers and sisters, friends and relatives, extolling the virtues of older sister Darlene in holding them together. Darlene arrived 28 minutes into the show, when we were doing what we called the "future." The subject was given merchandise, money, or other items that would help brighten life in the days to come. The show turned out well, but we were lucky because this particular story was of five children who stayed together and could be told through any one of them; however, it was a different show than we had planned—a one-of-a-kind, and once was enough for me!

Other programming began to take on the feel of what TV would become—the premiere entertainment source in the country. After 15 years on radio, *Your Hit Parade* brought the week's top popular songs to television. Jack Benny and Burns and Allen made the switch to television. *Your Show of Shows,* which set a standard

| UNIVAC is the first commercial business computer. | | | First thermonuclear test. |

| *See It Now* premieres on CBS television. | First live coast-to-coast TV networking. | | CBS makes first color telecast. |

for intelligent comedy and satire and starred Sid Caesar, began its run on television. The grandparent of subsequent audience participation shows, *Truth or Consequences*, moved from radio to television with its host of 10 years, Ralph Edwards. NBC proved that network afternoon TV could be successful with its introduction of *The Kate Smith Show*, and CBS followed suit a few weeks later with afternoon variety programs hosted by Garry Moore and Robert Q. Lewis. ABC's *Pulitzer Prize Playhouse* was the model for future drama series that would be called the Golden Age of Television Drama. And on Christmas evening in 1950, CBS started a phenomenon that is still continuing into the first decade of the 21st century: Steve Allen hosted a format that four years later evolved into *The Tonight Show* and its many counterparts.

The New York pilot stations of the networks and the regional networks that received their programs were doing well. But audiences were not yet national or large enough for advertisers to put much money into local stations. A musical variety show one of the authors of this book was producing for a station in the Midwestern network in 1950 failed to go on the air at the last minute because the sponsor refused to pay an additional $25 for each script, stating that the number of people who were watching didn't justify even that small extra cost.

There were now about 10 million television sets throughout the country. From less than 200,000 manufactured in 1947, some 140 companies produced more than 5 million sets in 1950. On the air in 64 cities were 108 TV stations, owned principally by radio licensees; 89 of these TV stations had radio stations in the same market. Though the networks and stations already on the air grew in terms of audience, the only new stations were those that already had construction permits prior to the freeze of 1948. In addition, the Korean War gave priority to the Armed Forces for electronic materials that might otherwise be used in radio and television.

STEVE ALLEN

COMEDIAN, HOST, AND WRITER _____

In a recently published work about *The Tonight Show*, written by a charming gentleman who has had long personal connection with the program, it is stated and will, sadly, now be accepted as fact by the thousands who will read the book that *The Tonight Show* was created by an NBC programming executive—oddly unnamed— and that its first host was Jerry Lester! Since these errors are not trivial and bear on the history of one of television's most important and successful programs, they naturally require correction. Incidentally, it's interesting that during the 1950s and 1960s

Color TV manufacturing takes a backseat to the Korean War.

I Love Lucy debuts on television.

I never had to mention the matter, for the simple reason that everyone knew the facts of the case. But new generations have now been born that never saw the original *Tonight*, millions who did see it have died, and a few of those who remain would appear to be suffering from what I call old-timer's disease; so, before the record is hopelessly obscured, it needs to be reaffirmed.

The unidentified NBC executive is Sylvester "Pat" Weaver, father of actress Sigourney Weaver. Pat and I have long constituted a mutual admiration society. He was kind enough not only to put me on his network for 90 minutes a night five nights a week, but at a later stage to ask me to do a far more important prime-time weekly comedy series. For my own part, I've always thought that Pat was one of the best programming executives in television's history. But it needs to be settled, once and for all, that he had nothing whatever to do with "creating *The Tonight Show*." The program, as I've described here, had already been created, with no input from the NBC

FIG 5.3 Steve Allen hosting his radio show in 1952, a precursor to *The Tonight Show*. *Courtesy Steve Allen.*

Mad magazine hits newsstands.

1952

American Women in Radio and Television founded.

Sixth Report and Order, issued by FCC, creates UHF band and reserves channels for educational TV stations.

Political use of television advertising increases dramatically.

programming people, over a year before Pat had the wisdom to add it to his late-night schedule. The only change that was made was that it was no longer called *The Steve* *Allen Show* but became known as *The Tonight Show*—or *Tonight*—because the network already had initiated its still-successful morning experiment called *Today*.

The FCC continued to deal with the key issue of color television. It approved the CBS system in 1950 despite its lack of compatibility; it was less expensive and was of higher picture quality than the RCA system. RCA and other manufacturers filed suit. Although a federal court upheld the FCC's right to approve the CBS system, it delayed adoption of the system as a national standard, pending RCA's appeal to the Supreme Court. The FCC followed suit, giving RCA additional time to perfect its system. CBS went ahead on a unilateral basis, knowing it had no guarantee of eventual adoption, and on June 25, 1951, telecast the first network color program. The Korean War, however, put the manufacture of color receivers in a nonessential category, and few CBS color sets were made. Further, the public did not want to have to scrap its personal investment in black-and-white receivers to receive the CBS color signal, even though monochrome as well as color picture quality would be improved.

The fight dragged on for a couple of years more, giving RCA time to utilize some of the previous work done by CBS, and eventually resulted in CBS joining RCA in the National Television Systems Committee (NTSC) efforts to find a suitable, compatible color system. Finally, in 1953 the FCC reversed its approval of the CBS system and okayed the new RCA system, and RCA became the principal manufacturer of color TV receivers. During CBS's promotional period for its system, it placed receivers in a number of public areas in New York where passersby could see the quality of its color television by observing two young, attractive performers whose principal duty was to "look pretty" in color. These performers were Buff Cobb and—prior to his image as a rough, tough news interviewer—Mike Wallace.

While the NTSC was convincing the United States to accept what was considered by many an acceptable standard for broadcast television picture quality, Philo Farnsworth knew TV could be considerably better. He began experiments with high-definition television and by the mid-1950s was demonstrating pictures with 1,100 and 1,200 lines of resolution. It would be a half century before the United States adopted a high-definition TV system.

Another early television phenomenon, pay TV, was dealt with by the FCC in 1950 as well. After several years of experiments, Zenith obtained FCC authorization to test its pay-per-view Phonevision system. Ostensibly, the system's purpose was to provide first-run movies for subscribers who would pay a few dollars to unscramble the signal.

THE FEARFUL '50S

Today Show debuts.   Communication Act amended.   NBC airs *Victory at Sea* documentary.

FIG 5.4 The technology of TV improves while receiver prices become more affordable.

Nixon's famous
"Checkers" speech is televised.

Although a Phonevision test in Chicago was fairly successful, movie companies did not want to encourage competition from this new medium and withheld the films Phonevision needed. Further, broadcasters were concentrating on building a viable advertiser base and were not then interested in pay-per-view TV. Phonevision's time had not yet come, but as we know now, several decades later, through cable, pay TV would begin its slow climb that could lead to eventual domination of the industry.

Continuing its concern with monopoly in the broadcasting industry, the FCC enacted its "Rule of Sevens" in 1950. Any one owner was limited to seven TV, seven AM, and seven FM stations. An event that would affect another FCC decision a couple of years later occurred in 1950 with the formation of the Joint Committee on Educational Television, which, with the backing of FCC Commissioner Frieda Hennock, rallied support for the reservation of television channels exclusively for educational purposes.

Radio still hung in, not yet totally affected by television, inasmuch as a coast-to-coast TV network was still a year away. Ninety-five percent of U.S. homes had radios, as did half of all automobiles. Radio had 11% of all the advertising in the country in 1950, with TV at only 3%; within 15 years the ratio would be almost reversed. It was AM, not FM, that was growing: Almost 100 FM stations folded in 1950. AM licensees co-owned 80% of the FM stations. Duplication of signals by co-owned stations (FM carrying, AM originating) and a lack of inexpensive FM receivers or AM/FM sets prevented FM from being a viable advertising medium. Newspapers owned some 20% of radio stations. Although most key radio shows were making the move to television, Ed Murrow and Fred Friendly began a news documentary series on CBS radio, *Hear It Now*, that would raise radio journalism to new heights.

1951

One year after it began on radio, Murrow and Friendly brought their highly acclaimed documentary format of *Hear It Now* to television: On November 18, 1951, *See It Now* premiered on CBS. "Good evening," Murrow said at the beginning of the program. "This is an old team trying to learn a new trade." It learned it well. *See It Now* was willing to deal with controversy, using investigative journalism to try to right wrongs, including some of the excesses of McCarthyism as blacklisting in the industry became institutionalized. *See It Now* was also innovative technically. On its opening show, it became the first network program to join the East and West coasts of the United States via television, showing the Golden Gate Bridge on one monitor and the Brooklyn Bridge on another, and then together on a split screen—although two months earlier, on September 4, a group of cooperating stations and networks had inaugurated the first national hookup with a telecast of President Truman's address in San Francisco at the conference on a peace treaty with Japan. The September 4 telecast had been seen in an estimated 95% of U.S. homes where television sets were on.

THE FEARFUL '50S

1953

TV Guide magazine is published.

Julius and Ethel Rosenberg executed for espionage as Cold War intensifies.

You Are There is hosted by Walter Cronkite on CBS television.

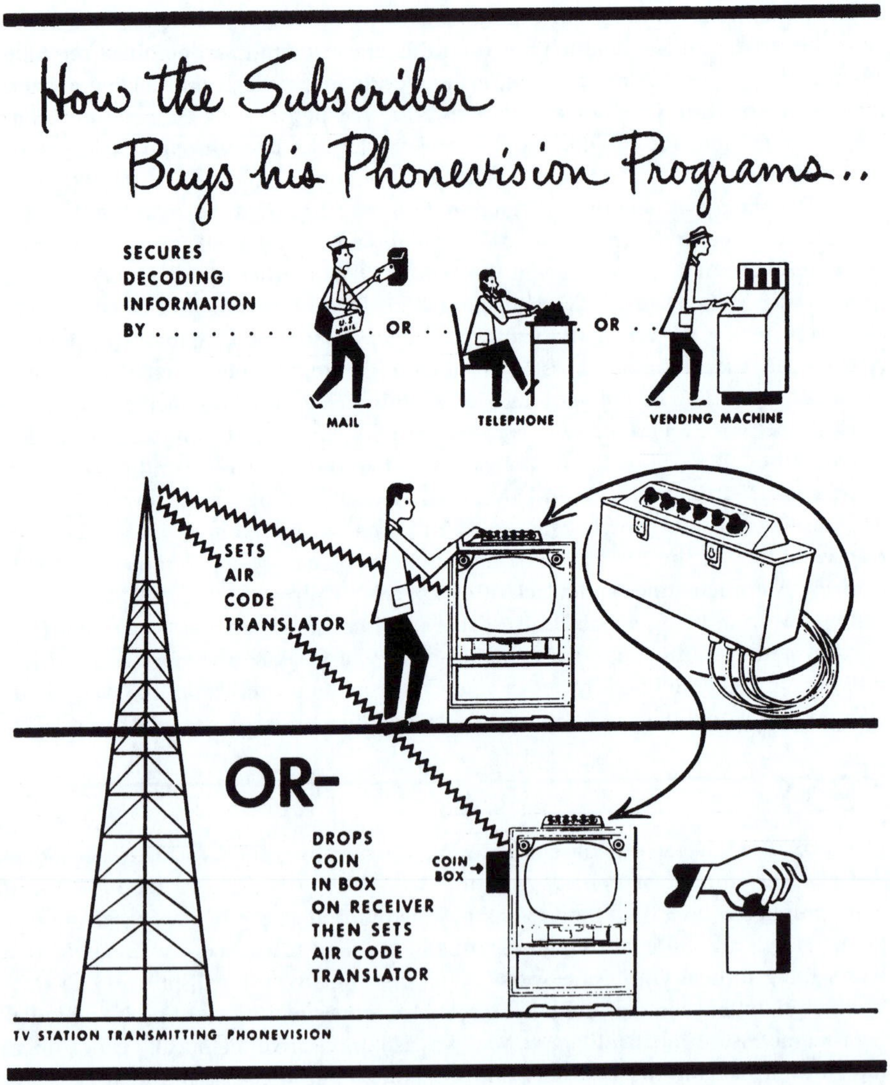
How the Subscriber
Buys his Phonevision Programs..
SECURES DECODING INFORMATION BY . . . .
OR . .
OR . .
MAIL
TELEPHONE
VENDING MACHINE
SETS AIR CODE TRANSLATOR
OR-
DROPS COIN IN BOX ON RECEIVER THEN SETS AIR CODE TRANSLATOR
COIN BOX
TV STATION TRANSMITTING PHONEVISION

FIG 5.5 Zenith's Phonevision promoted the idea of pay-TV in the 1950s.
Courtesy Zenith.

As television programming became increasingly attractive, movie attendance began to drop and rising numbers of movie theaters throughout the country began to close. The revenues of the major film studios suffered a one-third decline in the space of just a few years, and in 1951 more footage was being produced for television than for theatrical-release feature films. *The New York Times* stated: "The motion picture industry is worried, politicians are faced with learning a new art, and many

Korean War ends.

a face and many a scene that formerly we merely read about or listened to we will now be privileged to look at." This was true. Politicians soon learned that they had to become performers for the television camera if they were to influence the voters. Indeed, within three decades one actor was so successful in using the media in his role of President of the United States that he actually was elected to the office twice.

ED BLISS

FORMER EDITOR, WRITER, AND PRODUCER, CBS NEWS _____

I was privileged to work closely with both Edward R. Murrow and Walter Cronkite. Out of that experience it is inevitable that I compare broadcast journalism's two giants. As night editor at CBS News and later as writer-producer for Murrow, I came to know not only a reporter of reknown but an educator. He sought through commentary and documentary to shed light on the great issues: responsibility in government, Soviet intransigence, freedom of dissent, America's role in the world, and so forth. As a student at Washington State, Murrow majored in speech. He engaged in campus politics. He was popular. Later, in broadcasting, no one received more praise. Yet he was a shy man. Radio microphones and television cameras frightened him; they made him sweat. For most of the time, Murrow was troubled. Whatever he did, wherever we went, he carried heavy concerns: McCarthyism, the atomic bomb, the Cold War. And all the while, as he fought for social justice and understanding, he inhaled the Camel cigarettes that would kill him.

Working as a news editor with Walter Cronkite, I found a man equally devoted to

FIG 5.6 Ed Bliss.
Courtesy Ed Bliss.

the highest standards. But, unlike Murrow, he was comfortable with microphones and cameras. He could sit down before the evening news cameras after a tiring transcontinental flight and with each passing minute appear more refreshed. After his broadcast, Murrow tended to brood over the world's problems; it was more in Cronkite's

THE FEARFUL '50S

135

ABC brings baseball to
Saturday TV.

Paddy Chayefsky's
Marty televised on the
Goodyear Playhouse.

character to meet after the program with his wife, Betsy, and go dancing. A gregarious man, in contrast to Murrow, it is difficult to conceive of Cronkite ever being shy, and he eschewed cigarettes. On the evening news, it was Eric Sevareid who did commentary. When Cronkite spoke out most strongly, as when he declared the Vietnam War unwinnable, it was not on his program but on CBS News specials. Each evening, reporting as objectively as he could, he became known as the most trusted man in America. The great common denominator for these two [giants] is their integrity. Each brought to their informing roles their absolute best, which proved to be the best there was.

I Love Lucy began on television in 1951 and became the archetype for sitcoms, copied countless times but rarely equaled in popularity. *Dragnet* made a successful transition from radio and generated many cop-show clones. Well-known comedians, such as Red Skelton, and popular singers, such as Dinah Shore, began their own TV shows. CBS leapt in front of the other networks by bringing two of its top-rated radio soap operas to daytime television. The same year, CBS introduced its famous logo,

FIG 5.7 At work in a 1950s television control room.
Courtesy WTIC.

Edmund Hillary and Tensing
Norkay reach peak of Mt. Everest.

Academy Award ceremony is
telecast.

NBC and CBS attract a growing
audience with their nightly news
shows.

the Eye. Perhaps the most innovative artist in television history—one who used the
potential of the visual medium more creatively than anyone else—was Ernie Kovacs,
who got his first network job in 1951. As exciting and farsighted as Kovacs's work
was, though, it was too far ahead of its time for broadcast executives and advertisers,
and his sporadic career on network television ended with his death in an auto accident in 1962, at about the time television might have been ready to give him the
superstardom it had up to then denied him.

Not only was television badly hurting movies, but it began to take an even greater
toll on radio. Radio network revenues steadily declined and prime-time offerings
decreased. To survive, more and more radio stations turned to deejay formats, thus
presaging the reprogramming of the entire radio industry.

Captain Video and His Video Rangers

An early television hit among youngsters was this low-budget wonder, one
of a number of innovative creations that materialized on the perpetually
financially troubled Dumont Network. The show began in 1949, lasting until
the network itself folded in 1955. It was aired live but its scripts were so short
of material that good chunks of its daily 30-minute episode were filled with
clips from some old B movie, usually a Western. Although no one should ever
query the logic void in programming geared for children, this show stretched
the boundaries of credulity. Besides the usual shortcomings with narratives
dealing with alien beings (they persist in having humanoid form; hold similar
values and emotions as earthlings'; often go by a single name; their leaders
command an entire planet rather than nation-states), Captain Video's aliens,
with technology advanced enough for space travel at the speed of light, rely
on shields and swords as their weapons, wear first-century Roman outfits, and
rely on paper-written communications transported by rocket ships. And yet
this pre–civil rights era show would frequently interrupt its dramatic action to
air spots promoting justice, brotherhood, and tolerance of others who might
not look exactly like us.

1952

On April 14, 1952, the FCC issued its now-famous *Sixth Report and Order*, finally
resolving the matters it had begun considering in 1948 when, pending their resolution, it had imposed a freeze on applications for any new television stations. The *Sixth
Report and Order* solved some of the problems but created others. The freeze was
lifted, and hundreds of TV stations rushed to get on the air. The UHF band was established to provide for the growth of television, which otherwise would be stymied
because of an insufficient number of VHF channels. At first, UHF had channels

First educational (public)
TV station, KHUT, Houston, goes
on air.

ABC and Paramount
Pictures merge.

14 through 83; however, channels 70 through 83 later would be reassigned for special and safety purposes. The FCC decided on a system of intermixture—assigning VHF and UHF channels to the same community—as opposed to deintermixture—which would have provided for only VHF or only UHF in the same market. Consequently, with UHF not having the range of VHF, its frequencies were not as desirable as those of the already established VHF stations and, coupled with the lack of UHF receivers (it wasn't until 1962 that all sets manufactured were required to receive both VHF and UHF signals), there were few UHF viewers, very few advertisers, and even fewer network affiliations. Although UHF did grow after its initial authorization, within a few years the number of UHF stations on the air declined. In addition to making city-by-city assignments for TV channels, the FCC specified mileage separation distances for television stations in order to reduce the potential for interference.

Lifting the Freeze and Hurting UHF

UHF was the FCC's answer, in its *Sixth Report and Order*, to the lack of VHF space needed to accommodate the burgeoning demand for television. But UHF was fraught with complications. Most early TV sets were not equipped to receive UHF. Consumers would either need to purchase a new set (high priced and hard to find) when most had recently bought their first, or add an external tuner and special antenna. And even then reception was problematic. Succumbing to intransigently powerful interests such as broadcast giants NBC and CBS, which had established primary affiliations with VHF stations, as well the large electronic manufacturers such as RCA, which had already tooled up to produce VHF-only sets, the commission forced UHF into a competitive disadvantage, choosing intermixture in where UHF had to compete in the same market with established VHF stations. With smaller audiences, UHF operators struggled to attract network affiliations or advertisers, causing the lack of resources needed to acquire programming to entice viewers into purchasing UHF equipment. By the end of the decade nearly half of all UHF stations had failed. It wasn't until the passage of the All-Channel Receiver Act that required built-in UHF tuners on all new sets that the band began to recover. However, it took another 20 years before UHF became truly viable, thanks to the spread of cable that made UHF as easy to receive as VHF.

Educators won their fight. Of the 2,053 channels assigned to 1,291 communities in the *Sixth Report and Order*, 242 were reserved for educational stations. FM advocates lost their fight. The FCC assigned the more desirable audio frequencies for TV sound transmission, leaving FM where it was, with frequencies that FM's founder, Edwin Armstrong, believed were inadequate for the effective growth and full service of the medium.

UFO sightings increase.

First noncommercial television station begins broadcasts.

FCC authorizes color television.

As the politics within broadcasting accelerated, so did the political use of broadcasting. In his successful run for President against Adlai E. Stevenson in 1952, Dwight D. Eisenhower and his campaign managers made the first large-scale use of political ads on television. A series of 20-second spots concentrated on personalities rather than issues, much like the campaigns of the 1980s and 1990s more often than not concentrated on "sound bites" rather than substance. Eisenhower's running mate, Richard Nixon, charged with the misuse of campaign funds, his political career at the edge of a precipice, used television to convince the public, in his famous "Checkers" speech, that he was not a crook by shifting the charges into a discussion of the gift of a puppy that his daughter had named Checkers and that he vowed to keep. Nixon was eloquent in his use of the medium and remained on the Republican ticket, ensuring his political future. Joseph McCarthy also used television to his advantage, convincing the public of the dangers of international Communism, against which he was self-anointed to lead the fight.

While *I Love Lucy* shot to the top of the ratings charts in its second season, setting off a deluge of half-hour copycat sitcoms, programming centering on two wars and a frightening prophecy of what a future one would be like also attracted large numbers of TV viewers. *Victory at Sea*, a 26-episode documentary of the naval battles of World War II, with background music by Richard Rodgers, began on NBC and

FIG 5.8 The television equipment in this 1950s photo includes revolving slide drums, center, and larger movie projectors on each side. Images from all of these sources were multiplexed by means of movable mirrors into a single film-chain camera. *Courtesy David Richardson.*

THE FEARFUL '50S

Polio vaccine developed
by Dr. Jonas Salk.

Nautilus, the first
atomic sub, is launched.

1954

McCarthy reveals his
demagoguery on Murrow's
See It Now.

became one of the most popular and oft-repeated series in television history. Ed Murrow, one of the few reporters who attempted to bring the events and issues of the Korean War into U.S. living rooms, worked with Fred Friendly to produce a number of programs from Korea for *See It Now*. Among these offerings were the acclaimed "Christmas in Korea" shows in 1952 and 1953, programs that were especially courageous in the McCarthy era because they tried to be objective, show the truth about some of the horrors of war, and avoid phony patriotism and the exploitation of the country's Communist phobia. In addition, for an indication of what future wars might be like, the public saw on TV an atom bomb test in the Nevada desert.

Culture and religion entered television with a bang in 1952. The DuMont network put Bishop Fulton J. Sheen, a dynamic speaker, in a program without commercials entitled *Life Is Worth Living*, pitting this offering against Milton Berle. Although he did not displace Berle, Sheen stayed on the air for many years with respectable ratings. CBS took a chance with *Omnibus*, hosted by Alistair Cooke, which had been tried and dropped by other networks. It featured plays, poetry readings, documentaries, and even lessons in classical music by Leonard Bernstein. It did better than expected during the several years it remained on TV. NBC started a trend with the first *Today Show*, with Dave Garroway, one of the many stars who started in TV in Chicago. That same year, what was to be the longest-running daytime variety show on television, Art Linkletter's *House Party*, began on CBS.

RAY SCHERER

FORMER NBC WHITE HOUSE CORRESPONDENT (TRUMAN, EISENHOWER, KENNEDY, AND JOHNSON ADMINISTRATIONS) _____

When I started covering the White House for NBC, Harry Truman was President and radio was king. Television was little more than a gleam in General Sarnoff's eye. Network correspondents were not permitted to broadcast from inside the White House. They had to rush back to their studios in downtown Washington when news breaks came. Radio news on the hour was a long way away.

Broadcasting possibilities improved with the arrival of President Eisenhower and his

FIG 5.9 Ray Scherer.
Courtesy Ray Scherer.

Supreme Court, in *Brown v. Board of Education*, bans segregation in public schools.

McCarthyism at its height, broadcasting cooperates fully with blacklist.

The Tonight Show debuts.

news secretary, Jim Hagerty. Hagerty was open to new ideas. We began taping Ike's news conferences for radio and, in January 1955, filming them for television.

A breakthrough of sorts occurred when Hagerty gave NBC permission to do radio spots from inside the White House. The pressroom off the West Wing lobby was unsuitable. It was the province of the writing press and there were too many extraneous noises, including the slap of playing cards.

Where to set up a microphone and broadcast equipment? I convinced Hagerty I could do it from the phone booth behind the guard's desk in the lobby. I broadcast from there for about a week, my engineer perched over me like a giant praying mantis. I felt myself coming down with galloping claustrophobia and had my engineer set up the NBC radio mike in the photographer's film-changing room, a dingy cubicle just outside Hagerty's office.

It was hardly studio quality but it worked. I was the first to do a daily news program from the White House. In Kennedy's time the networks were given broadcast booths inside the pressroom, but by then TV was the big player and radio no longer claimed priority. By the Carter era, a White House TV reporter could get on the air within seconds, and in the 1980s with Reagan, the television President, the pressroom was turned into a television studio. Broadcasting had moved from the back row to the front row, but it took 40 years.

If you can't beat 'em, own 'em, and newspapers did just that, owning, in 1952, 45% of the country's television stations. Although the civil rights movement of the 1960s was almost a decade away, advertisers began to recognize the buying power of blacks in many parts of the country, and a number of radio "Negro stations," as they were called, went on the air, orienting programming and advertising to black audiences. Almost all of these stations were owned by whites.

1953

Anyone old enough to have watched television in 1953 will tell you they remember Lucy having a baby right on the air. In fact, she did; the *I Love Lucy* show decided to follow, on the sitcom, her real-life pregnancy through to the birth. Seventy percent of all television homes and 92% of sets in use that evening were tuned to the birthing episode. The first issue of *TV Guide* came out on April 3, 1953, and its cover featured a picture of Lucy's son, Desi Arnaz, Jr.

TV spectaculars—heavily promoted specials with many stars and usually an hour or more in length—came into being with the production of *The Ford Fiftieth Anniversary Show*. The radio documentary series *You Are There*, developed by

| Army–McCarthy hearings, Murrow programs on McCarthy lead to McCarthy's censure by Senate. | Senate votes to condemn Senator McCarthy. | U.S. Supreme Court strikes down public school segregation. |

| Edwin Armstrong leaps to his death. | Army–McCarthy hearings are televised. |

Robert Lewis Shayon years before for CBS radio, came to television, with Walter Cronkite serving as anchor in the simulated re-creation of historical news events. Adults and children alike were attracted to a new series right out of the comic pages, *The Adventures of Superman*. ABC brought major league baseball to television on a regular basis with the Saturday afternoon "game of the week," and DuMont brought professional football to prime-time television with Saturday night games. In addition to *See It Now*, Murrow and Friendly began a weekly *Person to Person* series that interviewed famous people, live, in their homes—a format copied many times since and honed to a fine point by Barbara Walters in the 1980s and 1990s. Pioneering the path for Walters and other women who would become prominent TV newspersons was Pauline Frederick, the first woman to become a full-fledged correspondent when she was hired by ABC in 1948. In 1953 Frederick moved to NBC, where she gained worldwide attention as a United Nations correspondent for the next 21 years.

Although anthology drama became a staple of television in the late 1940s, it wasn't until 1953 that the seminal play of the Golden Age of Television Drama, according to many critics, went on the air. The *Philco Playhouse* production of *Marty*, by writer Paddy Chayefsky, established the sensitive, realistic, in-depth, slice-of-life format that was to dominate anthology drama series such as *Goodyear Playhouse*, *Robert Montgomery Presents*, *Studio One*, *U.S. Steel Hour*, and *Kraft Television Theater* for years to come.

BETTY FURNESS

THE LATE BETTY FURNESS WAS ONE OF TELEVISION'S EARLY COMMERCIAL STARS _____

Those of us who worked in very early TV didn't know we were pioneers. We were just trying to earn a living. For the first few years [payment of] $25 a show was quite acceptable.

While I did some isolated shows at CBS, my first regularly scheduled program was *Fashions Coming and Becoming* at DuMont in 1945. It was 15 minutes once a week

and that was quite often enough. The studio was in an office building on Madison Avenue. It was, in fact, a converted office with the required very hot lights hung from the ceiling. Very hot meant that we had to dress like firemen for rehearsal, heads covered, dark glasses. The heat was almost unendurable. One day I laid a thermometer on a table. The temperature was 130 in five minutes. I wore combs with a metal edge in my hair at the time and burned my hand touching one. The program went off the air in the summer because of the outdoor heat!

In 1949 I played a small part on a new one-hour drama called *Studio One* at CBS. Westinghouse had just started sponsoring the show, and the ad agency asked if I'd

1955

Ninety-six percent of the
nation's homes have
radio sets.

The $64,000 Question
debuts.

FIG 5.10 Betty Furness.
Courtesy Betty Furness.

like to try [doing] the commercials the next week. $100. Sure I would. That started an 11-year job that made me rich and famous.

Studio One was live, like all shows at the time. I worked in a kitchen set in the same studio as the drama. Commercials, which now run from 10 to 30 seconds generally, were a minute and a half to three minutes. Everyone had to come out on time ... the drama and the commercials. The teleprompter had not been invented and I wasn't comfortable using cue cards; I wanted to look into the eye of the camera, therefore,

the eye of the viewer. So I memorized one three-minute and two minute-and-a-half commercials each week. Once I opened my mouth, there was no way out. I had to know [the lines] and say them correctly and promptly. It was quite stimulating.

In 1952, Westinghouse bought the TV coverage of the political conventions of both parties on CBS. The teleprompter had been invented, which was nice because I had a cycle of 96 commercials. Again I worked along with the "live" show in a studio adjacent to CBS News in the convention hall. I logged more air time than any speaker of either party, and because an enormous number of people had bought TV sets just to watch the first televised conventions, I became famous.

For those of us who started early, TV was never as much fun (or as terrifying) when everything was filmed or later taped and edited. It was too "safe."

I'm sometimes asked today if I miss live TV. Actually, because I'm a consumer reporter on a news program, part of what I do is still live, with the lifesaver of a smoothly operating teleprompter. We in news are still looking right in the eye of the viewer.

A new generation of playwrights was spawned by television. One of the authors of this book, as a young writer in the early 1950s, remembers a script competition for a first prize of $1,000 (a large sum then) offered by TV station WTVN in Cincinnati. When the results were announced in early 1953, this writer was pleased to learn that his entry was good enough to be awarded honorable mention status. But he was especially impressed with the obvious talents of another young, unknown playwright, who won two of the top awards, including first prize. That writer's name was Rod Serling.

DuMont television
network folds.

Subsidiary Communications
Authorization given to FM.

FIG 5.11 As network
radio declined in the early
1950s, local stations
became more involved
with program origination.
Here Allen Ludden hosts a
youth-oriented panel show.
Courtesy WTIC.

The NBC and CBS networks began 15-minute evening news shows. The Academy Awards were televised for the first time. A dramatic TV event occurred on the highly popular *Arthur Godfrey and His Friends* show, disillusioning many of Godfrey's fans. He fired, on the air, singer Julius La Rosa, a regular on the program. After La Rosa finished a song, Godfrey said to the startled singer and national audience, "That, folks, was Julie's swan song."

By 1953, 45% of U.S. homes had television. The number of stations on the air almost tripled from the year before, to 365. Advertising income increased by more than 35%. Network profits shot up at NBC and ABC. But ABC wasn't competing so well, and it merged with Paramount Pictures to provide greater resources for competitive programming. Most significant was the serious—and self-protective—entry of filmdom into television.

As a result of the *Sixth Report and Order*, the first noncommercial television station went on the air in 1953: KUHT at the University of Houston in Texas. Also in 1953 the FCC, as noted earlier, finally authorized color television, reversing its position on CBS and approving RCA's compatible system. Before the year ended, the first compatible color sets, made by Admiral, were being sold for $1,175, a price not too many people could afford, considering it represented more than half a year's salary for many individuals.

Meanwhile Senator McCarthy's power was growing, and he threatened both the VOA and the FCC, seeing to it that they hired people he designated as loyal and fired those he called subversive. Concomitantly, the organization that was to take

IBM introduces new line of computers.	"Ballad of Davy Crockett" is America's most popular song, coonskin caps most popular hat.
The Top 40 format is born.	*The Lawrence Welk Show* debuts on ABC television.

FIG 5.12 Arthur Godfrey kept audiences tuned to his radio (later, also television) shows throughout the 1940s and 1950s.
Courtesy Artist's Proof, Alexandria, Virginia.

FIG 5.13 A transition in recording techniques took place in the 1950s as disk recording made way for the tape recorder.
Courtesy WTIC.

THE FEARFUL '50S

1956

the lead in blacklisting in the broadcast industry, AWARE, Inc., was formed. Though broadcast executives cooperated fully with the blacklist, they weren't entirely insensitive to its effects. When it was revealed that Lucille Ball had once been a member of the Communist Party, CBS's head, William Paley, made certain that she was quickly cleared. How could America's favorite housewife be a Communist? Moreover, without her as star, the top-rated *I Love Lucy* show would stop making money for CBS.

What about radio? In 1948 a person listened to the radio an average of 4.4 hours a day; in 1953 that figure was down to 2.7 hours. News and music replaced the entertainment that had once dominated prime-time radio and had now moved to television. In 1948 radio prime time had 14% news and public affairs programs; in 1953, it had 40%.

1954

Although broadcasting capitulated to McCarthyism, broadcasting was also the key factor in McCarthy's ultimate demise. Three 1954 events revealed in close-up the senator's true nature. One was the Army–McCarthy hearings, in which McCarthy initiated an investigation of the U.S. Army on the grounds that it, too, had been infiltrated by Communist subversives. The others were Ed Murrow and Fred Friendly's two programs on McCarthy, one delineating McCarthy in his own recorded words and actions and the other giving McCarthy the opportunity to respond. These programs highlighted television's ability to get behind the facade and show "warts and all" and to affect the course of public affairs—when it wanted to.

During 1953 Murrow and Friendly's *See It Now* had gathered as much material as it could about McCarthy, to let the nation see the senator without the "Emperor's Clothes" protection the media had given him. Finally, after a cool reception from CBS management, the show was allowed to air on March 9, 1954. But CBS virtually washed its hands of it and refused to promote it, and Murrow and Friendly paid for their own advertisement for the program in *The New York Times*. At the end of the program showing McCarthy simply being McCarthy, Murrow added one of the few bits of commentary in the show, warning that this was no time for people who opposed McCarthy's methods to keep silent:

> As a nation we have come into our full inheritance at a tender age. We proclaim ourselves, as indeed we are, the defenders of freedom, what's left of it. But we cannot defend freedom abroad by deserting it at home. The actions of the junior Senator from Wisconsin have caused alarm and dismay among our allies abroad and given considerable comfort to our enemies. And whose fault is that? Not really his. He didn't create this situation of fear. He merely exploited it, and rather successfully. Cassius was right: "The fault, dear Brutus, is not in our stars, but in ourselves."

Bus segregation held
unconstitutional.

Ampex introduces video-
tape recorder (VTR).

John Henry Faulk
blacklisted by AWARE.

FIG 5.14 This early photo anticipated radio's aggressively promoted "mobility" image in the age of television. *Courtesy Westinghouse.*

On April 6, McCarthy was given a full half-hour of *See It Now* to respond. His vicious, clearly paranoid attack on Murrow as "the leader and the cleverest of the jackal pack which is always found at the throat of anyone who dares to expose individual Communists and traitors" was too much even for many of the viewers who until then had enthusiastically supported McCarthy's witch hunts. For the first time, mainstream America was beginning to question McCarthy's motives and stability.

The Army–McCarthy hearings began on April 22, and the glaring eye of television, given a bit of courage by Murrow and Friendly, did not now run away from the truth. ABC carried the hearings for their entire 187 hours over 36 days; NBC carried the proceedings live for two days and then switched to evening summaries; and CBS carried a 45-minute daily summary. As *Life* magazine stated, "Politicians, lawyers, and witnesses soon became as recognizable as movie stars." McCarthy's irresponsible, badgering, bizarre behavior during the hearings raised further questions in the minds of middle America about his methods and fitness to serve. As the premiere broadcast historian Erik Barnouw has written, "A whole nation watched him in murderous close-up—and recoiled."

THE FEARFUL '50S

147

The cordless television remote is introduced by Zenith.

The Western becomes a popular TV genre.

Before the end of 1954, two-thirds of the Senate voted to censure Senator McCarthy.

Murrow, because of the McCarthy programs, was now controversial, and CBS's head, William Paley, realized that the controversy was rubbing off on the network. *See It Now* was soon relegated to a less favorable time slot, a year later was changed from a weekly program to an occasional special (*See It Now and Then*, some Paley detractors called it), and eventually was forced off the air altogether.

The blacklisting continued. Censorship invaded the anthology drama, and more than one author took his or her name off the credits upon finding that the script had been changed to avoid anything controversial, particularly civil rights or civil liberties implications that much of America equated with Communist subversion. Nonpolitical, innocuous programming was preferred by networks and advertisers alike. The Miss America Pageant made it to television. *Dragnet, You Bet Your Life, The Jackie Gleason Show* (which spawned *The Honeymooners*), Bob Hope, and Walt Disney's *Davy Crockett* (which prompted a nationwide fad for coonskin hats) joined *Lucy* as the nation's favorite TV shows. At the same time, several anthology drama shows, such as *Studio One, Philco-Goodyear Television Playhouse*, and *Kraft Television Theater*, finished consistently in the top 10 in the rating charts. One auspicious debut was NBC's *The Tonight Show*, hosted by Steve Allen, which replaced an earlier version, *Broadway Open House* with comedian Jerry Lester. *The Tonight Show*, still going strong in the 2000s, would be hosted subsequently by Jack Paar, Johnny Carson, Jay Leno, and Conan O'Brien.

The public bought more and more sets. More than 30 million homes had television, compared with half that number just three years earlier—still only 27% of the population, but quickly growing. Prices of sets had fallen more than 50% in that time, averaging about $175 in 1954. More and more people watching TV in the early evening hours found it a distraction to have to make dinner, motivating a clever manufacturer to come out with a financial bonanza in 1954, the TV dinner. Although both NBC and CBS were broadcasting some programs in color, there were still very few color sets in use—the number was estimated at not more than 10,000.

The networks and advertisers were ecstatic about TV as a whole. More than $800 million was spent on television commercials in 1954. Because most programs had only one sponsor, advertisers, through their advertising agencies, had virtually total control over television programming, not only approving of scripts and performers but sometimes supervising production values and censoring dialogue and ideas as they wished.

Even in the noncivilian area, television grew; the Armed Forces Radio Service became the Armed Forces Radio and Television Service.

The Diary of Anne Frank wins the Pulitzer Prize for drama.

Grace Kelly marries Prince Rainier of Monaco.

Playhouse 90 begins its four-year run.

Most powerful "Personal" portable radio ever built!

FIG 5.15 To offset the effects of television, radio promoted mobility and intimacy. The prevailing slogan of the day: "Radio—your constant companion."

The year 1954 was the end of the line for Edwin Armstrong. He was depressed by what he felt was the FCC's destruction of FM's potential by its 1952 *Sixth Report and Order* assigning the best audio frequencies to TV instead of FM. After six years of his patent-infringement lawsuit against RCA and NBC, fighting the superior legal resources of his former friend David Sarnoff, who claimed that RCA and not Armstrong had been the principal developer of FM, Armstrong was physically and emotionally exhausted and almost bankrupt. He committed suicide by jumping out of the window of his 13th-floor Manhattan apartment, not living to see the subsequent growth of FM that enabled it to surpass AM and to reach its present dominant position.

Radio continued to change in order to survive, with basically only the soaps remaining as the audio medium's principal form of nonmusic entertainment. Localization, narrower demographics, local advertising, and the Top 40 music format seemed to be the answer for survival.

1955

While some of the rest of the United States in 1955 was beginning to question its devotion to McCarthyism as a result of the *See It Now* programs, the Army–McCarthy hearings, and the Senate censure vote, broadcasting didn't waver and held tight to its

FIG 5.16 Symbolic of the new video age was this futuristic Philco "Predicta," which graced the modern 1950s living room.

THE FEARFUL '50S

The *Huntley-Brinkley Report* is offered by NBC.

Premiere of *Twenty-One,* a major player in the 1958 quiz show scandals.

blacklist. Broadcast executives decided it was more important not to lose advertisers' dollars than to act on any personal or ethical beliefs in democracy they may have had. The business of broadcasting went on as usual.

The number of television sets manufactured continued to grow, reaching a total of 46 million, with 64% of America's households estimated to have TV sets. One factor for the increasing sales—almost 8 million in 1955—was the continuing drop in price: The average cost of a set was now $160. Although more and more programs were in color, only 20,000 color TV sets were purchased that year. A new video distribution system designed to bring TV stations to communities too isolated to receive a usable off-the-air signal showed signs of growth, too. Having begun in 1949 in rural Pennsylvania and Oregon, community antenna television (CATV) now served 150,000 households in 400 communities—only 0.5% of U.S. households but a foot in the door for what we now call cable television.

Ninety-six percent of the country's homes had radio sets, as did 60% of its automobiles. But only 4% of the sets were FM. The number of stations grew, too: 2,732 commercial AM, 540 commercial FM, 124 noncommercial educational FM,

FIG 5.17 Local TV stations expanded in-house programming efforts during the 1950s, and giveaway shows were among the most popular. *Courtesy Patricia McKenna.*

1957

Elvis Presley debuts on *The Ed Sullivan Show*, his performance is censored from the waist down.	Troops sent to enforce desegregation in Little Rock, Arkansas.	Nat King Cole becomes the first black performer to host his own network show.

458 commercial TV, and 12 noncommercial educational TV stations were on the air in 1955. While most of the economy was growing, however, radio was suffering. From billings that accounted for 11% of all advertising in the country in 1950, radio dropped to 6% in 1955 (from more than $600 million to less than $550 million); during the same period television's share rose from 3% to 11% (from only $171 million to more than $1.5 billion).

The expanding economy was reflected in programs. In the 1930s a popular audience participation quiz show was *The $64 Question*, in which a contestant could double the amount of money won by answering each subsequent question correctly, to a total of $64. A television version of that program, which became one of the most popular TV shows in America, made its debut in 1955, but now it was *The $64,000 Question*. At the other end of the programming scale, NBC's color telecast of *Peter Pan*, starring Mary Martin, was seen by an estimated 65 million viewers, the largest audience for a TV program up to that time. At the other side of the continent—New York was the center of television production—the first major movie studio decided to join rather than fight the television competition, and Warner Brothers broke the general ban on offering movies to TV by making TV series based on some of its famous films.

Programming breakthroughs were too late to help the DuMont network, however, the resources of which were simply not enough to compete with NBC and CBS, and in 1955 it folded. ABC barely survived. Radio tried to survive on whatever new approaches it could find. One such approach came to the fore in 1955, although few in radio would guess its ultimate impact. A recording by a pop music group called Bill Haley and His Comets became the number-one radio play. The song, called "Rock Around the Clock," ushered in the era of rock music on radio and, with it, a new audience that would prove to be radio's economic salvation. Around this time two radio programming innovators, Todd Storz and Bill Stewart, introduced the Top 40 format in Omaha, Nebraska. This would mark the intensification of the long and intimate relationship (some would call it a marriage) between the radio medium and the recording industry, as both relied on each other for their well-being and continued prosperity. The recording industry manufactured the popular, youth-oriented music radio wanted and needed, and the latter provided the exposure that created a market for this product. From the perspective of the recording industry, radio was the perfect promotional vehicle for showcasing its established, as well as up-and-coming, artists. FM radio, struggling to remain afloat, used a different kind of music to bring in some money. The FCC's Subsidiary Communications Authorization (SCA) permitted FM to use its subcarrier to transmit so-called "elevator" (and other kinds of) music to dentist's offices, supermarkets, waiting rooms, and, of course, elevators.

A national event that was to catapult television into a political and social change agent occurred in 1955. On the heels of the 1954 Supreme Court *Brown v. Board*

Nation's first solar-heated building shown.

Leonard Bernstein becomes new director of New York Philharmonic.

Number of color television programs increases as prices for sets go down.

BROADCAST EDUCATION BEA ASSOCIATION

The Broadcast Education Association (BEA) was formed in 1955 as an academic organization devoted to communications. BEA's founders recognized the importance of close interaction with members of the professional broadcast community. *Courtesy Broadcast Education Association.*

FIG 5.18 The Broadcast Education Association (BEA) was formed in 1955 as an academic organization devoted to communications. The BEA's founders recognized the importance of close interaction with members of the professional broadcast community. *Courtesy Broadcast Education Association.*

of Education decision that ruled "separate but equal" educational facilities unconstitutional and called for integration of the nation's schools, Rosa Parks's arrest for refusing to sit in the segregated section of a Montgomery, Alabama, bus led to a citywide bus boycott and was a key factor in the Reverend Martin Luther King, Jr.'s, ability to rally concerned citizens for nonviolent civil rights actions. At first the media ignored King, but by the end of the following year they had made him nationally known. Moreover, TV eventually played an important role in showing the public at large the brutality of segregationist practices and helped change people's attitudes into supporting equal rights for all Americans. Another event occurred in 1955 that years later would become the basis for a further example of TV's power to affect public opinion in extraordinary ways: The first U.S. military advisers were sent to Vietnam.

Despite the dynamic events in the rapid evolution of television, the medium's fourth network, DuMont, finally ceased operations due to growing debt and insurmountable competition from what would become known as the Big Three networks.

1956

Two rather diverse happenings in 1956 changed the course of broadcasting. On April 15, at the annual convention of the NAB, the Ampex Corporation introduced the videotape recorder (VTR), using 3M tape. Within weeks, backorders for the VTR and tape were piling up. Though not yet utilizing electronic editing, the VTR changed the process of television broadcasting, including rehearsal and performance schedules and time, studio use, and location shooting, and eventually put an end to the live show. (Although Bing Crosby Enterprises had demonstrated a videotape machine in 1952, it was not refined enough to go into production.)

The other event involved John Henry Faulk, a rising star at CBS who at the time was a vice president of the American Federation of Television and Radio Artists (AFTRA), the broadcast performers' union that took a public stand against the blacklist. AWARE, in an effort to discredit and silence AFTRA opposition, tried to pressure AFTRA members to name names and included Faulk on its list of subversives. Faulk sued. As noted earlier, Faulk eventually won, in 1962, but his principles and courage cost him his career.

Having given tacit support to McCarthyism and blacklisting, President Dwight D. Eisenhower understood the power of television. Running for a second term against Adlai E. Stevenson, Eisenhower tried an innovative campaign approach. His campaign organization bought the final five minutes of time on popular half-hour TV shows—the regular sponsor paying for the first 25 minutes—and presented appeals to an already watching audience.

VW Beetle big seller; Ford Edsel big flop.

Quiz shows account for 37 hours of weekly network programming.

FIG 5.19 Weather becomes a popular feature on TV.
Courtesy David Sarnoff Library.

More big-money quiz shows followed on the heels of the popularity of CBS's *The $64,000 Question*, including an ante-raising NBC program, *The $100,000 Big Surprise*. CBS countered with *The $64,000 Challenge*, on which winners on *The $64,000 Question* would vie for even larger prizes; one contestant won $264,000.

THE FEARFUL '50S

1958

Quiz show scandals
erupt.

Twilight Zone debuts,
gains cult following.

FIG 5.20 The look of portable TVs in 1956.

A new genre came to television, one that would ride the video range for two decades. *Cheyenne, Gunsmoke*, and *The Life and Legend of Wyatt Earp* made their debuts in 1956, and their successes spawned a plethora of Westerns that would dominate prime-time programming.

Another kind of legend-to-be also made a television debut in 1956; Elvis Presley's appearance on *The Ed Sullivan Show* got the kind of national exposure that guaranteed an idolization few other entertainers would experience.

All was not frivolity, however. One of the most successful of high-quality drama programs, *Playhouse 90*, began its four-year run. Perhaps the highest-quality children's program ever to be seen on commercial television, *Captain Kangaroo* began its 30-year TV history. NBC experimented with something new in news: two news anchors instead of one, with the *Huntley-Brinkley Report* and its tag line, "Good night, Chet," "Good night, David," becoming a household saying throughout the nation for many years.

1957

Although Senator Joseph McCarthy died in 1957, McCarthyism lived on. It continued to abuse the constitutional rights of many media personnel. Any reporter who deviated from the government party line became a *persona non grata*. In one of the most famous cases, the government was unhappy with CBS correspondent William Worthy's traveling to off-limits China and reporting from Peking, so the State Department took away his passport.

Some programming innovations succeeded, such as Dick Clark's *American Bandstand*, destined to be a TV staple for several decades. But others were too far ahead of their time. Nat King Cole was the first black performer to host his or her own show. Despite impressive responses from viewers and critics, racist attitudes resulted in no sponsorship and the program lasted only one season. Some types of programs became instant fads. Quiz shows challenged the popularity of Westerns, in

TV networks draw 95% of prime-time audiences.

FIG 5.21 Children's TV programming came into its own in the 1950s.
Courtesy David Richardson.

1957 accounting for 37 hours of network programming each week. But rumors of possible quiz show fixes began to circulate through the television industry, even as hints of payola (record companies bribing disc jockeys to play certain songs to make them bestsellers) made the rounds of the radio industry.

The price of color sets began to go down, the number of TV programs in color began to go up, and NBC introduced its new symbol of color, the famous Peacock.

1958

The big news in broadcasting in 1958 was the quiz show scandals. They broke with the assertion by a contestant on *Twenty-One*, a high-suspense competition in which participants answered questions from soundproofed glass isolation booths, that another competitor had been given answers in advance to beat him. The disgruntled contestant claimed that the producers had coached him and given him answers to be the long-running champion, and he felt he'd been double-crossed. Further revelations followed concerning this and other quiz shows, such as *The $64,000 Question*.

Charles DeGaulle becomes new
premier of France.

FCC Commissioner
Richard A. Mack is
charged with bribery.

United Press and International
News Service combine to
form United Press International
(UPI).

FIG 5.22 The practice of
program formatting took
hold in the 1950s. Radio
program clocks were
implemented to keep
things on their prescribed
course.

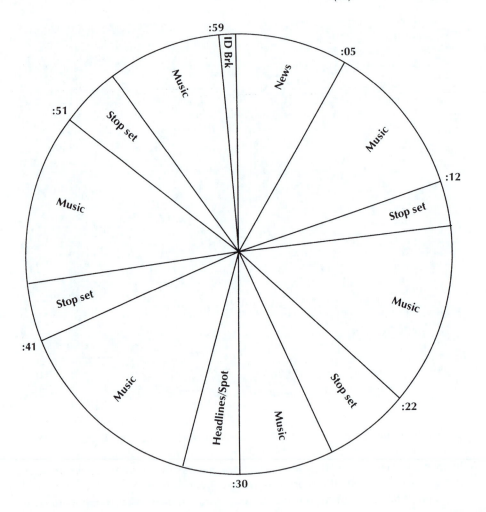

A grand jury investigation commenced, and New York newspapers began to dig into
the allegations. Before the year was out, several tainted quiz shows went off the air.

The scandals commanded national attention through 1958 and 1959, with millions of viewers feeling duped. In Washington, Congress convened a Special Committee
on Legislative Oversight to hold hearings on the exposures. Quiz shows all but disappeared from the air, and it was some years before the public again believed that
any of them were legitimate. The attractiveness of their format, however, remained,
and in this last decade of the broadcast century audience participation shows are the
highest-rated syndicated programs on television.

Paul Robeson returns to the United States from exile.	Fidel Castro ousts Cuban dictator Juan Batista.

1959

FCC decides it has no authority to regulate cable.

KIRK BROWNING

FORMER DIRECTOR, NBC SYMPHONY CONCERTS ──────────

I got to be director of the NBC Symphony concerts with Toscanini in 1950. They had a sports director doing them because it was a remote, out of studio, in Carnegie Hall. He'd read on the program that one of the selections was going to be *The Girl with the Flaxen Hair*, by Debussy. At the time I was working with Samuel Chotzinoff, the musical director for the National Broadcasting Company. I don't think I was any more than an assistant director at the time, but anyhow, I was watching the program on a monitor at Carnegie Hall with Chotzy as it was going on live. I'm looking at a picture of the maestro, Toscanini, conducting, and all of a sudden, supered over the maestro's face, is this picture of a girl sitting in front of a mirrored lily pond combing her hair with a brush. Chotzy turned to me and said, "Kirk, from here on, you're directing the Toscanini shows. I don't care what you do with the picture—just never be on anything but Toscanini." So that's how I started doing the NBC Symphony.

FIG 5.23 Kirk Browning directing a taping of a 1960s television program. *Courtesy Kirk Browning.*

The regulators as well as the regulated were not immune from scandal. Charges of bribery resulted in the resignation of FCC Commissioner Richard A. Mack.

Other than this unwelcome notoriety, the business of broadcasting continued as usual, television growing and radio slowly adapting to new music formats geared to narrow demographics. The TV networks were at their peaks, drawing 95% of prime-time audiences for the programs. *See It Now*, despite—or perhaps because of—its contributions to social and political justice and progress, was still controversial, and CBS's William Paley, after allowing it occasional specials during the previous few years, now took it off the air entirely. United Press and International News Service, both competing poorly against the Associated Press, merged into United Press International (UPI). Although cable continued to expand, few took it seriously, and the FCC decided that because cable was not broadcasting, the FCC did not have the authority to regulate it. It would not be until a dozen years had passed, when cable more clearly posed a threat to broadcasting, that the FCC would change its mind.

FCC mandates more
public affairs
programming.

FIG 5.24 Network
automation and routing
control area in the late
1950s.
Courtesy WABC, New York.

FIG 5.25 Technician at
work on a communications
satellite (COMSAT) in 1958.

1959

Networks in 1959 tried to refurbish their images tarnished by the quiz show scandals by putting more money into their budgets for public affairs programs. The FCC called for more public service programs. These factors resulted in a quick rehabilitation of Ed Murrow and Fred Friendly at CBS, who began *CBS Reports*, a documentary series that would make at least as many waves as *See It Now* had. Networks played up their news coverage, including extensive reporting of the cross-country visit to the United States of Nikita Khrushchev, the Soviet premier. Vice President Nixon, campaigning for the 1960 Republican Presidential nomination, got a boost from television when his "kitchen debate" with Khrushchev (literally taking place in an exhibition kitchen at a trade fair in Moscow) was widely covered by TV in the United States.

Soviet Premier Khrushchev
visits United States.

CBS Reports launched
by Fred Friendly and
Edward R. Murrow.

LYNN CHRISTIAN

BROADCAST EXECUTIVE AND FM PIONEER

A group of background music operators, who used their FM subcarriers for cost-saving delivery to save telephone line costs, gathered in the attic of the Palmer House Hotel in January 1959 to discuss changing the FM Development Committee into an FM broadcasting association. This band of part-time radio people—the main channel was only being programmed less than 12 hours a day in most cities—knew the potential of high-fidelity radio and perceived the possibilities of marketing stereo.

The National Association of FM Broadcasters [NAFMB] was founded at this meeting and met prior to the opening ceremony of the annual NAB convention each Spring (usually in Chicago at the Conrad Hilton Hotel). This initial band of independent FM "turks" grew and eventually held their own convention. In the early 1970s the group became the National Radio Broadcasters Association [NRBA] and with nearly 2,000 members merged with the National Association of Broadcasters in 1984. The lobbying of the NAFMB and NRBA allowed much of the FM explosion and creative experimentation in programming, promotion, and marketing in the 1960s, 1970s, and 1980s.

Prior to 1965, most of the FM dial was classical, esoteric, or beautiful music. There was very little talk, news, or sports on FM. The general public bought FM radios during the 1950s and 1960s because they liked the nonmainstream programming (very little pop-rock music), high-fidelity (stereo) sound, and low deejay presence; many assumed FM was a noncommercial band. Because so little commercial time was sold in the early years and because of the limited placement of low-key (nonjingle) spots, listeners made this erroneous assumption. Most listener surveys in the 1960s indicated that the primary reason people tuned to FM was the lack of both talk and commercials. In the late 1970s and 1980s this changed. In the mid-1960s, I led a national campaign for the NAFMB and the FM industry to convince Detroit to install FM radios in cars and trucks. Over 1,000 FM stations aired a free, one-year spot campaign to encourage listeners to ask for AM/FM car radios when they purchased a new car.

FIG 5.26 One of the pioneers of commercial FM broadcasting, Lynn Christian (right), gets help straightening his tie from commentator Paul Harvey. *Courtesy Lynn Christian and ABC Radio.*

THE FEARFUL '50S

Congress amends Section 315
(equal time rule) of the
Communications Act of 1934.

The pressure created by this major promotion was very effective in a couple of ways. First, it motivated General Motors and its Delco Division and Ford Motor Company and its Philco Radio Division to accelerate their plans. It also demonstrated FM radio's power to sell the consumer a new product. It was one of the first national FM spot campaigns and FM's first great success story. Happily, in 1969 I was awarded an Armstrong Foundation Award for this effort, as was David Polinger, who managed WTFM in New York. Initially, the NAB in Washington and state broadcasters' associations—dominated by the AM business folk—resisted the growth of FM. After the commission forced changes and broadcasters witnessed the development of new profit centers in their companies, they jumped on the FM bandwagon. The early commercial pioneers of FM and FM stereo were evangelical in their pursuit of success. They never doubted that FM would one day surpass AM in listenership, because they held to the belief that a quality product or service always finds its place at the top in the American free-enterprise system.

Courtesy Lynn Christian.

FIG 5.27 The 1950s saw many innovations in the design of portable radios.

Sun-Powered Radio

The Admiral radio with the "Sun Power Pak" is shown here. 32 silicon cells comprise the power pack which is shown in the small zippered case on the right.

The world's first commercial sun-powered radio is also completely transistorized and will work off 6 drycells.

Jack Kerouac and the "Beat Generation" set the stage for the 1960s.

Radio payola and plugola scandals break.

FIG 5.28 Portable radios with tubes were gradually replaced by transistor sets in the 1950s and 1960s.

On another political front, Congress amended Section 315 of the Communications Act of 1934 to exempt news programs from the requirement that stations provide equal time for all bona fide candidates for a given elective office. In adding that the news exemption did not relieve stations of the responsibility of presenting different sides of controversial issues, Congress established what many jurists, attorneys, and FCC officials interpreted as a specification of the Fairness Doctrine in the Act.

But no sooner did broadcasting think it was again on an even keel than another scandal broke—this time, payola in radio. FCC hearings and congressional investigations in 1959 and through much of 1960 showed clearly that a large number of disc jockeys, including some of the most respected ones, took bribes in exchange for promoting certain records. At the same time, there were charges of "plugola"—whereby program directors, producers, and personalities accepted products or services from companies in exchange for giving their wares free plugs on the air. The result was congressional legislation and FCC rules (1) requiring announcements of the sources of any cash or other remuneration received relating to program content and (2) banning deceptive programming. Although in the ensuing years no further serious allegations of rigged audience participation shows have occurred, charges of payola and plugola have surfaced many times and on occasion have prompted legal action by the FCC and other federal authorities.

Chapter SIX

The Soaring '60s

**Awakening,
Rebellion,
and the
Moon**

The 1960s saw the beginnings of conscientious FCC implementation of the "public interest, convenience, or necessity" provision of the Communications Act of 1934, an approach that lasted well into the 1970s. The reasons were twofold: (1) the election in 1960 of a new, young, liberal President, one whose efforts included appointing commissioners to the FCC who held proconsumer rather than proindustry philosophies, and (2) an environment in which large numbers of citizens rebelled against the previous decade's oppression of freedom and expression, with a leap toward individual choice, derision of hypocrisy, and greater sensitivity to the plight of less fortunate people and the will to do something about it. One manifestation of such commitment was the growing civil rights movement. Another, later in the decade, was the women's liberation movement.

The decade saw citizens' increasing and forceful participation in the legal and regulatory processes of their country, in an attempt to achieve equal opportunities and a redress of grievances. The media and the FCC were not immune. The public became aware that the exploding mass media industries were rapidly gaining increased influence over the information disseminated to the public and the ideas the public formed from that information. The electronic media's control of the nation's political process had begun.

The decade started with a remarkable demonstration of the power of television. Vice President Richard M. Nixon and Senator John F. Kennedy were the Republican and Democratic nominees, respectively, for the Presidency. Nixon seemed a sure winner, according to the early polls, as long as nothing dramatic happened to change the course of the campaign. He was therefore opposed to participating in television debates with Kennedy; however, he felt that his refusal could be used effectively against him and, hence, agreed to several debates. The first debate, on September 26, turned the election around. The largest audience to watch a single television program up to that time, an estimated 75 million, saw a fresh, vigorous, bright Kennedy and a seemingly unshaven, tired, scowling Nixon, the latter's gray suit fading him into the background. Kennedy had makeup and costume experts prepare his physical appearance; Nixon decided he didn't need theatrical trappings. Those who heard the debate on radio believed that, on the issues, Nixon had won; by contrast, those who saw it

DOI: 10.1016/B978-0-240-81236-6.00006-8

Greensboro, NC, lunch
counter sit-in.

U-2 spy plane downed
in Russia.

1960

Congress suspends the equal-time
provisions of the Communications Act to
accommodate the Presidential debates.

on television felt that Kennedy had won. Though Nixon regained ground by the time all four debates were over, the damage had been done and Kennedy was in the lead in the polls. Politics would never again be the same: Image would replace issues in reaching the public through television, and most of the public would thereafter vote on the basis of personality rather than policy.

To preclude debates among all of the 16 bona fide Presidential candidates on the ballot in one or more states that year, Congress suspended the equal-time provisions of the Communications Act, allowing the media to restrict their debate coverage to only the two leading eligible political parties. Another innovation in TV and politics that year was the networks' use, for the first time, of computers to predict the voting results on election day, even before the polls throughout the country had closed.

Another scandal rocked the FCC. President Eisenhower asked for the resignation of the FCC chairman, John C. Doerfer, following charges of (1) false billing of expenses and (2) accepting substantial gifts from the industry Doerfer was supposed to regulate. Increasing numbers of citizen complaints about broadcasting prompted the FCC to establish a Complaints and Compliance Division, the responsibilities of which continued, under different organizational names, into the 2000s.

Eighty-seven percent of U.S. homes had TV sets in 1960, with 440 VHF and 75 UHF stations on the air. More than 4,000 radio stations were in operation, 815 of them FM. Although sales of radio sets had doubled from 1955, only 11% of the public yet had FM receivers. Cable TV now had 650,000 subscribers—but that number was still only about 1.5% of the nation's households.

The networks developed programming to meet the overall growth, in the process starting to take back control of programming from advertising agencies. Instead of accepting shows that the advertisers provided, networks attempted first to get rights to programs and then to sell them to sponsors. This approach gave the networks better control of their schedules as well as of individual programs.

Television program content varied. On one hand, Edward R. Murrow and Fred Friendly's *Harvest of Shame* documentary on *See It Now* the day after Thanksgiving, with its theme, as stated by one of the farm supervisors, that "we used to own our slaves; now we just rent them," prompted public outrage and congressional legislation to protect migrant workers from cruel exploitation and inhuman living and working conditions. CBS wasn't the only network to deal with controversial issues. NBC's *White Paper* and ABC's *Close-Up* series documented and suggested humanistic solutions to problems that many people in the United States tried to pretend didn't exist.

On the other hand, the success of a new show, *The Untouchables*, with its 35-share of the audience (the percentage of sets on tuned to a given program), paved the way for a copycat deluge of similarly violent programs. Within a year the nightly spewing of violence from the TV screens was causing concern among many citizen groups and in several federal government agencies—anxiety and disapproval that have not stopped since.

| John F. Kennedy defeats Richard Nixon for Presidency. | FDA approves use of birth control pill. |

Nixon–Kennedy debates are broadcast on radio and TV.

FIG 6.1 This FM program guide cover reveals the fine-arts image characteristic of the medium in the 1950s and early 1960s. Leopold Stokowski poses for station KHGM, "Home of Good Music."
Courtesy Lynn Christian.

The Olympics were televised for the first time in 1960, and also for the first time a cartoon sitcom, *The Flintstones*, came to prime time. Whereas subsequent animated programs were only sporadically successful in prime time and for many years virtually nonexistent, in 1990 the unexpectedly high ratings of a comparable cartoon series, *The Simpsons*, suggested that it might again be time for prime-time animation.

GARRISON KEILLOR

Writer, Producer, Performer _____

I went into radio because it was my dream since I was a little boy to be invisible. I went into radio because it was magical, like ventriloquism—"Learn to Throw Your Voice and Mystify Your Friends," said the little ads for mail-order novelty stores. I went into radio because it was a novelty. I went into radio because I was broke and owed money to the University of Minnesota and they were talking about kicking me out, but I couldn't let them do it; they were the only ones who had liked me enough to let me in. (I was writing for *The New Yorker* at the time, but it wasn't aware of that.) Finally, I went into radio for love, for a tall girl with red hair and green eyes and long legs who sat behind me in American Literature. This was in October 1960, before so much happened in the world that made us skeptical, and to think

Echo I, first communications
satellite.

Frank Sinatra is once more the country's
most popular singer.

Murrow and Friendly produce
the landmark documentary
Harvest of Shame.

that a beautiful girl was looking at the
back of my head made me adventurous.
So when she asked me once if I was in
any activities, I said, "I'm in radio." "Oh
really," she said, "that's interesting." And
then I thought how bad I'd feel if she
found out I was lying, so I went into radio.

Radio station WUM was two little rooms
covered with green acoustic tile and a
transmitter in a closet across the hall, in
the basement of the women's gymnasium,
next to the squash court.

I went to a staff meeting. Men and
women sat on the floor and smoked
cigarettes and made sarcastic comments
about the Lutheran church, older men and
women in their twenties. They were so
cool, they laughed exclusively through
their noses, not overcommitting
themselves. It was the beginning of a new
decade and we were all anxious to make
the break out of Midwesternism into
something like atheistic nude Communist
avant-garde pacifist anarchism, just go as
far as we could. On the transmitter, which
looked like a large meat locker, someone
wrote the motto: "This Machine Destroys
Small Minds." It was an intense place.
They talked about doing a major
documentary about hypocrisy, and
everybody else wanted to work on it. It'd
be about four hours long and be finished
by spring and it'd knock the props out
from under everything as we knew it.

I was hoping for maybe a five-minute
newscast or something, so I was surprised
when the station manager, Don Olsen,
asked me, "Could you, uh, do an evening
show for like maybe five hours a night for,
say, seven nights a week?" I said, heck
yes. Everybody else would be busy on the
documentary, he said, and they needed
people to hold down the fort. "Maybe you

FIG 6.2 Garrison Keillor.
Photo © Cheryl Walse Bellville.

could contribute to the hypocrisy thing
later, by writing some stuff or something,"
he said, but I didn't care. I didn't want to
change the world; I only wanted to
impress one beautiful girl, and for that I
turned to glorious music written by great
men with names I learned to beautifully
pronounce in a voice I worked on so it
didn't sound so Midwestern, a voice that
might have spent some time at Oxford, a
voice whose mother may have been
French. Men with names such as Gabriel
Fauré, Andre Previn, Sergei Rachmaninoff,
Claude Debussy, Olivier Messiaen, Johann
Sebastian Bach—he was my favorite once
I got the "ch" right.

Every evening, seven to midnight,
sounds like a lot of work, but Beethoven
alone wrote many works over an hour in
length, and so did the others. All you
needed was five of those puppies and your
evening was complete. I learned to make
my voice deeper by talking with my chin

News and talk radio formats
debut.

RCA strikes a deal with
Japan to manufacture
television sets.

on my chest. It was a good deep solemn suave voice. It was thrilling for me, a boy from Anoka, to talk like that and to be intimately associated with greatness. Two months before, I was somebody who nobody ever invited to parties, and now I had my own show where great musicians appeared. I said, "You have just heard the *Symphony No. 5 in C minor* by Ludwig von Beethoven, Leonard Bernstein conducting the New York Philharmonic. Turning now to music of Johann Sebastian Bach, we hear his *Unaccompanied Suite for Cello No. 1*, played by Pablo Casals." And there he was.

Radio amazed me and I hoped it would amaze her, too. After class one day, I said, "You know, I keep meaning to ask you out, Renee, but I've got this radio show I've got to do." She said, "Yeah, I keep meaning to listen to that." I said, "I'd sure like to know what you think of it. I really would." She said, "Why don't you come over and we could listen to it together?"

I played Stravinsky's *Le Sacre du Printemps* over and over to impress her, and Poulenc, and Sessions, and *Nuage* by Delmer Gunsel, a local composer, avant-garde composers like Berio and Boulez, Ingmar Carlsson's *Four Choruses for Dying Orchestra on Themes of Soren Kierkegaard, Op. Posth*. Things of that sort.

As the year spun by, one by one the rest of the staff slowly disappeared, dropped out, sunk by failing grades in courses taught by professors they could not respect. The documentary on hypocrisy never got done. I never saw anybody actually record anything for it. March came, and the middle of April, a dreary cold month, and there were only three of us left, Clifford the engineer, Jim who did "Jazz in the Afternoon," and me. For some reason, without being aware of

it at the time, I seemed to have become the station manager. But I was happy. I was on the radio, in love, talking to her, playing great music, and my grades weren't bad either because, if I ever really needed to study, I'd just say, "We begin tonight's program with music of Johann Sebastian Bach, his *Mass in B-minor*, heard in its entirety and without commercial interruption." Almost three hours in the clear. I could run over to the library, check the reading list, sit down, get sort of an overview of the American Democratic Tradition, keep my eye on the clock, run back, and turn the record over, but even if it was stuck in the groove, nobody called up to complain. That's how good Bach is. There's so much there that one phrase repeated over and over just keeps showing you something else.

All spring I sat in the studio and played great music, imagining tonight would be the night she'd tune in and realize that this smooth voice was me and suddenly she'd be there! Waving, at the studio window! I'd wave her in and she'd say, "I heard your show. It's great. I love Bach!" and I'd say, "Hey, Renee, somehow I knew you had to love Bach as much as I love Bach and I knew that someday you and I would love Bach together."

But that evening never came. One night a guy appeared at the studio window, waving, and ran in and said, "We're off the air!" He wore a shirt that looked like old wallpaper with eight ballpoint pens in the pocket clipped to a white plastic pocket protector: I could see he was an engineer. It was Clifford. "When did we go off the air?" I said. He said, "I'm not sure but probably sometime before Christmas. That's when I went to California. Didn't you ever check the transmitter?" "No," I said,

Bay of Pigs invasion fails.

1961

Newton Minow
calls television a
"vast wasteland."

Minow establishes the
Educational Broadcasting
Branch of the FCC.

"I'm the station manager." And he reached down and turned off the turntable.

Suddenly I understood why nobody had ever called in to complain about *Le Sacre du Printemps*. I had been my only listener. I had spent six months talking to myself in a voice that wasn't even my own. If this happened to me today, it would probably kill me, but when you're 19, you bounce back from these disasters, and I picked up the phone and called the one person I knew who could comfort me at this terrible moment in my career. "Renee," I

said, "I need to come over and see you." "Okay," she said. So I did.

We talked for three hours—about life, for the most part—and she was wonderful, and I wished I really was in love with her, like you might wish you could play the piano, but I've thought of her ever since, especially when I'm near a microphone. All these years I've enjoyed talking to her out there somewhere. Thank you, Renee, wherever you are.
Courtesy Garrison Keillor.

Radio programming continued to change. The last four network soaps left radio, replaced principally by news shows. KFAX, in San Francisco, became the first all-news radio station, and in Los Angeles, KABC went all-talk. More prophetic was the change-over at WABC, the ABC radio network's pilot station in New York. Losing listeners and money, the station switched to a fast-paced, top-tune, musical ID rock-and-roll format. From a rating of 3 (the percentage of all radio homes tuned in) in its market, it jumped to a rating of 20 by the end of the decade. Stations throughout the country that followed its lead also found growing audiences. The nation's radio stations became primarily rock-and-roll operations.

Technical innovations helped both radio and television. Tape cartridges, or "carts," began to be used in more and more radio studios. The cordless microphone, or "mic," came into being. Transistors made possible the development of portable radios, a boon to radio's survival and FM's reemergence. To stay on the air by cutting personnel costs, a number of small radio stations tried automation. Television received a boost with Emerson's distribution of the first small, portable, battery-operated television sets, with 3-inch screens. Motorola's development of microwave communications made it possible for TV stations to carry remotes live from almost any site. Coupled with mobile TV units—which all the networks used at the 1960 political conventions—microwave greatly enhanced the immediacy of news broadcasts.

Its implications for the future escaping most of U.S. industry, RCA struck a deal with Japan, where workers' wages were lower than in the United States, to assemble RCA television sets in Japan from parts made in America. It seemed a good idea at the time because the savings in production costs enlarged RCA's profits. Eventually, however, Japan began to manufacture the entire set for RCA, then made sets for other companies, and finally made sets on its own, gradually taking world leadership away from the United States in the production and distribution of television and radio equipment. But back

Westerns dominate television programming.

then, U.S. industry looked on Japanese industry as something it could use for its own benefit, and even the following year, 1961, when the first Japanese-made television set, by Sony, went on sale in the United States, few people took it seriously.

1961

Within weeks after his appointment by President Kennedy to head the FCC, Newton N. Minow made his famous "vast wasteland" address at the annual convention of the NAB. Although the catchphrase was intended only as an incidental part of his speech, it became a symbol of Minow's efforts to push television toward more and better programming in the public interest. What concerned broadcasters more specifically was the section of his speech in which Minow said, "I understand that many people feel that in the past licenses were often renewed *pro forma*. I say to you now: renewal will not be *pro forma* in the future. There is nothing permanent or sacred about a broadcast license." The broadcast industry hadn't heard such tough talk from regulators since the *Blue Book* had been issued 15 years earlier.

NEWTON MINOW

FORMER FCC CHAIRMAN _____

In 1961, the FCC's brash, young, and newly appointed chairman, Newton Minow, created a stir when he delivered the following statement to attendees of NAB's annual convention: "I invite you to sit down in front of your television set when your station goes on the air and stay without a book, magazine, newspaper, profit-and-loss sheet, or rating book to distract you—and keep your eyes glued to that set until the station signs off. I can assure you that you will observe a vast wasteland."

Today, Minow is an attorney with a private law firm, but his famous rebuke lives on: "I recall a recent letter which came to me from a woman in a small town in the Southwest. She wanted to know what time the 'vast wasteland' came on."

FIG 6.3 Newt Minow. *Courtesy Newton Minow.*

Senator Thomas Dodd launches
an investigation into television
violence.

One of Minow's priorities was the development of noncommercial educational broadcasting, later on in the decade to be named public broadcasting. To facilitate the growth of this service, Minow established at the FCC an Educational Broadcasting Branch, which was to continue for almost two decades, only to be abolished, ironically, by another Democratic FCC chairman, President Jimmy Carter's appointee, Charles Ferris. Ferris began the process of deregulation that during the subsequent Reagan administration reversed most of the Kennedy-Minow regulatory actions regarding the public interest. Minow was also responsible for arranging for a commercial frequency in New Jersey to become New York City's first noncommercial educational television (ETV) station, in 1962. There were 51 ETV stations on the air, offering mostly cultural and instructional programming. An instructional television experiment that began in 1961, the Midwest Program on Airborne Television Instruction (MPATI), transmitted programs to classrooms in six Midwestern states from airplanes—an early version of today's satellite programs.

Minow attempted to strengthen the Fairness Doctrine, which was under continuous fire from the industry. His strong concern with monopolistic practices led to FCC rules that prevented networks from dictating, as they had been, even nonprime-time programming schedules for their affiliates. He was a strong advocate for the development of UHF. Two other early Kennedy FCC appointees, E. William Henry, who joined the FCC in 1961, and Kenneth Cox, who became a commissioner in 1963, were instrumental in carrying on Minow's strong regulatory policies after Minow left the Commission in 1963, shortly before Kennedy's assassination. During his Presidency Kennedy encouraged Minow's efforts, reportedly telling him on one occasion, "You keep this up. This is one of the really important things."

Kennedy used television not only for political purposes but to open up government operations to the public. He arranged for TV to cover every one of his press conferences with no restrictions. Just before Kennedy had assumed the oath of office, outgoing President Eisenhower used television to make a remarkable admission. During his Presidency he had supported McCarthyism and even jingoistic efforts of the military, the defense industry, and the CIA. Perhaps feeling he no longer needed the support of those organizations to maintain his Presidency, he used TV for his last address as President to warn the country of the dangers of the military-industrial complex.

In 1961 Westerns dominated TV programming, with such favorites as *Bonanza*, *Gunsmoke*, and *Wagon Train*. One could see 22 different Westerns on network television every week. Violence on television continued to concern the public, and a Senate committee headed by Senator Thomas J. Dodd began an investigation of the frequency and effects of violence on TV.

| Peace Corps launched. | Ernest Hemingway commits suicide. |

First live TV Presidential press conference.

During the Kennedy administration, Ed Murrow left CBS after 25 years to become head of the United States Information Agency (USIA), where his job was to present a positive picture of the United States to the rest of the world. One of the ironies of his USIA directorship was his request to the British Broadcasting Company (BBC) not to show his own *Harvest of Shame* because it gave such a negative picture of America. The BBC showed it anyway, and Murrow later expressed regret for having made such a request.

FM got a boost when the FCC authorized FM stereo in 1961. Within a few years, stereo, plus the clean sound of FM, began to attract many young music listeners to the service. Paradoxically, in a move that eventually permitted FM to overtake AM as the preferred sound medium, the FCC turned down a petition for AM stereo. This action kept the older medium at a significant competitive disadvantage when stereophonic sound all but replaced monaural. Within the next few years, first Germany and then Japan would ensure FM's future in the United States by exporting small, inexpensive, portable FM receivers.

1962

John Henry Faulk won his lawsuit against AWARE, Inc., and Laurence Johnson in 1962. The jury awarded Faulk $3.5 million—even more than he'd asked for. It turned out, however, that Johnson was virtually bankrupt, and so Faulk got little of the award—not enough to compensate for the fact that because he was controversial he never again worked for any network. Officially, the blacklist was now ended. Unofficially, broadcasting continued it in what was called a "graylist."

Both the President and the First Lady made television history in 1961. President Kennedy's ultimatum to the Soviet Union to withdraw its missiles from Cuba—his "Cuban Missile Crisis" speech—was carried on all three networks. Jacqueline Kennedy personally conducted an hour-long tour of the White House, carried by both NBC and CBS; the President joined her at the end to say good night to the viewers.

In other action related to the media, President Kennedy signed into law the All-Channel Receiver Act, which amended the Communications Act to authorize the FCC to require that, beginning in 1964, all TV sets made had to be capable of receiving both VHF and UHF. While UHF has still not achieved parity with VHF in this new millennium, this act did provide UHF with an opportunity to survive and indeed enabled many UHF stations to become very profitable.

Kennedy also signed into law the Educational Broadcasting Facilities Act, which provided, for the first time, federal grants to assist in the construction of educational television stations.

Roger Maris breaks Babe Ruth's
home-run record.

1962

Ed Murrow is appointed
head of the United States
Information Agency.

FCC authorizes FM
stereo.

LAWRENCE LAURENT

TELEVISION CRITIC (EMERITUS), *THE WASHINGTON POST*

By 1962 newspapers began to notice that networks were consistently running minutes ahead of the wire services. After the 1964 California primary, in which the AP was still declaring Nelson Rockefeller the winner over Barry Goldwater, even after Goldwater had been confirmed as the winner by the networks, the wire services and three broadcasting networks met to discuss creating a cooperative vote-counting agency. Shortly afterward the National Election Service was born. NES established machinery to furnish a quick running account to all of its subscribers, thus also protecting the newspapers, all of which were subscribers to one or both wire services. The new service was activated in time to furnish its organizing members full service for the fall election of 1964.

This quotation is from Sig Mickelson's excellent book, *From Whistle Stop to Sound Bite* (Praeger Publishers, New York, 1989, p. 145). Professor Mickelson is relying on a fine memory, and I would like to point out that he committed several errors. The news-gathering cooperative was first known as Network Election Service (NES) and later was called News Election Service. I know, for I was present at the creation.

The story begins on election night, 1962, at *The Washington Post*, where I had been the broadcasting critic for 12 years (and where I would remain for almost 20

additional years). My attention to election coverage was interrupted by a message that publisher Philip L. Graham wished to see me in the office of managing editor Alfred Friendly. I found the two of them sitting in front of a TV set, comparing the returns being displayed with the numbers fed into the *Post*'s teletype machines by the Associated Press and the United Press. Graham greeted me with a question: "Why are the results on television so far ahead of the wire services?"

FIG 6.4 Lawrence Laurent worked at *The Washington Post* for more than 30 years, covering television for 28 of those years. He retired from the *Post* in 1982 and was formerly vice president/communication for the Association of Independent Television Stations. He has taught broadcasting courses at four major universities and is also editor in residence at the Broadcast Pioneers Library.
Photo by Anna Ng, Washington, D.C. Courtesy Lawrence Laurent.

Benny Goodman plays
jazz concert in Moscow.

John Henry Faulk wins his
lawsuit against AWARE, Inc.,
and Laurence Johnson.

Kennedy's "Cuban Missile
Crisis" speech is carried by
all three networks.

Graham was an easygoing executive of enormous wit and great charm, but one learned quickly that his Harvard Law School training did not permit vague answers. I answered truthfully, "I don't know." Graham, who wore the staff worship with an easy grace, displayed his gap-toothed grin and asked, "How would you find out?"

"I would do a comparative study," I responded, "documenting the numbers that each offered in major elections over the election night."

"Good," said Graham. "You get your lazy self up to New York tomorrow and start that study." He paused and added, "And don't spend more than $50,000."

The following morning I was in New York, conferring with Bill Leonard, who was then running the CBS election unit. I thought CBS the best place to begin, for the simple reason that Philip Graham held the licenses to two television stations (in Washington, D.C., and in Jacksonville, Florida), both affiliated with the CBS television network. With Leonard I reviewed the vague aims of the study: Would it demonstrate that the networks were padding vote totals, as some California critics had charged? Would it show that the networks had developed new vote-gathering techniques? What were the limits a news organization ought to impose on the uses of computers? How could we improve the entire process of covering elections? Overall, I had no real idea of the ultimate use of the study I intended to do.

Leonard, who had been in television news since the end of World War II, nodded in agreement and said, almost as an afterthought, "I suppose I ought to clear this with Dick Salant?" Richard Salant, graduate of the Harvard Law School and a particular favorite of CBS President Frank Stanton, had

taken over running CBS News after Sig Mickelson's resignation. I responded to Leonard by saying, "Oh, I thought you had already done that." I remained in Leonard's office while he went to see Salant. Bill returned, looking unhappy. "Dick says for you to write him a letter, telling him what kind of study you intend to do and what use you intend to make of it."

I was stunned. This was a roadblock I had never considered. No point could be made by being angry with Leonard, the messenger, so I said: "Well, that takes this matter out of my hands. I will have to call *The Washington Post*." I used Leonard's telephone to reach Alfred Friendly and recounted the morning's happenings.

Friendly told me to go over to the wire services to set up that portion of the study, and he would have Graham talk to Salant. I spent the afternoon in the offices of the Associated Press and United Press. Cooperation was guaranteed. Each would make available to me the entire election night file.

A telephone call from Friendly to my hotel room awakened me the next day. He sounded disgusted. "Come on home," he said. "CBS refuses to cooperate, and that kills the project." I responded, "Before I come back to Washington I would like to see William R. McAndrew. He's the president of NBC News. He's a former print journalist and may be more sympathetic toward the answers we're trying to find."

"Go ahead," Friendly responded. "It can't hurt, but I wouldn't get my hopes too high."

I walked through the rainy Manhattan morning to 30 Rockefeller Plaza, NBC's headquarters, and went up to McAndrew's office without an appointment. I dripped rain over the carpet and chairs before I took a seat near a hostile, suspicious

Jacqueline Kennedy
conducts televised tour
of the White House.

President Kennedy signs into law the
All-Channel Receiver Act, requiring
all television sets to possess UHF as
well as VHF reception.

receptionist. "Mr. McAndrew is busy, and you have no appointment. You will have to wait." But McAndrew came to his door, spotted me immediately and insisted that I come into his office. He listened, sipping coffee, while I emphasized that I had already been turned down at CBS; that no one can limit a project or its uses before the work has been done; and that I thought both broadcasters and newspapers would benefit from such a study.

My shoes were drying, and I was warming to the task of convincing McAndrew. Yes, he and NBC might be taking a chance on the results, I argued, but McAndrew knew my work and should be certain that I wasn't out to do a hatchet job on anyone. Besides, all of us might learn something useful.

McAndrew said, "Fine. Now, let's bring in Julian Goodman, Elmer Lower, and Frank Jordan and see what they think." I told my story a second time, feeling more comfortable as the audience grew bigger. Goodman was McAndrew's chief deputy and a friend of long standing when he was NBC bureau chief in Washington. I knew Lower from his days in Washington. Frank Jordan and I were acquainted. All three agreed that the study would be a good thing.

I let out a sigh of relief, asked permission to make a collect call to Washington, and settled back while McAndrew chatted with my bosses at *The Washington Post*. NBC made everything available that I needed. With temporary clerical help, we made charts of vote reporting by NBC, the AP, and the UP in two-minute intervals for every senatorial and gubernatorial contest in the nation. (I made an arbitrary decision to eliminate

House of Representatives elections since interest tended to be local or regional and not national.)

By the time the charts were finished, the results were clear. Each time a wire service went head to head with NBC, the broadcast network was the winner. And the reasons weren't hard to find. First came the preparation and the organizing. Network-hired consultants had selected "key precincts" that were indicators of statewide returns. Also, networks had concentrated on elections that relied on the fast voting machines, ignoring the slower hand-marked, hand-tallied voting in some precincts. (This, almost alone, accounted for the swifter, higher totals in the California elections and put to rest charges in Los Angeles newspapers that the broadcasters were "padding" the totals.)

In some states, NBC had hired the League of Women Voters to staff every precinct and keep an open telephone line to the network. This was not expensive (NBC made a contribution to the league), and it outsped the conventional reporting methods.

In 1962, one must remember, computers were still comparatively primitive and huge. They still relied on vacuum tubes, which would be replaced within five years by the microminiature electronic circuits that grew out of transistor technology. Even in primitive form, however, the computers were a giant step in data processing. They were tailor-made for election night work. First, the computers could be programmed to prevent mistakes. For example, a computer was programmed with the exact number of registered voters in each precinct. If a total were received that was

U.S.–U.S.S.R. war averted in
Cuban missile crisis.

The Communications
Satellite Act of 1962
is passed.

Canadian professor Marshall
McLuhan says electronic media
have created a "global village."

greater than the number of registered voters, the computer would reject the report. An operator would be on the telephone to the reporter, asking that he double check the data and, perhaps, see if he had transposed a digit or reversed a few numbers. Computers in those days did swift calculations in seconds and displayed the results to a television camera. (By the 1970s, the computers had tiny new components and did the same calculations in nanoseconds, meaning a billionth part of a second.)

My own roots are deep into the print culture. I had been trained in typography, schooled to worship the printed word, and had done quite well working in this technology. As a consequence, I was able to stress the handicaps inherent in publishing compared to broadcasting. Networks receive direct benefits from election night coverage. Advertisers buy election night coverage on television while often avoiding a postelection newspaper. More important, election night offers one of the rare events in which the news departments of three major networks compete directly. (Impoverished ABC News didn't amount to much in 1962. It got its election results from the AP, and a valiant band of reporters did the very best they could.) The main point, however, is that an election night victory in the ratings or in published criticism could carry the winning news department through rough economic times. In short, in broadcasting, the winner of election night competition is rewarded.

Print, however, has a long list of opposites. Staffs are increased, overtime rates are paid, the hours are long, particularly for an East Coast newspaper with West Coast elections to cover.

Newspaper editors process vote totals, write and rewrite stories of fact and interpretation. Type must be set (and it was done by a manually operated Linotype machine in 1962). Type is assembled in page form to allow matrices to be made for stereotype plates that go into the pressroom. Still later, after the entire newspaper edition is assembled, it must be delivered across a city, throughout a county, or all over a state. The hours roll by, and television has already displayed the vote totals, interpreted the results, and often sent its audience to bed before midnight. In any race with newspapers, television will always win.

I concluded a 38-page report to Graham by advising that newspapers simply would have to harness computers and that, most of all, the competition between print and electronics was wasteful and foolish. One could be proud of its speed while the other could take pride in providing a permanent record. Finally, I advised the publisher of *The Washington Post* that a cooperative effort would be a real benefit to both competitors and, most of all, to the voting public, which is entitled to swift, accurate, meaningful voting totals.

Graham asked me up to his office after he had finished reading the report. "That's about what I thought you would find," he said. (Later, I was told, Graham arranged a meeting with the Antitrust Division of the Department of Justice.) After laying out his case for intermedia cooperation, which gave no competitive advantage to any of the participants, he got a favorable answer. In the archaic, impersonal language that is so dear to this branch of Justice, the antitrust division ruled it had "no objection at this time" to the unified coverage of voting.

Thalidomide cited in birth defects.

Astronaut John Glenn is first American to orbit earth; the event is televised.

Johnny Carson becomes host of *The Tonight Show.*

Philip Leslie Graham, who had so little time left in his remarkable life, was once described to me as "part prince and part Machiavelli." He showed both traits by having the study printed privately and distributed discreetly to newspaper editors, who needed to be convinced before a cooperative could be formed. Long-held grievances had to be forgotten for editors to agree to work with broadcasters. Out of this, in 1963, came the Network Election Service, or NES, and on election night in 1964 it worked quite well. The name News Election Service was adopted two years later.

Alfred Friendly, who rode herd on NES after Mr. Graham's death, told me several times that the study I did was vital to Mr. Graham's campaign of breaking down print resistance to the cooperative. He would add that the study would be remembered "as probably the most important thing you have ever done."

So, uh, pardon me, Mr. Mickelson, but I do have a different story about the formation of NES for the 1964 election and all the elections that have followed. I like my version better, too, for the simple reason that I lived it.

Courtesy Lawrence Laurent.

In combining his interests in space and in telecommunications, Kennedy pushed for enactment of the Communications Satellite Act of 1962. It was passed and signed just a month after the launch of the United States' first communications satellite, *Telstar I,* which debuted with demonstration programs between the United States and Europe. Although it would be many years before satellites were used for network transmissions across the United States, the Soviet Union in 1962 announced plans to use four *Sputnik* satellites for interconnection in its territories. The Communications Satellite Act of 1962 authorized a Communications Satellite Corporation (COMSAT, established in 1963) to coordinate and represent all U.S. telecommunications satellite operations.

The advances in satellite telecommunications opportunely occurred at the time that a new guru of communications, the Canadian professor Marshall McLuhan, began to have a worldwide impact on thinking in the field, including his concept that, because of electronic communications, "time has ceased, space has vanished . . . [and] we now live in a global village." His theory that "The medium is the message" would become both a pro- and an antitelevision slogan.

Perhaps the most dramatic proof of the world simultaneously expanding and getting smaller was the televising in 1962 of astronaut John Glenn's earth orbit in a space capsule, an event seen by some 135 million viewers.

Ninety percent of U.S. homes now had TV sets. What network shows were they watching? The top-rated program in 1962 was *The Beverly Hillbillies.* Number two was *Candid Camera.* A notable premiere was Johnny Carson's taking over from Jack

Paar as host of NBC's *The Tonight Show*, a job Carson held for 30 years, until 1992.
A notable special was Barbara Walter's first major assignment for *The Today Show*,
Jacqueline Kennedy's goodwill tour of India.

FM development got another boost from the FCC in 1962 when the commission
put a freeze on new AM stations. *Broadcasting* magazine's headline read, "For Radio,
Birth Control Begins at 40." Many applicants who wanted new radio stations reluc-
tantly switched to FM, little knowing at the time how fortunate a move that was.

1963

On November 22, 1963, President Kennedy was assassinated in Dallas, Texas.
Television was the principal news source of the tragedy. Americans stayed glued to
their sets for four days and watched with a mixture of horror and unbelieving
fascination as Lee Harvey Oswald, the accused killer of Kennedy, was murdered on
the television screen right before their eyes by Jack Ruby, in a police station, before
Oswald could be questioned about the assassination.

Earlier that year Newton Minow gave his final speech to the NAB convention,
stating, "You need to do more than feed our minds. Broadcasting must also nourish
the spirit. We need entertainment which helps us grow in compassion and understanding. Certainly make us laugh; but also help us comprehend. Of course, sing us
to sleep; but also awaken us to the awesome dangers of our time. Surely, divert us
with mysteries; but also help us to unlock the mysteries of our universe."

FIG 6.5 Newspaper headline reporting Kennedy assassination.
Courtesy of Smithsonian Institution.

1963

Newton Minow resigns
as FCC chairman.

When Minow left the FCC, Kennedy appointed as chair Commissioner E. William Henry, who carried on the administration's public interest philosophy. One of his initial efforts, to restrict the amount of commercial time on television—which was exceeding even the limits suggested in the NAB's own code—was frustrated when the House passed a bill forbidding the FCC from doing so. The FCC withdrew its proposal.

Television news expanded. Following a Roper poll that showed television to be the principal source of news for the U.S. public, the networks extended their evening news broadcasts from 15 to 30 minutes. ABC strengthened its competition with CBS and NBC by hiring Elmer Lower to head its news division. Television news helped move the country closer to civil rights legislation when in August it televised the March on Washington, in which the Reverend Martin Luther King, Jr., gave his famous "I Have a Dream" speech.

Sports made news, too, with the first use of the instant replay (in the Army–Navy football game). Before long, the technique was a standard feature in TV coverage of every athletic event.

How TV and Radio Flashed News

By Richard K. Doan
TV and Radio Editor

Reporting From The World Of Television and Radio

The national television and radio networks sprang yesterday to the task of informing the country of the tragic events in Dallas within minutes after news was flashed of the fatal wounding of President Kennedy.

All regular programming was immediately canceled to clear the airwaves for continuous coverage of the saddening developments. In New York, every TV channel turned to piecing together the details as the incredible story unfolded. Educational Channel 13 took video feeds from CBS and ABC.

No one at the networks gave any immediate thought to how long the all-out coverage would continue.

Everyone was too dazed by the emotional impact of the President's death to think beyond one moment to the next.

Veteran newshands like Walter Cronkite and Charles

Collingwood, Chet Huntley, and David Brinkley, were visibly moved as they grappled with the reading of bulletins and talked with correspondents in Texas.

Dallas and Fort Worth stations fed eyewitness reports to the networks. A Texas TV newsman said: "The eyes of Dallas are lowered in shame."

Plans for the first experimental trans-Pacific telecast via Relay satellite, scheduled for 3.30 p.m. yesterday, were shelved indefinitely. President Kennedy had videotaped a brief greeting to the people of Japan which was to have been in-

corporated into the historic telecast.

The program, which was to have been beamed from California to Tokyo, was to be shown in this country on ABC and NBC.

Earlier this week the three national TV networks had reached an agreement with the White House to tape a "rocking-chair chat" with the President on Dec. 20. It was to be televised simultaneously by the three chains, probably within 48 hours after the taping. President Kennedy had sat for a similar interview last Dec. 17.

The only other known date

President Kennedy had for a televised appearance was his scheduled speech here Wednesday night, Dec. 4, before a Joseph P. Kennedy Foundation dinner at the Americana Hotel. It was to have been televised live by Channel 5 and taped by the network for later showing.

An NBC news cameraman was in an automobile three cars behind President Kennedy's in the Dallas motorcade. He failed to get a picture of the President's car after the shooting, but showed people nearby crouching.

The ABC radio and TV networks announced cancellation of all commercial pro-

gramming through last night.

WABC Radio said it would broadcast liturgical music through the week end. WWRL, a station directed at Negro audiences, scheduled "sacred music" until the burial of the President, "however many days that is."

NBC expected at 7 o'clock last night to feed a 15-minute report on the day's tragic events to Japan via the Relay satellite.

Late yesterday, Dr. Frank announced that the CBS radio and TV networks will carry "no commercials and no entertainment programs until after the President's funeral." NBC said all commercial programming on radio and TV would be suspended "indefinitely."

Former President Eisenhower and United Nations Ambassador Adlai Stevenson were among shocked leaders of the nation who faced TV cameras during the afternoon to express their grief and their sympathies to the President's family.

FIG 6.6 Newspaper account of the electronic media's response to the assassination of President Kennedy. *Courtesy of Smithsonian Institution.*

| Electronic media provide unprecedented news coverage of the Kennedy assassination. | Roper poll shows television to be the principal source of news for the American public. |

Then as now, ratings drove broadcasting. Concern about the validity of ratings led to a congressional study, and the House Commerce Committee reported that several rating companies were providing inaccurate information. Thereafter a closer eye was kept on rating systems, though they continued to be the arbiter of all programming.

JULIA CHILD

CHEF AND TELEVISION HOST _____

Timing seemed to be a key factor in the success of my television show. World War II was over, air travel to Europe was suddenly affordable and accessible to the general public, the Kennedys were in the White House with a famous French chef, and European (particularly French) foods were very popular. I believe my informal style made this fancy upper-class cuisine seem less complicated. Since errors were not edited out of the programs, my shows had a credibility which provided viewers with a sense of identification.

Almost 10 hours of preparation and rehearsal went into each taped show. For most of the programs, recipes needed to be prepared several times, each one done to a particular point of completion so that the item was able to be used for illustration during the various stages of assembly. When expensive items such as suckling pig were used, the dish was auctioned off and the proceeds went to public television station WGBH; otherwise, the hungry television crew feasted on the day's taping results.

The early shows (circa 1963–1964) were filmed in the demonstration kitchen of a public utilities company. These black-and-white shows were filmed by two stationary cameras; and because television audiences wanted things to be literal, I was not able to skip around—I needed to methodically proceed step by step from the beginning to the end. This made the show seem very long. The later shows, filmed in color, were done with addition of a handheld camera. They were edited to show a series of short segments rather than the whole process in its entirety.

FIG 6.7 Julia Child.
Courtesy Julia Child Productions, Inc.

Networks expand their
evening news telecasts
from 15 to 30 minutes.

Dr. Martin Luther King,
Jr.'s "I Have a Dream"
speech is televised.

1964

Politics—party and public—interacted strongly with broadcasting in 1964. The election campaign between President Lyndon B. Johnson, who as Vice President had succeeded Kennedy, and Republican Senator Barry Goldwater introduced the kinds of negative television spots that would later dominate U.S. elections. So strong was one spot implying that Goldwater would start an atomic war that the Democrats voluntarily withdrew it. At the same time, both parties experimented with subtle ads designed to affect the viewer psychologically and to capitalize on the experiences of previous campaigns via commercials stressing personalities and biographical sketches rather than issues. Politicians were more sensitive than ever to the power of television, and where previously TV crews had full and free access to convention activities, the Goldwater contingent tried to maintain its control of the Republican Convention by controlling the movements of reporters. In one dramatic incident, NBC's John Chancellor was arrested, on camera, by the Goldwater forces for crossing into a forbidden area. As he was being dragged away, Chancellor signed off with "This is John Chancellor, somewhere in custody."

A public interest group, the Office of Communications of the United Church of Christ (UCC), monitored broadcast stations' services, especially in relation to the growing civil rights movement. Under its director, Everett Parker, the UCC Office of Communications investigated the programming and employment practices of WLBT in Jackson, Mississippi. It found the station racist in both respects and petitioned the FCC not to renew WLBT's license. The FCC renewed it anyway, rejecting the UCC's request for standing in the matter. In dissenting opinions, FCC Chairman Henry and Commissioner Cox insisted on the right of the public to participate in the FCC's licensing and renewal process. The federal district court overturned the FCC's action in 1965 and ordered WLBT's license revoked. The court's decision stated: "After nearly five decades of operation the broadcast industry does not seem to have grasped the simple fact that a broadcast license is a public trust subject to termination for breach of duty."

In 1964 the FCC issued a *Fairness Doctrine Primer*, which not only explained how stations could implement the Fairness Doctrine but reaffirmed their obligation to do so. Coincidentally in 1964, on radio station WGCB in Red Lion, Pennsylvania, a right-wing minister, Billy James Hargis, made a personal attack on the loyalty of Fred Cook, who had written a book critical of the Republican Presidential candidate, Barry Goldwater. Cook asked for free time to reply, under the Fairness Doctrine. WGCB refused but offered to sell him time. Cook complained to the FCC, which ordered the station to comply. The station continued to refuse, and the case wound up in the Supreme Court, which five years later, in 1969, issued its landmark *Red Lion* decision, upholding the Fairness Doctrine and the "scarcity principle" that justified government regulation of broadcasting. (The "scarcity principle" maintains that because there are

Jack Ruby kills alleged Kennedy assassin Lee Harvey Oswald; his murder is caught by live television cameras.

Congress passes Civil Rights Act.

1964

Instant replay is used for the first time in a live sports telecast.

EBS inaugurated.

a limited number of frequencies, the airwaves belong to the public and must therefore be operated in the public interest, under an agency established by the public's representatives.)

Other FCC actions in 1964 included hearings on payola and plugola and the establishment of fees for filling applications for licenses. Another FCC action had a

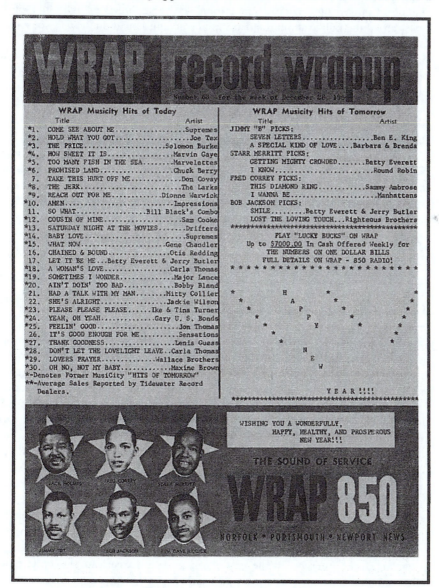

FIG 6.8 The number of radio stations programming exclusively to blacks grew in the 1950s and 1960s. *Courtesy Rick Wright.*

President Lyndon Johnson swamps
Barry Goldwater in election.

China tests A-bomb.

Political campaigns use
new strategies in television
advertising

Beatles appear on
the *Ed Sullivan Show*.

long-term effect on FM. The commission, believing that FM was now ready to survive on its own, eliminated some AM-FM program duplication, forcing FM stations to develop their own programming at least 50% of the time—a move that broadcasters protested but that we now know was in FM's best interest.

At another federal office an event occurred that would in a few years have a significant impact on broadcast advertising: The surgeon general, who in 1956 had first warned the public about the dangers of smoking, issued the now-famous *Report on Smoking*.

One thousand cable systems were in operation in 1964. Fred Friendly became president of CBS News. Cassette recorders became standard equipment in radio stations. While *Hello, Dolly* was a national hit, rock grew as the music of the Beatles began to dominate the airwaves. The first movie especially produced for TV, *The Killers*, was made, starring Hollywood actor Ronald Reagan. The movie never reached the air, however—it was considered too violent.

TV's revealing eye saw some results from its handiwork. The Civil Rights Act was passed and the Reverend King received the Nobel Peace Prize. TV would soon turn that eye on another matter that would galvanize public action: the United States' participation in the war in Vietnam.

1965

Surveys showed that color TV programs resulted in increased viewing and greater attention to commercials, and in 1965 all the networks were now broadcasting predominantly in color. Color film was being used in news programs. Among the news programs that were of most interest to Americans were those with reports from Vietnam. The networks expanded their coverage as U.S. forces expanded their participation in the conflict. Seeing the horrors of war and the body bags being carried virtually across their living rooms, more and more Americans, especially college students, began to rebel against their government's military involvement in Southeast Asia. Vietnam became not only an issue in campus discussions but an important theme in the folk music that captured the attention of the 1960s generation. Anger and protests grew as television began to include U.S. atrocities in its reports. One such report in 1965 that had a profound effect on many Americans was news correspondent Morley Safer's coverage of U.S. troops flicking their cigarette lighters and burning down a village of 120 huts because some of its residents had reportedly helped the Vietcong.

The Vietnam War and the continued hardening of the Cold War with the Soviet Union gave rise to a number of spy series on television. Two of the most popular were *Mission: Impossible* and *I Spy*, the latter breaking new ground in casting by costarring in an otherwise white cast a young African-American performer named Bill Cosby. Even comedy got into the TV spy act with *Get Smart*.

FTC orders cigarette
package warnings.

Marshall McLuhan says, "The
medium is the message."

Sidney Poitier first African-
American male to win an
Academy Award.

The United Church of
Christ accuses WLBT of
racist practices.

RICK SKLAR

THE LATE RICK SKLAR WAS
PROGRAMMER, WABC,
NEW YORK, AND HEAD OF
SKLAR COMMUNICATIONS _____

When I began to program WABC in 1962, it was the fourth Top Forty station in the market behind WMCA, WMGM, and WINS. Researching retail record sales, I noted that the top three songs sold more than twice as many copies as the next dozen, and below the top 24 hits, sales were scattered. Abandoning the 77 record playlist I had inherited from previous programmers and consultants, I cut the airplay list to an unheard of 18 to 24 singles per week (depending on what was selling), alternating with hits of the past from our existing library of the Top 100 rock-and-roll songs from 1954 to 1961. The top three songs were put on fast repeat cycles controlled by industrial timing clocks that activated PLAY THIS SONG NEXT lights in the studio. The number-one song was played every 60 minutes, number two every 75 minutes, and number three every 90 minutes. Every other song was from the Top 14 or a recurrent (recent hit).

To be certain listeners would report WABC and the time they heard it to the rating companies, I put the Top 14 songs on tape cartridges that were tagged with jingles that sung the call letters followed by a time chime to cue the disc jockey to give the time. The station was positioned as the home of "music power." The strategy worked. One by one WABC's competitors switched to another format. By the late 1960s WABC had a weekly reported audience of 6 million listeners, more than twice the circulation of the next largest station in America. In a market with over four dozen radio stations, WABC's share was often over 20%. On a typical Saturday night, more than one in every four radios was tuned to our "Cousin Brucie" show.

FIG 6.9 Rick Sklar with surrealist painter Salvador Dali, who served as the judge of a 1964 WABC contest.
Courtesy Rick Sklar.

At the FCC, the Kennedy legacy continued, with Chairman Henry getting the Commission to adopt public interest standards and service to the community as significant factors in judging to whom to award licenses in comparative hearings (those in which there were two or more applicants for the same frequency or

United States escalates
involvement in Vietnam.

1965

AM-FM program
duplication is modified
by the FCC.

All networks broadcast
predominantly in color.

FIG 6.10 The National
Association of FM
Broadcasters pushed for
parity with AM throughout
the 1950s and 1960s. An
FM receiver in every car
was a primary goal.
Courtesy Lynn Christian.

what this industry needs is an fm radio in every car!

AND YOU'RE ONE OF MORE THAN 500 STATIONS WORKING TO MAKE IT POSSIBLE!

Our thanks for your cooperation! We've included sample spot
copy with recommended production music in the folder hoping
to make your job as simple as possible. If you develop an
effective piece of copy or creative production technique,
won't you pass your version along to us? We'll send your
suggestions to all other cooperating stations so that the
ideas continue to flow.

You'll find a list of all the stations who have joined the
"Drive With FM" campaign as of August 5. We hope at next
mailing to report more than 1000 participants!

Included also is the first release sent to all major trade
and automotive press. We think it should get an impressive
play in all the papers. (See VARIETY; July 27, p. 40:
BILLBOARD; August 6, p. 24). You might want to send the
same information to your local newspapers.

Jim Perry of WEDA-FM, Grove City, Pennsylvania, has already
made concrete use of his station's participation in the
drive. A copy of his letter is enclosed. Perhaps you might
want to make a similar mail'ng, or even tailor a special
presentation to dealers in your area to turn up new revenue.

VOLVO Dealers in New York are already on the bandwagon!
The enclosed promotion sheets are designed by VOLVO for
dealer use as envelope stuffers, promotional mailers and
hand-outs in their showrooms. It's nice to know that an
auto manufacturer sees the importance of "an FM Radio in
every car"!

Our thanks again for your active and enthusiastic response
in this important venture. Won't you also keep us apprised
of how YOU use "Drive With FM"?

Cordially,

Lynn A. Christian

Lynn A. Christian, WPIX-FM
Director, "Drive With FM"

NAFMB · 45 west 45th street · new york city · 212 LT 1-2980

| Television offers increased coverage of the Vietnam War. | FCC authorizes COMSAT to operate commercial facilities. |

channel). The FCC gave satellite communications further encouragement by authorizing COMSAT to operate commercial facilities.

The industry was in good shape financially and statistically in 1965. More than 30 million radio sets were sold that year, about a fourth of them with FM. Almost 99% of all homes and 80% of automobiles had radios. Television was now in 93% of U.S. households. Four thousand radio stations were on the air, some 1,300 of them FM. Two hundred and fifty noncommercial educational FM stations were in operation. Five hundred and seventy commercial TV stations and 100 noncommercial educational TV stations were operating. In fact, the rapid growth and importance of educational television prompted efforts to build it into a system that could be a national alternative to commercial television. To study and determine such options, the Carnegie Commission on Educational Television was established.

But two rivals to broadcasting loomed large, one with its foot already in the door and the other on the horizon. The number of households with cable television had doubled in five years and now exceeded 1.3 million, served by more than 1,300 community cable systems. The National Cable Television Association (NCTA) made its presence known when it hired as its president a former FCC chair, Frederick W. Ford. The competition on the horizon came from the Far East, as the first videotape recorders (the VTR, later the VCR), the Sony Videocorders, which sold for $995 with a 9-inch receiver, came into U.S. homes.

Other horizons visually came closer in 1965. The previous year an international conference had established INTELSAT, a global satellite communications system. On June 28, 1965, it was inaugurated with INTELSAT I, called *Early Bird*, transmitting across the Atlantic Ocean. Not long after that, one of the authors of this book was invited to a gala event where, on a giant screen in Washington's Mayflower Hotel ballroom, he saw another miracle of the new satellite communications age: the first television transmission between Japan and the United States. For international telecommunications, it seemed that not even the sky was the limit.

1966

The war in Vietnam not only was a subject for television news but directly affected the operations of television in 1966. The networks continued to refuse to be critical of U.S. involvement, and sometimes they even distorted coverage to avoid stimulating negative public concern or embarrassing the administration. To do so at the time would have been considered controversial and, to some, even un-American. As *Variety*, the industry newspaper, finally put it, the networks were guilty of "no guts journalism." So many voters were outraged, however, that in early 1966 the Senate began hearings on Vietnam. After initial coverage of the hearings, CBS abruptly stopped and substituted reruns of *I Love Lucy* and *The Real McCoys*. The CBS News president, Fred Friendly—one of the few news executives who displayed consistent integrity as well as courage—resigned in protest.

Supreme Court rules state and local film censorship unconstitutional.	César Chávez hunger strike sparks grape boycott.	Watts ghetto explodes.

Communication satellite Intelstat 1 is launched.	The Carnegie Commission on Educational Television is established.

By the following year, antiwar protests had spread throughout the country, and network news programs were no longer able to ignore the demonstrations and marches by millions of Americans. Broadcasting provided more and more coverage, and finally individual journalists and news teams began to probe for the truth of what

FIG 6.11 Network coverage of the Vietnam War was extensive and had a profound effect on viewers.
Courtesy Irving Fang.

Ralph Nader consumer
crusade begins.

New slogans reflect a changing culture: "Flower power,"
"Make love, not war," "Drop out, turn on, tune in."

1966

Videotape recorders
(VTRs) enter
American homes.

Early Bird satellite
transmits across
the Atlantic ocean.

THE SOARING '60S

was happening. Their continuing efforts for honest coverage through succeeding years contributed to the government's eventually ending the war. It was television's stories on Vietnam and the public protests that reportedly persuaded President Lyndon Johnson not to run for another term. One account alleges that after he saw Walter Cronkite criticizing his military policy in Vietnam, Johnson decided that if Cronkite opposed him, then the average American couldn't be far behind and he had lost his base of support.

Citizen sensibility and outspoken action affected television programming directly. After 15 years on CBS television, the most recent ones as a variety program rather than in its original sitcom form, *Amos 'n' Andy* could not survive the civil rights movement of the 1960s, and public antipathy to its stereotyping and alleged racism forced it off the air for good. "People power" was reflected in other ways as well. A highly innovative show that made its debut in 1965 was the science fiction adventure series *Star Trek*. It bombed in the ratings, consistently finishing near the back of the prime-time pack, never higher than number 52. There was no way it could survive in bottom-line broadcasting. But a vociferous letter-writing cult developed around the show's essentially antiwar, prohumanistic story lines, reflecting the mood of much of the country. Accordingly, the series was kept on the air for three years, eventually

FIG 6.12 Network TV struck pay dirt in the mid-1960s with an adaptation of the comic strip favorite *Batman*. The show starred Adam West and Burt Ward. *Courtesy Artist's Proof, Alexandria, Virginia.*

Vietnam War protests spread across nation.

Miniskirts new fashion rage.

CBS News President Fred Friendly resigns in protest over network's unwillingness to deal with the Vietnam War issue.

ABC introduces prime-time movie blockbusters.

spawning a series of theatrical movies, a new *Star Trek: The Next Generation* TV series—which did better commercially than the first one—followed by more spin-off series and frequent syndicated repeats of the original one. Captain Kirk, Mr. Spock, and other characters remained household words through the remainder of the century, as did annual conventions of "Trekkies."

The so-called '60s generation was represented on the FCC as well. Appointed in 1966 by President Johnson, Commissioner Nicholas Johnson (no relation) vigorously and unabashedly symbolized the public interest—putting the needs of the consumer above the profits of the industry. For the next seven years, to the end of his term, Johnson would push for public interest rules and regulations that angered many broadcasters and annoyed his more conservative colleagues.

ANN LORING

ACTRESS AND WRITER _____

FIG 6.13 *Courtesy Ann Loring.*

Much maligned, too often ridiculed, soap operas have long been the butt of the TV critics . . . a reputation they do not deserve.

I have worked in soaps from the time they were shot in black and white, and "live," and little old men were careless with the prompting cards, when dinosaurs were nibbling the last green leaves from the trees, until ultimately I completed a 14-year leading role on *Love of Life*. This history, although it does inescapably "date" me, nevertheless does afford my hoary soul a maven's credibility.

Ergo the following statements:

a. Probably the toughest acting job that exists (and I have known them all . . . theater, film, radio) is playing a major role in a daytime drama, as they are now euphemistically called. Absolutely true!

Imagine committing 40 to 50 pages of dialogue to memory night after night, then struggling exhausted the next morning to face cold coffee, a minuscule three- to four-hour rehearsal, always digging deep into the recesses of your brain to find the words . . . oh, those words . . . then finally facing the ultimate terror: the invisible audience of some 26 million viewers ready to judge your performance for its emotional honesty and truth, developed within these bare bones of time.

Even more distressing, imaging being judged by critics as though one had had the luxury of a week's rehearsal or more, such as in extended prime-time shows. A consummation devoutly to be wished! I reiterate, it is the most taxing acting job of all, given these incredible circumstances.

b. My second statement bespeaks the courage of the various production staffs. Long before prime time dared, the soaps were already beginning to deal with such sensitive topics as abortion, mental illness, drug addiction, and teenage suicide. Soaps dared to make touch-and-go landings on the "untouchable" runways of general television fare.

Of course, the interplay of relationships: the unrequited love, jealousies, innumerable pregnancies, dalliances, spouse-stealing and spouse-switching and the consequent villainies were, and will continue to be, the thrust of most story lines.

But credit them, the soaps dared! They were the brave front, the very first to breach the ever-threatening enemy lines of censorship.

There is so much more to say had I but time and space. It is enough to remind one that soaps have molded taste, fashion, even behavior. The viewer, in a way that is almost beyond understanding, seems to identify and bond with his favorite character so powerfully, with such seriousness, that upon occasion he is unable to distinguish between his own life's reality and what appears on the screen.

Even after all these years, the influence of the soaps remains startling to me. Perhaps the strength of this influence is best illustrated by the following example: Some years ago, in our story line, a mature woman was in a hospital dying of a rare disease. It was the decision that this character would die after several months of suffering her illness. During this sequence, the producer received a letter from a doctor in a nearby New York hospital, who wrote that he was treating a patient ill with this same rare disease. His patient, he told us, unfailingly watched our show each day and reacted in precise parallel to the condition of the screen character. Knowing this, the doctor pleaded with the producer to be sure to keep the character alive—for surely if she were to die, he would certainly lose his patient.

Needless to say, a conference was called, [and] the story line rewritten so that the character began to grow better in a daily sequence of improvement.

One morning, a month later, a Jeroboam of champagne arrived at the studio. With it came a touching thank-you note. The real patient was rallying and the doctor would forevermore be grateful.

Need I say more?

Another Lyndon Johnson appointment was also a surprise but not at all controversial. When FCC Chairman Henry resigned in 1966, the President, instead of naming a Democrat to succeed him, named a sitting commissioner and a former chair, Rosel H. Hyde, a moderate Republican who had started his career with the old Federal Radio Commission. Because much of Lyndon Johnson's personal fortune was

Apollo 1 astronauts burn to death on launching pad.

Use of hallucinogenic drugs on the rise.

1967

FCC issues several regulatory actions, including applying the Fairness Doctrine to cigarette advertising.

ABC plans four radio networks.

based on broadcast holdings, some believed he was attempting to avoid charges of conflict of interest that might have been leveled had he appointed someone from his own party, politically beholden to him. Hyde kept the commission on an even keel for several years, leaving only when the next President, Richard M. Nixon, appointed his own chair.

Spy and war films were popular on TV and, to fill the "software" gap, NBC started to produce its own made-for-TV movies. ABC went it one better and paid millions to present the first blockbuster movie in prime time, *The Bridge on the River Kwai.* This action started a trend that still continues.

ABC, in third place and hurting financially, attempted to merge with International Telephone and Telegraph (IT&T). This arrangement would have provided the network with a needed infusion of money and created a new conglomerate with expanded media power. Although the FCC approved the merger, the Department of Justice fought it and the following year it was canceled. An attempt to establish a fourth commercial network failed, too. The Overmyer Network was established in 1966, became the United Network, and went on the air in 1967 with programs broadcast on 125 stations; a lack of advertisers caused it to fold in a month. Though regional and specialized networks (such as sports) were able to make it, another national network didn't come on the scene again for 20 years. Then, with the huge resources of its founder, Rupert Murdoch, to back it, the Fox network not only survived but began to grow.

Cable continued to expand, with national corporations such as GE, Time, Inc., and various regional telephone companies entering the field. The FCC, deciding it was time to assert strong jurisdiction over cable, mandated that cable systems carry all local broadcast stations and limit importation of distant signals. Meanwhile, the commission closely monitored and occasionally checked the medium's growth in major metropolitan markets.

In addition, that other future competition to broadcasting, still just a gleam, made a little headway as the price of VTRs came down to about $400.

1967

The FCC, spurred by Commissioners Johnson and Cox and responding to the public's assertion of its rights, issued a number of strong regulatory actions in 1967. Among them were rules requiring Fairness Doctrine implementation of time to answer personal attacks on any individual (the *Red Lion* case, still not decided by the Supreme Court), banning station identifications that misled the audience on the station's city of location, and—one of the most controversial rulings in the history of broadcast regulation—applying the Fairness Doctrine to cigarette advertising. Petitioned by John F. Banzhaf III, an attorney and professor of law, and relying on the findings of the surgeon general's office on smoking and health, the FCC ruled that stations carrying cigarette commercials had to present antismoking viewpoints or offer time to antismoking organizations. Despite vehement industry protests and lawsuits, the FCC had the backing of the Federal Trade Commission (FTC) and other government offices, and the courts found the FCC action to be constitutional. It was this ruling that led Congress, a few years later, to ban all cigarette advertising on television and radio, a ban that went into effect on January 2, 1971. Why January 2, instead of the more logical January 1? It gave the television industry and cigarette manufacturers a final huge audience to whom to sell their wares: those watching the January 1 football bowl games.

Cigarette Advertising's Last Hurrah

Following the Surgeon General's 1962 report confirming the deleterious effect of tobacco, mild notices were placed on these products. Antismoking groups sought to get these warnings on the air, with limited success. Broadcasters that complied often placed these public service announcements (PSAs) in the wee hours of the morning. Action on Smoking and Health (ASH), the group guided by Attorney Banzhaf, appealed to the FCC to invoke the Fairness Doctrine, eventually seeking a "fair" balance since there were no tobacco commercials airing at 2:00 A.M., and a 3:1 ratio between tobacco ads and antismoking spots. To their surprise, and without much further deliberation, the FCC consented. In effect, this meant the tobacco companies would be subsidizing the opposition; the more ads they ran, the more anti-smoking PSAs aired. When the idea of a ban on smoking ads in broadcasting surfaced, the tobacco companies vehemently resisted.

However, in 1968, the Federal Trade Commission indicated it might seek to prohibit all tobacco ads in other media and venues. In an effort to prevent the loss of all advertising, the cigarette companies opted to move out of the then high-profile radio and TV ads. The industry acquiesced to the broadcasting embargo on the ads, and in 1969, Congress passed the ban, which took effect on January 2, 1971 (the cigarette and broadcast companies pressured the FCC to allow the last ads to run during the New Year's Day football games). A few minutes before midnight, January 1, 1971, on NBC's *Tonight Show*, Virginia Slims ran the final cigarette commercial ever on television.

In cable, two companies were formed for the express purpose of providing regular programming to cable systems, going beyond simply carrying off-the-air broadcast stations. In radio, ABC was authorized to establish four news networks, an innovative approach to providing different kinds of news to different kinds of audiences. A dozen years later, other radio networks would follow suit, and a trend of multiple, short-form (as little as one program or one program series) and long-form (a continuous block of time, similar to the old radio structure) offerings of various specialized formats to affiliates developed. This scheme helped radio networks to survive and grow.

First heart transplant, performed
by Dr. Christiaan Barnard.

Corporation for Public
Broadcasting is
established.

The rebellious nature of much of the country was reflected in radio by what was to become known as the underground rock format. Tom "Big Daddy" Donahue, a former disciple of "more music king" Bill Drake, inaugurated underground radio's precursor, progressive radio, at KMPX in San Francisco. While vacationing at home, Donahue arrived at the conclusion that only one or at best two cuts on any hit album were getting airplay and that the remaining cuts were being ignored. This realization led him to implement an album cut–intensive format at a time when AM Top 40 was the reigning monarch of the airwaves. Several months after Donahue's programming innovation, Boston's WBCN-FM initiated a free-form (anything goes) progressive format. Soon there were dozens of such stations across the country.

Owing in part to their nonconformist image, derived from the unorthodox mix of music and announcers who often sounded sedated—what one observer referred to as "those voices from the purple haze" (a reference to a popular rock song of the period)—many of these stations became part of the much-ballyhooed counterculture movement. The term *underground*, with its clandestine and subversive connotations, was ascribed to stations that gave the impression (if nothing more) of being outside the mainstream of American thinking on such issues as war, sex, and drugs. The so-called underground stations—a phrase that prompted a snicker from the leader of the Black Panthers, Eldridge Cleaver, who thought it an absurdly inappropriate name when such stations could readily be tuned in on any radio receiver, from the White House to Shaker Heights—were also later referred to as "acid rockers" because of their heavy emphasis on music associated with the psychedelic drug movement. The climate of social unrest that existed, at a time when rock music was becoming more diffused and a substantial segment of the radio audience was disenchanted with the predominance of the highly formulaic Top 40 sound, gave real impetus to the album rock format.

In the meantime, educators had convinced both President Johnson and Congress that it was time for the establishment of an educational television network. The congressional plan was based on the Carnegie Commission's report, *Public Television: A Program for Action*. After many months of lobbying, radio was included, and the Public Broadcasting Act of 1967 was passed. Its principal provision was to establish the Corporation for Public Broadcasting (CPB), which, with federal funding and an independent board of directors—somewhat along the lines of the BBC—was to set up one or more national systems of public television and public radio. Within a few years CPB had created, for television, the Public Broadcasting Service (PBS) and, for radio, National Public Radio (NPR). Whether President Johnson's key role in getting the legislation passed was for political or educational reasons—or both—has been debated by public broadcasting historians. One of the authors of this book, who was involved in the Public Broadcasting Act legislation, was at the bill-signing ceremony at the White House and chatted briefly with the President about his role and the fact that inasmuch as the first public television station was KUHT in Texas, it was appropriate that a President from Texas should be responsible for this next historical step.

Antiwar sentiment forces President
Johnson not to seek reelection.

Martin Luther King, Jr.,
assassinated in Memphis.

1968

FCC authorizes
pay TV.

Apollo 7 sends first live telecast
from manned spacecraft.

Outlandish Sitcoms Follow TV's Golden Age

The appellation of television's Golden Age refers to the abundance of mostly live original and classical dramas that dominated prime time in the 1950s, frequently with a lone sponsor who insisted they steer clear of socially and politically controversial themes. By the close of the decade critics began ruminating that these idealistic morality tales were becoming stale and repetitious. Additionally, television was spreading from its East Coast, more cosmopolitan, base to the rest of the country. Early in the 1960s, as the nation began to experience the societal upheavals that would define the decade, the medium turned to bizarre fantasy sitcoms marked by the likes of talking horses and cars, genies, benign witches, flying nuns, friendly ghouls, millionaire hillbillies, and the introduction of prime-time animation. What prompted this switch from serious, albeit narrowly prescribed, dramas is not clear, but three factors may have contributed: (1) major Hollywood studios became more involved with television production and its facilities allowed for more audacious plots; (2) a perceived need to appeal to a growing, more heterogeneous mass audience; (3) and a yearning to evade reality, assassinations, the violent repression of civil rights marches, and a growingly unpopular and endless war.

1968

The year 1968 was a high-water mark of protest, of going underground to fight the establishment, of trying to make changes in the structure of the country. There were underground newspapers, underground magazines, and underground radio stations. People fought not only against the war abroad but against poverty and discrimination at home. When they did so openly, they suffered, sometimes by harassment and beatings and sometimes worse, as in the government's predawn raid in 1969 of a Chicago apartment where the leaders of the Black Panthers were sleeping, killing two of them in their beds. Blood, death, and tears galvanized America, especially its youth.

Television covered student demonstrations on college and university campuses all over the country. Urban demonstrations became violent. "Revolts," some called them; others said "riots." "Burn, baby, burn!" was a battle cry heard frequently on TV news, as desperate, underprivileged people, facing hopeless poverty and racism, futilely torched and rioted.

Not only were militant protesters attacked, but two mainstream leaders, the Reverend Martin Luther King, Jr., and Senator Robert F. Kennedy, were assassinated that year. The latter happened virtually in our living rooms, on TV, on Presidential primary day in California. Television also showed us, live, the police violence against protesters at the Democratic National Convention in Chicago, shocking America just

Robert F. Kennedy assassinated in Los Angeles.	Richard Nixon defeats Hubert Humphrey for Presidency.

Extensive television coverage of the King and RFK assassinations and police violence against protesters at the Democratic National Convention in Chicago.	Handheld cameras are used at the national political conventions.

as the police violence against protesting civil rights marchers in the South had done only a few years before.

Though television was now willing to report more of the truth of America's rebellion, it was unwilling to take a controversial viewpoint itself, as Murrow and Friendly would have done. Public television, through PBS's predecessor, National Educational Television (NET), tried to, with an *Inside Vietnam* documentary that was promptly attacked by a number of members of Congress as being un-American and pro-Communist. Two young comedians who had quickly risen in the ratings with their *Smothers Brothers* TV show tried to reflect the mood of the country and angered their network, CBS, by insisting on putting on the folk guitarist and singer, Pete Seeger, playing his popular anti-Vietnam War song, "The Big Muddy." The Smothers Brothers continued to inject political and social humor and comments into their programs until the following year, when CBS, still headed by William Paley, abruptly threw them off the air for not being, as the network put it, sufficiently "mainstream." Was Joe McCarthy laughing in his grave?

The Tet Offensive in Vietnam in early 1968—a bloody, massive assault by Vietcong and North Vietnamese forces into South Vietnam—revealed an enemy stronger than the military had led the public to believe. Key opinion makers like Walter Cronkite began to express misgivings about the war. Given the turmoil and the mood of the country and the erosion of his popular support, President Johnson made a television address in which he described the state of the war, announced a halt to the U.S. bombing, and then, unexpectedly, stated he would not run for reelection.

The "Birth" of Public Television

Public television in the United States has never been as vibrant as most of its foreign counterparts, primarily because it was the "second child," emerging long after commercial broadcasting had been entrenched as the primary system. Even when it moved from a loose confederation of local and generally poorly funded noncommercial, educational television stations into a more cohesive structure called National Educational Television (NET) in 1963, it was still teetering on the edge of irrelevance, relying on mostly stale prerecorded programming. Some feared it would follow the path of educational radio, which began with great enthusiasm, then through a combination of events fell into near total neglect. Public television's fortunes began to turn in 1967, when, with the backing of the Ford Foundation, it was able to interconnect a number of educational stations with several hours per week of live programming featuring a weekly Sunday night news and feature program, the *Public Broadcasting Laboratory*. It was also in 1967 that the Carnegie Commission on Educational Television issued its seminal report that defined the mission for a public broadcasting system, and political leaders began to take serious notice, eventually leading to the passage of the Public Broadcasting Act of 1967.

Jackie Kennedy marries Aristotle Onassis.	*Hair*, with nude performances, debuts; first rock musical.	911 emergency telephone system inaugurated.

Action for Children's Television (ACT) is formed.

PACIFICA RADIO NEWS

WASHINGTON D.C.

Pacifica Radio News: National & International Coverage

Pacifica Radio News provides 7-10 national and international daily stories, Monday through Friday covering breaking news with analysis and producing feature stories and follow-up pieces.

To help you plan your newscast, we send pre-broadcast DACs messages with story slugs, reporters names, story lengths and suggested leads when available.

Pacifica reporters Elaine Korry and Judy Shimel at the Washington Bureau.

k Reinhard

As a subscriber, you'll have full rights to use the feed in whole or in part, to rebroadcast any segments and to reuse the actualities in other productions.

Pacifica's 29 minute daily newscast is distributed by satellite. Rates are set on a sliding scale. A sample cassette is available.

Pacifica Radio News: Since 1968

In 1968 Pacifica Radio News was established to provide provocative, detailed and alternative news coverage for the five Pacifica stations. Today Pacifica Radio News is still committed to these same goals, featuring stories and perspectives from around the world.

Our reporters have won awards for their coverage—the battle of DaNang and anti-war protests, to name a few. We cover contemporary issues before a crisis brings them into the commercial media. For example, Pacifica was reporting on health risks of low-level radiation and covering the nuclear industry long before the nuclear accident at Three Mile Island. And we reported on "private" Contra connections way before it became "news" on other broadcasting services.

Washington Bureau Chief Dan Collison hosting the newscast.

Rick Reinhard

We provide live, daily coverage of congressional investigative hearings–of Vietnam, Watergate, and more recently the Iran-Contra affair. And we've been on the campaign trail since 1972, producing gavel to gavel coverage of the Democratic and Republican Conventions as well as following the Women's and Minority Caucuses.

Pacifica's half-hour daily newscast is independent, critical. We use a wide range of sources and look outside officialdom for perspectives ranging from the far right to the far left and everything in-between. With correspondents across the United States and throughout the world, our coverage is thorough and provocative.

Pacifica Radio News Covers:

• The Reagan Courts: Are civil rights and Roe vs. Wade history?

• Intimidation and harassment of government opponents.
• What's really behind the Middle East peace process.
• Racism in the 80s: Howard Beach to Forsythe County.
• The southern African Front Line states fight back.
• The Sanctuary movement: roots & roadblocks.
• Big Mountain: Native American genocide?
• Corporate takeovers and the mass media.
• The growing gap between rich and poor.
• The Gulf War & U.S. escort diplomacy.
• AIDS: public policy and private pain.
• The Washington/Pretoria partnership.
• The Soviet Union: Wither Glasnost?
• Arms control: formula for build-up?
• Organized labor in the Eighties.
• Philippines: Is it people power?
• Covert action at home & abroad.
• Chernobyl: Can it happen here?
• Realities of the Contra war.
• Apartheid on the West Bank.
• Toxic Waste: Who gets it?
• The Salvadoran air war.
• Lesbian and gay rights.
• And more . . .

FIG 6.14 Pacifica Radio has presented some of the medium's most innovative and controversial programming since its inception in 1949. *Courtesy Pacifica Radio.*

The nation's attitudes spurred some changes in broadcasting. In Boston, a group of mothers concerned about the increasingly low quality of children's programs, including violence, sexism, racism, and the cupidity of advertisers, formed Action for Children's Television (ACT), which during the next few decades proved to be a thorn in the side of the FCC, Congress, broadcasters, and sponsors in its attempts to improve the quality of children's programs and reduce the avarice of commercials. ACT continued into the 1990s under the leadership of one of its original founders, Peggy Charren.

One of the emerging gurus of underground broadcasting was Lorenzo Milam, who, frequently without compensation, helped radio stations get on the air and develop programming that reflected the attitudes and dissent of large, voiceless segments of the populace.

Daytime programs for "housewives" began to change, with less emphasis on the stereotypes of clothes, cooking, and cosmetics and increased attention to the political, social, and economic concerns of the community, including its women members.

U.S. lands first humans on moon.

Woodstock concert draws almost a half million.

1969

Sesame Street begins its telecasts.

The number of talk shows, discussing the furious controversies of the time, increased, with 18 such programs in syndication in 1968. One irony: Although changing attitudes toward sex and violence were key aspects of a changing America, networks censored the sex and violence aspects of films shown on TV.

After lengthy consideration, the FCC officially authorized pay TV. Pay TV's potential supplanting of advertiser-supported "free TV" was still not given serious credence. One technical development strengthened TV's ability to cover and disseminate the news: A handheld camera developed by CBS was used with great success at the national political conventions.

Television's Role in the Civil Rights Movement

In the 1960s, television lent a new urgency to the decades-long struggle for basic human and civil rights. There's no denying the transcendental eloquence of Dr. King or the rhetoric of President Kennedy, particularly his spontaneous address to the nation in June 1963 reacting to the governor of Alabama standing in the doorway of the state university to block the registration of black students. But what possibly moved white America to support civil rights legislation was seeing, for the first time, the visceral, visual brutality of the racist hierarchy in the South in contrast to the serene demeanor of the protestors. The drama and sensationalism of peaceful civil rights protestors in defiance of the violent, despicable behavior of the segregationists was not lost on news producers who needed to fill their expanded newscasts. Among the nearly everyday confrontations, the brutal murder of three civil rights organizers and an all-white jury's eventual acquittal of their accused murderers, the frequent burnings of black churches, and the particularly vile oppression directed by Bull Connor, the Birmingham, Alabama, Commissioner of Public Safety were fed nightly into the 90% of U.S. households with television sets and may have done more to move public opinion than any glowing oratory.

1969

The year 1969 witnessed both Woodstock and people on the moon. Woodstock was reported in the media as the epitome of the 1960s "hippie" or "flower child" generation; 500,000 people arrived at a farm in upstate New York to listen to contemporary music's greatest stars and rebel against the establishment with the slogan and action "Make love, not war."

On July 20, 1969, all the networks televised the first landing of human beings on the moon, from the *Apollo 11* spacecraft. Neil Armstrong's "One small step for man, one giant leap for mankind" entered the lexicon of famous quotes. People who didn't have TV sets at the time of the event rented them so they could watch. While Vietnam was tearing the country apart, for a moment the moon landing brought it together.

Nuclear nonproliferation treaty approved.

Electronic media report on Woodstock and the moon landing.

The Smothers Brothers TV show is canceled.

FRED ROGERS

THE LATE FRED ROGERS WAS A PERFORMER IN AND PRODUCER OF CHILDREN'S PROGRAMMING _____

When I reminisce about my career, I think fondly of my days as a "gofer" at NBC in New York, about the *Hit Parade*, *The Kate Smith Show*, the *NBC Opera Theater*, the first color telecast—all of which I helped floor-manage back in the early 1950s. I recollect, too, the stories about beginning WQED in Pittsburgh (before it even went on the air), our first children's program, *Children's Corner*, which ran between 1954 and 1961. Of course, a very vivid recollection is the launching of *Mister Rogers* in Toronto, which was broadcast by CBC. I always smile when I think back to serving as floor manager at NBC (after being a gofer) in Studio 3K, where

cameras were telecasting in color. There were only three color sets in all of New York that could receive such transmissions. General Sarnoff had one, Niles Trammel another, and I think some vice president had the third. Anyway, I was the first floor manager for those telecasts—and I'm color blind!

FIG 6.15 Fred Rogers.
Courtesy Fred Rogers.

America watched a wide variety of television programs that year. The Children's Television Workshop (CTW) was established and promptly produced *Sesame Street*, arguably the most popular and meaningful children's TV program in history, still continuing in the United States and many foreign countries into the 21st century. *Sesame Street* was designed to provide preschool learning for disadvantaged children. Although the show has often been criticized for catering principally to children of the relatively affluent middle class in terms of its materials and values, it has nevertheless had a demonstrated impact on the early learning of language and numbers on the part of all children who watch and has inculcated understanding of different cultures, races, and beliefs.

With *The Smothers Brothers* dropped, another show, building on the comedy approach of *The Smothers Brothers*, made its debut. *Rowan and Martin's Laugh-In* introduced the burlesque, blackout-skit format to television and, while avoiding any

Police kill Black Panther leaders in Chicago raid.

Public Broadcasting System (PBS) begins operation.

Vice President Spiro Agnew accuses media of bias.

highly charged controversial topics, nonetheless included bits of topical satire. *Laugh-In* was so popular that Presidential candidate Richard Nixon appeared as a guest in 1968, uttering the show's "Sock it to me" tag line. Although some viewers thought his appearance ludicrous, enough people felt he proved he was a "regular guy" and he gained many votes. The show became the model for later successful programs of this genre, principally *Saturday Night Live*. Another comedy event, although for the participants perhaps not intended as such, was the highly hyped marriage of performer Tiny Tim and Miss Vicki on Johnny Carson's *The Tonight Show*.

A new network got under way, with CPB establishing PBS as an alternative to commercial broadcasting, using federal funds and a generous grant from the Ford Foundation.

The FCC was busy. A conservative Republican, Dean Burch, who had been manager of the 1964 Goldwater Presidential campaign, was appointed new FCC chair by the new President, Richard Nixon. The days of consumer-oriented, tough regulation might soon have ended, but the times prompted the FCC to continue its public interest standards for some years more. For the first time, the FCC voluntarily revoked the license of a TV station on the grounds of monopolistic cross-ownership: Boston's WHDH, co-owned with the *Herald-Traveler*, a daily Boston newspaper. Earlier violations of rules by WHDH regarding *ex parte* undue influence on commissioners were also considered factors. After appeals by the stations failed—the company also owned local AM and FM radio stations—the revocation became final in 1972.

Revocation of the license of WLBT, Mississippi—finally ordered in 1969 by the Supreme Court, which chastised the FCC for not doing it sooner following the 1965 federal district court's order—gave heart to a number of citizen organizations representing multicultural groups traditionally denied equal access to or programming by the media. As a result, a number of citizen petitions to deny license renewals were filed at the FCC.

The commission affirmed a three-year trafficking rule, which required the purchaser of a station to hold it for at least three years before selling it. This requirement precluded buying a station for a quick turnover and profit without regard to programming in the public interest. The FCC authorized cable to carry commercial advertising on systems of more than 3,500 subscribers, provided that the income was used for original programming.

In 1969 the Supreme Court upheld the FCC's Fairness Doctrine, and the privilege of replying to personal attacks, in its *Red Lion* decision (see years 1964 and 1967), stating, "It is the right of the viewers and listeners, not the right of the broadcasters, which is paramount."

One of the hallmarks of the new Nixon presidency was its continuing confrontations with the press and its attempts, on several occasions, to browbeat the media and influence news coverage of the administration. Such actions began early, with a

198

televised address by Vice President Spiro Agnew attacking the media as biased. Although the media responded that the charges were themselves biased and untrue, Agnew's continued attacks had a chilling effect on media news commentary. The press was objective and even relatively kind to Agnew when, a few years later, he was forced to resign to avoid the possibility of impeachment because of corruption.

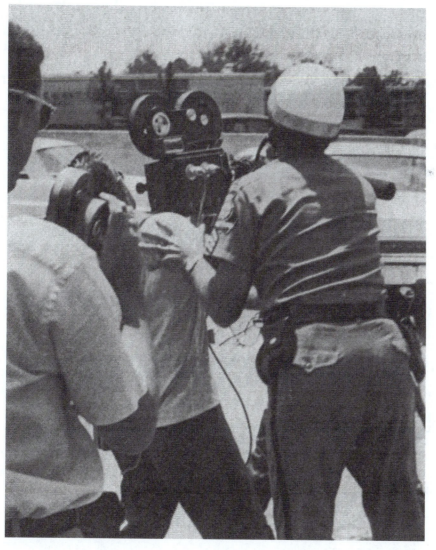

FIG. 6.16 Television film crews and the law sometimes clashed during the heated 1960s. *Courtesy Irving Fang.*

Chapter SEVEN

The Shifting '7O s

Q and A and Jiggle

The new decade began as the previous one had ended. Vietnam was topic number one in 1970, with broadcasting expanding its coverage of nationwide protests as the protests themselves escalated. There was much to cover, including the National Guard's killing of student protesters at Kent State and Jackson State universities. Kent State, where the students were white, received then and still receives strong media attention; Jackson State, where the students were black, was and is still largely ignored by the media.

President Richard Nixon was unhappy with broadcasting's coverage of events. Believing that television and radio were distorting his policies and purposes for political reasons, he did not hesitate to attack the press—electronic and print—as biased. Nixon established a new governmental communications organization, the White House Office of Telecommunications Policy (OTP), appointing Clay T. (Tom) Whitehead as director. The OTP was designed to be both an initiating and a coordinating point for the nation's communications development. Through the OTP, Nixon was in a position to determine long- and short-range policy, including policy toward broadcasting. Tom Whitehead threatened broadcasters that if they didn't "correct imbalance or consistent bias" toward the administration, they would be held "fully responsible at license renewal time." Believing that the PBS network was also guilty of liberal bias in its programming, Nixon had Whitehead attempt to drive a wedge between the nation's public broadcasting stations and PBS. Although some broadcasters cooperated with the administration, most were unwilling to be intimidated.

PLURIA MARSHALL

CEO OF THE NATIONAL BLACK MEDIA COALITION, WHICH "MADE A DIFFERENCE" _____

I came into the field of broadcast activism through my work with the Southern Christian Leadership Conference (SCLC) in Houston. In 1971, I was heading Houston's "Operation Breadbasket," one of the SCLC operations that Jesse Jackson had headed. We were doing what we could in Houston— lawsuits, citizen pressure, boycotts—to get racist companies to hire some black employees. And we got a lot of jobs opened up. But the media, which were, after all, controlled by big business and big businessmen, were against us and made

Four students killed by National Guard at Kent
State, two at Jackson State in antiwar protests.

1970

Electronic media cover
Kent State massacre.

First black in title role
in TV sitcom: Diahann
Carroll in *Julia*.

President Nixon attacks
media for alleged
distortion and bias.

FIG 7.1 Pluria Marshall.
Courtesy Pluria Marshall.

everything we did look sinister. They refused
to acknowledge our successes or even be
fair in their coverage of our activities.

That didn't surprise us, because radio
and television stations by and large had
few or no black or Hispanic employees and
weren't providing programs that recognized
the needs of the large black and Hispanic
populations of the Houston area. So, in
1971 we challenged the licenses of 11
stations, and in 1974 we challenged eight
more, under an organization that was
called Black Citizens for Media Access.

A number of civil rights activists like
myself throughout the country realized how
important the media were in efforts for civil
rights and equal rights for blacks,
Hispanics, other people of color, and
women. A man named Bill Wright had been
traveling throughout the country training
people like me, in various cities, how to
fight for media access and fairness. He
was then heading an organization called
BEST, Black Efforts for Soul in Television.

Under Bill Wright's leadership, a group of
us gathered in Washington, D.C., in 1973 as
the organizing body of NBMC, the National
Black Media Coalition. Bill Wright was the
"Godfather" of the whole movement.

Jim McCullough became the head of
NBMC. At the end of 1974, I moved from
Houston to Washington to become NBMC's
unpaid executive director, and in 1975 I
became CEO when McCullough left. But we
still had little monetary support and in
1976 I moved back to Houston, from where
I continued to run NBMC.

We filed hundreds of petitions with the
FCC, challenging stations' licenses. The
Citizens Communication Center was getting
grant money to act as attorneys for us. But
we didn't get a share of the money, which
kept them afloat, to help keep us afloat. In a
way we were being used, and in 1978 we
broke off with Citizens Communication Center.

We managed to get some funding and in
1980 I returned to Washington as the paid
CEO of NBMC. One of our major successes
was with the Gannett Company. They
wanted to buy Combined Communications.
While most citizen groups were against
extending their monopoly power, we were
able to come to an agreement to support
Gannett; they would see to it that Ragan
Henry would become the first black to own
a TV network affiliate. This was a huge step
forward that no other organization had
given us.

The first big grant for NBMC was from
Gannett in 1981, and they've been
providing grants since. Gannett is one of 40
or 50 companies that have been giving us
support. By 1984 we were making big
strides. We were suing any broadcasting
company that discriminated against blacks.
One of our big actions for equal opportunity
was against the Times-Mirror Company.

Nixon creates Office of
Telecommunications
Policy, appointing Clay
T. Whitehead director.

"Frito Bandito"
commercial is banished
from airwaves.

FCC institutes EEO
requirement for stations.

They agreed to provide about $2 million to facilitate black station ownership and fund communications scholarships for black students, among other things, and they increased their number of black employees to 10% in three years.

We managed to really change the attitudes of media owners toward blacks in the industry. Even lack of cooperation from other groups that should have helped us, such as the National Association of Black Journalists—too many of them were dependent for their jobs and promotions on the very companies we were suing—didn't keep us from keeping our eye on the prize.

After a while even the FCC—maybe because it knew we'd continue to kick butt if they didn't act—was sometimes willing to take action on its own against stations. For example, there's the case of WXBM-FM, in Milton, Florida. We brought it to the attention of the FCC, and the FCC found the station guilty of discriminatory practices. The station then corrected those practices, but the FCC didn't let it off the hook, and set it for hearing because of its past practices.

Another example: NBMC led the way in the only major affirmative action victory against broadcasting in the Supreme Court. In the recent Shurburg case, out of Hartford, Connecticut, and the Metro case, from Orlando, Florida, the Supreme Court upheld the FCC's minority preference policy. I want to note that both of these were Hispanic cases—the NBMC doesn't only deal with black cases but acts on behalf of all groups denied equal opportunity in employment, ownership, and programming.

One of our most significant ongoing projects is our Employment Resource Center, where we match employment opportunities in the communications industry with qualified black professionals. Through our Resource Center we receive information on several hundred media employment opportunities during a month, and we are in touch with a network of black professionals who we advise, counsel, and refer to these positions. Through our referral activities we have probably helped well over 5,000 persons in their employment endeavors.

We've made a helluva lot of difference. People either love us or they hate us. We think that's just fine!
Courtesy Pluria Marshall.

THE SHIFTING '70S

While the White House was unhappy with some broadcasters, broadcasters were unhappy with some segments of the public. The fervor of the 1960s civil rights revolutions spawned a number of citizen groups seeking an end to discrimination and stereotyping—racism and sexism—in electronic media. Black organizations filed petitions to deny license renewals of stations they believed were not providing equal opportunities in employment and fairness in programming. Hispanic groups protested negative images of Hispanics on the air; an example was their forcing the removal of the "Frito Bandito" commercial. Asian-American groups, heretofore generally uninvolved, began to express their concerns. Women's organizations began to take action against sexist portrayals of females in advertising and in programs and to push the industry to hire and promote on the basis of merit rather than gender. The FCC

Plane hijackings proliferate.

FCC rejects requests by antiwar organizations and environmental groups for equal time.

Prime Time Access Rule is approved by FCC.

National Public Radio (NPR) is formed.

instituted Equal Employment Opportunity (EEO) requirements for stations, including the filing of annual reports on employment and affirmative action policies. An EEO office was established by the FCC to monitor licensees; it continued into the 1990s. Fearing the possibility of delay of license renewals as well as excessive legal expenditures, a number of stations made agreements with the petitioning groups to provide more equitable employment opportunities and to be more sensitive in their programming.

The continuing war in Vietnam and growing environmental problems prompted other citizen groups to seek what they felt would be fairer media coverage of their concerns. Their attempts to invoke the Fairness Doctrine were unsuccessful. The FCC turned down antiwar organizations' requests for airtime to counter the generally supportive approach to the Vietnam War taken by broadcasting. Stations wouldn't even sell commercial time to antiwar groups. One organization that tried to buy time, Business Executives Move for Peace, appealed to the FCC, which ruled that advertising did not fall under the Fairness Doctrine. Friends of the Earth, an environmental group, filed a complaint with the FCC after it was unable to obtain free airtime or paid advertising time for antipollution messages to counter the ads placed by gasoline companies and automobile manufacturers; the FCC turned the group down.

It was a busy year for the FCC. It approved a Prime Time Access Rule (PTAR), which limited stations in the top 50 markets to no more than three hours of prime-time (7:00–11:00 P.M., EST) network programming, excluding news, beginning September 1, 1971. It also barred networks from acquiring financial and syndication rights (called *finsyn*) to independently produced programs. For producers, this step opened the door to the big bucks from syndication of successful shows and to a continuing controversy that in the early 1990s brought attempts to repeal or modify finsyn.

The FCC also began to crack down on what it felt were the evils of broadcast monopolies. Relying on the scarcity principle—unlike newspapers, which can proliferate as long as there are enough printing presses, the number of broadcast stations is limited because the available spectrum for broadcast frequencies is limited—the FCC established the duopoly rule. The duopoly rule prohibited the operator of a full-time TV, AM, or FM station from acquiring another station in the same market.

A challenge to a previous FCC ruling authorizing pay TV reached the Supreme Court in 1970; the FCC was upheld. Although broadcasters were unhappy with some FCC actions, most FCC rulings supported the broadcasting industry. For example, one FCC policy statement affirmed that an existing licensee would be given priority in the event that one or more other applicants contested its license at renewal time. This policy was challenged by a public interest organization, the Citizens Communications Center, and was overturned by a federal court the following year. The policy had been designed to allay licensees' fears following the unprecedented revocation of the license of WHDH; but now licensees had to pay special attention to serving the public interest.

The FTC pushed stations and advertisers, too. It acted against misleading and fraudulent advertising on TV and issued a ruling that gave offenders the choice of

FIG 7.2 The U.S. Postal Service commemorates early broadcast innovations.

FCC establishes duopoly rule.

FTC cracks down on false advertising.

either stopping their commercials for a year or admitting their past erroneous claims by posting corrective ads.

The broadcasting industry continued to grow, even as it aged, with some of it passing into history—such as David Sarnoff's resignation as chairman of the board of RCA due to ill health, and his replacement by his son Robert, who had been president of RCA—and some of it presaging the future—such as the founding of the NPR network.

In 1970, 95% of all U.S. households had television. Commercial TV was reaching the saturation stage, with an increase of only little more than 100 stations from 1965 to 1970, for a total of 677. Public television, given the impetus of the Public Broadcasting Act, the facilitating work of the FCC's Educational (Public) Broadcasting Branch, and a surge of federal funds, almost doubled its presence in five years, from 99 stations in 1965 to 188 in 1970. Although only 8% of U.S. homes yet had cable, that was three times as many as five years earlier, and cable TV was on the edge of taking off. Auto radios reached the 90% mark for the first time. Radio, finding its new niche, grew.

FIG 7.3 National Public Radio becomes a vital new broadcast service. *Courtesy NPR.*

THE SHIFTING '70S

WHAT'S DIFFERENT ABOUT NATIONAL PUBLIC RADIO?

Our Programs. ALL THINGS CONSIDERED*, MORNING EDITION*, WEEKEND EDITION* — NPR's news programs are a regular, reliable source of national and international news. Millions of NPR listeners tune to these newsmagazines for in-depth coverage, for analysis beyond the headlines, for news they trust as thorough and balanced.

NPR's arts and performance programs celebrate the richness of the arts in America and abroad. Perhaps best known for its classical and jazz music, NPR also presents folk, bluegrass, and new music, in addition to humorous variety programs and radio drama. Conversations with writers, musicians, and other artists provide listeners with varied opinion and reflection on all that is current in the arts world.

Acknowledging the diversity of American society, NPR provides programs which focus on minorities, the elderly, and the disabled. NPR is designed to encourage broad participation. The resulting programs are as original and varied as those who contribute, who in turn are as diverse as the American public.

Our Sound. Always a little ahead of our time, challenging our listeners, challenging ourselves. On location with NPR correspondents, NPR's engineers contribute to the creation of audio portraits, bringing to life the ideas, personalities, tensions, and debates of radio news, demanding and insuring the highest quality sound.

National Public Radio's arts and performance programming takes listeners to the great concert halls of the world, to avant-garde performances off-off Broadway, to crowded jazz clubs tucked away on Bourbon Street. The high-tech special effects which animate Ruby the Intergalactic Gumshoe, the chalky voice of the playwright Sam Shepard, a soaring aria sung by Kiri Te Kanawa, the clarity of Itzhak Perlman's violin — NPR's sound is of the highest calibre.

But it's the absence of some sound that distinguishes our programs from anything on any other radio network. No advertisements. No hard sell — no soft sell. We're not trying to sell our listeners on anything.

Our Partnership. National Public Radio is more than the program-producing center based in Washington, D.C. National Public Radio is also a partnership with more than 350 stations. Highly independent and autonomous, stations respond to the specific needs of their communities and determine how to present NPR's programming.

Stations produce many of the performance programs that are presented nationally by NPR, and stations' news reporters regularly file stories heard on NPR's newsmagazines. And it is through NPR stations that the public directly participates in National Public Radio — as volunteers, contributors, and listeners.

Our Structure. A private, not-for-profit membership organization based in Washington, D.C., National Public Radio was incorporated in 1970 with 90 public radio stations as charter members. Since then, NPR has grown to include 350 stations located in 48 states, Puerto Rico, and the District of Columbia. In addition to programming, NPR provides stations with support services such as marketing assistance; a computerized satellite-delivered communications system; and engineering training and advice. NPR also works with stations to represent their interests before the Federal Communications Commission and other federal agencies.

Our Funding. Funding of public radio is a team effort. NPR stations contribute more than half of NPR's operating budget. National Public Radio makes up the difference with grants and underwriting from national corporations, foundations, associations, and individuals to support both its programming and general operations. NPR stations are supported by their communities: listeners, universities, and state governments. And the Corporation for Public Broadcasting (CPB) makes federal money available to public radio stations in the form of grants.

Our Listeners. The weekly audience for all public radio programming is 10 million people. The weekly audience for all NPR news programming is six million. NPR's programs — both news and performance — attract an audience most notably distinguished by its level of education, professional success, and community involvement.

Our Mission. "Radio is a personal medium of incalculable impact. Realizing that potential is perhaps the most fundamental responsibility National Public Radio can fulfill. As information continues to transform our world at an incredible pace, our responsibilities to one another are more important than ever. The need for a touchstone — for clarity, continuity, a renewed sense of community — is becoming increasingly essential. National Public Radio, at the leading edge of the very technology that has created these new needs, has as its mission to be that touchstone."

— Douglas J. Bennet
President, National Public Radio

NATIONAL PUBLIC RADIO®

Lt. William Calley found guilty in
My Lai massacre.

1971

David Sarnoff retires as
RCA chairman.

*The Selling of the
Pentagon* is aired
by CBS.

Electronic media probe
My Lai massacre.

There were 4,300 AM stations in 1970, 250 more than in 1965. But it was FM that emerged from a painful childhood into a blossoming adolescence, with an increase of 1,270 stations in five years, for a total of 2,200 in 1970. This growth was attributable in great part to FM's gradual move toward more mainstream, pop music formats. Sixty percent of the radio sets in the country now had FM reception.

1971

The rebellion against the establishment grew. CBS broadcast *The Selling of the Pentagon*, a documentary showing how the U.S. military spent huge sums of money to propagandize the public to support higher military budgets. Coming at a time when Americans were more and more outraged over the U.S. military action in Vietnam, the documentary angered both the public and the Congress. The House held hearings and subpoenaed all CBS footage prepared for the documentary. CBS's president, Frank Stanton, refused to comply. Despite pressure from Vice President Agnew, the FCC, and many members of Congress, broadcasting's First Amendment rights were upheld.

A further blow to the integrity of the Pentagon and the White House was publication of the so-called "Pentagon Papers" by *The New York Times*. Taken from official files by whistleblower Daniel Ellsberg, and their release facilitated by U.S. Senator Mike Gravel, the documents showed how the government was deliberately misleading the public regarding the conduct and status of the war in Vietnam. The Supreme Court upheld the First Amendment and refused to allow the government to exercise prior restraint of the press. Broadcasting covered the scandal. An even stronger blow against the U.S. action in Southeast Asia was television's coverage of the trial of Lieutenant William L. Calley, whose platoon massacred civilians at My Lai in Vietnam. With indications that this was only one of a number of atrocities by U.S. forces, more Americans turned against continuing U.S. involvement in Vietnam.

Citizen groups got a boost in regard to broadcasting's coverage of controversial issues when the federal courts (1) overturned the FCC's ban on the sale of time to present alternative viewpoints on controversial issues and (2) ruled that ads for automobiles and leaded gas fell under the Fairness Doctrine, entitling environmental groups to respond. These court decisions posed additional problems for the increasingly beleaguered White House, and President Nixon's director of OTP, Tom Whitehead, called for abolition of the Fairness Doctrine. Such calls would be heard often in subsequent years, but it wasn't until President Ronald Reagan vetoed a Fairness Law in 1987 that the Fairness Doctrine was actually abolished by the FCC.

The FCC, pressured by more and more groups throughout the country filing renewal challenges against more and more stations, enacted an Ascertainment of Community Needs rule. All stations were required to determine the 10 most significant issues in their communities of service and at the end of each year report to the FCC on the extent to which they had dealt with those issues in their programming. This requirement was also eliminated in the later deregulatory period.

Eighteen-year-olds gain right to vote.		Charles Manson "family" sentenced to death.

	FCC imposes "ascertainment of community needs" requirements on broadcasters.		Drug-related lyrics opposed by FCC.

In response to strong public support of a petition from Action for Children's Television (ACT), the FCC proposed rules relating to quality and advertising practices on children's programming. The FCC didn't actually issue any such rules, however, until Congress passed a bill in 1990 limiting the amount of advertising time on children's TV shows and requiring the FCC to consider children's programming in its renewal process.

The FCC also tackled another problem—one that is still unresolved in the 2000s—when it issued a policy warning broadcasters against playing songs that contained drug-related lyrics. The commission was immediately attacked—as it still is on this issue—from a number of sources on grounds of censorship and violation of the First Amendment.

New kinds of programs made a mark in 1971. In commercial television, Norman Lear's *All in the Family* made its debut, showing that a sitcom with content and controversy could be successful. Lear generated the prototype, motivation, and economic justification for the social-reality sitcom on U.S. TV. *The Mary Tyler Moore Show*, also debuting in 1971, established the genre of sophisticated sitcom comedy, seen in later years in successors such as *Murphy Brown*. Besides Lear, producers such as Grant Tinker and Garry Marshall put their stamp on the decade by contributing a myriad of popular (if not profound) sitcoms, many of which were spinoffs of the originals.

THE SHIFTING '70S

Norman Lear Changes the Landscape of Television

With the sound of flushing toilet, Norman Lear's *All in the Family* rocked the world of American television. *All in the Family* altered the conventions of television comedy by tackling subjects and using heretofore blasphemous language that had been assiduously avoided. Debuting in January 1971, *All in the Family* may have been the beginning of "reality" programming, snubbing the conformist belief that audiences would not take to programs dealing with real, often controversial issues. Following the bland, idealized families that ruled 1950s sitcoms and the weird fantasy plot lines of the 1960s, *All in the Family* tackled subjects that reflected what was actually occurring in a country undergoing a seismic cultural shift. With cunningly scathing dialogue, *All in the Family* exposed the ills of contemporary society by addressing such hot-button topics as menopause, rape, impotency, homosexuality, racism, women's rights, the Vietnam War, and the Nixon Administration, with its main protagonists, the conservative, head-of-the household Archie Bunker and his liberal, live-in son-in-law, Mike Stivic. After a slow start, *All in the Family* proved a ratings winner for many seasons during the 1970s and spun off an entire cottage industry of Lear-produced topical shows such as *The Jeffersons, Maude, Sanford and Son,* and *Good Times* that forever changed the face of television sitcoms and perhaps the entire medium.

Ban on radio-TV
cigarette advertising
begins.

All in the Family
debuts.

In radio, NPR began broadcasting with a network of 90 stations. Although its programming was applauded, its criteria for network membership, supported by the Corporation for Public Broadcasting (CPB), were criticized and continue to be criticized even today. Using federal funds, NPR provides its services only to those stations wealthy enough to have five full-time, paid staff members plus NPR-designated power and time on the air. The less affluent noncommercial radio stations—including low-budget college and university licensees, many of them predominantly black institutions with marginal public support and needing the tax-supported services more than the richer stations—continue to be denied NPR network membership.

As part of its franchise requirements, cable opened the doors to public participation in the media with the establishment of access channels in New York City. For the first time, any and all members of the public had the opportunity to present their ideas and talents to the rest of the public through the media on a regular, supported basis.

Two archrival broadcast pioneers died in 1971: Philo Farnsworth, generally recognized as the father of American television and who got his first patent for electronic television in 1927, passed away at 64; David Sarnoff, credited with building the RCA and NBC communication empires, died at 80.

1972

Live international television coverage via satellite was established in 1972 through three significant events. *Broadcasting* magazine called the broadcasts by all three TV networks of President Nixon's landmark visit to China a "milestone in broadcast history." A few months later the networks did the same for Nixon's trip to the Soviet Union for a summit meeting in Moscow. ABC kept its cameras going as the coverage of the Olympic games turned from triumph into tragedy when Palestinian terrorists took 11 members of the Israeli team hostage and later killed them.

The FCC entered a crossroads of regulatory policy. It was deluged by mass filings from many citizen groups challenging the license renewals of hundreds of stations across the country. In most cases the challenges resulted in agreements between the stations and the citizen groups, principally in the areas of providing equal employment opportunity and more sensitivity in programming in multicultural and women's areas. Concomitantly, Benjamin L. Hooks became the first African American to be appointed to the FCC—or, for that matter, to any federal regulatory agency. Reflecting the mood of the country, Commissioner Hooks began pushing for equal employment opportunity action in the communications industry. Some of his attempts were successful; others were not. For example, one of the authors of this book worked with him on a proposal to study the racial composition of the boards of directors of public broadcasting stations, many of which at the time appeared to have even fewer minorities than commercial stations did. The public broadcasting establishment, including such organizations as the National Association of Educational Broadcasters (NAEB),

Millions of Americans march against
U.S. involvement in Vietnam War.

President Nixon visits
People's Republic of China.

1972

Farnsworth and Sarnoff
die.

Live international television
coverage through satellites
takes place.

and some of the other commissioners were furious, and their opposition caused the study to be abandoned.

The beginning of reregulation took place that year when the FCC dropped a number of technical requirements regarding station operations. Within the decade, reregulation would become deregulation.

Television breathed a partial sigh of relief when the surgeon general's report on television violence came out. The report found no definitive causal relationship between violence on TV and aggressive behavior in the average child; it did, however, find that TV violence could trigger aggressive behavior in some children, especially those already prone to violent acts. The report generated concerns that continue today. The FTC did its part to try to protect children, monitoring ads on "kidvid," as children's television was called, as well as continuing to take action against misleading advertising in general.

Television Violence: Forty Years after the *Report*

Nearly 40 years after the release of the massive (six-volume) congressionally funded probe, collectively referred to as the *Surgeon General's Report*, the issue of the effects of television violence remains contentious. The weight of the evidence from the thousands of studies, of varying precision, seems to affirm the connection. Yet there are still doubters who find the evidence inconclusive or contradictory. So, what's the answer? There doesn't seem to be an all-encompassing one. A leader of the confirmative side is media scholar George Comstock, who was with the Rand Corporation, which produced much of the scientific research for the surgeon general (*Television and Human Behavior*, 1975). Recently Comstock concluded an exhaustive meta-analysis that confirmed a statistical causal relationship between television and aggressive or antisocial behavior. A meta-analysis is basically an "analysis of analysis," a quantitative aggregation of a large body of disparate studies. Comstock found that though the overall variation may be small (there is no perfect cause and effect connection), which suggests televised violence is just one among numerous causes, the direction of the findings is undisputedly in the same positive direction. Skeptics point to the large degree of unexplained variation, meaning the many nontelevision contributors to violent behavior.

Unable to intimidate most broadcasters into presenting the news as he thought it should be presented, President Nixon had the Department of Justice filed antitrust suits against all three networks. The suits were later dismissed. While not letting up on what it believed were the left-leaning prejudices of commercial broadcasters, the Nixon administration took dead aim at public broadcasting as well, the public affairs

THE SHIFTING '70S

programs of which the White House considered harmful to the government and, in fact, Communist tainted. President Nixon tried to end funding for public broadcasting and succeeded in seeing its support reduced, even vetoing one of the CPB budget bills. Nevertheless, public broadcasting continued to develop new programs, one of which—hardly controversial—made its debut in 1972 and became a household favorite, Julia Child's *The French Chef*. (See Child's comments in the 1960s chapter.)

Vietnam was not forgotten, and its horrors were reemphasized in a new sitcom, set in Korea, that became a brilliant, bitter satire on war: *M*A*S*H*.

The year 1972 saw technical advances that forecast the kinds of competitive communication systems that would result in serious challenges to broadcast television, including a drastic drop in prime-time network viewing, within 20 years. A number of firsts took place:

- The first demonstration of a videodisc using laser-beam scanning, by MCA and Philips
- The first home videogame on the market, Magnavox's *Odyssey*
- The first prerecorded videocassettes for rental and sale to the public
- The first pay-cable channels for public subscription, including Home Box Office (HBO would also be the first cable system to use satellite distribution, in 1975)
- The new technical equipment that dominated that year's NAB convention was, ironically, the computer

Monday Night Football Transforms the Prime-Time Audience

If *All in the Family* revolutionized the content of television, *Monday Night Football* (*MNF*) forever altered the composition of the prime-time audience. Conventional wisdom held that women controlled television during evenings, and they did not like football. The National Football League (NFL) relationship with television began modestly, highlighted by the ill-fated DuMont Network's Saturday night package over its tiny collection of affiliates in the early 1950s. However, it was the league's regular Sunday afternoon schedule that attracted broadcasters, which needed something other than religious and political programming to make the day profitable. Soon double-headers and pre-game shows pushed "public service" programming to the periphery. The NFL had longed for a weeknight prime-time series and found a willing partner in ABC, which, as a constant distant third in the ratings battle, had little to lose. Under the tutelage of Roone Arledge, president of ABC Sports, the venture proved to be a rousing success. Arledge, recognizing that he needed more than a football game to attract viewers, stressed entertainment over athletics, focusing on personal vignettes combined with a compelling cast of characters in the broadcast booth that attracted enough non-NFL aficionados to become a staple of prime-time television each fall.

Benjamin Hooks becomes the first black to serve on FCC.

Reregulation era begins.

First Native American radio station, KTDB, goes on the air.

President Nixon directs Department of Justice to file antitrust suits against all three TV networks.

BILL SIEMERING

RADIO EXECUTIVE PRODUCER, *SOUNDPRINT*, AND CREATOR OF NPR'S *ALL THINGS CONSIDERED* —

FIG 7.4 Bill Siemering.
Courtesy Bill Siemering.

Gunpowder was invented in a Chinese kitchen when charcoal, sulfur, and salt peter accidentally came together. In like manner, elements came together at WBFO in Buffalo, New York, to form the essential values of public radio. The station, the university, and the city were in the cauldron of the cultural and political revolution of the times. An exceptional staff was the catalyst in this mixture, which resulted in new assumptions about the content and sound of radio that became NPR. The mixture included a spirit of learning by doing, concern for people and ideas, and the sound possibilities of radio.

As a university station, experimentation and risk taking were natural. We did this, for example, with the composition *City Links WBFO*, by Mary Anne Amacher, which brought the sounds of the city on five lines live into the studio, where they were mixed and broadcast for 28 hours. Listeners also heard broadcasts of the city council and writers John Barth, Leslie Fiedler, and Robert Creely reading and talking about their writing.

WBFO pioneered in multicultural programming. We established a storefront broadcast facility on Jefferson Avenue, where African-American and Hispanic residents planned and produced 25 hours of programming a week. We sponsored a Black Arts Festival with photographers, paintings, live jazz, and a mural in the studio depicting the history of Afro-American

communications, ending with the satellite facility. "The Airwaves Belong to the People" was given new grassroots meaning and was the slogan of the staff. We traveled to the Tuscarora reservation and produced a series on the Iroquois Confederacy.

These and other experiences informed the mission and goals statement of NPR, which I wrote in 1970. Before *All Things Considered* had a title, I wrote that it "... will not substitute superficial blandness for genuine diversity of regions, values, cultural and ethnic minorities which comprise American society; it will speak with many voices and many dialects.... There may be views of the world from poets, men and women of ideas, interpretive comments from scholars."

Our commitment to these ideals was grounded in experiences in the community. We saw how commercial media ignored conditions of minorities on the east side; we witnessed the results of anger at injustice; we saw familiar store windows

Break-in occurs at Democratic
headquarters in Watergate building.

M*A*S*H debuts.

Videocassettes become
available to the public for
rental and sale.

INTV is formed.

shattered and then covered with dull plywood; we smelled the acrid smoke of burning buildings; we felt the tear gas burn our eyes; we knew the fear in the streets.

Later, unrest came to the university during a long student strike and 300 police occupied the campus. Reporting on the turmoil within the university—as a university-licensed station—tested our journalistic independence and our professional skills and shattered some old assumptions. Truth, we discovered, was reflected through different perceptions of reality, and we broadcast a full spectrum of opinion. Amid tear gas in the building and some administration objections, we stayed on the air, and the [local] *Courier Express* commended the coverage as a "beacon of light" amid the chaos. WBFO emerged with a new professional respect within the community and the university.

Even though similar events were going on in other parts of the country, it was the exceptional group of people at WBFO who saw public radio as an active participant in the process of this change and worked to define public radio as more than an alternative to commercial radio. Five WBFO staff members joined NPR. Many others went on to distinguish themselves in journalism and other professions. I wrote in the NPR mission statement:

The total service should be trustworthy, enhance intellectual development, expand knowledge, deepen aural aesthetic enjoyment, increase the pleasure of living in a pluralistic society and result in a service to listeners which makes them more responsive, informed human beings and intelligent, responsible citizens of their communities and the world.

We tried to do that first as a kind of laboratory experiment at WBFO. Now, after 20 years of programming, that's what public radio does nationally.

Courtesy Bill Siemering.

The FCC issued, finally, its definitive cable rules in 1972. These included requirements that a local cable system must carry all local broadcast stations (those within a 60-mile radius); must delete network and syndicated programs of any distant stations it carried if such programs were on a local station (called *syndex*, or syndicated exclusivity); must offer a minimum of 20 channels in the top 100 markets; and must provide free-access channels for the public, education, and municipal government as well as a system-operated, local origination channel. The FCC also claimed jurisdiction over rate structures. A dozen years later, virtually all the FCC cable rules would be eliminated with the passage of the Cable Communications Policy Act of 1984.

In an attempt to generate support as they tried to compete with the stronger, principally VHF network affiliates, independent nonnetwork, mostly UHF, stations formed the Independent Television Association (INTV). In radio, AM saw that it might soon find itself in the same disadvantageous competitive position. One-third of the nation's listeners now tuned in to FM, whose greater fidelity and stereo capacity made it superior to AM in music. Some AM stations began to move to more talk shows,

Nixon wins reelection by beating
Senator George McGovern.

American war activity
in Vietnam ends.

1973

FCC issues its definitive
cable rules.

Electronic media report
Watergate break-in.

and a number of those with sagging ratings saw these new talk formats hold the line and even increase their ratings. A few stations tried all-news formats for the first time, in New York, Washington, D.C., and Los Angeles.

President Nixon seemed to be overly concerned about the challenge to his reelection by Senator George McGovern, the Democratic nominee; perhaps remembering his 1960s debate against another vibrant opponent, Senator John F. Kennedy, Nixon turned down requests for TV debates with McGovern. In June 1972, the media reported what seemed like a routine story of five men caught breaking into the Democratic headquarters in the Watergate office building in Washington, D.C. The implications of that story, and the media's subsequent role in reporting it, couldn't even have been guessed at the time.

1973

The Vietnam War finally came to an end in 1973. Television played no small part in bringing to the American people many of the events in Southeast Asia that the government had withheld from the public, as well as bringing to the attention of government leaders citizens' demands and actions to end the war. Watergate replaced Vietnam as the number-one topic of conversation and media coverage.

The Watergate scandal became full blown, and the networks devoted more than 300 hours of time from May to August to the Senate Watergate hearings chaired by Senator Sam Irvin. The American people saw the very worst of their political system. But the system survived. President Nixon's statement, "I have never heard or seen such outrageous, vicious, distorted reporting in 27 years of public life," did not fool the public; nor did his "I am not a crook" plea.

To add even more coals to the fire that was consuming the Nixon White House, television viewers watched with morbid fascination as Nixon's attorney general, Elliot Richardson, resigned rather than obey the President's orders to fire Archibald Cox, the special Watergate prosecutor who was getting closer to learning Nixon's role in the crime; Nixon had an assistant attorney general, Robert Bork, do the dirty work. (Bork became a federal judge and was subsequently nominated by President Ronald Reagan to the Supreme Court, but he was not confirmed by the Senate.) As though that weren't enough, the public saw even more corruption in the White House as they watched the resignation, in disgrace, of Vice President Agnew amid corruption charges.

The rebellion and scandals were too much for Americans, who began to yearn for the placidity of the 1950s, slowly turning to the conservative acquiescence of the Eisenhower years. The soaring, highly sensitive 1960s glided to a flat-bellied landing of 1970s insensitivity. CBS, under pressure from its affiliates, canceled *Sticks and Bones*, a highly regarded anti–Vietnam War drama about a blinded veteran. The Supreme Court overturned the lower courts and decided that the Fairness Doctrine did not after all apply to television and radio advertising and that no one had the

Vice President Spiro Agnew resigns
in disgrace for corruption.

Watergate scandal shocks nation.
First ENG camera is unveiled.

Networks devote
extensive coverage to
the Senate Watergate
hearings.

"Topless radio" is taken
to task by the FCC.

right of paid access to present alternative viewpoints. The FCC modified the PTAR, giving the networks a bit more leeway. The commission cracked down on what was called "topless radio," a short-lived phenomenon in which talk-show hosts encouraged people at home, principally women, to call in and talk about their sexual problems, experiences, techniques, and fantasies. The ratings of stations carrying these shows shot up. Finally, fines and the threat of fines and possible loss of licenses brought topless radio to a halt—though in later years, similar shows would be permitted on radio and television when the talk-show personality had a "Dr." in front of his or her name.

Carl McIntire, the owner of WXUR-AM-FM in Media, Pennsylvania, the principal in the infamous *Red Lion* case, lost his appeal to the Supreme Court to retain his stations' licenses, and within a few months he opened a pirate radio station offshore, in the Atlantic Ocean; it lasted only about two weeks before its operations were stopped by a court injunction.

Public broadcasting was undergoing an upheaval, encouraged by the Nixon administration in its attempt to make public stations more locally oriented to reduce what the administration believed was the left-leaning content of network-controlled programs. After a bitter battle for control between CPB and PBS, a compromise was reached that gave the PBS stations more autonomy over programming decisions.

Black participation in the media made some advances in 1973. The first black-owned television station in the country, WGPR-TV in Detroit, began operations. And the National Black Network, primarily a radio news organization, started with 41 affiliates.

Technical advances continued apace in 1973. The first small portable TV camera, the Ikegami HL-33, made its debut. The first fiber-optic system was installed. Panasonic gave the first demonstration of high-definition television (HDTV). The first *multipoint distribution service* (MDS) system began operating; now called *multichannel multipoint distribution service* (MMDS), it operates a point-to-point microwave service as a commercial common carrier and is sometimes referred to as *wireless cable*. In addition, Western Union received the first authorization for a domestic satellite.

Commercial time continued to grow more expensive, requiring an increasing number of sponsors to support a given program and resulting in the virtual disappearance of ad agencies' absolute influence over programs. A sponsor could, of course, still threaten to withdraw, but with multiple sponsors such threats had less effect on networks than in previous years, and rarely did they succumb to such pressure. More often the networks cooperated with large conservative citizen groups, such as the Rev. Jerry Falwell's Moral Majority, whose membership could, on short notice, generate thousands of letters of protest against programs or performers that were not in agreement with the organization's religious, political, or other beliefs. It was not a 1950s-style blacklist; it was more a stifling of viewpoints other than those of a self-styled moral majority.

Top Nixon aides indicted and/or resign.

Pulitzer Prize to *Washington Post's* Woodward and Bernstein for Watergate stories.

Initial fiber-optic system is installed.

RICK WRIGHT

PROFESSOR, SYRACUSE UNIVERSITY, AND RADIO PERFORMER _____

FIG 7.5 Rick Wright.
Courtesy Rick Wright.

In the early 1970s, I deejayed at several stations, most of which featured Afro-American–oriented programming. Many black radio pioneers helped pave the way for minorities in the medium. I'm currently at work on a book that will tell the story of this important aspect of the broadcast century. Among those who made a unique contribution to black radio and broadcasting in general are Jack Gibson back in the early 1920s in Chicago; B. B. King and Rufus Thomas at WDIA-AM in Memphis; Jack Holmes and Mrs. Leola Dyson at WRAP-AM and Starr Merritt, King Hot Dog the Great, and Bob Jackson in Norfolk; Rodney Jones at WVON-AM and Sid McCoy and Merrie Dee in Chicago; Joko Henderson, Frankie Crocker, Chuck Leonard, The Dixie Drifter, Del Shields, Hank Spann, Martha Dean, Gary Byrd, and Hal Jackson in New York City; Martha Jean the Queen in Detroit; The Magnificent Montaque and Herman Griffin in Los Angeles; Norfley Whitted in Durham; Ben Miles and Tiger Tom Mitchell in Richmond; Georgie Woods and Jimmy Bishop in Philadelphia; Bill Haywood in Raleigh; Daddy O. and Larry Williams in Winston-Salem; Merrill Watson in Greensboro; Doctor Jive and Wild Child in Boston; Bob King, Cliff Holland, Jerry Boulding, and The Nighthawk in Washington, D.C.; Hoppy Adams in Annapolis; and The Moonman and Hot Rod in Baltimore. There are a host of other great Afro-American air personalities who left their special mark on the medium, and I salute them all.
Courtesy Rick Wright.

1974

What were people watching on television in 1974? Politics, scandal, resignation, soap opera, and violence—both make-believe and real-life.

The real-life versions came out of the Watergate hearings of 1973. In August 1974 the networks covered the House impeachment proceedings against President Nixon. A week later the television cameras shifted to Nixon himself, who became the first U.S. President to resign in disgrace. More than 40 million people watched his resignation speech, and probably more than 100 million saw it repeated on later news

THE SHIFTING '70S

| Supreme Court's *Roe v. Wade* decision legalizes abortion choice. | Pet rocks become a national fad. |

1974

First multipoint distribution system (MDS) begins operating.

Networks cover House impeachment proceedings against President Nixon.

specials. A federal judge ordered the Watergate tapes—the "smoking guns"—released to broadcasters, but the high drama itself was over and the tapes were anticlimactic.

Other real-life dramas on TV were the Senate Communications Subcommittee's hearings on televised violence and the intensive media coverage of the kidnapping of heiress Patty Hearst, a story that would stay on broadcasting's top burner for years. Whose words and images did the public hang onto, to learn of the important events of the world? First and foremost, Walter Cronkite at CBS, then John Chancellor at NBC, and finally Harry Reasoner and Howard K. Smith at ABC.

Make-believe violence was expensive. NBC paid a then-record $10 million for the right to show the movie *The Godfather*. Make-believe soap operas cost less but lasted longer. A new series from Britain, *Upstairs, Downstairs*, made its debut on public television's *Masterpiece Theatre*. For 68 weeks the public stayed glued to the tribulations of an Edwardian English family, the Bellamys, and their entourage of servants. For many Americans, however, the highest drama of the year was broadcasting's coverage of Henry Aaron breaking Babe Ruth's home-run record.

The FCC had its ups and downs under a new chair, Richard E. Wiley, who succeeded Dean Burch. On one hand, the FCC received the plaudits of many citizen groups when it ordered revocation of the station licenses of the Alabama Educational Television Commission on grounds of racial discrimination in programming and employment. On the other hand, it was cited by the U.S. Civil Rights Commission as one of five federal independent agencies guilty of not protecting the civil rights of minorities and women in the industries it was supposed to regulate.

Technical advances in broadcasting continued. Satellites made news with the launch of Western Union's *Westar*, the country's first domestic satellite, and with RCA's use, for the first time, of a domestic satellite for communications services. Forebodings to some and good tidings to others of things to come was the use of an IBM computer to run the WLOX-TV (Biloxi, Mississippi) transmitter by remote control, under special approval from the FCC.

Cable, continuing its slow but steady growth, got a boost from the Supreme Court, which ruled that the Copyright Act did not apply to TV broadcast signals carried by local cable systems. Cable could legally carry broadcasting's copyrighted programs without paying a fee.

1975

The FCC's most significant action in 1975 was its approval of a cross-ownership rule, which affected newspapers as well as broadcast stations. The rule barred future joint ownership of a daily English-language newspaper and a radio or television station in the same market. It gave owners of such information-monopoly combinations in small markets five years in which to divest one of the media properties. Court rulings in subsequent years made the prohibition even more stringent than the Commission initially intended. Other tough actions by the FCC that year were (1) revocation of

President Nixon resigns in disgrace; nation views resignation speech on TV.

CIA admits illegal secret files on many Americans.

Hank Aaron sets home-run record on network television.

FIG 7.6 Automation systems have been a mainstay for many radio stations since the 1960s. *Courtesy IGM Communications.*

THE SHIFTING '70S

some radio stations' licenses because of misconduct, such as news slanting and false advertising, and (2) denial of approval of a cable system on grounds of bribery.

Everything grew: television, radio, and cable. Cable now claimed 15% penetration of the country's TV homes. About 96% of U.S. households now had TV sets. AM had added some 150 stations since 1970, for a total of 4,450, but FM had added 450, to reach 2,600 stations on the air. Noncommercial FM did better percentagewise, adding more than 300 stations, for a total of 717. Commercial television grew more slowly, increasing by only 30 stations in five years, to 706. Noncommercial, or public, television did better, adding more than 60 stations, for a total of 247. The bottom-line statistic is the one that pleased broadcasters most: TV advertising increased 50% from 1970 to 1975, to $5.2 billion; radio advertising grew by the same percentage, to $2 billion.

Radio's comeback was by now well established, and new, specialized radio networks appeared. In 1975 NBC set up a news and information service to 33 stations. Ironically, Canada's Radio-Television Commission (CRTC) proposed AM and FM uses diametrically opposite to what was occurring in the United States: AM for popular music and general information; FM for in-depth information and culturally significant programming.

Television's program innovation was a new NBC show with risqué, irreverent satire and farce that launched such personalities as John Belushi, Gilda Radner, and Eddie Murphy into stardom—*Saturday Night Live.* CBS offered a technical innovation:

Cultural revolution in China.		Heiress Patty Hearst kidnapped by SLA.

First domestic satellite, *Westar*, is launched.		Supreme Court rules that Copyright Act does not apply to television broadcast signals carried by local cable systems.

FIG 7.7 TV becomes portable.
Courtesy David Sarnoff Library.

electronic news gathering (ENG), with portable minicameras and recorders that took TV journalists into places where few had gone before. Cable, too, proposed something new, one of its many threats to broadcasting: satellite transmission by HBO to local cable systems. Satellite-to-home possibilities—called *direct broadcast satellite* (DBS)—frightened broadcasters, and the three networks opposed such possibilities in hearings at the FCC.

1976

Three more presidents were replaced in 1976. Lawrence K. Grossman succeeded Hartford N. Gunn, the first president of PBS; CBS's president, Arthur Taylor, was fired by William Paley because he was allegedly "too big for his britches"; and the nation's Republican President, Gerald Ford, was replaced by the American people because, according to some pundits, he wasn't big enough for his, and thus Jimmy Carter, a Democrat and Georgia governor, became the new head of state. During the campaign Ford and Carter engaged in three highly publicized television debates, the first since 1960. An estimated 90 million to 100 million people saw the first debate, but for 28 minutes they didn't hear it. It was suspended for that length of time when the sound went out; the networks had neglected to provide backup equipment.

On another government communications front, in the legislative branch, the new chair of the House Communications Subcommittee, Representative Lionel Van Deerlin, began a series of unsuccessful efforts to write a new communications act. He argued that the Communications Act of 1934 was obsolete because it was not designed to address the problems of the many new and emerging technologies. Another legislative action affecting communications was passage of a revised copyright law that, for the first time, required cable and public broadcasting to pay royalties. A "compulsory license" that entitled cable to retransmit copyrighted TV programs for a statutory fee paid to a copyright tribunal for distribution to broadcasters was still a matter of controversy in the 1990s.

In the executive branch of government, following years of controversy with Nixon appointees, the White House OTP moved toward moderation with the appointment of a moderate Republican, Thomas Houser, as director. In another corner of the executive branch, the FCC was again in trouble with the third branch of government, the judiciary. In 1975 the new FCC chair, Richard Wiley, had worked out an agreement with the networks and the NAB for what was called *family viewing time*. Programs with sex and violence or other content deemed inappropriate for family viewing would not be aired between 7:00 and 9:00 P.M. (EST), and this provision was incorporated into the NAB's television code. Protests from producers, civil liberties organizations, creative artists, and others filled the nonbroadcast air until, in 1976, a federal court ruled that the family viewing time agreement was in violation of the First Amendment; having been instigated by and implemented because of government, it was deemed unconstitutional. The FCC's *faux pas* was not quite ameliorated by its opening of 17 more citizens band (CB) channels for the more than 20 million CB users in the country.

FIG 7.8 The role of women in network news gradually increased in the 1970s.
Courtesy Irving Fang.

THE SHIFTING '70S

GEORGE HERMAN

FORMER CBS NEWS REPORTER

My first election night at CBS News was 1944 and my task was lowly. My bosses said: "Herman, you were a math major at Dartmouth, you do the math." This was before computers, so I became a computer. Side by side with my colleague Alice Weel, I received all election copy from the wires of the AP, UP, and INS. Typically it would read: "With 154 precincts reporting out of 2,347, Franklin D. Roosevelt leads Thomas E. Dewey 123,457 to 107,658." With a quick slip of my slide rule (remember, I *was* a math major), I would figure out the percentage of precincts reporting and, later on, the percentage of votes for each candidate. I then scribbled those numbers on the copy and passed it along the chain of command. There two things happened. The numbers were added to already known totals for that state and the new total read through a phone line to a page, wearing a headset and standing on a scaffold in front of one of the huge blackboards arcing across one whole side of the huge studio. The page would hastily erase his old numbers and chalk the new total onto that state's line on the board so

Spanish dictatorship ends
with Franco's death.

Nonsexist terminology
advances in United States.

Saturday Night Live
debuts on NBC.

HBO uses satellites to
reach local cable
systems.

FIG 7.9 George Herman.
Courtesy George Herman.

our anchormen could see it. And if the reporting region was important enough and the returns exciting enough, the slip of paper with my scribbled figures went to an anchorman to read on the air.

A series of us, adding, dividing, scribbling numbers on slips of paper and passing them along by hand and by headset, served as the computer—the pages and blackboards were the digital readout from which anchormen and analysts noted trends, figured totals. This was before television came back from its wartime freeze and we worked in our shirtsleeves, proud of our informality and sneering to each other about NBC, where President Sarnoff had made the election-night crew dress in tuxedos to impress the visitors he brought in.

It was the same drill in 1948—informal, but neatened up for the occasional TV shot of the crowded studio and its busy chalkboards.

I had noticed that at the conventions the delegate totals were displayed by the simple expedient of gluing 3- × 5-inch unlined pads to the wall: a pad, then a painted-on comma, then three pads, a painted-on decimal point, then two more pads. A stage hand wrote a single digit on each pad to show the total figure. When it changed he quietly tore off the top pages, crayoned the new digits on the fresh sheets and let the old ones fall out of sight to the floor.

In 1952 as a war correspondent I listened to the returns in Korea as they came in over Armed Forces Radio. But in 1956 I was back in the election-night studio. This time there was a new gimmick. Instead of pads glued to the wall, the TV people had cut pairs of tiny slits in the wall and inserted endless belts of flexible plastic film in through the top slit and out through the bottom one. Digits were painted top-to-bottom on the belts, and stage hands behind the wall pulled the belts through the slots so that the single appropriate digit was visible on the camera side of the wall. Presto! Digital readout (from the digits of the stagehands).

It's hard to realize that today the digits, the actual numbers, don't exist anywhere in reality, aren't written or painted or displayed by alphanumeric gadgets. They are merely strings of electric charges hidden inside a computer and displayed on the monitors of the reporters and, at the discretion of the director, displayed in fancy artwork on the home TV screen, updated, manipulated, all percentages neatly inserted by the computer. Goodbye slide rule, goodbye pencil and paper.

Courtesy George Herman.

1976

Networks commemorate the bicentennial.

In the realms of programming and personalities, two significant events occurred. *Rich Man, Poor Man*, based on the Irwin Shaw novel, was the first miniseries, with six two-hour programs airing over seven weeks. According to *Life* magazine, "It paved the way for serialized dramas such as *Roots, Shogun, Brideshead Revisited*, and *The Jewel in the Crown*." ABC and Barbara Walters struck a blow for equal rights—even as a federal equal rights constitutional amendment was failing—when ABC lured Walters away from NBC with a $1 million contract to become the first female network news anchor.

ABC had another coup with its *Eleanor and Franklin*, winning 11 Emmys, the most ever for one program. CBS did well with its bicentennial-year *Bicentennial Minutes*, vignettes of U.S. history. Indeed, all the networks had a number of specials commemorating America's 200th birthday. Public broadcasting got into the programming act with an antidote to the increasingly "infotainment" news programs of the commercial networks, *The MacNeil Report*. Public broadcasting and viewers with hearing impairments got help from the FCC when the commission approved vertical blanking interval lines for closed captions, which are visible on TV sets with special decoders.

A more widespread technical advance was Sony's new 0.5-inch Betamax video-cassette deck for recording TV shows off the air and for playback. Its price of $1,300 was less than the record-and-play unit with integrated monitor that Sony introduced the previous year for $2,300 and that seemed to be going nowhere. The Betamax was the first step in what has become a national phenomenon, causing profound changes in TV viewing habits and creating a new high-profit industry.

Cable also made a breakthrough when Ted Turner's WTCG (now WTBS) in Atlanta became the first TV station to be distributed via satellite to cable systems throughout the country. Radio didn't do so well. NBC Radio's News and Information network, which had begun with high hopes only a year before, folded after huge monetary losses.

Any history of broadcasting has to make note of an event dedicated to broadcasting history. In 1976, with its first five years of funding guaranteed by William Paley, the Museum of Broadcasting opened in New York City.

1977

The year 1977 clearly signified the end of the social conscience era of the 1960s. Entertainment was king, the king died, long live the king: to many Americans, the most important radio and television broadcasts in 1977 were the reports of Elvis Presley's death from a drug overdose. The ethical attitudes of the times were clear. Rather than being vilified for his role in intensifying a drug culture among the nation's youth, Presley received media canonization. Considerably less attention was paid to the official pardons in 1977 of people whose consciences led to their refusals to fight in the discredited Vietnam War.

"Legionnaire's disease" strikes.

Representative Lionel Van Deerlin proposes new Communications Act.	Legislative action requires cable and public broadcasting to pay royalties.	"Family viewing time" agreement deemed in violation of the First Amendment.	Barbara Walters becomes the first female network news anchor.

The FCC reflected the lack of social concern of much of America, as more and more of its actions tended to serve the private rather than the public interest. For many broadcasters, the FCC's new deregulatory attitude was a breath of fresh air, relieving the business of broadcasting from what it felt was the too-heavy hand of government. The commission repealed its radio rules from 1941, issuing a new, less rigorous policy statement; it modified the equal time rules; it put its inquiry on network station relations, as *Broadcasting* magazine couched it, "in deep freeze" (the U.S. General Accounting Office later began its own network investigation); the U.S. Court of Appeals affirmed the FCC's policy of leaving children's television to self-regulation; the FCC eliminated several cable rules; the Civil Rights Commission again criticized the FCC and the broadcast industry for inadequate equal employment opportunity action, and a federal court stopped the FCC from exempting stations with fewer than 10 employees from filing EEO reports. In the fall of 1977 public interest groups looked for better times, from their points of view, with President Carter's appointment of Charles D. Ferris as chair of the FCC, although Ferris's lack of experience in communications had been raised at his Senate confirmation hearings. Their high hopes were not to be realized, however; the Ferris FCC moved even further away from the heyday of public interest regulation and toward the proindustry deregulation of the 1980s.

Although television programming included innovative social content, the medium was attacked for what appeared to be increasing emphasis on violence and sex. However, social content was found both in comedy and in drama. *Soap* was a satire with social commentary and included—rare for that time—an openly gay character, played by newcomer Billy Crystal. *Roots*, based on Alex Haley's book, became the most watched program in TV history over its eight-day schedule. The saga of a family, from its roots as kidnapped Africans forced into slavery in the United States, had ratings in the middle 40s and shares in the high 60s, with its final episode watched by an estimated 80 million people. This series helped ABC win the prime-time ratings race for the first time, ending 20 years of CBS domination. Its success reinforced the miniseries concept, and networks moved ahead with plans for more of them.

Violence was nothing new, but "jiggle," or "T and A," introduced the previous year with the *Charlie's Angels* series, now became TV's principal ratings booster. Criticism about violence and sex grew from citizen and professional organizations such as the National Parents-Teachers Association and the American Medical Association. To its television code the NAB added prohibitions concerning obscenity and profanity; however, the voluntary nature of the code resulted in little impact.

With the media coverage of the Hanafi Muslims' taking of hostages in Washington, D.C.—one of the first modern-day terrorist acts on U.S. soil—broadcasting was criticized for encouraging violence through its news approach. Broadcasters were accused of exacerbating the problem and were urged not to provide a platform for terrorists.

Portugal becomes a democracy.		Howard Hughes's forged wills flood nation.		

	MacNeil Report debuts.		FCC approves closed captions.	Sony introduces its Betamax videocassette deck.

Other broadcasting-related events in Washington, D.C., were President Carter's increased use of the media, including a call-in, question-and-answer program; approval by the House of Representatives to allow broadcast coverage of its proceedings; and a failed attempt by Representative Lionel Van Deerlin's House Communications Subcommittee to rewrite the Communications Act. Internationally, the World Administrative Radio Conference (WARC) set aside spectrum space (11.7–12.2 GHz) for DBS.

The National Association of Television and Radio Announcers (NATRA), established in the 1960s as an alternative for black broadcasters to what was perceived as the racially discriminatory American Federation of Television and Radio Artists (AFTRA), had been ahead of its time and was no longer an important factor in broadcasting. But the time seemed right for another minority organization. The National Association of Black Owned Broadcasters (NABOB) was formed. By the end of the year, however, blacks, Hispanics, and other minorities owned only 1% of the almost 10,000 television and radio stations in the United States.

On the technical front, broadcasting conventions saw demonstration of a new technology: digital audio. Still, it wouldn't be until the 1990s that *digital audio broadcasting* (DAB) would be established as the wave of the immediate future. In Columbus, Ohio, Warner Cable began an experiment that many thought would revolutionize video for the home: interactive, two-way cable. The experiment, QUBE, though highly touted and praised, never obtained enough subscribers to be successful, and it folded in 1984. The subsequent development of newer transmission technologies and sources of software suggests that in the near future interactive video, through such systems as videotex, will begin to take its place in U.S. homes.

1978

Technological innovations seemed to occur almost every other week in 1978. Computers were beginning to be critical factors in broadcasting. Microprocessors revolutionized audio consoles, switchers, character generators, and other equipment. PBS became the first television network to move from terrestrial to satellite distribution of its programs, with *Westar* providing feeds to 280 public television stations. Cellular telephones made their debut in Chicago. The first laser videodisc players were unveiled. So were the first home rear-projection TVs. It had taken a quarter of a century, but for the first time, in 1978, the number of color television sets in use in the United States exceeded the number of monochrome sets.

The jokes about violence on television—"And that's only the news"—were validated with network coverage of such events as the mass suicides in Jonestown, Guyana, and the murders of San Francisco's mayor and a gay member of the city council. Another kind of violence was perceived by the FTC: the effects of

Jimmy Carter defeats Jerry Ford for Presidency.

Elvis Presley dies of drug overdose.

1977

Presidential candidates Ford and Carter engage in televised debates, losing sound for 28 minutes during the first debate.

FCC repeals its radio rules from 1941 and modifies the equal-time rules.

commercials on children. Under Michael Pertschuk, its new chair dedicated to the public interest, the FTC proposed rules that would eliminate commercials from children's programs. Such rules, some of them aimed at curtailing the potential medical harm caused by the high sugar contents of breakfast cereals that ads encouraged children to eat, never reached fruition. Pertschuk was disqualified by the courts from participation in the rule making; Congress ordered the FTC to stop the proceedings, and, when the FTC refused, the House of Representatives voted the commission a "zero" budget for 1979, thus putting the FTC out of business. The FTC dropped the rule making. To be certain that it would not be resumed, in 1980 the Senate passed a resolution forbidding the FTC to take further action on the matter. The power of industry over government and communications has rarely been exemplified more effectively.

NORMAN CORWIN

RADIO'S POET LAUREATE, WRITER, PRODUCER, TEACHER _____

First a panel lit up, reading ON THE AIR
A shingle hung out in the sky, denoting
　　Open For Broadcast.
Then words and music.
That embarkation is barely started toward
　　Andromeda
Cruising at the speed of starlight
And already we are ripe for jubilee.
Babes born on that night
Show gray, show wrinkles where they
　　should be showing,
Are not as fast afoot as once they were
But since they ride together with us on the
　　float we call our home
They join the party.
Years of the electric ear!
The heavens crackling with report: far-
　　flung, nearby, idle, consequential,
The worst of bad news and the best of
　　good

Seizures and frenzies of opinion
The massive respirations of government
　　and commerce
Sofa-sitters taken by kilocycle to the ball
　　park, the concert hall, the scene of the
　　crime
Dramas that let us dress the sets
　　ourselves
Preachments and prizefights
The time at the tone, the weather will be,
　　and now for a word,
The coming of wars and freeways
Outcroppings of fragmented peace
Singing commercials and The Messiah.
And then the eye.
Cyclops the one-eyed giant put to work
As picture-maker to uncountable galleries
No longer the imagined but the living face
　　in the glowing mosaic
Not only the tap of the dancing foot but the
　　swirl of the twirling skirt
Not only the bounding arpeggio but the
　　dazzle of running fingers.
No eye has roved like the video eye
Away and beyond the reach of earth
Out to the moon and onto it
Footprints in primordial dust umbilical
　　walks in the deeps of space

Star Wars captures movie box office.	Vietnam draft evaders pardoned.

Roots becomes the most watched program in television history.	President Carter engages in a call-in, question-and-answer program.	Broadcast coverage of the House of Representatives is approved.

Sprayed on the tube in front of the chair or
    up on the wall in the bedroom.
Blood, too.
Between that night and this
The cruellest half of the cruellest century:
The resentful atom, furious when
    provoked
Depots of extermination
Bomb blasts and body counts
Corpses on campuses
Terror the diplomat
Olympic torch flaring over a funeral bier
Gunsights on the boulevard the motel porch
    the hotel kitchen the parking lot
Murder on camera: the shot seen round the
    world.
Is it any wonder the eye of Cyclops
From time to time was bloodshot?
But look out across the anniversary:
Antennae like stubble on rooftops
Drawing light and shadow and polychromes
    out of the general yonder
Galvanic clouds raining anchormen and
    action
In-laws of the sitcom, outlaws of the west
Contagions of laughter
Pandemic widows of the football weeks
Guesses and giveaways: riches on the
    instant: Cinderella liveth!
The stubborn noble enterprise of human
    rights
Whodunits and doves
Hawks and ferrets:
Now sir will you tell the committee
Well sir at that point in time
Protocols of mayhem
Animated mice men messages
By authority of the Commission.
Babes born on this night will,
By our second jubilee
Find few of us now here, still in the flesh,
But all summonable out of silence.
To you, then, sons and daughters:

Members of tomorrow's weddings and the
    families to follow:
Play us back not as a quaintness but a
    memoir of a contentious time
Sift out past and you will find among the
    gravel, gemstones of a kind,
But do not dwell on us: instead,
Enter the future as the future enters you
And what you see, the lens will see
And what you do, the ribbon will record
And what you say, be stored with every
    inflection in its place.
In cribs tonight, what ballerinas playing
    with their toes?
Yowling for the nipple, what incipient
    Homer?
What toddler picking up her dolls and
    baubles
Will write a poem or find a cure to make
    an epoch happier?
Who on a scooter-car will transfer to a
    wagon set for Mars?
Meanwhile Cyclops will not be indifferent
For he is worked by mortals made of
    malleable metals;

FIG 7.10 Producer and writer Norman
Corwin cues his performers during a
1940s radio program.
Courtesy Norman Corwin.

Digital audio is demonstrated.

The National Association of Black Owned Broadcasters is formed.

And glass can weep and dust fall on a
   lens.
This is the eye in which our inheritors will see
   themselves as in a vibrant mirror
With all their pores and passions.
We whose celebration runs out in this
   hour
Send you benisons to last you to the year
   2000 and far beyond:
May you give shelter to the muses
Melt down your barriers
Pay no more dues to war
Make liberty a cult, and love of liberty a
   deep addiction
Adorn yourselves with sunny aspects and
   ornaments of honor.
There end our greetings,

But we must send a postscript to
   Andromeda:
When at last this reaches you
Know that it went out from a small planet
With one moon and a billion families
A globe with salted oceans and green
   mantles.
We on this spinning outpost share with you
The same infinity of time and space
So when you spot us on your sets and tune
   us in
And ponder what you see and hear,
We ask this only:
That you do not judge us yet,
For there is more to come.
*A poem written in honor of CBS's fiftieth
birthday. Courtesy Norman Corwin.*

While one of the FTC's most famous tribulations began in 1978, one of the FCC's ended. In 1973 the FCC had received a complaint from a father that he and his young son (then 15) heard on their car radio an indecent program from WBAI-FM, a Pacifica station in New York. The material in question was performer George Carlin's "Seven Dirty Words" routine. The case reached the Supreme Court in 1978. The Communications Act, the Court, or the FCC had not up to that time designated what kind of specific language or material was "indecent" or "obscene." Previous court decisions had used such phrases as "community standards," "no redeeming value," "appeals to prurient interests," and similar generalities. An indecency case in broadcasting, however, had never reached the Supreme Court before, and both the FCC and broadcasters hoped that finally a clear definition and designation of what was considered indecent and obscene would be forthcoming. The Court, however, didn't go beyond the "seven dirty words." It stated that the FCC did have a right, under the obscenity, profanity, and indecency provision of the Communications Act, to take action against any station that it deemed was in violation of that standard. It also decided that the FCC was correct in judging the "Seven Dirty Words" presentation to be indecent because its references to sexual and excretory functions violated community standards. Moreover, the Court said it would

Hundreds in cult commit suicide in Jonestown, Guyana.

San Francisco mayor, gay counselor murdered by homophobe; "gay pride" spurred.

1978

Two-way cable, known as QUBE, is offered to Ohio cable subscribers.

Computer use in broadcasting grows.

PBS becomes the first network to move to satellite distribution of its programs.

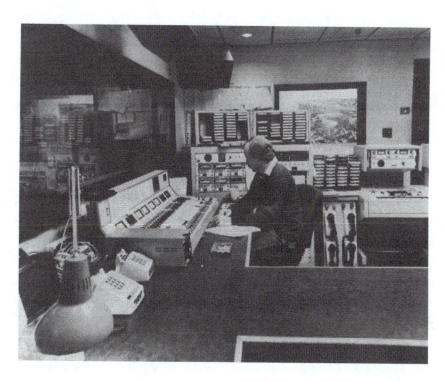

FIG 7.11 The look of the radio production studio in the late 1970s.

judge each future case on its individual merits. Other than the "seven dirty words," then, the FCC is still unable to tell inquiring broadcasters whether any specific piece of questionable material they propose to air would or would not be in violation. The FCC simply says that the licensee must make the judgment, and that if there are complaints and if the FCC investigates and finds that the material in question was indecent or obscene, then the station may be punished; clearly, a Catch-22 for broadcasters. In the late 1980s the FCC established stronger anti-indecency rules, but, as discussed in the 1980s chapter, still without specific usable definitions.

Another FCC action in 1978 that was not successfully resolved in the 1990s was the authorization of AM stereo broadcasting. AM stations continued to lose ground to FM's better fidelity, and prognostications did not include much of AM in radio's future. AM stereo was one possible competitive solution. Although in 1980 the FCC approved the Magnavox AM stereo system, out of a number of applicants, as the standard, strong objections from the industry and a general lack of interest

Laser videodisc players are unveiled.

in the Magnavox system resulted in the commission's reevaluation of other potential systems. AM stereo was put on hold. Finally, in 1982 the FCC decided not to decide. It approved five different systems and would let the marketplace decide; presumably, the best one would eventually win out. But AM radio couldn't wait for "eventually." Because the systems were not all compatible, neither stations nor the public could move ahead until one system emerged. As FM continued to outstrip AM, AM owners asked the FCC to designate one system; the FCC refused to do so. As *Broadcast Engineering* magazine stated some years later, "That's where AM stereo still is—waiting for the marketplace to decide." In the 1990s, except for some scattered markets, stereo still had not fully come to AM radio. Whether the marketplace theory in practice has made it too late for AM's revival still remains to be seen.

In other government actions in 1978, the National Telecommunications and Information Administration was established in the Department of Commerce, replacing the old White House OTP and its successor, the Office of Telecommunications Policy of the Commerce Department.

Van Deerlin's House Communications Subcommittee made another attempt to rewrite the Communications Act of 1934 and approved and sent to the floor of the House a bill to do so. Highly charged lobbying began by industry, citizen groups, and even government officials. The bill, which would have abolished the FCC and created a new regulatory structure, failed to pass.

While the FCC attempted to resurrect some consumer-oriented actions, it also nullified others. It reopened the 1977 inquiry it had dropped on network-affiliate relations; it was criticized by the U.S. Court of Appeals for giving incumbent licensees automatic preference over challengers at renewal time; and it eliminated certificates of compliance with FCC requirements for cable systems.

One FCC action in 1978 was the adoption of a policy making it easier for minorities to become licensees of broadcast stations. Minority applicants were given preference in obtaining licenses for new stations and in buying stations up for sale. In subsequent years, attempts were made to abolish such preferences. Although for a period the FCC suspended application of the rules, public and congressional pressures forced the commission to reinstate them. The Reagan administration attempted to abolish the minority-preference rules but was blocked by Congress. The Bush administration asked the Supreme Court to declare such rules unconstitutional. In 1990 the Supreme Court held the rules to be constitutional. Even so, in the early 1990s minorities held only 3.5% of all broadcast licenses.

In 1978 another part of the past of broadcasting died and part of its future arrived. Clarence Dill, coauthor of the Dill–White Act—the Radio Act of 1927—and a contributor to the Communications Act of 1934, died at the age of 93. The first pay-per-view option on television, for classic movies, began at KWHY in Los Angeles. Additionally, the first video rental/sale store opened.

1979

| National Telecommunications and Information Administration is established. | FCC requires networks to sell Carter–Mondale campaign 30 minutes of airtime. | ITU authorizes extension of U.S. AM band to 1,705 kHz. |

1979

The saga of the Communications Act continued in 1979. Two Senate bills and one House bill rewriting the act were introduced. None succeeded. By the end of the year, Representative Van Deerlin, who had taken the lead in seeking a new act, gave up and decided to concentrate on changing the common carrier provisions of the old act.

Under the old act, the FCC began consideration of broad deregulation of radio, to let the marketplace substitute for government guidelines. The Supreme Court mandated deregulation for one of the FCC's rules, the one that required cable systems to provide free-access channels for the public, education, and local government. The FCC implemented Section 312 of the act by requiring the networks to sell the Carter–Mondale campaign 30 minutes of airtime, which the networks had previously refused to do. The FCC contended that reasonable access was necessary to prevent the networks from deciding who and how much the public may hear in Presidential races. The networks took the FCC to court, contending that it had violated broadcasting's First Amendment rights. In 1981 the Supreme Court upheld the FCC. Nevertheless, as subsequent events would prove, networks and individual stations—through their acquiesced manipulation by political campaigns, their use of money as a criterion for coverage, their adoption of "sound bites" as opposed to substance, and the weakening of the political equal time rules of Section 315 in the 1980s—effectively gained much control of the political process by deciding which candidates would get exposure and what the exposure would be like.

Another FCC action was prompted by the International Telecommunications Unions' (ITU) extension of the AM band in the United States to 1,705 kc. With support of the NTIA, the commission began a series of rulemakings to compress individual station bandwidth and, with the new spectrum space, add additional frequencies. Radio broadcasters, as might be expected, fought against the creation of new competitor stations, but by mid-1991 the new bandwidth had been established although there was little interest in it because of changes in the market.

The FCC took a stand on children's television. Prodded by citizen groups, including ACT, and motivated by the regulatory attempts of the FTC, in 1979 the FCC released a report criticizing the industry's compliance with the FCC's 1974 guidelines. The commission expressed concern over the failure to increase children's educational programming, to eliminate manipulative practices in presenting commercials, and to decrease the amount of advertising. One network, ABC, did reduce commercial time on its children's shows. Nonetheless, the 1974 guidelines were just that—guidelines. There were no enforcement provisions, and despite its critical report, the FCC did not propose rules that would have required compliance.

Notwithstanding its long experience covering the news and its new equipment, including electronic news gathering (ENG), broadcasting failed the American public

THE SHIFTING '70S

Nuclear accident at Three Mile Island.		Iranians seize U.S. embassy, hostages in Tehran.

Presidential commission finds media ill-prepared for nuclear accident at Three Mile Island.		Electronic media provide extensive coverage of Iran hostage crisis.

in reporting the most potentially catastrophic event of the year in the United States: the nuclear accident at Three Mile Island. A Presidential commission found that the media were unprepared for and unable to give the public effective coverage of this story.

TERRY GROSS

HOST OF NPR'S *FRESH AIR* _____

Nothing on radio had ever surprised me more than hearing one of my roommates proclaim she was a lesbian. It was 1973, and she was appearing as a guest on *Womanpower*, a feminist program on WBFO, Buffalo's NPR affiliate on the state university campus. I was puzzled and a little offended that she would go public to strangers who happened to be listening, before letting her own roommates know. Somehow, in a radio studio she felt secure enough to reveal intimacies she was not yet comfortable confiding to her own friends.

I desperately wanted to work in a medium that could have this effect on someone, and for a program that went that far. I was lucky. My roommate's new lover was one of the producers of the feminist program, but she was leaving for the lesbian-feminist show. My friend gave me the name and phone number of one of the remaining producers and encouraged me to call.

It didn't matter that I had no radio experience. The producers were almost as committed to training other women as they were to getting the program on the air. They were convinced that the mass media would continue to ignore or misinterpret

the women's movement until women were in a position to make editorial decisions and report the stories. And that couldn't happen until there were women who knew their way around the studio and control room.

The women I worked with became my closest friends. But things didn't always go as well with the men at the station. Some men were threatened by feminism, some were just terribly confused. Just as our parents believed that marijuana inevitably

FIG 7.12 Terry Gross hosts *Fresh Air*, a national radio magazine featuring a lively look at the arts and contemporary culture. *Fresh Air* is produced by WHYY-FM/ Philadelphia and distributed by National Public Radio.
Courtesy Terry Gross. Photo by Alejandro.

Antinuclear protests sweep United States.

ABC reduces commercial time in its children's shows.

Second Report of the Carnegie Commission on the Future of Public Broadcasting is issued.

Compact disc (CD) is demonstrated.

led to hard drugs, there were men who suspected feminism was the first step to lesbianism. Their confusion occasionally saved us from behavior we might have found infuriatingly sexist. On the night of my going-away party, I was warmly embraced by a male colleague who had always been cold to me, even a little hostile. As we said goodbye, he apologized for never having come on to me, and explained that he had assumed I was a lesbian. I guess he didn't want me to leave town feeling cheated.

These were the days before public radio had become as professionalized and formatted as it is today. There was a crazy quilt of programs produced by dozens of eccentric people, only a handful of whom were paid. Jazz, rock, blues, classical, and avant garde music; gay, lesbian, feminist, Latino, black, and student issues; comedy, advocacy, poetry, and Dada all had regular places on the schedule. The infighting could drive you mad, but at the same time you wondered if you'd ever experience such camaraderie again. Passion and skepticism were always present, and these are two instincts that I've since come to think of as essential to the production of any program worth putting on the air.
Courtesy Terry Gross.

Broadcasting did, however, provide continuing coverage in depth of an American crisis overseas: the taking of hostages at the U.S. embassy in Tehran by the new Ayatollah Khomeini regime in Iran. In fact, the continuing emphasis on this story by the media during the ensuing year was a factor in the public's rejection of Jimmy Carter after his single term as President.

New technological advances in 1979 included the first demonstration of the Philips compact disc (CD); in a dozen years, the CD would be well on its way to replacing records and tapes. The Ampex Corporation introduced the first digital VTR, and Sony came out with the Walkman, the first personal headset stereo, a system that would become an extension of virtually every teenager's persona.

The Carnegie Commission on the Future of Public Broadcasting issued a report entitled *A Public Trust*, advocating changes that would include abolition of the CPB and establishment of a trust that would equitably distribute funds from national license fees. But the report did not result in congressional action, nor did it change or affect the structure of public broadcasting.

The 1970s were eclectic in terms of programming, ranging through cop shows, crime, adventure, Westerns, science fiction, nostalgic sitcoms, jiggle, and war. Among the television programs that found the largest mainstream audiences during the 1970s were *M*A*S*H, Happy Days, The Waltons, McMillan and Wife, Little House on the Prairie, Laverne and Shirley, Six Million Dollar Man, Kojak, Three's Company*, and *Starsky and Hutch*. By the end of the 1970s television programming had made some democratic progress. Racist stereotypes had all but disappeared. The civil rights

Margaret Thatcher first woman to be elected
prime minister of United Kingdom.

Nicaragua dictatorship
overthrown by Sandinistas.

Sony Walkman is
introduced.

revolution of the 1960s; the organization of citizen associations, especially those representing black interests; and the early 1970s FCC regulations stemming from the Kennedy appointees' legacy—all had an impact on broadcast practices. While Huxtable-type families had not yet reached the TV screen, *Sanford and Son*, with Redd Foxx; Norman Lear's *The Jeffersons*; and other shows building on earlier attempts at sitcoms featuring black lead characters—pioneered by Diahann Carroll, who starred in the first sitcom about a black family, *Julia*—were not only accepted but popular. *The Flip Wilson Show*, featuring a black performer in a variety series, was successful; but the way had been paved years before by Nat King Cole, who could not get advertising support at that time. The public, broadcasters, and advertisers now seemed ready to see at least a few African Americans in nonstereotyped lead roles.

Conversely, sexism continued strongly. Despite efforts by the National Organization for Women (NOW) and other groups, television commercials and programs by and large still stereotyped women as sex objects for men or in roles solely to serve the needs of males in a household. Sexism in children's programs was, and in the 2000s continues to be, standard practice. With few exceptions, males always take leadership roles in children's programs, including cartoons. Most characters are male. When females are shown in leadership roles, most often they are saved from their error or predicament by a male. The self-fulfilling prophecy of women having second-class status was reinforced in the 1980s, the "Me Decade," and still is a part of children's TV programming, although to a lesser degree, in the 2000s.

Chapter EIGHT

The Techno-Edged '8()s

Teflon, Tinsel, and Me

Were the 1980s a replay of the 1920s? The similarities between the two decades were remarkable. For the media, both decades were marked by technological advancement. In the 1920s radio technology advanced and television technology arrived; in the 1980s cable and satellites advanced and fiber optics, high-definition television, digital broadcasting, and other new technologies were introduced. In the 1920s the business of broadcasting grew by leaps and bounds and managed to survive the economic crash of 1929; in the 1980s the broadcasting business—including record sums for sales of properties as well as record advertising revenues—reached its highest peaks before the economic recession began at the decade's end.

Both decades were eras during which the rich got richer and the poor got poorer. Wealthy stations got stronger; poorer stations fell by the wayside. Government turned a blind eye to unethical entrepreneurs who exploited their country—in one era, oil barons and bootleggers; in another, savings and loan operators and military contractors. Public officials violated the Constitution and federal laws with impunity. Teapot Dome scandals in the 1920s vied for infamy with Iran-Contra scandals in the 1980s. In both decades millions of people were plunged into poverty, hunger, illness, and homelessness. For most of the 1920s, broadcasting operated with no regulations requiring service in the public interest; in the 1980s, deregulation moved toward nonregulation. In the 1920s, responsible radio news was just beginning; in the 1980s, broadcast news was often criticized for abandoning its responsibilities and allowing itself to be manipulated by politics and politicians, making news more "infotainment" than information. If there were any Ed Murrows around in either decade, they were kept well hidden.

If the 1920s reflected the "I don't care generation," the 1980s were called the "me generation"—and both generations overindulged in a national orgy of spending. In the economic euphoria of both decades, the middle class ignored the huge national debt that it would one day have to pay off, the artificial prosperity that would end in joblessness and bank failures, and the tax laws that decreased the taxes of the upper-income groups while increasing the burden of lower- and middle-income taxpayers. In the early 1980s, the United States was developing a polarization that it had not experienced since the early 1930s, a déjà vu of profiteering and free-spending insensitivity that pretended that the less fortunate part of America didn't exist.

DOI: 10.1016/B978-0-240-81236-6.00008-1

U.S. hockey team wins dramatic
Olympic victory over U.S.S.R.

Mount Saint Helens volcano
erupts.

1980

CNN debuts; first 24-hour news
program.

Home ownership of TV at all-time
high.

In most of its programming, broadcasting reflected and even encouraged that fiction. By the end of the 1980s, as in the 1920s, as broadcasting's profits reached record heights, the economic bubble burst.

Both television and radio continued to grow in the 1980s. At the beginning of the decade 98% of the nation's households had television sets, the highest figure the medium would reach. Cable had 20% penetration. Although fewer than 100 new AM radio stations had gone on the air during the previous five years, more than 650 new FM stations were in operation, for a total of 8,750 radio stations, including 763 noncommercial FMs. Television had begun to reach its saturation point, with only 28 new commercial and 30 new noncommercial stations in five years; nevertheless, for the first time they added up to more than 1,000 TV stations on the air. Soon another dimension would be added as the FCC authorized the development of low-power television, which by the end of the decade would have more stations on the air or with more construction permits than full-power TV. Television advertising revenue had more than doubled in the previous five years, to almost $11.5 billion; radio advertising had almost doubled in the same period, to more than $3.7 billion. FM continued to do better than AM; in 1980 it captured 52.4% of the total national radio audience age 12 and over.

Home Ownership of TV Receivers, 1946–1980

YEAR	HOUSEHOLDS WITH TV (%)
1946	0.02
1950	9.0
1955	78.0
1960	87.0
1965	93.0
1970	95.0
1975	97.0
1980	98.0

SOURCE: U.S. BUREAU OF THE CENSUS.

The nation's highest-rated television program was a prime-time soap opera, *Dallas*. It hit its peak in 1980—two years after its debut—when more than 41 million homes tuned in to see one of the most hyped single episodes in television history—"Who Shot J. R.?" It received the highest numbers for any individual show up to that time, a 53.3 rating and a 76 share. The second most watched TV weekly show was a news feature, *60 Minutes*. In the early 1990s *Dallas* ended its long run; *60 Minutes* was, and is, still going strong.

FCC authorizes low-power
television.

TV viewers saw new personalities in 1980. Walter Cronkite, the "uncle" of network news anchoring, retired, and Dan Rather succeeded him at CBS. Roger Mudd, who had wanted that job, accepted the same position at NBC. ABC countered with an expansion of topics on a late-night news feature program that had begun the year before with special reports on the Iran hostage crisis; in 1981 the program would officially be titled *Nightline*, with Ted Koppel. The longevity of all three news personalities in their jobs suggests that the networks had made good choices.

While variety and music programs had all but disappeared from television, radio had settled deeper into its specialized music programming formats. A number of different types of rock stations, for example, could be found in almost every market, sharing highly fractionalized and targeted audiences.

On the technical side, the commercial TV networks followed PBS's lead and instituted closed captioning for people with hearing impairments. On the business side, RCA and CBS made a deal reminiscent of the early days of radio: CBS was licensed to produce and distribute videodiscs using RCA's SelectaVision system.

In this last year of the Carter–Ferris FCC, the commission mixed hard regulation with deregulation. It rescinded the licenses of three RKO TV stations—WOR (Newark), KHJ (Los Angeles), and WNAC (Boston)—because of business misconduct by RKO's parent company, General Tire and Rubber. The decision sent shock waves through the broadcasting industry, which felt that now the children were being held responsible for the sins of the parents.

The FCC also changed clear-channel designations for certain day and night stations, causing havoc for some and increased opportunities for others. It began a telco inquiry, a matter still debated in the 1990s. *Telco* is simply an acronym for *telephone company* and refers to the issue of telephone companies seeking the right to own and operate cable systems in communities where they also provide telephone service. Broadcasters and cable operators grew increasingly wary of telcos throughout the 1980s because of their potential as both delivery services (using fiber optics) and information entertainment providers. In the early 1990s, telcos could not engage in area-of-service activities beyond those of supplying common carrier services to companies that wanted to provide programs; but federal court and FCC rulings in 1991 suggested that telcos might soon receive cable operation authorization, which ultimately they did.

Beginning in the late 1990s, once-strict restrictions on telcos' provision of news or entertainment programming in their main area of (telephone) service were relaxed in an effort to promote intermedia competition. Critics argued that such changes merely strengthened the monopoly position of the four surviving Bell regional operating companies.

During 1980, following intensive investigation, the FCC staff drew up a report and recommendations on the Reverend Jim Bakker and his PTL television network. Violations of many FCC rules, including the filing of false reports and the defrauding

THE TECHNO-EDGED '80S

235

of viewers, made it clear that Bakker's licenses could be revoked, that he would be subject to fines, and that he was open to prosecution by the Department of Justice. The FCC order was ready to go. But for some reason FCC Chairman Ferris decided not to go ahead with the action and instead let it carry over for President-elect Ronald Reagan's FCC to deal with in 1981. Yet the Reagan FCC did nothing about it, either. Coincidentally, it was reported that Bakker and some of his colleagues had contributed heavily to the Reagan campaign. It wasn't until the late 1980s that action finally was taken against Bakker.

The FCC's pre-Reagan deregulatory efforts in 1980 included the ending of requirements for a number of station reports and filings and the abolition of two of its offices, the Office of Network Studies, which for years had been a watchdog on network-station relations, and its Educational (Public) Broadcasting Branch, which had served as the facilitator and advocate for the growth of public broadcasting and other educational-oriented media services within the FCC. A federal district court upheld an FCC order that modified the syndex (syndicated exclusivity) rules; the order permitted cable systems not to black out "significantly viewed" distant signals that duplicated the programs of local stations. A few months later the FCC repealed the syndex rule entirely. The U.S. Court of Appeals stopped FCC implementation of the repeal, pending its consideration of the case; the following year, 1981, it upheld the FCC's ruling. (In 1990 the syndex rule was reinstated.)

Yet as Al Jolson, were he still alive, might have said, "You ain't seen nothin' yet." In November Ronald Reagan was elected President decisively over Jimmy Carter and an era of deregulation moving toward unregulation was at hand.

1981

The year 1981 began with a deregulation bang. President Reagan's nominee to chair the FCC, Mark Fowler, was expected to immediately implement the new President's marketplace philosophy and deregulate the broadcasting industry, to "get the government off broadcaster's backs." In the several months that it took him to be confirmed by the Senate, two predecessors paved his way.

First was, as *Broadcasting* magazine wrote, "the laissez-faire legacy of Charlie Ferris." The Carter FCC chair, a Democrat who had been expected to represent the public interest, had been attacked by public interest citizen groups at various times during his years as head of the FCC because of his deregulatory policies. Ralph Nader, for example, denounced the FCC under Ferris as one of the worst agencies in Washington. Second was Robert E. Lee, a forthright conservative Republican, who was in his 28th year as an FCC commissioner—the longest tenure of anyone on a federal commission, surpassing Rosel Hyde's 23 years on the FCC when Hyde retired in 1969. Lee planned to retire later in 1981. He was first named interim chairman, then chairman, until Fowler's arrival in May.

Iran hostages freed.

U.S. space shuttle orbits earth.

1981

FCC modifies clear channel designations, abolishes third-class license, and initiates telco inquiry.

Deregulation eliminates public service programming and program log requirements.

Ferris and then Lee oversaw the following FCC deregulatory actions in the first four and a half months of 1981:

- Radio was deregulated, its public service programming requirements discontinued.
- Radio was allowed to exceed 18 minutes per hour of commercial time.
- Applications for license renewals were shortened to the size of a large postcard, replacing forms and reports designed to make a station show it had operated in the public interest during its preceding license period.
- Third-class radiotelephone licenses were abolished.
- "Ascertainment of community needs" requirements for radio were dropped.
- Program log requirements for radio were rescinded.
- Public broadcasting stations were permitted to broadcast logos and identify products of underwriters.

Within months after Fowler took over, the FCC asked Congress to revise the Communications Act to eliminate the comparative renewal process, eliminate the "reasonable access" provision of the equal time rule, repeal the requirement for equitable distribution of radio service throughout the United States, and initiate other changes that would make the marketplace rather than the government the regulator of broadcast services. Although Congress was not cooperative, during the next few years Fowler managed to accomplish virtually every one of his deregulatory goals. In 1981 Congress extended the license period for radio stations from three to seven years and, for television stations, from three to five years. The U.S. Court of Appeals ruled that scrambled pay-TV signals were protected and that any user must obtain permission and pay whatever fee was required to unscramble and use such signals. The Supreme Court opened courtroom doors to electronic journalists by ruling that states could—but were not required to—allow broadcast coverage of criminal trials, even if the defendant objected.

Some 1981 news coverage showed how effective broadcast journalism could be. One of the biggest stories was the release of the American hostages in Iran, even as Ronald Reagan was being sworn in as President. Later in the year, five ENG cameras were in operation as the nation saw live the attempted assassination of President Reagan. Broadcasting also covered fully the assassination attempt on Pope John Paul II.

Entertainment programming made new paths in drama and music. *Hill Street Blues* began on NBC, its in-depth, slice-of-life story lines reminiscent of the Golden Age of television drama but with more characters and episodic continuity. It would revolutionize TV drama formats. And MTV was born, not only providing teens with countless new hours of TV viewing and Michael Jackson with countless moonwalks but also helping shape video and film content and style, as well as other aspects of society, for years to come.

FIG 8.1 For many young people, MTV was the most important television innovation of the 1980s. *Courtesy MTV Networks.*

President Reagan shot, survives assassination attempt.

IBM introduces its first PC.

Broadcast license periods are extended.

ENG cameras record the assassination attempt on President Reagan.

Supreme Court opens courtroom doors to electronic journalists.

A new high for viewing was reached in 1981, with an average of 6 hours and 36 minutes per day per household. More people watched and listened to more television and radio stations than ever before; the total on the air broke the 10,000 mark by the end of January 1981.

Some people, however, were unhappy with television's programming. The Reverend Donald Wildmon and his organization, Coalition for Better Television, threatened to boycott advertisers who continued to support programs Wildmon and his group deemed offensive. The increasing conservatism of the times encouraged the growth of this and other groups similar to the already powerful Moral Majority.

The business of broadcasting boomed. Mergers of media giants, takeovers of communications companies, and buying and selling of stations escalated. One 1981 sale represented the largest price paid up to then for a single station: $220 million from Metromedia to Boston Broadcasters, Inc., for WCVB-TV in Boston. The largest merger in cable TV up to then also took place: Westinghouse Broadcasting Company bought TelePrompTer Corporation for $646 million. The recorder of the business of broadcasting, the bible of the industry, *Broadcasting* magazine, also celebrated; it was its 50th birthday. Time and people passed: Robert E. Kintner, the former president of NBC and ABC, died, as did Marshall McLuhan, the guru of mass communications.

Public broadcasting was now well established, with yearly budgets from Congress and with a strong structure in CPB, PBS, and NPR. Having done its job of promoting the development of the system, including the Public Broadcasting Act of 1967—perhaps too well for its own survival and unable to adapt creatively to the new noncommercial broadcasting structure—the NAEB, which had been formed in 1934 and traced its roots back to 1925, went out of existence.

Technical innovations continued. The first professional one-piece camcorders went on sale. The Japanese HDTV system was demonstrated in the United States, initiating the beginning of a dramatic change in the U.S. system. Although not then associated with the living-room television set but to have a profound effect on U.S. communications within a few years, the first IBM personal computer, or PC, became available.

Broadcasting reported both belligerence and humility. Ronald Reagan started his Presidency by escalating the Cold War, threatening to nuke the U.S.S.R. (in an offhand remark at an open mic prior to a radio address). By contrast, he ended his Presidency by making an accommodation with the U.S.S.R. and helping bring the Cold War to a close. Nuclear conflict was the last thing the American public wanted as it soberly remembered its last war with the 1981 unveiling of the Vietnam Memorial in Washington, D.C.

MTV

Everything changed when cable came along. Prior to cable, which more than doubled its household penetration to nearly 60% during the 1980s, Americans had lived in a network broadcasting era in which there was a single popular culture served by the few major radio, then television networks. From 1920 through the 1980s, the broadcast era was something unprecedented in human history, a culture that had nearly everyone sharing the same media fare. Cable changed that dynamic by breaking up the audience into many popular cultures (now called "niche" audiences), with each faction sharing experiences different from those of other segments of the population. At first audiences were reluctant to abandon free television for the unproven content of cable. But that changed on August 1, 1981, with the launching of Music Television (MTV) and its prophetic first song, "Video Killed the Radio Star." MTV produced a generation of screeching kids echoing the channel's mantra of "I Want My MTV," for whom cable would become an absolute necessity. Kids *needing* their daily dose of artists like Michael Jackson, Culture Club, and Duran Duran harassed their parents into getting their homes wired and may have, more than any other single factor, made cable a necessity.

1982

In 1982 the FCC removed its limits on commercial time per hour for television. It abolished its three-year trafficking rule, which had prevented a station from being resold within three years after its acquisition. This rule had been designed to prevent stations from being bought and sold for immediate profit taking, thus neglecting programming or other operations in the public interest. As noted earlier, the FCC authorized AM stereo in 1982. Yet the commission refused to designate one of the five approved systems as the standard, thereby leaving AM stations waiting for an eventual marketplace determination. Subscription television was deregulated. Some public TV stations were given special authorization to experiment with actual advertising.

The FCC also authorized DBS, but implementation, other than short-lived experiments, was a long way off. The commission began accepting applications for cellular radio. And low-power television (LPTV) stations, which had been authorized earlier, began going on the air, with large numbers of applications for more pending. Congress amended the Communications Act to reduce the number of FCC commissioners from seven to five.

A combined government–industry deregulatory action was the abolition of the NAB's radio and television codes for programming and advertising. After the courts, following a Justice Department suit, found part of the NAB's advertising code unconstitutional, the NAB hastily dropped all its codes, including its guidelines for children's programs.

THE TECHNO-EDGED '80S

239

Reagan administration designates ketchup a vegetable in school lunches.

Vietnam Memorial dedicated in Washington.

1982

IBM introduces its first PC.

FCC removes its guidelines on commercial time per hour for television and authorizes DBS.

NAB drops its codes.

FIG 8.2 In the 1980s AM broadcasters saw stereo as a way to gain parity with FM.
Courtesy KDES, Palm Springs, California.

Perhaps the most significant implementation of an earlier FCC-prompted action was the settlement of the Department of Justice's suit against AT&T, divesting AT&T of all its local telephone companies, effective in 1984. AT&T would, in return, receive permission to enter other new technology fields. Although many public interest groups hailed the breakup of Ma Bell as a step forward in reducing industry monopolies, it would take years to resolve some of the immediate problems of chaos, inefficiency, and higher costs. Another government action related to broadcasting was a report by the National Institute of Mental Health, Television and Behavior, which found that televised violence did affect some viewers' behavior.

While violence may have come from some television programs, violence was done to one. Ed Asner, star of the *Lou Grant* show, which had for some years been successful artistically and in the ratings, became politically controversial when he participated in raising funds for medical supplies for rebels fighting the dictatorial government of El Salvador. He was attacked by politically conservative sources, including the Moral Majority and the actor Charlton Heston, who had recently been beaten twice by Asner in bitter fights for the presidency of the Screen Actors Guild. Pressure was put on advertisers, and several withdrew from the show. Although the show's ratings had begun to decline, they were still highly respectable; nevertheless, CBS decided to cancel the program anyway. Asner himself later stated he did not liken this situation to the blacklisting of the 1950s; now it seemed sufficient simply to be controversial.

PAULA LYONS

Consumer Editor, WBZ, Boston; former consumer editor, ABC's *Good Morning America*

FIG 8.3 Paula Lyons.
Courtesy Capital Cities/ABC, Inc.

Great moments in television cannot be planned. They just happen! One happened to me back in 1982. It was a typical scenario. A housing company had taken deposits from consumers, promised to put up manufactured homes on specified lots of land in Southeastern Massachusetts, and never delivered. I was on the empty lots about to interview three of the aggrieved couples when a representative of the housing company showed up, with a customer, trying to sell the same lots all

National Institute of Mental Health issues its report *Television and Behavior.*

"Psychographics" becomes newest market research buzzword.

over again! The victims I was about to interview went crazy! They attacked the saleswoman and the new customer—verbally—warning the customer not to be the next chump. And for a moment I wondered, What is my role? What do I do here? And the answer was nothing, nothing at all. The photographer kept rolling. The argument was a beaut! And I ended up with a piece of award-winning television!

Courtesy Paula Lyons.

While *Lou Grant* went off the air, two new shows that went on the air were to make their marks. *St. Elsewhere*, though never a ratings leader, was praised over the years for innovation and funkiness. *Cheers* became a national institution and until it went off the air in 1992 was still at or near the top of the ratings every week.

In seeking higher ratings, ad agencies began to stress an additional aspect of market research. Going beyond demographics, they now worked with "psychographics" as well, seeking to determine attitudes and beliefs as well as age, gender, and affluence of viewers and prospective purchasers.

Cable continued to expand, now reaching 29% of all homes, and nonentertainment channels such as C-Span and the Home Shopping Network appeared.

Another broadcast pioneer, RCA's longtime star inventor, Vladimir Zworykin, who had vied with and lost out to Philo Farnsworth for the title of father of American television, died at age 94.

1983

Less regulation and more technology dominated 1983. The FCC allocated eight Instructional Television Fixed Service (ITFS) channels to MMDS and was deluged by thousands of applications for the commercial service. The commission decided how to determine to award new LPTV licenses—not on the basis of proposed service to the public but by lottery. The FCC authorized teletext—visual data that can be ordered for transmission to an individual television screen—but, as it did with AM stereo, refused to designate a standard. Previously authorized videotex—two-way interactive television, computer coordinated—was experimented with in two communities.

The FCC watered down the political equal-time rule. It permitted stations to set up their own political debates, thus allowing a station to include those candidates it favored and to exclude those it didn't. That, and the relaxing of the definition of news—exempt from the equal-time rule—also made it possible for a station to carry news features and news interviews with candidates it favored and to virtually rule out of contention, by lack of exposure, those it didn't. This situation gave broadcasters

THE TECHNO-EDGED '80S

241

FIG 8.4 VCRs and CD players became the hottest new home entertainment technologies in the 1980s. *Courtesy TEAC.*

unprecedented influence on local and state elections, especially party primaries having a number of candidates. Broadcasting's control of the U.S. political process was virtually complete.

In a policy statement regarding children's television, the FCC once again refused to issue any rules; rather, as it did in its 1974 policy statement, it recommended voluntary self-regulation by the industry.

ABC, CBS, and NBC radio network feeds went satellite. Compact disc players, with considerably better sound quality than long-playing records or tapes, began to make inroads in the home audio market—though it wouldn't be until 1987 that full marketing of an improved version would take the country by storm. The shift from analog to digital radio began, and there was much talk about digital television and HDTV in the near future.

The amazing ratings success of *Roots* continued to prompt more network television miniseries, including *The Winds of War*, which set a new record for numbers of viewers, and *The Thorn Birds. The MacNeil Report*, which had been on the air since 1976, enhanced PBS's status as it became *The MacNeil-Lehrer Report*. The final episode of *M*A*S*H* was a 2.5-hour special, garnering the largest audience up to that time for a single program, a 60.3 rating and a 77 share.

A 1983 special generated overtones of 1950s McCarthyism. *The Day After* was a docudrama portraying what might happen were there an atomic war. The early 1980s were a time of antinuclear protest and a national nuclear freeze campaign, reminiscent of the anti–Vietnam War protests of more than a decade before. *The Day After* was labeled unpatriotic, even Communistic by some groups, and, coupled with its graphic depiction of nuclear effects, it was highly controversial by the time it aired. Indeed, there were rumors that it might not be shown at all. ABC, which showed courage in airing it, added a disclaimer, and a panel discussion followed the program. Rating surveys showed that more than 50% of potential adult viewers saw *The Day After*. For some, the horrors it presented were devastating; for others, it didn't go far enough.

Controversy attended NBC's miniseries *Holocaust* as well. It presented, also in docudrama form, what happened to a Jewish family in Germany before and during World War II. Here, too, some viewers felt that the program opened wounds that should have remained closed; others felt that it should have done more to prick the consciences of those who permitted the Holocaust to happen and of a current generation that might forget its lessons.

Station sales set one record after another. No sooner did TV station KTZA in Los Angeles sell for a record $245 million than KHOU-TV in Houston sold for $342 million.

Ethics raised its disturbing head in 1983. In Alabama, a camera operator for WHMA filmed a man who set himself on fire; the cameraman did so rather than interceding and possibly saving the man's life. The question of the journalist's role in such situations continues to be discussed today. In Kansas City, a former TV news anchorwoman, Christine Craft, was awarded $500,000 by a jury in a sex-discrimination suit that found Craft's firing had been based on physical looks—she allegedly didn't look young and pretty enough—and not on competence. Although the decision was later reversed, Craft's courage in standing up against gender bias at the potential cost of her future career motivated many other women in broadcasting to stand up for equal opportunities and their personal rights. The treatment of Christine Craft was counterpointed that same year with media coverage of the treatment given another woman, Dr. Sally Ride. Based on ability and performance, Ride became the first American woman astronaut in space.

TV's Versions of *The War of the Worlds*

Following the 1938 *The War of the Worlds* broadcast, the FCC banned pseudo radio newscasts. But the format had a go on television with little public uproar or comment by the FCC. NBC's 1983 *Special Bulletin* opened with benign promos on the fictional RBS Network before an ominous graphic "Special Bulletin" appeared. What followed was a faux newscast detailing antiwar terrorists holding a homemade atomic bomb outside Charleston, South Carolina, demanding the government disable its nuclear stockpile. The program followed events as though it were an actual newscast, shot on videotape, stumbling dialogue, and frequent technical glitches, all enhancing the "live" feel. But television permitted on-screen scrawls noting that the show was fictional. Still there were isolated reports of panic as some made snap judgments on what they were seeing between disclaimers. And as we learned from *War*, those affected failed to make a simple "reality check" by flipping the dial to see what other stations were covering. In a similar vein, CBS's 1994 *Without Warning* featured a "live" news break-in during an ostensible network movie, reporting on an unfolding alien invasion, and as homage to Orson Welles, also airing on Halloween eve in the same fictional village of Grover's Mill but this time situated in Wyoming.

1984

Cable's deregulatory turn came in 1984 as Congress passed the Cable Communications Policy Act of 1984. Rates for subscribers were no longer limited to those agreed to in franchise contracts, and within a few years they shot up 50%, 100%, and more in many parts of the country. Percentages of gross revenue fees to cities previously agreed to between cable systems and cities were no longer valid, and a cap of 5% was set. Access channels no longer had to be provided free. These specifications and other amendments to the Communications Act gave cable additional freedoms to compete more effectively against broadcasting. Within five years, complaints from cable subscribers nationally—complaints predominantly related to service and rates—prompted Congress to begin work on a cable reregulation bill. Threats of a veto by President George H. W. Bush, however, caused Congress to drop cable legislation in 1990, though it was expected that some kind of cable reregulation would nonetheless occur in the early 1990s.

Another controversial action in 1984 was the FCC's relaxation of the multiple-ownership rule to allow any one entity to own up to 12 TV, 12 AM, and 12 FM stations nationwide—an increase from 7-7-7. The original rule was adopted to "maximize diversification of program and service viewpoints as well as prevent any undue concentration contrary to the public interest." Congress, however, was concerned with the extension of media monopolies and information control, and a series of compromises between Congress and the FCC resulted in a 25% cap on the total U.S. population any one TV conglomerate could reach. Exceptions were made for the maximum number of stations for minority owners, and population percentages were discounted for UHF stations. The new "Rule of Twelves" went into effect in 1985.

The deregulation of ascertainment, program logs, public service, and other requirements for commercial radio of a few years before went into effect for television and public broadcasting in 1984. Although broadcasters saw these FCC rulings as a boon, over their shoulders they saw other developments with which they were not happy. One was a Supreme Court decision in favor of Sony, reversing the finding of a lower court. The high court ruled that it was legal for a VCR owner to copy programs off television. For the two preceding years, that activity had been illegal. The 15 million U.S. VCR homes that had been doing so had, in fact, violated federal law. But, of course, such criminal actions—which they technically were—were impossible to monitor. Technical developments included the arrival of the first digital videodisc recorder, the first HDTV recorder, for sale by Sony.

In television programming, *The Cosby Show* came to NBC. It immediately became a national favorite and in the early 1990s was still near the top of the rating charts. With one of the few nonstereotyped portrayals of a middle-class black family—the father was a physician, the mother an attorney—*The Cosby Show* was lauded for establishing highly positive role models.

In radio, specialized music formats in some markets began to lose ground. By the end of the year a number of stations had revived the Top 40 format (by now referred to as Contemporary Hit Radio, or CHR), with its emphasis on personalities (Rick Dees and Scott Shannon, to name a couple of CHR superjocks) as much as on the music. It recalled for some listeners the 1960s, when such deejays as Alan Freed, Cousin Brucie, Wolfman Jack, and Murray the K reigned over the audio airwaves.

The power of advertising took an unusual turn when the TV commercial slogan for Wendy's fast-food chain—"Where's the beef?"—spoken by an 80-year-old performer, Clara Peller, became a critical catchphrase in the 1984 Democratic Presidential

1984

A TV news anchorwoman, Christine Craft, wins initial sex-discrimination suit.

M*A*S*H* ends run with record audience.

Congress passes the Cable Communications Policy Act of 1984.

primary. One candidate used the slogan to denigrate another candidate. In the Presidential campaign, especially at both party conventions, satellite news-gathering (SNG) equipment made possible more thorough television coverage than ever before, permitting individual broadcast stations and cable networks like CNN and C-Span, as well as broadcasting networks, to report. It was in this campaign that special attention and probing were given to the first female ever to be on the Presidential ticket of a major party—Geraldine Ferraro, the Democratic Vice Presidential candidate.

Whereas broadcast journalists received full cooperation from political parties, they didn't fare so well with the military. The military, having learned from television coverage of Vietnam that one should not let the public know what it is doing if the public might not like it, barred the press from covering the U.S. invasion of tiny Grenada. Only after several days were news teams allowed in. Such control and censorship of the press would reach a peak less than a decade later in the Persian Gulf.

1985

This was the year of the networks. In 1985 GE announced it was buying RCA and, with it, NBC, for $6.5 billion (the sale was completed in 1986). Ownership had come full circle since 1919, when GE established RCA to operate radio stations so that GE could remain solely on the manufacturing side of the business. Also in 1985, ABC was purchased by Capital Cities Communications for $3.5 billion. The Mutual Radio Network was sold to Westwood One for $39 million. CBS almost had a new owner, too, but Ted Turner's bid to buy up controlling stock in the network failed. Rupert Murdoch purchased six television stations from Metromedia for $2 billion and formed a new network, Fox, which began operations the following year. Even cable got into the act, with the formation of a new network conglomerate, Viacom International, buying the Showtime, Movie Channel, MTV, and VH-1 cable networks for $690 million. To top it off, the networks took to the sky, transmitting programs by satellite to their affiliates.

Under deregulation, television licenses continued to increase in monetary value, and Tribune Broadcasting paid a record $550 million for one station, KTLA, in Los Angeles. Television advertising revenues nationally had zoomed almost 100% since 1980, to surpass $20 billion annually. Radio's five-year increase was more modest by comparison, under 90%, but reached an annual total of $6.5 billion. The number of AM stations increased only 10%, to 5,973; commercial FM stations went up just a bit more than 15%, to 3,282; and noncommercial FM up less than 5%, to 797. Commercial TV stations increased by fewer than 150, to 883, and noncommercial TV stations by only 37, coming close to their saturation point, for a total of 314. Cable saw accelerated growth and was now in almost 40% of U.S. television homes.

FCC relaxes multiple ownership rule.

Programming was eclectic, as varied new sitcoms such as *The Golden Girls*, the first pay-per-view cable service, and national distribution of the Home Shopping Club. To some, the most significant program of 1985, and the one with the largest audience, was the "Live Aid" concert from Philadelphia and London featuring the leading popular music performers of the time. Fourteen communication satellites carried the program to more than 1,200 countries and by tape delay to almost 50 more. "Live Aid" was watched by as many as 400 million people worldwide. It raised about $75 million for relief to famine-stricken lands (see Tony Verna in the next chapter).

Syndication of video programming grew for a number of reasons. More network programs became available. The increasing number of cable networks and new, independent television stations, including LPTV operations, required more program material. The increased use of satellite and other new technologies facilitated program distribution.

A most important court decision regarding a regulatory matter shook the broadcasting industry. In its 1972 cable rules the FCC had asserted the "must-carry" principle, whereby cable systems were obligated to carry all local broadcast signals—"local" defined as stations within a 60-mile (later 50-mile) radius. Quincy (Washington) Cable Television and Turner Broadcasting (which wanted less competition from local signals in order to facilitate carriage of its Atlanta "national" station) had brought suits against the FCC on the grounds that the must-carry rules were unconstitutional. The U.S. Court of Appeals found that the must-carry principle did violate the First Amendment. A subsequent attempt by the FCC to institute a must-carry provision was also ruled

FIG 8.5 In the 1980s pop-rock music stations enhanced their hold on audiences by sponsoring spectacular concert events.
Courtesy WLS, Chicago.

Indira Gandhi assassinated.

1985

Supreme Court authorizes over-
the-air home videotaping.

The Cosby Show debuts.

Breakup of AT&T.

unconstitutional. Finally, agreement was reached (1) requiring carriage only of public television signals, based on cable system capacity, and (2) providing subscribers, at a fee, with A/B switches whereby a subscriber could switch from cable to off-the-air reception if the cable system were not carrying a local broadcast signal the subscriber wanted to see. Although broadcasters' worst fears were not realized, in fact a number of local stations were dropped by cable systems that could make more money by substituting a distant channel or an additional cable network. Some marginally subsisting television stations, with the loss of advertising revenue, did not survive. (For example, in a 50% penetration market, loss of cable carriage removed 50% of a station's viewers except for those who used the A/B switch, in turn causing advertisers to withdraw or pay an equivalent discounted rate for commercials.)

A sign of economic times yet to come was foreign competition, which in 1985 forced the RCA Broadcast Equipment Division—producers of broadcasting equipment almost from the beginning of radio—to close down.

The Twistings and Turnings of "Must-Carry"

The FCC first mandated must-carry rules in 1972, but it wasn't until the 1980s that cable operators complained. With the growth of cable-only networks, operators, particularly those with limited capacity, felt they would be less marketable if they had to devote considerable portions of their space for stations consumers could receive free, over the air. Some operators offered subscribers an A-B switch in which one terminal linked to the cable and the other to the antenna but found viewers reluctant to leave the comfort of their couches to manually switch between cable and local feeds. Over the years the federal courts have frequently rejected must-carry on First Amendment grounds, only to have it resurface. The current version, known as *retransmission-consent*, is an odd arrangement wherein local stations can force carriage if they don't request reimbursement, but if they do, even if it is some barter deal, the cable operator can refuse to carry. Must-carry more often affects independents and minor network affiliates that are at a program-popularity disadvantage. The problem has been further confounded with the transition to digital that offers broadcasters the ability to send multiple content streams but finds cable operators balking at how many they must carry.

1986

Hard times were coming to broadcasting, despite its expanded revenues. In 1986 all the networks, faced with increasing competition from cable, VCRs, and other home technologies and steadily losing prime-time audiences, reorganized under new ownership and/or changed leadership. They tried to become more business efficient by

GE announces plans to purchase RCA and NBC.

ABC is acquired by Capital Cities Communications.

cutting back staff and paying more attention to the profit and loss columns. CBS, for example, which had been responsible for some of the key technical innovations in broadcasting, closed its technology center.

A television-linked service received a setback. The Knight-Ridder Company's experiment with videotex in Miami, Viewtron, closed down with a loss in excess of $50 million. Five years later videotex still had not yet made expected headway, although the number of videotex services and subscribers was growing.

Pay-cable companies tried to protect themselves from piracy. Led by HBO and Cinemax, most pay-cable channels were, by the end of the year, scrambling their signals. Illegal decoders and unscramblers were easily available, however, even through mail-order services, and many were sold.

Despite the problems, TV viewing was the highest it had ever been, an average of 7 hours and 10 minutes per day per home. A spate of Cosby-clone sitcoms hit the air. Few of them survived. A successor to *Hill Street Blues* did: From one of the same creators, Steven Bochco and Terry Louise Fisher, but set in a law office and courtrooms instead of in a police station and patrol beats, *L.A. Law* started high on the charts and stayed there.

A bright spot for network television was sports. Live coverage drew larger and larger audiences each year, with advertising revenues to match. By 1991, for example, a 30-second commercial on the National Football League Super Bowl broadcast cost $800,000.

Technical advances stressed the coming digital revolution, including continued development of digital audio tape (DAT), laser videodiscs with digital sound tracks, and digital TVs and VCRs. A number of new satellites were launched for the principal purpose of reporting. SNG was now an essential part of broadcast journalism. The importance of cable news as an alternative to broadcast news was demonstrated when the space shuttle *Challenger* blew up shortly after its launch from Cape Canaveral. Only CNN was covering the event live, although the network news teams came in almost immediately after the disaster.

The year 1986 was the beginning of the end for the Fairness Doctrine. Controversial since its development through the *Mayflower* decision and the *Red Lion* case, its demise was urged by most broadcasters, who believed it violated their First Amendment rights by restricting their privilege to say what they wanted on their stations without the government requiring them to present opposing viewpoints. Its retention was urged by those who believed that rather than restricting freedom of speech and ideas, it made them more available for a broader U.S. constituency—those who, under the Fairness Doctrine, had an opportunity to put them on the air and those who heard views they would not otherwise have heard. FCC Chairman Fowler, implementing President Reagan's marketplace philosophy, had stated that one of his priorities was to abolish the Fairness Doctrine.

The doctrine's opponents got their chance, ironically, because the FCC upheld a Fairness Doctrine complaint brought by the Syracuse (New York) Peace Council

Terrorist hijackings of planes, ships continue.

United States votes sanctions against South Africa.

U.S. Court of Appeals votes against "must-carry" rules.

Mutual Radio Network is sold to Westwood One.

Choosing a Parental Control Code

In order to fully secure the Parental Control feature, you may wish to choose and program a Parental Control code into the converter. This capability allows you to "teach" the converter a code that must then be used to remove Parental Controls. Again, the converter must be disabled prior to code programming (see page 8).

Enter Parental Control Code

Action	Converter Display
1. Press "LEARN."	L E
2. Press "*" or "PC/PM."	L P
3. Press "ENTER."	L P *(flashing)*
4. Enter code (up to four digits).	L P *(remains flashing)*
5. Press "ENTER." (Selected channel is displayed.)	1.2

Any break in the above sequence will cause the converter to revert to the current channel display.

The code you select can be any number from 0 to 9999, but cannot exceed four digits. If the code selected exceeds four digits, the converter will recognize only the last four digits entered.

To help you remember your code, write it here, and keep this handbook in a safe place.

To Change a Parental Control Code

Action	Converter Display
1. Press "LEARN."	L E
2. Press "*" or "PC/PM."	L P
3. Enter old code.	L P
4. Press "ENTER."	L P *(flashing)*
5. Enter new code.	L P *(remains flashing)*
6. Press "ENTER." (Selected channel is displayed.)	1.2

Any entry error in the above sequence will cause the converter to revert to the current channel display.

To remove Parental Control from the channels you have chosen, follow the "Parental Control Deactivation" instructions on page 8. Then, tune to each parentally controlled channel and press "*" or "PC/PM." The indicator light (a small red "dot" shown between the channel numbers on your channel selector) will disappear.

FIG 8.6 As cable entered more and more homes in the 1980s, concern that children would have access to adult-oriented programming prompted systems to offer "lock-box" features to subscribers.

THE TECHNO-EDGED '80S

against the Meredith Broadcasting Company station, WTVH, in Syracuse. WTVH was found to have denied the council time under the doctrine to respond to false statements by the station regarding a controversial Syracuse nuclear power plant referendum. In a sequence of events from 1986 to 1987, Meredith Broadcasting refused to honor the FCC's invocation of the Fairness Doctrine and took the case to court. The U.S. Court of Appeals, in a 2–1 vote, decided that there was no statutory Fairness Doctrine requirement and that the commission did not have to implement it. (The two votes against the doctrine, coincidentally, were by Justices Anthony Scalia and Robert Bork, both of whom would be nominated to the Supreme Court by President Reagan, the former to be confirmed, the latter not.) Congress then passed a Fairness Law, codifying the doctrine. President Reagan vetoed it, and although the veto would have been easily overridden in the House, the Senate count indicated it would be one or two votes short. Congress therefore let the veto stand, whereupon the FCC abolished the Fairness Doctrine.

1986

Ted Turner attempts CBS takeover.

"Live Aid" concert is broadcast internationally.

TV networks employ satellite for affiliates.

1987

When Mark Fowler left the FCC in January 1987, he had put through virtually every deregulatory action he had promised. The major action not yet completed was that of the Fairness Doctrine, which was not officially eliminated until later in the year. But during his almost six years as FCC chair, Fowler's record was impressive (that is, if you were pro-marketplace; it was depressive if you favored public interest regulation). During Fowler's stewardship the commission took the following actions:

- Authorized AM stereo without setting a standard
- Dismissed a proposal requiring divestiture of colocated AM-FM stations owned by the same licensee
- Eliminated filing of annual financial reports by broadcasters and cable operators
- Shortened station application and transfer of ownership forms
- Authorized paid, promotional announcements for nonprofit groups by public broadcast stations
- Eliminated the three-year antitrafficking rule
- Authorized MMDS while taking away ITFS channels
- Eliminated the requirement that a station ID be that of the community of license, thus permitting station identification with any community
- Exempted cable systems from rate regulation of tiered services
- Modified the equal-time rule to authorize broadcasters to hold their own political debates
- Eliminated most of its regulations regarding station call signs
- Eliminated a "regional concentration" rule that prohibited ownership of three stations when two were located within 100 miles of the third
- Relaxed the policy even more for children's TV, giving producers full leeway
- Broadened multiple-ownership limitations from 7-7-7 to 12-12-12
- Eliminated restrictions on AM-FM combinations' duplication of programs
- Relaxed the policy of judging the character of an applicant for a station license
- Rescinded cable system requirements of compliance with technical-quality performance standards
- Permitted tendered offers and proxy contests in sales of stations
- Eliminated the "ascertainment of community needs" requirement for TV and public broadcasting (having done so for radio earlier)
- Eliminated commercial ad limits
- Shortened program reporting requirements

Whereas all these actions might be considered clearly deregulatory, a number of others during that period were deregulatory in that they opened the media to new

CBS closes its technology center.

Network audience numbers are affected by cable and VCRs.

FIG 8.7 Talk studios have become more commonplace than deejay studios in AM radio.

THE TECHNO-EDGED '80S

technologies but regulatory in that they established new rules and regulations. With respect to these combined kinds of actions, the FCC did the following:

- Authorized LPTV
- Authorized DBS
- Authorized teletext
- Reduced satellite orbital spacing
- Applied criteria used for broadcasting in reviewing cable EEO practices
- Authorized TV stereo
- Permitted quadrupling of the nighttime power of local AM stations
- Gave daytime AMs preference in the FM application procedure

Although deregulation was *de rigueur*, the FCC became a hard-nosed regulator with its indecency rules. Revived "topless radio" programs were the primary targets. Although unable to establish a specific definition of what it meant by "indecency," "obscenity," or "community standards," the FCC stated it would not permit material that "depicts or describes, in terms patently offensive as measured by contemporary

| United States bombs Libya. | Wall Street insider trading scandal. | Iran-Contra scam by high U.S. officials revealed. |

| Fox TV network debuts. | HBO and Cinemax scramble their signals. |

community standards for the broadcast medium, sexual or excretory activities or organs." While not permitting obscenity at any time, the commission established what it called a "safe haven" for "adult" materials between midnight and 6:00 A.M., presumably when children would not be watching or listening. At President Reagan's urging, the safe haven was removed by Congress in 1988, and a 24-hour ban went into effect. This was one of the few issues on which broadcasters and citizen civil liberties groups generally agreed: They opposed such restrictions. In 1991 the U.S. Court of Appeals ruled that the full 24-hour ban was unconstitutional, a violation of First Amendment protections of freedom of speech.

News grew. The industry-supported public information arm, the Television Information Office (which would be abolished in 1990), reported that twice as many network affiliates increased their news coverage as decreased it. There was much ado about one news event in 1987. When the CBS live telecast of the U.S. Open tennis championships ran over into *The Evening News*, anchor Dan Rather protested the sports-versus-news priority by walking off the set. The result? Six minutes of dead airtime for all CBS affiliates—and sharp criticism of Rather.

Game shows became the most watched syndicated programs. Talk shows hit new daytime peaks, with *Donahue* clones such as *Oprah* and *Geraldo* becoming highly successful. Music shows on cable continued to attract large youth audiences, a phenomenon much like Dick Clark's music shows on television had been decades before. One widespread complaint about programming involved Ted Turner's colorization of old movies his company had acquired when he bought MGM.

The technical development of digital and HDTV continued apace. A *Boston Globe* headline said, "Digital May Make FM Obsolete." The expectation was that digital sound would be to FM what FM sound was to AM. Presuming that digital would become the standard for all radio stations, it was predicted that by the year 2000 AM and FM would be equal, necessitating entirely new structural and programming changes in the radio industry.

The FCC took a hard look at HDTV through a joint FCC–Industry Advanced TV Advisory Committee and through the industry's own Advanced Television Systems Committee. The time was nearing when the FCC would have to choose between HDTV (high-definition television) and EDTV (enhanced-definition television). ATV (advanced television) is the generic term referring to any system of distributing television programming that results in better video and audio quality than the current U.S. NTSC standard of 525 lines. HDTV offers about twice the number of lines, with picture quality comparable to that of 35mm film and audio quality similar to that of CDs. EDTV refers to systems that are an improvement over NTSC but are not as good as HDTV. In 1990 the FCC determined that it preferred an HDTV system that could operate in the present broadcast television spectrum and be compatible with the NTSC system—that is, permitting existing sets to receive the new signal in the 525-line mode while the public gradually switched over to HDTV sets, similar to what was done when color TV was authorized in 1953.

Stock market takes biggest
plunge in history.

1987

Space shuttle *Challenger*
explosion is aired live by CNN.

Fowler completes tenure as
chairman of the FCC.

Fairness Doctrine is abolished.

DICK CLARK

PERFORMER AND PRODUCER _____

I've always striven for sincerity and
believability on mic and on camera. In the
old days when radio announcers used to
listen to their voices with a cupped hand
held over their ear, they were listening for
deep tone and resonance. The most sought-
after qualities in those days were authority
and command. The male voice needed
maturity and depth. Things have changed
since then. These days, whether it's a male
or female voice, the quality that works best
is naturalness—believability. One does not
have to possess a super-mature, super-
resonant voice to succeed. Since starting in
broadcasting in the 1950s, I've tried to
come across as a "real" person.
Courtesy Dick Clark.

FIG 8.8 Dick Clark's career as a
broadcast performer spans five decades.
Courtesy Dick Clark.

Broadcasting's competition continued to grow in 1987: Cable and home video
recorders were each in more than 50% of U.S. households, and the fourth network,
Fox, officially started its program schedule. Throughout the 1980s, complaints about
rating methods grew, not only from some of the public but from networks, stations,
and advertisers. The ratings systems, including leading companies A. C. Nielsen and
Arbitron, tried various new approaches. One of Nielsen's was a "People Meter" that
purported to determine who and how many were watching, not just what number
of sets were tuned to what programs. The networks soon expressed dissatisfaction
with the People Meter, which showed lower ratings for their programs than they
thought they should have. Some critics stated that the networks were trying to ignore
the fact that the competitive media had generated a steady increase in viewing for
their own programs, with a concomitant serious drop in viewing of networks' prime-
time schedules. In the early 1990s network prime-time viewing continued to drop,
rating companies were still blamed, and an acceptable method of measurement had
not yet been found.

Televangelist Jim Bakker scandal breaks.		"Safe sex" is new slogan as AIDS spreads.

FCC targets "shock radio" for indecency.		Ted Turner is criticized for colorizing old movies for broadcast.

The power of television was shown in its coverage of the Senate's Iran-Contra hearings. The Contras were the U.S.-founded armed forces trying to overthrow the socialist government of Nicaragua. Some of the funds sent to the Contras were sent illegally, siphoned by government officials and others from illegal arms sales to the United States' enemy, Iran. Lieutenant Colonel Oliver ("Ollie") North was a major figure in these transactions. Was Lieutenant Colonel North a hero or an antihero? North, who admitted actions that many considered subversive of the democratic processes of American government and even traitorous to the U.S. Constitution, was nevertheless transformed into an instant hero by the media.

Also in 1987, another moment dealing with the history of broadcasting occurred: the American Museum of the Moving Image (film and television) opened in Astoria, New York.

Cable Television Systems, 1955–1987

YEAR	NUMBER OF SYSTEMS
1955	400
1960	640
1965	1,325
1970	2,490
1975	3,506
1980	4,225
1985	6,600
1987	7,900

SOURCE: U.S. BUREAU OF THE CENSUS.

1988

Technology continued to dominate broadcasting developments in 1988. Broadcasters looked at HDTV with increasing interest, as a way of helping the quality of their off-the-air signals compete with cable. The industry's Advanced Television Systems Committee approved a 1,125-line, 60-Hz signal standard. The FCC's new HDTV Advisory Committee met for the first time, with a commission directive that any HDTV system chosen must be compatible with receivers currently in use. HDTV innovations in 1988 included release of the first HDTV videocassette and production of the first HDTV movie.

Two potential threats to both television's and cable's current structures moved forward. First, AT&T demonstrated its latest development in fiber optics. Modulated by lasers, the beams provided a wider bandwidth and an excellent signal. Second, Congress passed a bill facilitating delivery of satellite signals to backyard dishes—television receive-onlys (TVROs).

FIG 8.9 Radio stations—more than 12,000 strong—dot the U.S. landscape today. *Courtesy KNEW, Oakland, California, and Metromedia.*

Stereo advanced in one medium but struggled in another. More than a third of the nation's television stations were now in stereo; however, only 10% of AM stations were in stereo, not all of them compatible. The FCC recognized AM's problems by eliminating its AM-FM nonduplication rule, and within a year some 1,000 pairs of stations were duplicating programs. AM continued to try new formats to stay alive. The SUN Radio Network offered AM 24-hour, talk-information programming. FM moved ahead, concerned principally with what music format might provide a new edge; in 1988, the adult contemporary format topped the ratings.

Television programming was a mixed bag. A 22-week writers' strike forced cancellation of some series programs and compelled the networks to offer an "interim" fall schedule. The growing number of made-for-TV movies did well, and one miniseries, *War and Remembrance*, 18 hours in length, started in 1988, took a hiatus, and finished months later in 1989. "Trash TV" was in. Programs like Morton Downey, Jr.'s, with physical altercations provoked on the show, and Geraldo Rivera's, in which the host actually got his nose broken during a fight on the program, drew large audiences.

Sometimes the news was almost as confrontational. While not Downey and Rivera, the U.S. Presidential candidate, George H. W. Bush, and journalist Dan Rather

President Reagan visits Soviet Union.

FCC's Advanced Systems Committee recommends a 1,125-line, 60-Hz television signal standard.

Congress passes satellite/TVRO bill.

FCC eliminates its AM-FM nonduplication rule.

almost came to blows during a CBS interview. Bush and Rather "Spar Live on Network News," headlined *Broadcasting* magazine. The last few months before the election gave the networks their final chances to cover President Ronald Reagan, whose television presence and "Teflon" image the networks continued to polish by emphasizing his positive actions, as in the excellent coverage given to Reagan's summit meeting with Soviet President Gorbachev in Moscow. Broadcasters usually downplayed Reagan's negative actions, such as his "I can't remember" approach to the Iran-Contra scandal and his frequent "misspeaks." The networks did, though, have one confrontation with the White House, which attacked them when all three declined to give the President prime-time coverage for a speech advocating aid to the Contras.

The election itself set off further criticism of the networks, principally from the public. The networks' naming Bush and Quayle the winners even before all the polls closed resulted in calls for legislation mandating uniform voting hours nationwide. The networks were also accused of being the pawns of the politicians in going along with a highly negative Presidential campaign, including derogatory advertising against the Democratic nominee, Michael Dukakis, for which the Republican campaign director, Lee Atwater, apologized a few years later. The networks were criticized as well for allowing themselves to be manipulated by "spin doctors," a phrase given to campaign officials whose jobs entail convincing journalists to give the "right" slant to stories about their candidates. Broadcast journalists seemed content to stress "sound bites" instead of issues and substance. Was it coincidence that public broadcasting stations won the most national Emmy Awards for 1988 news programs? Lawrence Grossman, the head of NBC News, urged television to be an "instrument of truth." Was it also coincidence that, shortly afterward, he was fired?

Cable moved forward. Twenty stations copied Ted Turner's WTBS and became superstations, reaching the entire country on cable via satellite. Turner added a new national station, Turner Network Television (TNT), designed to compete directly with the broadcast networks. Cable also added new, specialized channels, such as health and fitness. Pay-per-view grew, although the growth of VCRs did slow it down. Cable penetration and viewing went up, whereas prime-time broadcast viewing was down to 65%, continuing to drop steadily from its 90%-plus of not too many years earlier.

The regulators at the FCC, in the courts, and in Congress were busy. The FCC warned broadcasters about allegations of new payola scandals. It paid decreasing attention to citizen challenges to broadcast stations, renewing the licenses of a number of stations whose renewal applications had been challenged by the NAACP. In the courts, the FCC wasn't doing as well as it would have liked to. In the preceding two years, 40 of its rulings had been overturned by the federal courts, ranging from must-carry provisions to policies regarding children's TV programs. The FCC got what it wanted, however, from one negative court decision. A law initiated by Senators Edward Kennedy and Fritz Hollings had enjoined the commission from acting on a request from Rupert Murdoch for an extension of the waiver that would permit him

Drought, heat wave, Yellowstone
Park fires plague United States.

George H. W. Bush uses TV, "sound
bites" to defeat Michael Dukakis
for presidency.

SUN Radio Network offers 24-hour
talk-information AM programming.

Adult contemporary is the top
radio music format.

to continue to own both a daily newspaper and a television station in the same communities, New York and Boston; such an arrangement was prohibited by the cross-ownership rules. A federal appeals court found the law unconstitutional. Murdoch challenged the cross-ownership rule itself in the courts.

Congress took a number of broadcast-related actions in 1988. It approved a rider by Senator Jesse Helms to the appropriations bill that established a 24-hour indecency ban, removing the midnight–6:00 A.M. FCC window for "adult programming." Congress passed a bill limiting the amount of commercial time on children's TV programs and requiring the FCC to consider informational and educational children's programming at renewal time; however, President Reagan vetoed the legislation. In the House, Representative Edward Markey, chair of the Telecommunications Subcommittee, let the industry know that he would seek strong public interest regulation.

That didn't deter the industry. Prices of stations continued to rise. However, not all was well: The stirrings of economic unease arrived as new owner GE began to break up the RCA radio-television empire, selling off parts of it in an economy move, radio going first. The NBC radio network was sold to Westwood One—which two years earlier had purchased the Mutual Radio Network—for $50 million (see Kenneth Bilby in the next chapter). ABC officials began to worry when ABC's investment in covering the Olympics turned out badly—a loss of $50 million. The media were still solvent, however, at least according to the value of communication properties. Telephone companies were worth a total of $240 billion; cable, $90 billion; and broadcast television, $40 billion.

FIG 8.10 During the 1980s, UPI tottered on the edge of insolvency. It filed for bankruptcy in 1985 and, after restructuring, again in 1991.
Courtesy Irving Fang.

1989

Broadcasting began to worry seriously in 1989. For some time, networks had been tightening staff costs through attrition and layoffs. Advertising revenue had dropped in 1988; in 1989 it stayed just about even. This was unusual for an industry that for years had seen commercial revenues rise at rapid rates. A combination of the economy and cable competition made it a difficult time. Some cable companies had begun to put commercial programs, such as syndicated sitcoms, on their local origination channels, directly challenging local broadcast stations. In 1990 the Rochester, New York, cable system programmed a half-hour local daily news show, competing head to head with broadcast stations having the same type of program at the same hour for the community's available ad dollars. A national survey found that viewers rated cable program quality and diversity higher than those of broadcasting. Broadcasting initiated an extensive "free-TV" campaign.

While some belt-tightening occurred, expansion also took place. Westinghouse bought 10 group radio stations for a record $360 million. The merger of Time and Warner created the world's largest media company, renewing concerns about industry monopoly. One approach taken by producers to expand their businesses was to

THE TECHNO-EDGED '80S

257

Benazir Bhutto, Pakistan president, first woman to lead a Moslem country.

United States invades Panama.

1989

Congress acts against "adult programming" hours and limits commercial time in children's shows, but President Reagan vetoes the legislation.

"Trash TV" reaches its peak.

seek more international coproduction, thus simultaneously cutting costs and opening new markets. As Eastern European countries opened up to the West, they became a target for coproduction.

Broadcast programming was often controversial, sometimes in entertainment, sometimes in news. "Trash TV" looked like it might be a fad, as 1988's hottest show, hosted by Morton Downey, Jr., was canceled because ratings and advertising dropped. Dramas dealing with real-life issues frightened advertisers, as always. *Roe vs. Wade*, NBC's TV movie docudrama on the famous Supreme Court abortion rights case, was critically praised, but its controversial nature caused several sponsors to withdraw. CBS took a chance with a format that years before had virtually disappeared from prime-time television: a Western. It paid off: *Lonesome Dove*, a four-part miniseries, received the largest prime-time ratings in two years. Would Westerns now return to TV?

Broadcasting news was at times excellent, at times disappointing. TV did a good job covering the student revolt in Tiananmen Square in Beijing until transmission was shut down by the Chinese authorities. On-the-spot coverage of the San Francisco earthquake was as unexpected as the quake itself; it came principally from the ABC-TV crew on hand to cover the World Series. Broadcasting provided in-depth coverage of the fall of the Berlin Wall. Broadcasting did try to cover the U.S. invasion of Panama, but the military did not allow the press freedom to report the early days of the conflict. Some journalists said that at least they were given more opportunity to cover the story than they'd been afforded at the U.S. invasion of Grenada. Strangely, the electronic press made little outcry about what many considered was a restriction of their First Amendment rights of freedom of the press.

Some news shows tried to fake their stories during 1989. By the end of the year, the television networks were apologizing for having used simulations in news reports. Radio, which once had been a bastion of news reporting, was its old self in 1989 with highly praised coverage of the *Exxon Valdez* oil spill in Alaska.

Gradual breakthroughs into the male-dominated and -controlled broadcast news field saw a number of women, such as Jane Pauley, Connie Chung, and Diane Sawyer, in key reporting and anchor positions in network and local news.

The networks were willing to pay big for big ratings. Live major competitive sports drew such audiences for broadcasting, cable, and, already beginning to make huge sums of money, pay-per-view TV. In 1989 CBS paid $1 billion for seven years' rights to the NCAA basketball tournament games. Major league baseball did even better, getting $500 million from radio and television for just one year, 1989.

It was a busy year for the FCC. It hung tough as a regulator when it investigated many and fined some radio stations for violations of its indecency rules. It wasn't so tough, however, when it granted a number of waivers of its one-to-a-market restriction, at times appearing to dismiss its duopoly rule with impunity, including a waiver to the Boston Celtics basketball team to buy both a TV and a radio station in the Boston market. It voted to repeal the compulsory license whereby cable was authorized to

| Chinese students demonstrate, attacked by army in Beijing. | Gorbachev cuts troops, enables Eastern European countries to move toward democracy. | Berlin Wall comes down. |

Electronic media cover Tiananmen Square confrontation and offer live coverage of San Francisco earthquake.

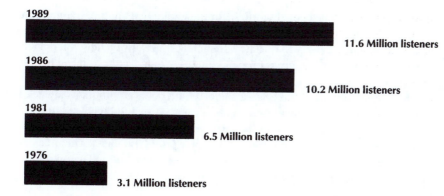

1989

11.6 Million listeners

1986

10.2 Million listeners

1981

6.5 Million listeners

1976

3.1 Million listeners

FIG 8.11 National Public Radio has enjoyed steady growth in listenership. *Courtesy NPR.*

use copyrighted material of the stations it carried by paying one statutory fee. Broadcasters sought such repeal in order to force cable to negotiate for each station or program on an individual basis. Any final change, however, would have to be made by Congress. Also in 1989 the FCC affirmed its new syndex rules, to go into effect in January 1990; it authorized 200 new class C (25-kW) radio stations; and eliminated a 44-year-old rule limiting network-affiliate contracts to two years. Further, unable to reinstate a must-carry rule, the FCC temporarily settled for the requirement that cable companies offer subscribers an A/B switch.

The FCC and the courts continued to back away from the affirmative action practices of the late 1960s and early 1970s. The U.S. Court of Appeals found unconstitutional the FCC's "distress sale" policy, under which a station in danger of losing its license, thus forfeiting a chance to sell its station, could sell at a reduced rate to a minority or female applicant. The FCC reduced the impact of challenges by citizen groups through petitions to deny in license renewal proceedings: It banned settlement payments made by stations to petitioning groups in order to get the groups to withdraw in exchange for voluntary changes on the part of the station.

Congress, throughout much of the year, was involved in hearings and bills that reflected a proregulatory attitude. Among its concerns were children's television, Fairness Doctrine codification, cable reregulation, and violence, sex, and drugs on TV. The only major law to come out of this activity, though, was enacted the following year, 1990, and concerned children's TV.

Noncommercial and formal and informal educational television reached a few milestones in 1989. CPB and public television station organizations agreed to a new program-funding plan. Television programming into the schools, something that had been going on for about 40 years, had taken a new twist with Channel 1, a Whittle Communications concept, providing receiving equipment and news programs free to schools. The catch? Commercials to a captive audience, which raised the hackles

FIG 8.12 CDs have replaced LPs as the preferred sound medium at home and in the broadcast studio.

259

Another earthquake in San Francisco.	*Exxon Valdez* oil tanker pollutes Alaskan coast.

Networks continue to lose ground to cable.	Channel 1 offers programming and commercials to schools.	FCC fines stations for violations of indecency rules.

of some educators but seemed worth it, for the equipment and programming, to others. Other groups, including Turner and Monitor, began to offer programming comparable to Channel 1 but without the commercials. A relatively new phenomenon in communications—public access programming controlled and produced by the public—had come about in 1972 when the FCC required cable systems to offer such access channels; by 1989, there were some 10,000 hours of programs a week being carried over cable public access channels on more than 1,200 cable systems.

Key technical developments in 1989 included the first 100% 3-D television broadcast; the demonstration by Panasonic of a prototype digital video camcorder; the first regularly scheduled HDTV in the world—in Japan, using DBS; and the FCC's facilitation of satellite television by granting flexible use of frequencies to DBS applicants.

Chapter NINE

The Cyber '90s

Toward a New Century

By the latter half of the 1990s, the decade had already become a communications anomaly. It was a decade of cyberspace and censorship, indecency and irreverence, technology and testament, dogmatism and deregulation, polarization and politics, economic bust and boom, merger and monopoly. Early in the decade, the country's voters appeared to support a proconsumer, liberal agenda, the public seemingly ready to relive the late 1960s and early 1970s. Many observers therefore anticipated strong *re*regulation of the broadcasting industry when Bill Clinton was elected President in 1992, countering the Reagan-era deregulation, or "*un*regulation," as a former Republican FCC chair once put it. But within a couple of years the reverse was true as a Republican Congress included a strong marketplace philosophy in its "Contract with America." Within another couple of years, public attitude began to change again as many people began to perceive the Republican actions as a "Contract *on* America." Some accused both the Republican and Democratic parties of hypocrisy: The Republicans were calling for more freedoms for the industry, at the same time implementing greater censorship and control of media content; the Democrats claimed to represent the consumer but at the same time backed legislation that vitiated the role of the consumer in the regulatory process and strengthened the control of the industry.

By mid-decade the die was cast. The Telecommunications Act of 1996, endorsed by both political parties, reversed virtually all the remaining proconsumer legislation, rules, and regulations that had been accumulating for some 50 years and that had not already been eliminated in the 1980s, as described in the previous chapter.

In 1990 and 1991 the deficit-spending indulgences of the 1980s began to catch up with the United States. Banks failed, jobs were lost, and millions more Americans were thrust into poverty. There was less money for consumer products and services and, therefore, less advertising money. Production costs, however, continued to increase, and broadcasters tightened their collective belts. The broadcast industry had one important ray of hope: Although almost every other industry suffered during the economic depression of the 1930s, radio grew because it was the principal source of free entertainment and information.

DOI: 10.1016/B978-0-240-81236-6.00009-3

| Cold War ends. | East and West Germany unify. |

1990

Syndex re-enacted.

FIG 9.1 At the beginning of the 1990s the NAB published these facts about broadcasting.

Broadcasting employs 216,033 people, less than 1% of the nation's civilian work force. Broadcasting is more diverse in number and dispersion of outlets than the daily print media. There are 10,794 radio stations and 1,469 television stations in the United States, compared to 1,626 daily newspapers.

Radio: The Listener

► The average household has 5.6 radio sets.

► Radio reaches 96% of persons 12 + each week.

► Persons 12 + spend 3 hours daily listening to radio.

► 3 of 4 adults listen to radio in their cars each week.

► Radio reaches 99% of teenagers (12-17) weekly.

► Radio reaches 21 million people with walk-along sets.

Television: The Viewer

► 98% of TV households own color sets.

► 65% of TV households own two or more sets.

► The average TV household can receive 30.5 channels, including those available via cable services.

► The average TV household views an estimated 7 hours and 2 minutes a day.

► Television is cited as the main news source by 65% of the public.

Radio Stations

	Commercial					
	AM	FM		Non-Commercial		Total
1980	4559 + 3155		=	7714 + 1038	=	8752
1985	4754 + 3716		=	8470 + 1172	=	9642
1990	4984 + 4372		=	9356 + 1438	=	10794

Television Stations

	Commercial					
	VHF	UHF		Non-Commercial		Total
1980	517 + 229		=	746 + 267	=	1013
1985	539 + 365		=	904 + 290	=	1194
1990	552 + 563		=	1115 + 354	=	1469

Female and Minority Employment
Full & Part-time Employees

	All Employees	Women	Minorities
1980	176,704	58,175 (32.9%)	26,213 (14.8%)
1985	206,135	74,906 (36.3%)	32,634 (15.8%)
1989	216,033	81,638 (37.8%)	36,489 (16.9%)

1989 Radio and Television Financial Profile

Type of Station	Revenues	Expenses	Full-time Employees
TV Network Affiliate*	15,809,909	12,365,172	95
TV Independent*	14,906,352	14,684,601	62
Full-time AM Radio**	1,006,660	902,707	11
FM Radio**	1,536,129	1,457,622	15

*Average values as reported in *NAB 1990 Television Financial Report*.

**Weighted average values as reported in *NAB 1990 Radio Financial Report*.

Acknowledgements for "Facts about Broadcasting": American Newspaper Publishers Association; Bureau of Labor Statistics; Federal Communications Commission; Nielsen Media Research; Radio Advertising Bureau; Television Bureau of Advertising.

In the 1990s, however, broadcasting no longer had the monopoly on electronic communication. By 1991 cable TV was in 60% of U.S. television homes, and growing. Videocassette recorders (VCRs), compact discs (CDs), and direct broadcast satellite (DBS) were reducing even further the television broadcast networks' domination of prime time, and broadcasting's share of all TV viewers was dropping steadily.

Recession spurs barter in program acquisition.

Infomercials grow.

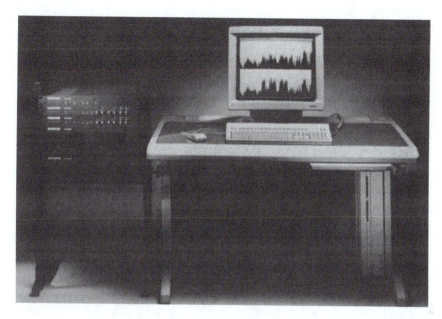

FIG 9.2 As the broadcast century came to a close, the computer—with its Internet potential—became more and more of a threat to broadcasting and other electronic media as a source of entertainment, education, and information in the home.

Also, something new had entered U.S. homes, although in the early part of the decade not yet seriously competing for vast numbers of viewers' and listeners' time but beginning to develop entertainment and information services that might someday become a major threat to previously existing video and audio distribution systems. That, of course, was the home personal computer and its CD-ROM and Internet potential.

1990

With the end of the Cold War—the fall of the Berlin Wall, the "velvet revolutions" in the countries of Eastern Europe, and the transformation of the Soviet Union into a loose confederation of independent states—the world in general opened up for satellite communication. Reuters, BBC, Murdoch, ABC, CNN, and other groups raced to place their news and entertainment signals into as much of the world as possible. News, in particular, was given an international impetus. Eastern Europe, in particular, became an open market for U.S. video producers and distributors. Although the Cold War with the Soviet bloc was over, it continued with Cuba, and the United States launched Radio Martí, a shortwave propaganda station aimed at that nation.

The deregulatory actions of the 1980s remained in force, with the deregulation trend itself continuing. Some challenges to the 1980s actions were dismissed by the

THE CYBER '90S

263

| Iraq attacks Kuwait. | Congress censors Mapplethorpe art exhibit. | Dr. Kevorkian helps first terminally ill patient "die with dignity." |

FIG 9.3 Cable continued to expand in the 1990s. *Courtesy Storer Cable.*

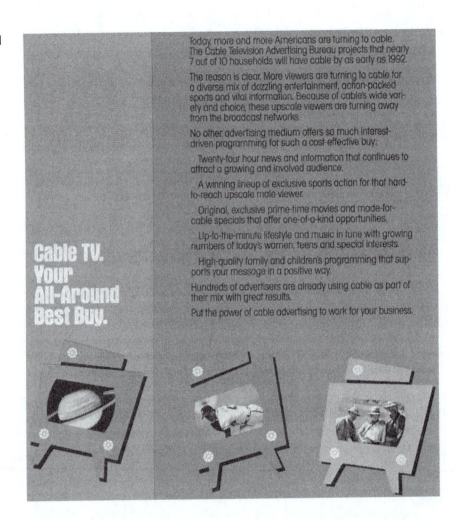

Today, more and more Americans are turning to cable. The Cable Television Advertising Bureau projects that nearly 7 out of 10 households will have cable by as early as 1992.

The reason is clear. More viewers are turning to cable for a diverse mix of dazzling entertainment, action-packed sports and vital information. Because of cable's wide variety and choice, these upscale viewers are turning away from the broadcast networks.

No other advertising medium offers so much interest-driven programming for such a cost-effective buy:

Twenty-four hour news and information that continues to attract a growing and involved audience.

A winning lineup of exclusive sports action for that hard-to-reach upscale male viewer.

Original, exclusive prime-time movies and made-for-cable specials that offer one-of-a-kind opportunities.

Up-to-the-minute lifestyle and music in tune with growing numbers of today's women, teens and special interests.

High-quality family and children's programming that supports your message in a positive way.

Hundreds of advertisers are already using cable as part of their mix with great results.

Put the power of cable advertising to work for your business.

Cable TV. Your All-Around Best Buy.

courts; some were upheld. For example, the Supreme Court affirmed the minority preference distress sale option for stations in danger of losing their licenses; and the court refused to consider a challenge to the 1987 elimination of the Fairness Doctrine.

Growing concern about excessive cable rates and insufficient cable services, among other complaints, created rumbles in Congress for reregulation of cable, which had been almost completely deregulated in 1984, as noted in the previous chapter. It would be another two years before Congress took final action on the matter.

Free elections in Eastern Europe.

Children's Television
Entertainment Act passed.

Television Decoder Circuitry Act
passed (closed captions).

FCC gives "TEETH" to the 1990 CTA

In 1996 the FCC crafted rules that strengthened and clarified the way that broadcasters were expected to comply with the conditions of the 1990 Children's Television Act (CTA). It defined educational, what it termed "core programming," any program that furthers the educational and informational needs of children 16 and under, including issues dealing with a child's intellectual/cognitive or social/emotional growth. It set a minimum of three hours per week for such programming, airing between 7:00 A.M. and 10:00 P.M., required on- and off-air labeling, and imposed commercial limits of 10.5 minutes per hour for weekend shows and 12 minutes per hour on weekdays. Television stations were required to provide consumers with advance information about these shows as well as displaying an E/I (educational/informational) icon throughout their airing. Each show must be at least 30 minutes long, and the commercials cannot be for a product related to that program, nor be promoted by an actor or character that is featured on that program, defined as "host selling." All licensees must file with the FCC and place in their public inspection files a quarterly *Children's Television Programming Report* (FCC Form 398) identifying their core programming and other efforts to comply with their educational programming obligations.

KENNETH BILBY

FORMER RCA EXECUTIVE AND CHIEF BIOGRAPHER, *THE GENERAL: DAVID SARNOFF AND THE RISE OF THE COMMUNICATION INDUSTRY* —

FIG 9.4 Kenneth Bilby with a research assistant in the Harvard Library.
Courtesy Kenneth Bilby.

As far as the networks are concerned, I believe they're continuing to provide a necessary service, and as long as they continue to do so they will continue to exist, despite the steady erosion of their total audience. Even if this erosion continues, the viewer will not suffer because there will be ample cable services to pick up the slack.

In the broader perspective of the electronics industry, I fear lasting damage has been done through the merger and

Jean-Bertrand Aristede becomes president
of Haiti, then is ousted by military.

Desert Storm, U.S.–U.N. action in
Gulf War.

1991

William S. Paley, longtime head of
CBS, dies.

THE CYBER '90S

acquisition binge of the 1980s. The phasing out of famous companies, the piling up of huge junk bond debts, and the lessening of emphasis on electronics research were among the results. Electronics leadership passed to foreign enterprises, primarily Japanese. I am particularly sensitive to this because of the fate of RCA, the company with which I spent more than 30 years. In my view, it's a corporate tragedy.

Founded in 1919 as a wireless offshoot of the English-based Marconi Company, RCA was created at the government's request so that America would never be dependent on other nations for wireless communications. From that small beginning, under the leadership of David Sarnoff, RCA exploited virtually every new development in the infant science of electronics and became America's premier company in that field: creating a whole new range of products and services, always in the vanguard of technology, producing in American factories to make America a stronger nation.

As RCA created new wealth in the Sarnoff era, that wealth was put back into the company in the pursuit of innovative new products and further scientific inventions. The laboratories at RCA were, as Sarnoff put it, "our life blood."

Nothing took precedence over scientific invention and development while General Sarnoff was running RCA. I think the company got off the track when successor managements began plunging into diversification. The company became, in effect, a conglomerate, going into businesses as remote as frozen prepared foods, chicken plucking, carpeting, rental cars, financial services, and greeting cards—all unrelated to the electronic core.

After Thornton Bradshaw took over a reeling company at the start of the 1980s, he sought to return it to its heritage by selling off nonelectronic businesses and steering the same course that Sarnoff had originally chartered. The company resurged as an electronics leader.

But then, inexplicably, Bradshaw merged RCA with General Electric. The rationale was that RCA's strength, coupled with GE's, would prove that one plus one equals three. It would strengthen America's waning capacity to compete against the Japanese, the Germans, the Dutch, and the French in the electronics marts of the world.

Unfortunately, it proved to be a merger in name only. As events have shown, GE promptly embarked on a course of dismemberment. The core RCA Consumer Electronics Division was sold to the French, the historic RCA Records Division to the Germans. The scientific labs were disposed of and other operations phased out. The company that had given America world leadership in electronics was consigned to oblivion.

Courtesy Kenneth Bilby.

Coup fails, but Soviet Union falls,
Gorbachev resigns.

Government censorship of press
in Gulf War protested.

Total ban lifted, safe harbor
ordered for adult programming.

Another cable matter, however, was dealt with in 1990. Syndex—syndicated exclusivity, which required a cable system to black out any distant station or cable network program it carried that was already being aired by a local TV station—was reenacted. Local broadcasters were happy; cable operators were furious.

The economic recession that ended the 1980s and began the 1990s hit broadcasters hard. Barter boomed. Barter is the system whereby a local station, lacking the upfront cash to pay for syndicated programs, pays less cash in exchange for the syndicators using some of the avails—the available advertising time spots—to sell their own ads. What had been largely a cash transaction market turned to cash-plus-barter and, in some instances, all barter for programs. Although it began as a stop-gap measure in a recession, barter took hold and continues today.

The recession also affected affiliates as well as independent stations. With less advertising revenue, the networks cut back on their compensation to affiliates, thereby forcing the affiliates to cut back on programming, find barter sources, or obtain more local advertising support. Further, in-house programming at the networks was decreased, and new production jobs at the networks virtually disappeared. One growing source of income was program-length commercials. The abolition during the Reagan deregulation era of all restrictions on the length of commercials gave way to the proliferation of entire programs devoted to commercials on broadcast television, competing with the already proliferating similar programs on cable, such as home shopping networks, which had not been under FCC jurisdiction.

Programming became more eclectic on both radio and television. Official antidrug campaigns resulted in more public service announcements (PSAs) on the subject and more antidrug content in entertainment programs. Spanish-language programming grew, especially on radio and cable. Radio syndicators and networks were shifting their demographic focus from the 12- to 34-year-old target audience to the emerging dominant buying power of the baby boomers, 25 to 54. While sitcoms and drama, including evening soaps, still dominated the ratings, one special attracted a broad audience and gave PBS its best ratings to date—Ken Burns's *The Civil War*.

Congress enacted the Children's Television Entertainment Act of 1990, a culmination of years of effort by Action for Children's Television and other consumer groups. It reduced the amount of advertising time permitted per hour on children's TV shows and required stations to air "educational and informational" programs, directing the FCC to take this into account at license renewal time.

Congress also passed the Television Decoder Circuitry Act of 1990, which required all sets 13 inches or larger sold after July 1993 to be capable of decoding closed-captioned transmissions.

Having learned the power of the press and the public in a free democratic society during the Vietnam War, the Pentagon continued to receive criticism for its restrictions on freedom of the press and the public's right to know in its invasion of Panama and finally admitted, in 1990, that it had hampered media coverage in that conflict.

FIG 9.5 *Soundprint* suggested the potential of a renaissance in radio programming in the 1990s—perhaps the medium's second Golden Age. *Soundprint* was a weekly documentary series of compelling sound pictures that provoked thought, fired the imagination, and stirred the sense of possibility. Each week the series provided an intense, thorough exploration of a single issue, subject, or place in meaningful context. *Soundprint* exploited the intimate, personal qualities of radio to take listeners into the lives and experiences of people, places, and cultures uncommon and common, unique and universal. The series combined journalistic excellence with state-of-the-art technology to create an engaging and compelling presentation of contemporary issues.

THE CYBER '90S

MMDS gets more spectrum space.

The Department of Defense (DoD), it appeared, had been obsessed with secrecy and was guilty of poor planning. This problem would be further exacerbated by the DoD less than a year later with almost total restriction and censorship of the press covering the Gulf War.

As the last decade of the 20th century began, the life of one of the century's giant figures in broadcasting ended. William S. Paley, head of CBS and creator of what many called the "Tiffany Network," died.

1991

By the time a shackled and angry press filed suit against the U.S. government for violating its First Amendment rights during the Gulf War, the war was over and the court case was declared moot. But the damage done to America's traditional democratic freedoms of the press during that war were so deep that even five years afterward, a *New York Times* feature article, "The Gulf War Story Is Still Being Told," included journalists' continued criticism of the Pentagon's restrictions. They objected to the military's decision to "conduct the war largely out of the camera's view, restrict access to troops, and showcase the most favorable gun-camera film from Allied bombings." The Vietnam War lesson was cited by both the military and the journalists. The former claimed, stated *The Times*, that "unchecked television exposure could jeopardize war plans and stoke opposition back home if casualties piled up." The journalists said, "full and open disclosure would help prevent a senseless war." Many journalists are concerned about future restrictions by the military, especially because advancing technology would make it possible to provide even fuller and more extensive coverage of a war than ever before (see Chapter 10 for further discussion on this topic).

CNN continued direct reports from Baghdad on the U.S. destruction of civilian targets, angering the Pentagon and some others in the United States. CNN's courage, however, resulted not only in dramatically increased ratings for its news but spurred television news in general.

FIG 9.6 During the patriotic fervor of the Persian Gulf War, most stations waved Old Glory, too.
Courtesy WMZQ, Washington, D.C.

DAB gets reserved spectrum
space.

FCC expands AM band by 100 kHz.

Some early press coverage of the war, especially that of CNN, was highly praised. For the first time, Americans saw on television and heard on radio a number of women reporting directly from the forward war zones. In the first few days, the war was broadcast to the United States on an intensive, minute-by-minute basis by most networks. But even as its efforts were being praised, the press's independence was being questioned. It was not informing the American public of alternative policies, of behind-the-scenes activities, of world points of view that might differ from the official U.S. position, or of widespread protests by citizens in the United States and abroad. While reflecting public condemnation of the totalitarian regime in Iraq, the press did not report concerns that the United States was sacrificing soldiers to save a totalitarian government in Kuwait. The press seemed to be repeating its largely

The centerpiece of CNN's news and information programming is 13 hours of comprehensive news reports each weekday and more than 12 hours each weekend. With up-to-the-minute national and international news and extended reports on the latest developments in business, sports and weather, CNN is able to give viewers in all time zones, virtually worldwide, unmatched depth and immediacy of live news coverage.

As the morning hours unfold, CNN's morning news program, *Early Bird News* (co-anchored by Molly McCoy and Rick Moore) is the first newscast available for East Coast viewers. *Daybreak* (also co-anchored by McCoy and Moore along with Norma Quarles and Bob Cain) and *CNN Morning News* (with Quarles and Cain) deliver fresh and constantly updated live morning news to every region of the country–the only live network news available mornings on the West Coast. *Daywatch* (co-anchored by Mary Anne Loughlin and Ralph Wenge) includes interviews with guests and viewer call-ins on a variety of topics.

At noon on the East Coast, *Newshour* is co-anchored by Bobbie Battista and Reid Collins. Weekday afternoons follow with *Newsday* (co-anchored by Loughlin, Catherine Crier and Don Miller) and *Early Prime* (co-anchored by Sharyl Attkisson and Lou Waters), bringing CNN's viewers timely and accurate coverage of the day's unfolding events, including expert financial analysis when Wall Street closes at 4:30pm ET.

At 6:00pm ET, CNN airs network television's first evening newscast, *The World Today*. Co-anchored by Catherine Crier and Bernard Shaw, *The World Today* covers global news far more comprehensively than 22-minute newscasts produced by other commercial networks and keeps abreast of breaking stories with live reports from the scenes of the day's major stories. *(cont.)*

Principal Washington anchor Bernard Shaw presents The World Today *and* PrimeNews.

Norma Quarles anchors reports from New York on Daybreak *and* CNN Morning News.

Lou Waters anchors Newswatch *and* PrimeNews *from network headquarters in Atlanta.*

Turner Broadcasting System, Inc. • One CNN Center, Box 105366, Atlanta, GA 30348-5366 • (404) 827-1500

FIG 9.7 Cable TV's premier news service is CNN, which enhanced its growing reputation with its coverage of the Persian Gulf War.
Courtesy CNN.

THE CYBER '90S

Yugoslavia falls apart, siege of Sarajevo begins; Serb, Muslim, Croat atrocities.

Anarchy and U.S. troops in Somalia.

1992

Murphy Brown vs. Dan Quayle.

unquestioning and sometimes acquiescent role from previous recent conflicts. It agreed to let the U.S. military determine where and what it could cover and, on grounds of national security, permitted its reports to be censored. Protests from various sources, including Walter Cronkite, effected no change. A *Time* magazine correspondent, Stanley Cloud, summed up a growing feeling among journalists that "this is an intolerable effort by the government to manage and control the press. We have ourselves to blame as much as the Pentagon. We never should have agreed to this system in the first place." Neither the United States nor the press was willing to take a stand on the distinction between censorship of sensitive information for military security purposes and censorship of information for political manipulation of the public.

A number of consumer concerns were addressed by Congress, the FCC, and the courts, some pleasing consumer and First Amendment rights groups and some pleasing industry. The U.S. Court of Appeals threw out an FCC 24-hour ban on indecent or so-called "adult" programming on television and ordered the FCC to establish a "safe harbor" for such programming. The saga of the safe harbor would not be finally resolved for another four years. Shortly after Clarence Thomas was confirmed to the U.S. Supreme Court, the Court of Appeals released a decision he had delivered months

FCC OFFERS THREE SPECTRUM OPTIONS FOR DAB
Commission seeks comments on different suggestions for new audio service prior to 1992 WARC; proposals are 728-788 mhz, 1493-1525 mhz, 2390-2450 mhz

DAB Comments Pour Into FCC
by Charles Taylor

WASHINGTON When a broadcasting issue is sweeping enough to attract comments not only from the NAB and National Public Radio, but also from the ... would be a substantial advance in radio sound and service." Behind the zeal, however, was a unanimous disdain among those commenting toward any threat DAB may bring in the near future to the current heavy losses on national/regional revenues would not likely be evenly distributed among local broadcasting stations. The impact would most likely fall hardest on the class of stations must vulnerable at this time—AM stations." While the majority of those filing agreed that terrestrial delivery held the most advantages, some acknowledged the value of satellite-based service. National Public Radio (NPR) said *(continued on page 12)*

Digital audio broadcasting was anticipated by the radio industry as the key to establishing a level playing field between AM and FM.

BROADCASTERS, COMMERCE OFFICIAL DEBATE DAB
NAB members fear NASA, VOA and USIA support for satellite-delivered systems; NAB research shows need for new FCC propagation measurements for DAB

FIG 9.8 Digital audio broadcasting was anticipated by the radio industry as the key to establishing a level playing field between AM and FM.

Los Angeles explodes after police acquittal in Rodney King beating.

Olympic pay-per-view fizzles.

Infinity–Howard Stern hit by huge fines for indecency.

The Power of Radio

Thousands of New Englanders, darkened by power blackouts, got much of their news about the Gorbachev ouster and Hurricane Bob from battery-operated radios. It was a reminder of the immediacy and power of this medium.

A friend of ours, who lost power at 2 P.M. Monday, was relieved to find that public radio station WBUR picked up the audio from WCVB-TV, Channel 5. "I didn't miss a thing," he said. "Who needs to look at another multicolored radar display, anyway? And there's not much information conveyed by a picture of a reporter in Goretex being tossed about by the wind."

As the outage continued throughout the night, radio provided skillful coverage of the Moscow coup. "The only strong visual image was of Boris Yeltsin on a tank, and that happened early in the morning," our friend said. "After that, it was mostly talk. You don't need to know the color of a Soviet expert's suit when he gives his opinions."

Our friend's experience was a reminder that many memorable moments in TV reporting could have been done equally well on radio. Our memory of John F. Kennedy's assassination is mostly of Walter Cronkite's television presence. Arthur Godfrey's radio broadcast of Franklin Roosevelt's funeral was equally compelling.

TV news has had its moments: the murder of Lee Harvey Oswald; the suppression of the protest in Beijing; the tracer fire in Baghdad as US bombers made their first attacks.

Their images, replayed over and over on videotape, were illustrations of events better reported by the human voice. Amid the bombing in Baghdad, three reporters for the Cable News Network gave an audio account that was reminiscent of Edward R. Murrow's broadcasts of the German air raids on London.

Television pictures are attention-grabbing, but the true communications revolution occurred not when the first TV news was broadcast but a generation earlier, when radio discovered its voice.

FIG 9.9 While multimedia video services grew, radio not only remained a basic entertainment and information service, but many observers agreed with this 1991 *Boston Globe* editorial, "The Power of Radio." *Reprinted courtesy of the Boston Globe.*

earlier in which, ironically, he struck down the FCC's affirmative action requirement in granting broadcast licenses to women.

The recession, which continued to reduce advertising income for both broadcasting and cable, promoted attempts by larger stations or group owners to take over small stations, and the FCC increased the granting of waivers of its one-to-a-market rule. The FCC also attempted to level the political playing field by requiring stations to sell political advertising time at the "lowest unit cost." The FCC opened more spectrum space to multichannel multipoint distribution systems (MMDS), also called *wireless cable*, through a lottery.

The electronic press had one door opened for it when the federal courts approved television coverage of civil trials on an experimental basis, at the discretion of the individual case judge.

Radio multiple ownership raised to 18 and 18, duopoly rules eased.

One of the newer technologies, digital audio broadcasting (DAB), emerged as a key concern and expectation of media executives and operators, and the FCC set aside spectrum space for DAB. The FCC expanded the AM band by 100 kHz, making it possible to accommodate about 250 additional stations nationally. In ferment were a number of issues that would become the keys to changes in the entire communication industry in subsequent years. Digital video compression was developing as a future system for both conventional and high-definition television (HDTV). An industry committee continued its work on developing a standard for digital satellite television. Perhaps most important, as it turned out five years down the road, were the court decisions and the increasing pressures on and discussions in Congress and at the FCC that were bringing telcos (telephone companies) closer to being authorized to operate cable systems.

Radio fared somewhat better than television in coping with the difficult economy. Perhaps having learned how to do this when it survived the sudden dominance of TV decades before, radio had a resurgence by concentrating on an increase of news and talk shows and on more precise targeting of audiences. Radio also experienced a growth with urban formats aimed at the 25- to 54-year-old age group. On both television and radio, talk shows proliferated in syndication. With the frightening spread of AIDS, the pubic and the industry were slowly being forced to acknowledge its existence, if not do something about it. Radio and TV stations, which generally had refused to carry condom ads, now began to consider doing so.

TONY VERNA

PRODUCER _____

In my book, *Globalcasting*, I expanded on perhaps the newest development of the broadcast century. I detailed for future broadcasters the patterns developed as I executive-produced/directed international shows such as Live Aid, Sport Aid, Prayer for World Peace, Earth 90, The Goodwill Games, etc. An executive director directs the work of other directors functioning separately around the world. The increased amount of preparation and communication required to unify a globalcast has to be organized on a scale to match the

FIG 9.10 Tony Verna in a control room at the 1990 Goodwill Games.
Courtesy Turner Broadcasting and Tony Verna.

challenge. Understanding satellite coverage and how to order it is just one of the new technical challenges. The "what ifs" of any broadcast expand to match the increased size of globalcasting. Also, the complexity of languages and customs involved highlights

Tony Kushner's *Angels in America* lights up Broadway theater.

Boxing champ Mike Tyson convicted of rape.

Cable regulated in Cable Television Consumer Protection and Competition Act; must-carry reinstated.

the increasing role of globalcasting in unifying the world's nations and peoples.

Whether it is news coverage of an event like the Persian Gulf conflict or a musical celebration like Live Aid, globalcasts—both radio and TV—cross national boundaries as few other methods of communication have been able to do. And they are changing the way the world works. Having worked in television since its first decade, I view this decade of the '90s as laying the groundwork for the next very exciting broadcast century.

Courtesy Tony Verna.

Public broadcasting experienced another flap about censoring controversial material. Although in many cases PBS provided alternative and even controversial programming eschewed by commercial television and was ostensibly immune to outside vested interest pressures, it did cancel a *P.O.V.* (point of view) documentary, *Stop the Church*, about a gay rights protest against the Catholic Church.

Exactly 30 years after his "vast wasteland" speech, former FCC chair Newton Minow, in another speech to the industry, gave television an "A-plus" for technological advances and a "C" for using that technology "to serve human and humane goals." Last, perhaps a most significant sign that the Cold War was really over, Russia became a member of INTELSAT.

The Commercialization of Public Broadcasting

Ever since the Nixon Presidency, Republican administrations have had a vendetta against public broadcasting, primarily on ideological grounds, a perceived liberal bias by PBS/NPR. Public broadcasting was established in 1967 as an alternative to what was a growing homogeneity in the commercial world. For-profit stations actually favored this public option, for it relieved them of providing programming that was creative, innovative, in-depth, or educational, all of which lacked the broad mass audience advertiser-driven commercial broadcasters desired. Over the years conservatives have been successful in reducing funding to the point that PBS/NPR has increasingly turned to market-driven content to attract "enhanced underwriting," virtually indistinguishable from commercials. Audience size, the common denominator for commercial broadcasting, has become a major consideration for public broadcasting. By the late 1990s PBS/NPR more and more resembled just one more commercial outlet, abandoning its strong community orientation and reducing its diverse content along with its educational elements save for children's programming. The trend toward commercialization of the public sector has occurred so gradually that few notice the transformation, but there is little doubt that a colossal sea change is taking place on the venue that was intended to offer unconventional programming that lacked a mass appeal.

THE CYBER '90S

273

1993

Clinton elected President,
Reagan–Bush era ends.

1992

In the musical *Fiorello*, the song "Politics and Poker" satirized politicians and political campaigns. "Politics and Programming" might well have been an appropriate tune title for 1992 because broadcast programming played a significant role in this Presidential election year. First, somewhat reminiscent of the first 1960 Kennedy–Nixon Presidential debate in which personality played a key role in determining public reaction, a three-way debate among President George H. W. Bush, Democratic challenger Bill Clinton, and third-party candidate Ross Perot showed Clinton to much greater advantage than his rivals. Some critics credit that debate with swinging voters to Clinton, much as the 1960 debate swung the tide to Kennedy.

Political talk shows on both radio and television grew. By the end of 1992, 16 syndicated talk shows were being stripped—that is, appearing every day, five days a week, in the same time slots—and the number was growing. Prognosticating the subsequent conservative attitude in the country was the phenomenal success of right-wing commentator Rush Limbaugh, who was being carried on 480 AM stations alone. Although the material he presented as fact was revealed frequently to be fiction, he was taken seriously by the public.

Conversely, *Murphy Brown*, a sitcom that was presented as fiction, was sometimes confused with fact. The principal character, Murphy Brown, decided to become a single, working mother and gave birth to a child. She drew the ire of the Vice President, Dan Quayle, who publicly objected to the character's lifestyle as though she were a nonfictional person. While it is the sitcoms that are usually rather inane, in this case it was the Vice President who came off as somewhat doltish. Was this a high-level example of the growing belief that more and more people are under the impression that television is the true reality and that if it isn't on television it doesn't really exist?

There was, of course, more than political programming in 1992. A most significant event was the Olympic Games. Believing that there was gold in pay-per-view (PPV), television put some of the Olympic coverage on a paying basis. The results were dismal. On the other hand, there were large audiences for the free TV coverage.

There were also large audiences for programs cited by the FCC as indecent, most particularly those of Infinity Broadcasting's Howard Stern. Refusing to abide by the FCC's indecency rules, Stern's programs were fined—first a record $105,000, and when they continued to violate the FCC's indecency standards, further fines totaling $600,000 were levied. Infinity challenged the constitutionality of the indecency standards. The fines mounted up. How did it end? Tune in next year (in the next chapter of this book)!

The FCC fined other stations as well for indecency violations. Its 24-hour ban on adult programming reached the Supreme Court, which struck it down, reiterating the lower court's order for a safe harbor.

The FCC continued to levy fines, some quite large, against a number of TV stations that exceeded the advertising limits of the Children's Television Act of 1990.

Telcos move closer to cable.

Some finsyn rules relaxed.

FIG 9.11
Ultraconservatives ruled the radio airwaves in the last decade of the broadcast century, in stark contrast to programs such as "shock jock" Howard Stern's.
Courtesy of Westwood One Entertainment.

In addition, in still another area of program content violation, where stations used hoaxes to promote their ratings, the FCC established a $250,000 fine for "knowingly broadcasting false information." Less controversial was the continuing growth of programming for minority groups, especially Spanish-language programs.

N.Y.P.D. Blue sex and violence: art or indecency?

Letterman switches to CBS, competes with Leno.

FIG 9.12 The television studio of the 1990s employed highly advanced, cutting-edge equipment. The inset shows a stereo audio time compressor/expander.
Courtesy Lexicon.

PEGGY CHARREN

FOUNDER OF ACTION FOR CHILDREN'S TELEVISION _____

For a very long time, I believed there was a need for a child advocacy group dedicated to increasing choice, diversity, and delight in children's television—a group whose goal was to stop the worst of commercial manipulation and exploitation. In 1968, this resulted in the creation of ACT. Since then the organization has been very active in lobbying for the upgrading and overall enhancement of existing children's programs as well as campaigning for an

FIG 9.13 Peggy Charren.
Courtesy Peggy Charren.

increase in quality television for young people. In 1990 we successfully lobbied the U.S. Congress to pass the Children's Television Act, which mandates that local television stations provide educational programs for children. Although ACT was dismantled in 1992, the work to make television a valuable and positive medium for children continues.
Courtesy Peggy Charren.

Two program-related milestones were reached in 1992. The sitcom *Cheers* went off the air after 11 seasons, and after 30 years Johnny Carson retired as host of *The Tonight Show*. It was an up and down year for broadcasting. The courts struck down the FCC's new, more relaxed finsyn (financial syndication) rules, giving the networks greater participation, although not full control, in the production and syndication process of programs, but permitted a stay pending an appeal. Congress cut back another FCC action, one that increased the multiple ownership of radio stations from 12 AM and 12 FM stations nationwide to 30 and 30, and allowed ownership of six stations in a given market; Congress limited it to 18 and 18, and a duopoly of two plus two in large markets, and two of one and one of another in small markets. Radio mega-combos grew, with more and more duopolies. The FCC set forth a maximum of five years for TV station conversion to HDTV once a national system was approved; industry pressure forced the FCC to change it to 15 years. The most serious problem for broadcasting, however, was the continuing recession, with ad revenues continuing to fall.

For cable, it was a bad year. Most important, Congress finally acted on what seemed like an avalanche of constituent complaints and reregulated cable once again in the Cable Television Consumer Protection and Competition Act of 1992. Among the key provisions was a retransmission consent/must-carry requirement. This allowed TV stations to charge cable systems a fee for carrying their signals. However, if such a fee were demanded, cable systems could opt not to carry a station. Conversely, if a local station did not demand a fee, it could require the station to carry it. Before the provisions went into effect, the networks and most larger stations decided that they would demand a carriage fee. But most cable systems stood firm, and when the deadline for decision arrived in May 1993, almost all stations opted for the no-fee, must-carry requirement, and few cable systems paid fees to stations. Other provisions of the act established a cap on rates charged to subscribers and in some instances mandated a rollback, required prompt and better service to customers, and regulated service and equipment costs. Before the new cable rates went into effect in 1994, many cable systems raised their rates, so even with cutbacks that were supposed to

European Union ratified.

Mandela elected President in South
Africa's first all-race election.

1994

Motorola chosen by FCC for AM
stereo transmission.

average about 15% nationwide, rates did not go down for many subscribers and actually went up for many others.

The FCC also let TV networks into ownership of cable systems and allowed cable systems into broadcast activities, with some restrictions.

Technical advances and anticipations continued, waiting for the political world to catch up with the technological. For example, fiber-optic video dial-tone systems were all ready to go and needed only FCC approval. Also, more and more satellite programmers were investing in digital compression equipment to multiply their video capacity.

JUDY WOODRUFF

NEWS REPORTER, EDITOR, AND PRODUCER

FIG 9.14 Judy Woodruff.
Courtesy MacNeil/Lehrer News Hour.

Over the two decades of my experience as a television reporter, about the only phenomenon of broadcast journalism that has remained the same is that the picture still flashes off the surface of a glass screen in the home of the viewer. In 1970, there were a mere handful of women in front of the camera; in the 1990s women are a common sight.

Twenty years ago, it took hours, and even days, to transfer film from the camera to the processor, to the editing room, and, finally, to the projector to be broadcast out over the airwaves. Today, thanks to portable microwave units and low-cost satellite, people who live in Wichita, Kansas, can watch live pictures of missile attacks on Riyadh, Saudi Arabia, shot by lightweight videotape cameras.

In the early days, TV reporting mimicked print: Visuals took a backseat to information and analysis. Today, pictures frequently drive the story; and too many news directors worry more about profits and ratings than they do [about] informing the public.

As we head into the 21st century, I would hope that the wizards who have produced all this marvelous technology and these mind-boggling returns on the dollar will turn their attention to the content of what is being broadcast. As the world shrinks and as news and

Israel and PLO sign historic agreement to establish
Palestinian autonomy in Gaza and Jericho.

Bloodbath in Rwanda.

Super Bowl broadcast attracts
largest TV audience to date—
134.8 million viewers.

information hit us at a dizzying pace, we feel we should know as much about our neighbors in the Middle East as we do about our neighbors in the Midwest, not to mention down the street. It will be tempting to slip into a "gossipy" form of news coverage—focusing on personalities and their foibles. Unless we receive more thoughtful analysis, historical perspective, and context from our friends behind and in front of the broadcast news cameras, it'll be very hard to keep up. Hard to keep up with issues from nuclear weapons treaties to preschool education—all of which affect the sort of lives our children and grandchildren will live. If we don't stay informed about these issues, who will?
Courtesy Judy Woodruff.

1993

With a liberal Democrat President in office, many citizen groups believed that the deregulation tide that had eliminated many of the rules and regulations that had protected consumers for decades would be stopped. But it was not to be. The FCC, if anything, moved further toward allowing the wealthiest communication players to merge and monopolize at the expense of the smaller players and the public. In fact, Democrats fully cooperated with the Republicans in what became, three years later, a telecommunications policy that placed virtually no restrictions on big business and virtually eliminated cable rate caps, program diversity, and other consumer protections.

Minority-owned radio stations already were being squeezed by the growing number of duopoly giants authorized through waiver of the FCC's rules. The future of telco growth was in the cards with the FCC's authorization of a public test of video dial tone, which would enable telcos to provide video services. A *Broadcasting* magazine headline stated, "Telcos Closing In On Video," noting the plans of many key companies, including Bell Atlantic, GTE, NYNEX, Southwestern Bell, Pacific Telesis, and US West.

The FCC relaxed the rules on cable ownership. A federal court lifted all finsyn rules, authorizing broadcast networks to contract for domestic and foreign rights, including syndication, for all of its shows, whether in-house or out-of-house productions. This ruling was appealed, however, and it was a while longer before total elimination of finsyn would occur.

Although the FCC expanded some of its Equal Employment Opportunity (EEO) requirements, the commission was strongly criticized by civil rights and minority groups because the new rules did not go far enough toward solving some of the key continuing problems. Once more the Fairness Doctrine was taken to the courts, and once more the FCC's 1987 elimination of the doctrine was upheld. As the Republicans left and the Democrats arrived at the beginning of 1993, Commissioner James Quello,

THE CYBER '90S

Computer multimedia services,
Internet move forward.

a strongly conservative and pro-industry Democrat, was appointed interim chair of the FCC, pending nomination and confirmation of Clinton's new choice for chair, Reed Hundt.

The most important indicator of continued deregulation under the new administration, however, was its announced plan to introduce into Congress a telecommunications bill that would codify and extend deregulation.

Program content was on the minds not only of program executives, who vied with each other to create the most successful clones of the most successful new shows, but on the minds of many citizens and members of Congress who expressed concern over what they felt was rampant indecency and violence on television. Howard Stern was the premier *bête noir*, with personal attacks as well as his usual descriptions of sexual and excretory organs and activities. After his principal talk-show rival, Don Imus, was hospitalized with a collapsed lung, Stern said, on the air, "I hope he dies." His indecent material resulted in further fines for Infinity of $500,000, bringing the total to more than $1 million.

In the continuing saga of a safe harbor, which was not finally resolved for another couple of years, the FCC established, again, the time of midnight to 6:00 A.M. for adult programming. The federal courts struck down this safe harbor time. But the FCC, resolved to restrict adult programming, set a new time of 8:00 P.M. to 6:00 A.M. This was also changed not too long afterward.

One new network program was the focus of protests about its alleged sex and violence by a number of conservative citizen groups, especially those representing the religious right wing, even before they had seen the program. A number of ABC affiliates succumbed to the pressure and refused clearance to *N.Y.P.D. Blue*. Nevertheless, the program immediately shot up in the ratings, had heavy advertising demands, and received critical acclaim for its artistic and entertainment value. Reality TV was spreading rapidly, the four networks presenting 14 weekly reality programs. Action-adventure shows also grew, spurred by the success of *Star Trek: The Next Generation*. Infomercials continued to take advantage of the lack of advertising time restrictions, and shopping channels, already a fixture on cable, made the jump to broadcast TV as well.

Late-night television saw its greatest competition ever. Unhappy that he didn't get *The Tonight Show* host job vacated by Johnny Carson, David Letterman crossed over to CBS to rival the new NBC host, Jay Leno. Fox got into the act, too, with a competing late-night show hosted by Chevy Chase. Chase's show faded quickly. Letterman's ratings immediately began to outpace Leno's; it would be several years before Leno would catch up and pass Letterman.

Ratings of all kinds, however, were under fire. After 44 years Arbitron stopped its TV ratings, leaving the field entirely to Nielsen. Network and station complaints about the accuracy of Nielsen's work continued to rise.

U.S. news and entertainment programming expanded to more corners of the world through satellite, such as Fox's establishment of a Latin American channel.

Merger mania, monopolies hit
broadcasting and cable.

But domestic news was becoming more and more infotainment, to the chagrin of many critics. Former Massachusetts governor and Presidential candidate Michael Dukakis described the sorry state of local news trends: "If it bleeds, it leads."

In radio, country music expanded nationally, including urban markets. So did political content. President Clinton began a regular series of Saturday morning addresses to the nation via radio, reminiscent of President Franklin D. Roosevelt's "fireside chats." Clinton got his message out to the people over local radio stations, asking support for his political agendas such as a health care bill to cover all Americans. At the same time, however, conservative to far-right talk shows continued to grow, and both Clinton and the President's wife, Hillary Rodham Clinton, were attacked mercilessly. One critic described President Clinton in his first year in office as "the most bashed individual in talk show history."

Technological advances continued. The so-called Grand Alliance of technology companies announced a tentative agreement on HDTV standards. It was estimated, however, that conversion of a television station to the HDTV digital standard could cost as much as $1.7 million. HDTV proponents continued to push for it, however, and rival HDTV companies agreed to work together to get HDTV into homes in time for the 1996 Olympic Games. Do you remember seeing the 1996 Olympics in HDTV? That's right, it didn't happen!

There was much talk of 500-channel cable systems appearing within a few years. How many cable channels do you get now, this many years later? There was also much talk of DBS providing multiple channels and replacing cable and terrestrial broadcasting in the near future. An increasing number of production companies, including Disney, Paramount, Time Warner, Viacom, and Turner, offered their programming to DBS distribution companies.

The AM stereo drama went on. The FCC finally designated the Motorola system as the standard. However, it also allowed the Kahn system to be sold, inasmuch as it appeared to be favored by most broadcasters.

1994

By 1994 almost all U.S. households had television; in fact, more had television than had telephones. More than four out of five households had VCRs, adding increasing competition to both broadcast and cable services. Nevertheless, cable also continued to grow, serving almost two-thirds of all U.S. homes. Home computers were in about one third of U.S. homes, and that number was increasing rapidly. The age of multimedia communication was upon us. But even then, almost midway into the last decade of the 20th century, few people realized how much multimedia would dominate us by the beginning of the 21st century.

The networks talked about recapturing their audiences through interactive multimedia systems. More and more program producers, including large companies such

THE CYBER '90S

281

Abortion clinics attacked, prochoice
advocates murdered by right-to-lifers.

O. J. Simpson saga begins.

FCC okays first VDT system.

as Disney, were adding CD-ROM productions. Online computer services were growing, with companies such as Microsoft entering the field. The Home Shopping Network added an Internet service, and even *TV Guide* went online. In fact, there was such demand for new multimedia services that the FCC held it first-ever auction of frequency space, for narrowband personal communication services and for interactive video data services, with the expectation of more frequency space auctions to come. Of course, the wealthiest companies were able to obtain the most space. There was much concern about where the "information superhighway" was going. The larger companies, with their Cadillac bankrolls, were able to ride on it easily, while the smaller companies were obliged to hitchhike.

Critic Tom Shales took a look at the coming predominance of interactive multimedia and suggested—with tongue in cheek, we presume—that we will no longer have real experiences, but "only virtual experiences."

The newly elected Republican Congress pledged even greater deregulation of the communication industry and promised to abolish funding for public broadcasting. The FCC cooperated. It gave Bell Atlantic the okay to build the first video dial-tone system. The FCC approved VDT networks for GTE in four states, and within a year, in 1995, some 100 operations were ready to go. Digital video took another step forward with the unveiling of a digital video storage system to take the place of tape. More telcos announced that they were ready to move into cable as the federal courts continued to relax anti-telco cable rules.

The FCC extended the multiple ownership limits to 20 AM and 20 FM stations. Since the duopoly rule changes in 1992, more than 2,000 of the 10,057 commercial radio stations on the air had already entered into duopolies or local marketing agreements (LMAs).

In other significant actions, a federal appeals court stayed repeal of the domestic part of the finsyn rules. MMDS—wireless cable—continued to grow as another player on the multimedia board. DBS also moved ahead, with 27 domestic communication satellites in orbit. Further attempts to resurrect the Fairness Doctrine failed. And merger mania took a big step forward, with Viacom buying Paramount Communications.

To accommodate the rapidly changing communications landscape, both domestic and global, the FCC changed its own structure, adding a new International Bureau and renaming and giving new duties to others. In addition to the International Bureau, the major operating arms were the Mass Media, Common Carrier, Wireless Telecommunications, Cable Services, and Compliance and Information bureaus.

Programming, especially in television, was both controversial and eclectic. Censorship reared its ugly head. A survey of viewers showed general support for censorship of violence and sex on television, but there was little agreement on definitions of these areas. The U.S. attorney general threatened federal action. Although there was general objection and concern among media professionals, few were willing to risk harming their careers by speaking up on behalf of the First Amendment. Self-censorship

Republicans look for political dirt
in Whitewater affair.

U.S. Major League Baseball strike.

Broadcast and cable programming
dominated by O. J. Simpson saga.

of controversial content that might offend lawmakers, advertisers, and some of the viewing public—which had always been prevalent—became more noticeable as public attitudes began to change. ABC, for example, threatened to cancel an episode of *Roseanne* in which Roseanne kisses another woman. The episode was eventually aired as gay-lesbian themes and characters continued to edge their way into program content, although networks and advertisers by and large continued to reflect the homophobia of much of the U.S. population. The saga of the safe harbor took another twist and turn when the FCC went back to a midnight–6:00 A.M. time. And PBS was once more under fire for allegedly suppressing programs that might alienate the country's new conservative political attitudes and congressional funding.

Programming became concentrated on the O. J. Simpson murder trial. "O. J. mania" began in June with live coverage of the white Bronco chase and accelerated as time went on. Larry King continued to expand the reach of his talk show, which became a launching pad for a number of politicians and political endeavors. The Fox network continued to grow with its programming emphasis on youth demographics. Sports were popular on two fronts, with local baseball live coverage rights increasing to $375 million and Ken Burns's PBS series, *Baseball*, receiving much acclaim. Native American radio joined African American and Latino radio programming as growing formats.

The economy had steadily improved since the election of Bill Clinton, and the three major television networks' profits were up 6%, to more than $9 billion. Total TV advertising topped that of newspapers for the first time. And radio was doing something right, too, with its advertising income reaching a record $10 billion.

Aside from the dominance of the O. J. saga, the networks and stations catered to and promoted viewers' tastes throughout the globe as well as in the United States, with extensive continuing coverage of two other world-shaking events: the Nancy Kerrigan–Tonya Harding ice-skating clash and the Lorena Bobbitt penis-amputating caper.

1995

There was good news and bad news for broadcasters in 1995. Although prime-time TV network shares continued to decrease, down to 57%, ad revenue and profits for both TV and radio continued to go up. Television LMAs grew, making money for the more powerful companies despite complaints that such local conglomeration raised the price of advertising in given markets.

Mergers brought more money into the networks. Disney bought Cap Cities/ABC for the second highest price ever paid for any U.S. company—$18.5 billion. Westinghouse bought CBS, saving that network from potential bankruptcy. Time Warner bought Ted Turner's Turner Broadcasting System (TBS). Group radio and TV station buying grew under relaxed FCC rules that would be even more vitiated in 1996. Some $8 billion was paid for individual radio and TV stations sold in 1995.

THE CYBER '90S

1995

Country top radio format.

More mega-mergers: Disney buys Cap
Cities/ABC, Westinghouse buys CBS,
Time Warner buys Turner's TBS.

FIG 9.15 The future of broadcasting includes Native American stations. Dozens of radio outlets have served the country's Native American population for decades and plan to continue to do so. "Some radio stations that 'ring' the reservation offer 1–3 hours of Navajo programming daily," notes Dale Felkner, the operation director at KNDN in Farmington, New Mexico. "Stations in Gallup, Flagstaff, Holbrook, and Cortez block out portions of certain dayparts for the Navajo listener, but KNDN does so around the clock. We serve approximately half of the total population of the Navajo Indian Reservation, the largest of all U.S. reservations with its total land mass of 25,000 square miles. Our station serves about one-half the land area and one-half the population. All program elements—news, commercials, features— are done in native tongue. The Indian format should remain viable for a long time. We're a unique brand of radio."
Courtesy KNDN-AM.

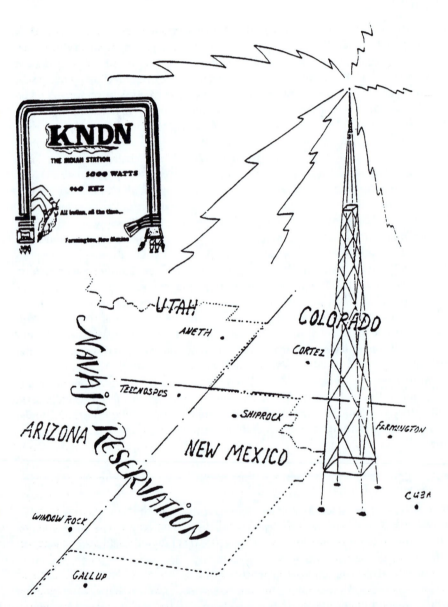

While posing potential competition for the four existing networks but attesting to the belief that broadcasting was far from dead, two new television networks made their debut in 1995: WB (Warner Brothers) and UPN (United Paramount). Rupert Murdoch's Fox empire was safe after an FCC investigation determined that the funding of Fox stations by Murdoch's Australian company did not constitute foreign

Two new broadcast TV networks,
WB and UPN, debut.

ownership. Congress ended the tax certificate program for selling stations to minority groups, while Murdoch, Viacom, and 17 others were in the process of such sales. Murdoch got a special waiver from Congress to complete his sale; Viacom and the 17 others did not. Some cynics suggested that Murdoch's close friendship with House Speaker Newt Gingrich might have had something to do with that. Public broadcasting didn't fare quite so well. Although the new Republican-controlled Congress tried but failed to eliminate all public broadcasting funding, it did decrease it.

After eight years of work, testing was completed on an HDTV standard, and a digital advanced TV system was recommended to the FCC. To permit a changeover without interrupting operations, stations were given a second channel free for 15 years. Networks were happy when the FCC voted (once again) to kill the finsyn rules and to abolish the Prime-Time Access Rule (PTAR), while independent producers and syndicators had nightmares of Porsches being repossessed from their driveways. Radio got a technical boost when the FCC approved the building of a digital audio radio system, although the commission had not yet officially authorized the service.

The affiliate news services of NBC, ABC, and CBS all grew, for three major reasons. One was the increase in live coverage: In 1995 there were about twice as many live shots on news shows than in previous years. Another reason was an attempt to compete more strongly with the proliferating cable news networks, which at the end of 1995 had several new entrants with 24-hour cable news services. Perhaps the main reason news boomed was the O. J. Simpson trial. Coverage was both praised and condemned. The case dominated TV time throughout the year, not only in extended broadcast coverage, but programs devoted to the trial consistently finished at the top of the cable ratings—usually 8 or 9 of the top 10 rated cable shows each week. Some 150 million people were watching when the "not guilty" verdict was handed down.

There was, perhaps to the surprise of some, programming other than O. J. in 1995. Television prime-time fare continued to consist, in large part, of *Seinfeld* and *Home Improvement* clones. The three larger networks borrowed from Fox's successful shows and maintained a spate of innocuous and sometimes silly sitcoms oriented to the 20-something audience. Many of them got consistently high ratings. The late-night Leno–Letterman competition heated up, and in 1995 Leno began to catch up with, and finally passed, Letterman. Spanish-language programming, on both television and radio, continued to expand. Not surprisingly, radio surveys confirmed that AM listeners tended to be older and FM listeners younger.

Indecency was still "topic A" in some circles. Both Congress and the White House backed the inclusion of a V-chip provision, allowing the screening and blanking out in the home of programs deemed by the household to be violent or indecent. Infinity and Howard Stern, who had protested the FCC fines to the federal courts, voluntarily dropped their lawsuit and paid $1.7 million to the FCC to end the proceedings.

Cable, like broadcasting, had both good news and bad news. More and more original programming appeared on cable networks and the networks themselves multiplied, attesting to the health of cable. Some of the new cable networks, their content and target

THE CYBER '90S

285

Kobe, Japan, hit by devastating
earthquake.

Tax certificate to spur minority
group ownership abolished by
Congress.

PTAR abolished.

audiences implied by their name, were the American Political Channel, America's Health
Network, Auto Channel, Black Shopping Network, Classic Arts Showcase, Conservative
TV Network, Ecology Channel, Game Show Network, Golf Channel, Language Network,
Military Channel, Premiere Horse Network, Women's Sports Network, and World African
Network. New music networks, clones of MTV, also came to the fore.

FIG 9.16 A popular show
among television viewing
youth in the 1990s.
Courtesy MTV.

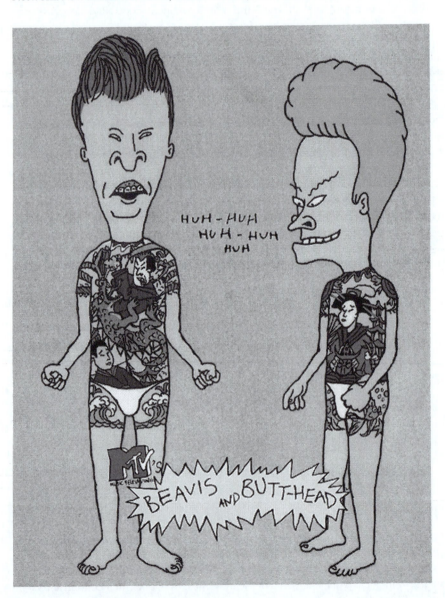

Budget battle shuts down U.S. government.

Finsyn rules lifted.

Infinity–Stern pay $1.7 million fine to end indecency proceedings.

Local cable systems were given greater jurisdiction over their public access and leased channels by the Supreme Court, which allowed them to ban what they considered indecent material on those channels.

Mergers and buyouts were also rampant in cable as well as in broadcasting. Comcast, for example, bought the Scripps cable empire. The big got bigger.

Bad news for cable was the increasing encroachment by telcos on their de facto monopolies in municipalities. In early 1995 the FCC reached a tentative conclusion

FIG 9.17 A flashback. This newspaper column written by one of this book's authors in 1953 suggests that the need for the V-chip existed even during television's infancy.

THE CYBER '90S

Oklahoma City Federal Building bombing linked to U.S. right-wing radicals, militias, neo-Nazis.	Ebola virus outbreak in Africa.

Internet and CD-ROM eat into TV viewing time.

The Learning Channel
The smart choice on cable.

FIG 9.18 The Learning Channel (TLC) was the nation's third-fastest-growing basic cable network in the 1990s and is cable television's premiere educational channel. The network delivers formal and informal educational programs; pertinent business and career information; stimulating hobby, how-to, self-improvement, and personal enrichment series; plus award-winning "Independents" series from independent film and video producers. TLC Excel and the Electronic Library offer programming designed for use in the classroom and geared to promote literacy in all areas of language, math, and science. TLC provides a lifelong learning experience for everyone as it delivers more educational programming nationwide than any other television network. *Courtesy TLC.*

that telcos could offer video dial-tone systems. That tentative determination would be codified into law a year later.

The map was changing, however, for all travelers in the communications world, including broadcasting and cable. Multimedia, computer-based communications were developing faster and faster. The global information society was virtually here. More companies were bringing shows to CD-ROM. Interactive television was becoming multimedia. Microsoft predicted that mini-digital broadcast receivers carrying broadcast and cable television soon would be built into personal computers. Broadcast and cable networks were creating Websites on the Internet. With the increased sales of the dinner-plate–sized satellite receiver dish, the digital satellite system was beginning what many believed to be a revolution in the way TV and other video programming would be delivered.

CATHARINE HEINZ

DIRECTOR, BROADCAST PIONEERS LIBRARY

In the reporting of history, only broadcasting can depict sight and sound with the capability to instantly record it. Broadcasting in its documentation of world events should be responsible, just as print journalism media are, for preserving the heritage it creates. Frequently, however, that incredible product is being destroyed after having been seen or heard only once. Surely the technically perfection-oriented industry that has evolved can find a way to preserve its unbelievable product, if not for posterity—then selfishly for its own use. Most "bottom line" followers will say preservation is much too expensive, will take up too much room, and will not be used. Is that necessarily true in this age of sophisticated telecommunications technology? Consider

now in this age of nostalgia how production companies and all manner of collectors search worldwide for past events such as a 1940 Winston Churchill speech at Dunkirk. *Courtesy Catharine Heinz.*

FIG 9.19 WCBS Phil Cook Book Drive, New York City, 1948. *Left to right:* Roy E. Larsen, president, Time, Inc.; Catharine Heinz, director, hospital libraries, United Hospital Fund; G. Richard Swift, program manager, WCBS Radio; and Phil Cook. *Courtesy Catharine Heinz.*

1996

Pay-as-you-go spectrum access proposed as replacement for exclusive licensing.	WJDM in New Jersey is first station on expanded AM band.	Telecommunications Act of 1996 becomes law; entire communications landscape changed; most proconsumer rules abolished.

While all this was going on, Congress was working on an instant revolution, a new telecommunications act. Throughout the year there was expectation of sweeping deregulation. Most of the deregulatory proposals were supported by the FCC. House Speaker Gingrich pledged to "liberate" the telecommunications marketplace, including no cable rate regulation, open telco–cable competition, entry of power companies into the telecom business, and no antimonopoly rules for broadcasters.

1996

President Clinton, in his 1996 State of the Union address, talked about this "age of technology information and global competition." Shortly afterward, a headline in the *Boston Globe*, commenting on the new Telecommunications Act of 1996, stated: "New telecommunications law puts billions of dollars up for grabs in new era of competition . . . firms rush to a revolution."

FIG 9.20 In 1991 Black Entertainment Television's (BET's) subscriber base reached 30 million in 2,400 markets. It is clear that African Americans and other people of color will play a major role in the next broadcast century. *Courtesy BET.*

THE CYBER '90S

| U.S. profits, executive salaries up; workers' jobs, benefits down. | Shaky peace in Bosnia. | Terrorists, conflict threaten Mideast peace process. |

Both of these comments heralded the most important developments in telecommunications, not only in 1996, but for the past half century. And they were inescapably interrelated.

First, global information technology. Everyone who could was getting on the bandwagon. Increasing numbers of companies were building information Websites on the Internet. Syndicators of video and audio programs established Web pages. *Broadcasting & Cable* magazine went on the Web. AT&T entered the Internet access business.

Internet usage rose 50% in the first six months of 1996, with about 36 million people in the United States online. More radio news producers were planning to put their materials on the Internet. An increasing number of television, cable, and radio networks and stations, and even individual producers, were putting their programs on Websites. Musical artists looked toward the Internet as a means of marketing their music, an approach that some would rue several years later.

With cross-media ownership rules virtually eliminated in the new Telecommunications Act, AT&T and other companies were developing one-stop full-service offerings, to include cable, Internet, and telephone and other local and long-distance common carrier services. Continuing plans were made not only for international distribution of entertainment programs via satellite but for 24-hour-a-day news services to as much of the world and from as much of the world as possible. Murdoch's "birds" were fast approaching total global coverage, with BSkyB covering Europe and part of Africa, Star TV covering Asia, and a new satellite service expected to cover Latin America before the end of the year. Murdoch also achieved more effective coverage of North America, joining with MCI at an FCC DBS auction to get the last DBS slot to cover all of the United States. The auction, a new approach to fundraising by the government, raised a total of $735 million. Auction of wireless telephone spectrum at the beginning of 1996 garnered $10 billion, and plans were under way to auction spectrum space for digital TV as well.

The key word was *digital*, as part of the advanced or HDTV system expected within the next few years. The White House, pushing for progress in the electronic media, called for the establishment of digital TV standards, and the FCC set a November deadline for its adoption of digital standards that were not yet agreed on by the marketplace. In the meantime, Fox's new 24-hour news cable network adopted a digital videotape format, the first model station to try out a UHF HDTV transmitter began operation, and television station WRAL in Raleigh, North Carolina, began broadcasting some programs in HDTV under an experimental license from the FCC.

By mid-1996 the skies were getting crowded with satellite services. In the United States three companies—DirecTV, Primestar, and United States Satellite Broadcasting (USSB)—were in operation, and two more were preparing to follow. About 5 million homes had satellite receiver dishes, with about half paying monthly fees for signal

V-chip provides home censorship.

descrambling, most of the remainder content to pick up clear, unscrambled signals, and the rest pirating the DBS signals.

Cable companies were worried. DBS companies were adding subscribers who otherwise might have chosen cable. In part, this was cable's own fault. First, the average monthly cable bill jumped 7.8% in 1996. Second, cable's promise of 500 available channels by the end of 1996 didn't happen. A survey showed that 30% of all cable subscribers were dissatisfied with their cable services, and of those who knew of alternatives to cable, 53% were considering switching.

The Telecommunications Act of 1996 legislated the most sweeping changes in telecommunications in the United States in more than 60 years and reversed laws, rules, and regulations that had been built up over decades. The antimonopoly rules were virtually totally eliminated, specifying no caps on the number of radio stations owned by one entity, and expanded dual ownership in individual markets, depending on the market size. The 12-station limit on one entity's TV ownership was also eliminated, with the FCC charged with developing new, broader standards. Reversing the 1941 network duopoly rule, the act permitted ownership of two networks, provided one was not purchased by another. *Broadcasting & Cable* headlined a story on the lifting of ownership limits for radio thus: "Radio Supergroups: They're Off."

And indeed they were! In just one week in March, Infinity Broadcasting Corporation bought 12 stations for $410 million, giving it a nationwide total of 46, and Clear Channel Communications, Inc., bought 13 stations for $130 million, giving it a total of 52. A Sinclair–River City merger resulted in a holding of 29 television and 34 radio stations.

A Westinghouse/Infinity/CBS merger resulted in a super-giant radio ownership company. Television super-giants were formed by Time/Warner acquiring Turner Broadcasting and a Westinghouse/CBS merger. But there were still some limits on TV ownership. With virtually none on radio, by the end of the year some $25 billion had been spent on radio acquisitions.

The act allowed common ownership of broadcast networks and cable systems. It allowed cable–MMDS cross-ownership under certain conditions. Broadcast license terms, for both TV and radio, were extended to eight years. VDT rules were repealed and telcos were permitted to deliver video signals. Conversely, cable systems were permitted to enter the area of telephone service. Atlantic Bell and NYNEX merged, providing a huge conglomerate that offered cable as well as local and long-distance telephone service.

Between the Congress and the courts, censorship was imposed on several fronts. The safe harbor issue finally reached the Supreme Court. Despite objections from civil liberties groups and ACT—which argued that First Amendment freedoms of speech and press were the best protections for children—the court ruled that the FCC has the right to establish a safe harbor for adult programming, ostensibly to

THE CYBER '90S

291

protect child viewers. The hours of 10:00 P.M. to 6:00 A.M. were designated, based on the presumption that children are not watching television during that period. Conversely, programming that is deemed "adult" may not be broadcast between 6:00 A.M. and 10:00 P.M.

The new act required cable systems to scramble any programs the subscriber deemed unsuitable for children. All new sets sold were required to have a V-chip, and the industry was required to develop a ratings system within a year as a guide for parental use of the V-chip or the FCC would itself set up a rating system. Congress seemed to be obsessed with indecency. Fines for broadcast or cable obscene programs were raised from $10,000 to $100,000. Congress also managed to pass a Communications Decency Act, in which anyone using the Internet for alleged indecent material could be fined up to $25,000 and jailed for two years, although it was not clear what exactly would be considered indecent. Anyone even under suspicion of sending or receiving indecent material on the Internet could have their phone lines tapped by the FCC. The moment the bill was signed by the President, a number of citizen organizations, such as the American Civil Liberties Union (ACLU), filed suit, and the federal courts stayed implementation of the cyberspace indecency provisions pending First Amendment review by the Supreme Court.

Renewal of licenses was made virtually automatic, and competitive applications would not be allowed. Cable rates were deregulated beginning in 1999. The act also limited advanced TV licenses to incumbent broadcasters. Murdoch was one of the first on the bandwagon, stating that he would convert the Fox-owned stations immediately, although there was still a need for integrated production and operations components linked to high-speed computer networks.

And these were only some of the key changes in the telecommunications landscape. Consumer groups were outraged by both the bill and by the media's—presumably acting in their own vested self-interests—refusal to report to the people the potential negative impact of the new telecommunications law on the public. An article by Justin Twergo in *Censored*, by Carl Jensen and Project Censored, stated that "America's marketplace of ideas, upon which our democracy rests, began shutting its doors in the summer of 1995. The harbinger of the bad news for the public was aptly titled the Telecommunications Regulation Bill . . . under the guise of encouraging competition [the bill will create] huge new concentrations of media power." Consumer advocate Ralph Nader stated that the new law would provide "fewer choices for consumers."

A somewhat different view was expressed by Annenberg Washington Program Fellow Anton Lensen, in "Concentration in the Media Industry: The European Community and Mass Media Regulation." Lensen wrote, "The trend toward concentration leads to concerns that the free flow of information will be reduced or that interlocking media ownerships will jeopardize news operations' independence.

Camelot goes on the auction
block at Jackie O. auction.

Mega-mergers in television and
radio.

Cyberspace indecency laws
stayed by court on First
Amendment appeal.

However, media concentration can also help provide less expensive, high-quality information in greater quantities and improve the effectiveness of media enterprises."

Cable, now facing serious competition, attempted to strengthen individual network images, and more targeted cable networks, such as History, Home and Garden, The Learning Channel, and Cartoon Network, made their appearance. With PTAR gone, syndicated shows were fearful of their future, but *Wheel of Fortune* and *Jeopardy* continued to dominate syndication ratings, with talk shows such as *Oprah* and sitcoms such as *Seinfeld* and *Home Improvement* right behind.

Talk shows, which had exploded in 1994 and 1995, began to fade in 1996, principally because the "sleaze" factor that dominated so many of them finally began to turn audiences away. An exception was the *Rosie O'Donnell Show*, which had the highest rating for a talk-show debut since Oprah Winfrey had gone on the air 10 years earlier. Magazine formats grew on TV. Gradually, nonstereotyped gay and lesbian roles were added to dramas and sitcoms, in great part spurred by the revelation of actress Ellen DeGeneres's sympathetic character on the sitcom *Ellen* as a lesbian.

Meaningful programming for children got a boost from the FCC, which ruled that beginning in the fall of 1997, commercial TV stations would be required to provide a minimum of three hours a week of "educational" children's programming as a condition of license renewal. Minority programs also got a boost—from the marketplace. Univision and Telemundo strengthened their programming as they vied for the largest share of the Spanish-language television market.

Despite objections from many broadcasters, Seagram's distillery ended a 40-year-old voluntary ban on advertising hard liquor. As subsequent years proved, the expected windfall of ad dollars and sales profits did not materialize. Through all this, network prime-time shares of the audience continued to fall. One response, to some observers justifiable, of the big four television networks was to call for changes in the Nielsen rating system.

Some long-time shows ended their run in 1996: *Murder, She Wrote* after 12 years, and the father of talk shows, Phil Donohue, retired after 30 years as a host. The networks made a move considered highly positive by most observers: They provided, for the first time, some free time for Presidential candidates in that 1996 election year to present their views to the public, unhampered by limited commercial time or distorted by sound bites. A few years earlier, in a speech at Harvard's Kennedy School of Government, Walter Cronkite had said, "In emphasizing political manipulation, rather than issues, we of the press have probably contributed to public cynicism about the political process," referring specifically to the use of "photo ops" and "sound bites" in place of substance. The TV networks also agreed, under pressure from the public, the White House, and Congress, to provide a minimum of three hours per week of children's educational programming.

Following the media circus of the O. J. Simpson trial, many judges became leery of cameras in the courtroom; they believed that the practice encouraged grandstanding

THE CYBER '90S

293

| Talk shows hit by "sleaze" factor.

| Supreme Court okays "safe harbor."

FIG 9.21 This program was one of a few hit dramas on network television as the end of the century neared. *Courtesy Warner Brothers.*

by attorneys and other participants and weakened the Sixth Amendment's fair trial provisions. The Judicial Conference of the United States, which establishes procedures for the federal courts, had banned cameras in the courtroom, although several years of experiments had resulted in positive recommendations for continuation. In early 1996 it reversed itself and allowed individual federal district court systems to decide;

Westinghouse buys Infinity Broadcasting.

MSNBC debuts.

electronic media journalists hoped this decision would level the playing field with newspapers in federal trial coverage.

In 1996 there were more than 4,900 commercial AM, 5,290 commercial FM, and 1,810 noncommercial (or educational/public) radio stations on the air. There were more than 560 commercial TV VHF and 623 UHF stations and 123 noncommercial TV (educational/public) VHF and 240 UHF stations in operation. Low-power TV (LPTV) had more than 565 VHF and 1,215 UHF stations. Cable systems throughout the country totaled more than 11,660, with total subscribers over 62.5 million; cable passed almost 92 million homes, with a penetration of more than 65%.

The cultural and historical importance of broadcasting was further acknowledged with the opening of still another Museum of Television & Radio, this one in Los Angeles.

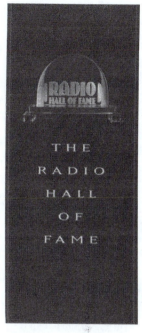

FIG 9.22 In recent years, radio's greats have been inducted into the Hall of Fame.
Courtesy Museum of Broadcast Communications.

THE CYBER '90S

Evaluating the Age and Content Ratings System

Approximately four years after the passage of the 1996 Telecommunications Act that implemented the V-chip and led to the age-based program rating system (TV-G, TV-PG, TV-14, etc.), along with content descriptors (the S, L, V, D, and FV) that were added following complaints that the age labels did not provide enough information, a collection of researchers[1] analyzed the validity of the television industry's self-applied labeling practice. Because no centralized agency or governmental authority checks the authenticity of these ratings, it was important to investigate how accurately they were being applied. The researchers found that the age-based ratings reasonably reflected the content, but the content descriptors were a problem. The results suggest that these inaccuracies limit the V-chip's ability to work effectively, because needed information is lacking. The most problematic designator was violence, with approximately 80% of the programs studied containing excessive violence but sans the V label, whereas the majority of programs without the D designator possessed exorbitant sexual dialogue. In the children's programming arena they found only a paltry 11% of the shows displaying the fantasy violence label, despite the fact that content analysis revealed violence widespread across the terrain of children programs.

1997

Programming changes, innovations, and challenges marked much of the year in all the electronic media. News and special event coverage played significant roles. The year had barely started when the network news divisions faced a dilemma: During President

[1]Kunkel, D., Fannola, W. J. M., Farrar, K., Donnerstein, E., Biely, E., and Zwarun, L. (2002). Deciphering the V-chip: An examination of the television industry's program rating judgments. *Journal of Communication*, 52, 112–138.

Increased Mideast terrorist bombings.

Death sentence recommended for Timothy McVeigh in Oklahoma City bombing.

1997

TV documentaries on rise.

Clinton's State of the Union address, the O. J. Simpson civil trial verdict came in. Most news teams stayed with the President; others opted to interrupt with the verdict.

Just weeks later the media covered Clinton again, this time with almost all broadcast and cable networks carrying his inauguration live. The biggest news story, milked for all it was worth by news media worldwide, was Princess Diana's death in a car crash. Ironically, most of the news divisions that criticized the role of the "paparazzi" in connection with Diana's death shamelessly exploited her personal life and speculated about the circumstances surrounding her death, seeking as much sensationalism as had the paparazzi.

The public itself laid the groundwork for the growth and, in subsequent years, proliferation of news and public affairs programming—although many of these programs were personality and human interest oriented, some even frivolous, rather than serious news shows. A survey showed that 62% of the public believed that it was very important for television to provide news and information, whereas only 42% believed that it was very important for television to provide entertainment.

Serious television documentaries saw a resurgence, principally on PBS and on cable, with networks such as A&E and the History, Discovery, and Learning cable channels among the leaders. In an effort to stem the decrease in numbers of

FIG 9.23 Shock radio and trash TV continued to enjoy huge audiences throughout the decade.

Debate on V-chip continues.

prime-time viewers, the television broadcast networks promoted new drama venues, including cop and sci-fi shows, and a heavy schedule of sitcoms, with concentration on 20-somethings to draw the coveted young adult demographics, and on new comedies with an emphasis on kids and families.

Television programmers capitalized on whatever appeared to attract more viewers. Courtroom reality shows became favorites. A new talk show, *The Jerry Springer Show*, moved steadily up in the ratings, proving once again that sensationalism sells. Even syndicated video games such as *Mortal Combat* found distribution on television and cable channels.

But all of this didn't help much. Prime-time TV network viewing dropped to a 62 share, from a 65.2 share the previous year. Both cable and the incipient mega-giant Internet proved to be effective competition for viewers' time. Cable's prime-time share increased from 29.5 to 32.4 for the year—despite its rates going up about 10%. Cable nets were doing more original programming to attract viewers.

Although the picture quality of entertainment on the Internet was still quite inadequate, the future was clearly in view as an increasing number of entertainment programs, including game shows, comedies, dramas, and music programs, were being streamed into cyberspace. NBC, for example, was putting more prime-time dramas on the Internet, and it established a new cyberspace network, linking affiliates in 40 communities into what it named an "Interactive Neighborhood."

Radio remained solid. Its revenues continued to increase. Country music continued as the top radio format, with adult contemporary next, followed by news/talk stations.

The Supreme Court played a significant role in establishing freedoms for Internet programming. It reaffirmed a lower court's 1996 ruling and found the Cyberspace Decency Act unconstitutional. Conversely, however, it affirmed another lower court ruling concerning television: Adult video programming must be scrambled between 6:00 A.M. and 10:00 P.M. In another decision, it upheld the must-carry rules that required cable systems to carry local broadcast stations.

One aspect of the Telecommunications Act of 1996 still plagued broadcasters. Arguments continued as to whether the V-chip designations and on-screen warnings should be solely age based, similar to the film rating system, or whether content information should be included with SLV (sex, language, violence) specifications. All but one of the networks went along with providing viewers with the additional information; NBC held out.

The merger mania fallout from the Telecommunication Act of 1996's elimination of most, and the relaxing of other, antimonopoly regulations continued apace. Broadcast networks were increasingly becoming big cable system owners. The acquisition of stations made it possible for Bud Paxson to form a seventh television network, PAX, with a "family values" orientation, even though the two existing smallest networks, UPN and WB, were experiencing tough going. Rupert Murdoch's News Corp. expanded with the acquisition of the Family cable channel. The FCC granted waivers for local TV-radio cross-ownerships pending a possible rule change permitting

THE CYBER '90S

Digital channels assigned by FCC.

Reporting on O. J. verdict and Princess Di's death draws huge audiences.

this practice. LMAs, which had marked radio's approach to getting around the local multiple ownership restrictions, were increasing for television, with more than 70 TV markets having LMAs. Mergers and monopolies spread rapidly in the international arena as well, with the big players becoming even bigger and the small players being forced out of the global game. As a *Broadcasting & Cable* magazine headline stated, global "Satellite Operators See Untapped Overseas Markets."

FIG 9.24 National talk radio personalities became superstars invited to host Presidential roasts, sometimes with scandalous results.

DON IMUS
Monday-Friday 5am-9am

Time Magazine labeled him as "One of the most influential people in America." His radio show is heard in over 90 markets across the U.S. His best-selling novel **God's Other Son** spent 3 months on The New York Times Best Seller's List. His charitable efforts have raised nearly 13 million dollars to benefit the C.J. Foundation for SIDS and The Tomorrow's Children Fund. And as host of America's Best Morning Show...Don Imus has only just begun!

Don is **SERIOUS!**...A show blending news, music, sports and bawdy humor...where politicians and journalists mingle to be heard by an audience of chattering peers. His guests have included President Clinton, CBS News Anchors Dan Rather and Walter Cronkite, Senators Bob Dole and Alfonse D'Amato, Comedian George Carlin, NBC's News Anchors Tom Brokaw and Jane Pauley, Former Pittsburgh Steeler's Quarterback Terry Bradshaw and countless others.

Winner of 4 Marconi Awards, an inductee into the NAB and Emerson Radio Hall of Fame and recognized by Billboard Magazine as Major Market Personality of the Year...there is nobody like Don Imus. His goal..."To goad my guests into saying something that will ruin their life!"

Yes...the **I-MAN COMETH**...and he's **Don Imus.** Hear him every weekday morning from 5 to 9am on the new **LA TALK 1110!**

Prime-time TV audience
continues to dwindle.

Preparation for digital HDTV continued, although the promise was still well ahead of the pace. The FCC assigned digital TV channels in preparation for broadcast station transitions. NBC produced the first live network HDTV program on experimental station WHD-TV in Washington, D.C.; it was, appropriately, the venerable *Meet the Press*. The MTV and Lifetime cable channels introduced new digital networks. And the industry as a whole increased its use of disc-based video storage and playback equipment, digital acquisition formats, and editing equipment.

Deregulation continued to affect employment as well as other areas of broadcasting, with minorities and women having more and more difficulty not only in breaking through the artificially imposed ceilings but in even getting their feet through the office, control room, and studio doors. A study found that women cable executives were paid an average of 15% less than males doing the same jobs. There was one bright spot for women: For the first time women were general managers of stations in the top three markets—all of them Fox stations.

1998

Mega-deals! Mega-mergers! Mega-profits! The Telecommunications Act of 1996's elimination of most restrictions on media monopolies continued to result in the big and wealthy getting bigger and wealthier and the smaller being gobbled up or forced out of business. The number of combined TV-radio deals in 1998 increased 254% from 1997. The monetary amount reached $6.54 billion. TV-alone deals accounted for $7.12 billion. Radio AM deals went up 65% from the year before. Altogether, total deals in 1998 reached $22.8 billion. One of the largest deals in broadcasting history was Clear Channel Communication's acquisition of Jacor Communications for $6.35 billion. Despite decreasing numbers of prime-time viewers, the four major television networks' combined revenues rose by 14% from the previous year, to $24.7 billion. Combined profits were up only 3%, but that was due in part to Fox's huge losses in covering the 1998 Olympic Games; CBS profits, for example, were up 41%.

Cable monopolies increased, too. In 1994, the 10 largest cable multiple system operators (MSOs) controlled 45% of the country's total cable subscriptions; in 1998, the 10 largest controlled 74%. AT&T, flush with the 1996 act's removal of restrictions on telcos owning and operating cable systems, took over TCI, one of the largest cable MSOs, pending FCC approval, which would come the following year. One part of America, however, was still in the back of the media bus: Station ownership by racial minorities and women had increased only 1.5% in the 20 years since 1978.

The year 1998 might also be called the "Year of Digital." After so many years of preparation for the still-to-come high-definition television age, digital HDTV finally got off the starting line. The FCC authorized more power and additional channels for

1998

EAS replaces EBS.

UHF, to provide matching digital channels to stations for the HDTV transition. More cable networks went digital. CBS broadcast National Football League (NFL) games in digital. And for one of the big human interest news stories of the year, television initiated broad HDTV coverage, with 24 stations showing John Glenn's October space launch using high-definition technology. In November, 41 stations began initial, although limited, broadcasting in digital high-definition. *Broadcasting & Cable* magazine made the digital age official for the telecommunications industry with a 60-page supplement on digital in its November 18, 1998, edition, stating, "The race to digital has begun."

Competition for all media increased. DBS continued to grow, with two out of every three new video subscribers choosing DBS over cable. DBS's Echo Star experimented with beaming local broadcast signals into local markets, a process that was expected to remove one of the major hurdles for DBS to compete much more strongly with cable. It would be another year, however, before DBS would receive the congressional approval needed for regular local-signal distribution. Residential Communications Network (RCN) increased its overbuild (more than one cable system in a community) in cities from Washington, D.C., to Boston, creating serious competition for existing cable operators, especially where the subscriber base in a given community was too small to provide a profit margin for more than one company. As cable systems increased, so did cable networks, with 109 new companies offering a broad variety of programming. Cable continued to do well with the same high-income, high-rating type of programming that worked for broadcast television, sports, but combined it with a prepared entertainment factor: The highest-rated programs on cable were professional wrestling shows. Meanwhile, Congress continued to express concern over cable's ever-rising rates—but declined to do anything about it.

Through all the changes that were occurring, radio not only survived but was on very solid financial ground. A panel of Wall Street analysts described radio as being in "the best of all worlds today." The top format for radio was a combination of adult contemporary (AC) formats, which selectively incorporated in their lists some country music performers whose styles were compatible with AC preferences; country had previously been the most popular format.

Television broadcast networks continued to seek ways to stem the tide of increasing competition from other distribution systems, of higher costs, and of decreasing audiences. In January the networks paid a record sum of $18 billion for the rights to carry NFL games. They revived game shows, some of them reincarnations of quiz shows that had disappeared in the wake of the scandals of almost 40 years before. Adult (but not pornographic) cartoons were expanded, with the success of Fox's *The Simpsons* generating the usual clones. *King of the Hill* and *South Park* became almost instant successes and, in turn, generated more clones over the next few years.

Radio revenues still on rise.

25 YEARS WITH
ARNIE "Woo Woo" GINSBURG

Fabulous 50's

Swinging 60's

Super 70's

108 PLATTERS THAT MATTERED

FIG 9.25 Interest in the good ol' rock-n-roll days of radio was high in the last decade of the century. *Courtesy KISS-FM.*

NBC took a big hit in its dominating Thursday night schedule and in its ratings when *Seinfeld* ended its remarkable run. However, syndication sales for *Seinfeld* broke all previous records for cost in a single market.

The FCC tried to encourage an additional aspect of news and public affairs programming for broadcast stations: free air time to bona fide political candidates. But Congress—why would an incumbent who already was getting coverage want any rivals to obtain time, too?—pressured the FCC to back off its efforts under threat of not funding the commission. The FCC backed off.

The year's biggest news story, however, dealt with politics. For much of the year the media exploited the Clinton–Lewinsky affair and the President's impeachment trial to its zenith, to daily bated-breath audiences. Most foreign countries and media didn't understand why Americans made such a fuss over a politician's personal life, but at home the media reports drew huge audiences and concomitantly increased revenues. Even after the President's impeachment acquittal by the Senate early the following year, the stories continued.

Despite the increasing number of TV homes nationwide and, concomitantly, more viewers, TV networks' prime-time TV audiences continued to decline in the 1990s. In fact, only five of the 25 most watched broadcasts since 1960 occurred in the 1990s—and three of those were football Super Bowls. None of the top nonsports shows of the late 1980s and 1990s made the list, including the number-one series between

Merger mania continues unabated.

1985 and 1989, *The Cosby Show*, which twice got an annual rating above 30, or *ER*, the leader in the 1995, 1996, and 1998 seasons, with a 22 as its highest annual rating and only a 17.6 for the 1998–1999 year. The following chart indicates that the heyday of network TV individual shows was in the late 1970s and early 1980s.

Top 25 TV Shows by Audience Rating

RANKING	PROGRAM	DATE	NIELSEN RATING
1	*M*A*S*H* finale (CBS)	February 28, 1983	60.2
2	*Dallas*—Who Shot JR? (CBS)	November 21, 1980	53.3
3	*Roots*—final episode 8 (ABC)	January 30, 1977	51.1
4	Super Bowl XVI (CBS)	January 24, 1982	49.1
5	Super Bowl XVII (NBC)	January 30, 1983	48.6
6	Winter Olympics XVII (CBS)	January 23, 1994	48.5
7	Super Bowl XX (NBC)	January 26, 1986	48.3
8	*Gone with the Wind*—movie, part 1 (NBC)	November 7, 1976	47.7
9	*Gone with the Wind*—movie, part 2 (NBC)	November 8, 1976	47.4
10	Super Bowl XII (CBS)	January 15, 1978	47.2
11	Super Bowl XIII (NBC)	January 21, 1979	47.1
12	Bob Hope Christmas Special (NBC)	January 15, 1970	46.6
13	Super Bowl XVIII (CBS)	January 22, 1984	46.4
14	Super Bowl XIX (ABC)	January 20, 1985	46.4
15	Super Bowl XIV (CBS)	January 20, 1980	46.3
16	Super Bowl XXX (NBC)	January 28, 1996	46.0
17	*The Day After*—movie (ABC)	January 20, 1983	46.0
18	*Roots*—episode 6 (ABC)	January 28, 1977	45.9
19	*The Fugitive*— final episode (ABC)	August 29, 1967	45.9
20	Super Bowl XXI (CBS)	January 25, 1987	45.8
21	*Roots*—episode 5 (ABC)	January 27, 1977	45.7
22	Super Bowl XXVIII (NBC)	January 30, 1994	45.5
23	*Cheers*—final episode (NBC)	May 20, 1993	45.5
24	*Ed Sullivan Show* (CBS)	February 9, 1964	45.3
25	Super Bowl XXVII (NBC)	January 31, 1993	45.1

Media entrepreneurs continued to move toward the new millennium as the old one was running out. The future was, of course, the Internet. It seemed clear that it wouldn't be too many years before the programming on now-traditional distribution systems would be going through cyberspace. More and more programs from networks, stations, cable, and other media sources were put on the Internet. CBS went online

Media frenzy about
Clinton–Lewinsky affair grows.

with material from 154 affiliates. NBC expanded its Internet programming. Individual popular programs went on the Internet; *Saturday Night Live*, for example, presented sketches from its past 23 years.

Music programs became a staple of the Internet, but the radio and music industries were increasingly concerned about "pirates" stealing their copyrighted material and presenting it for downloading without their permission, presaging lawsuits that were to be filed within the next couple of years as pirating increased. Although a Digital Millennium Copyright Act was enacted in 1998, lack of immediate implementation of its provisions encouraged easy larceny.

The FCC pushed for greater diversity in broadcasting as more women and minorities lost their positions to the continuing resurgence of white male control following the vitiation, which had begun during the Reagan administrations, of equal employment requirements and affirmative action rules. The number of women on the 10 most popular nightly news programs dropped in four years from three to zero. Women in cable earned 20% less than their male counterparts. During 1998 a number of top women television executives lost their jobs, prompting *Broadcasting & Cable* magazine to headline a story, "Men Are Still Running the Show in TV." The FCC's efforts were in vain. The U.S. Court of Appeals decided that the FCC's EEO rule that required stations to recruit minorities and women was unconstitutional.

Even with all the new media developments, television, in one form or another, continued to dominate and strongly affect people's lives. As Bart Simpson said to his elders in one of the episodes of the video cartoon, "It's just hard not to listen to TV. It's spent so much more time raising us than you have."

1999

Mega-deals continued to dominate the business of broadcasting and all the other electronic media. The top 25 television group owners controlled 471 of the 1,200 commercial TV stations on the air—almost 40%. Fox's 23 stations alone reached more than 40% of the U.S. population. (The FCC's formula of counting UHF signals at 505 of their population reach put Fox within the FCC 35% nationwide reach limit—at 34.5%.) The FCC opened up even larger monopoly possibilities with its authorization of ownership of two television stations and cross-ownership of up to six radio stations in the largest markets. One giant grew even more as AT&T added to its empire by acquiring Media One, giving it not only the largest telephone but also the largest cable conglomerate in the country. The largest media merger in history up to that time took place in 1999 as Viacom announced it would buy CBS for $34.9 billion, putting it in second place as the world's largest media conglomerate behind Time Warner, but ostensibly as the world's leading company in producing, promoting, and

THE CYBER '90S

distributing entertainment, news, sports, and music. Media critic Robert W. McChesney wrote that "the new Viacom would be one of only nine massive conglomerates . . . that dominate the U.S. media landscape."

Radio was not left behind, with increasing consolidation of that medium's stations. Early in the year the top 25 radio station owners in the United States controlled 19% of all stations in the country. Clear Channel Communications owned 484, AMFM 480, Cumulus Media 248, and Infinity 163. But that wasn't enough. Later in the year the largest company, Clear Channel, bought the second largest company (which had the largest revenues), AMFM. Even though the FCC required divestiture of some stations, Clear Channel retained a total of 830.

There were plenty of audiences for radio. Joel Brinkley wrote in *The New York Times* that "Americans bought more than 58 million radios for the home last year . . . most homes have at least eight of them. If car radios are included, that number rises to 9 or 10 per home, making radios easily the most ubiquitous consumer electronics device in the nation."

The FCC strengthened monopolies by holding a broadcast license auction. No longer basing license approvals on how the programming and technical facilities of the applicant would serve the public interest, convenience, and necessity, as mandated in the amended Communications Act of 1934, the FCC now awarded licenses on the basis of wealth—to those who were richest and could outbid other applicants at an auction.

The FCC did seek more diversity in one area: employment in administration, production, and casting. The commission was supported by a number of public interest groups, including those seeking equal opportunities for racial minorities and women.

However, the Republican-controlled Congress pushed the Democratic majority on the FCC to more deregulation and less policy making, to act principally on technical matters rather than on broader matters that might affect the public interest. The broadcast industry agreed with Congress. At one national public interest meeting on the need for more diversity in television, all the networks—except CBS—stayed away. Perhaps in reaction to its frustrations, perhaps as a means of presenting a different face but maintaining the same policies, the FCC began a five-year plan of internal restructuring.

The media romance with the Internet continued to grow. More and more video services and music were on the Internet. More and more cable companies and broadcast stations were streaming programs, especially news, onto the Internet. Plans were moving ahead for interactive television, which would include the Internet on TV sets and video-on-demand. Broadcast companies employed techniques to build Internet audiences. CBS, for example, attracted audiences to its Website with sweepstakes prizes of up to $10 million. *The Washington Post* and *Newsweek* decided to set up a joint Website for news. Disney enterprises offered news and entertainment on the

FIG 9.26 Spanish Radio
led the ratings in many
U.S. cities as the
millennium approached.
Courtesy Radiolandia.

In Spanish...

Radiolandia 1330 AM (WRCA)

408 South Huntington Ave., Boston, MA 02130
(617) 522-5060 (617) 524-5886-fax

Radiolandia Broadcasting was established in 1973, as a Spanish-language radio format programmer for the purpose of serving the growing Hispanic population of Metropolitan Boston. Coupled with the backing of EL MUNDO SPANISH NEWSPAPER, Massachusetts' oldest and most respected Hispanic publication, (another division of CARIBE COMMUNICATIONS) it is recognized as one of New England's most consistent and credible broadcasters of quality ethnic programming.

FORMAT:

RADIOLANDIA provides the Latino community of Massachusetts with the very best in music, news, entertainment, sports and public affair programming...*all in Spanish!* The focus of RADIOLANDIA's varied programming allows it to reach listeners in *virtually every age group.*

AUDIENCE:

RADIOLANDIA targets its programming to adults 18+ with a concentration in the 18-59 year segment. Our audience is Spanish-speaking, representing over 20 Latin-American countries, from the Caribbean, Central and South America and Spain.

FACILITIES:

WRCA AM, 5000 watts, 1330 KHZ, (6AM-7PM)

COMMERCIAL POLICY

:30 and :60 spots available. Must air in Spanish.

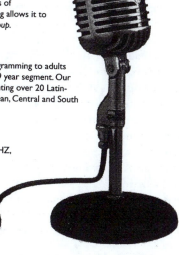

Internet. CBS put prime-time shows on the Internet. Cablevision used its system to begin linking schools to the Internet. Arbitron began its initial dissemination of Internet ratings.

Radio and the Internet moved in together and found domestic and global bliss. About half of the country's 12,000 radio stations were on the Web as sound quality in cyberspace rapidly improved. In addition, another 5,000 or so radio stations internationally were also on the Internet, giving small stations worldwide access and people worldwide access to stations they would never be able to hear otherwise. Billboard Online introduced the first cyberspace program on which audiences could choose on demand from the 100 most popular song hits of the week.

Perhaps a key indication of the growing importance of the Internet was Arbitron's initial dissemination of Internet ratings and the entry of Nielsen into the Internet ratings field, to compete with the company already doing cyberspace research, Media Metrix.

Technical advances also continued in the digital-HDTV field, including automated software for HDTV, datacasting, and multichannel broadcasting. However, the cost of HDTV sets remained prohibitively high—between $5,000 and $10,000—and few homes were ready to invest in them. Although some stations were already providing programs in high definition—66 stations were broadcasting digital signals to more than 50% of the U.S. population—and many others were about ready to do so, it would likely be some years before the price of the receivers went down far enough, as happened with VCRs when they first came in the early 1970s, for a substantial HDTV audience to develop. Other technical developments included video servers and automated software for cable systems.

Radio, too, advanced technically. Digital radio tests began in five markets, an important step toward leveling the radio playing field for both AM and FM. One sad nostalgic note for radio in 1999: The Mutual Broadcasting System—which interestingly never had any owned-and-operated stations but solely provided programs to affiliates—closed down after 64 years on the air.

Broadcast network shrinking audiences continued to create problems for both the networks and their affiliates. Each network was sharing approximately $200 million among its affiliates to carry the network's programs. The networks wanted a pullback on the payments. The affiliates agreed, but only on condition that they get exclusive rights to the network programs. However, the networks sales to cable systems provide them with necessary revenue that they don't want to lose. The problem continued.

Though revenues for the TV broadcast networks fluctuated, with the smaller ones losing money, some cable networks were reaping large profits. ABC, NBC, and CBS led in total media revenues, but two cable channels—QVC, a shopping network, and ESPN, a sports network—were in fourth and fifth places, followed by Fox and then by other cable nets, led by HBO, HSN, TNT, and Nickelodeon.

Growing number of video and music sources on Internet.

Cable reached virtually the saturation point with subscribers. There were 66 million cable homes out of the nationwide total of 99.6 million television homes. Cable concentrated on increasing its share of audiences with more original programming. Some original shows, such as *The Sopranos*, were not only attracting substantial audiences, they were winning Emmy Awards. Eighty-four new cable networks offered programming to what was still an insufficient number of channels for the number of available products. Among new cable networks was one, Oxygen, devoted to women's needs and issues. The highest-rated format on cable continued to be wrestling.

Cable was significantly affected by two legal rulings. Congress authorized DBS systems to retransmit local station signals back into local station markets under the Intellectual Property and Communications Omnibus Reform Act of 1999, thus ending one of cable's key advantages. But the must-carry rules were interpreted to permit cable to exclude fringe stations, thus freeing up some channel space for more lucrative program sources.

Broadcasting fought back with an increase in three types of popular programming. Reality programs found large audiences. Court shows, essentially promoted as reality programs, were very strong in syndication. Judge Judy, Judge Joe Brown, Judge Wapner, and others were attracting loyal audiences. Quiz shows were back with a vengeance. The phenomenal ratings success of *Who Wants to Be a Millionaire* led to multiple presentations each week and a number of clones. Given the low level of information required to answer the show's questions, its success validated the premise that reaching the lowest common denominator is indeed the way to the highest ratings.

Ordinarily, the Academy Awards tended to draw the biggest audiences each year, behind the Super Bowl. But not in 1999. Which show finished second? You guessed it: Barbara Walters's exclusive interview with Monica Lewinsky.

News and public affairs investigative reporting received an assist when the $5.5 million verdict a jury awarded Food Lion against ABC's gathering of materials for its documentary expose on the grocery chain was reduced to $2 by the U.S. Court of Appeals, thus reinforcing the First Amendment's press freedoms. The California Supreme Court upheld the state's "shield law" for journalists, thus strengthening their rights not to reveal confidential sources. Reality programs with a news base had one important legal setback: The courts ruled that journalists accompanying police on raids and other police business violated people's right to privacy under the Fourth Amendment.

One extremely significant development in media, most important on the Internet but also to a great extent on radio and cable, was brought to the fore by the publication of a new book in 1999, *Waves of Rancor: Tuning in the Radical Right*, which revealed for the first time how more than 300 radio stations and as many as 2,000 Websites were being used by extremist groups to foment hate and violence against people whose religion, skin color, ethnic background, lifestyle, or politics they did

THE CYBER '90S

Cable penetration at all-time high.

Viacom plans purchase of CBS.

Arbitron and Nielsen initiate
Internet rating services.

FIG 9.27 Despite sweeping deregulation following the Telecom Act, the FCC was still very active in levying fines.

Fine Guide

Violation	Fine
Construction/operation without authorization	$10,000
Failure to comply with prescribed lighting/marking	$10,000
Violation of public file rules	$10,000
Violation of political rules (reasonable access, lowest unit charge, equal opportunity, discrimination)	$9,000
Unauthorized substantial transfer of control	$8,000
Violation of children's television commercialization or programing requirements	$8,000
Emergency Alert System equipment not installed or operational	$8,000
Alien ownership violation	$8,000
Failure to permit inspection	$7,000
Transmission of indecent/obscene materials	$7,000
Interference	$7,000
Importation/marketing of unauthorized equipment	$7,000
Exceeding of authorized antenna height	$5,000
Fraud by wire, radio or television	$5,000
Use of unauthorized equipment	$5,000
Exceeding power limits	$4,000
Failure to respond to FCC communications	$4,000
Violation of sponsorship ID requirements	$4,000
Unauthorized emissions	$4,000
Using unauthorized frequency	$4,000
Failure to engage in required frequency coordination	$4,000
Construction/operation at unauthorized location	$4,000
Violation of requirements pertaining to broadcasting of lotteries or contests	$4,000
Violation of transmitter control/metering requirements	$3,000
Failure to file required forms or information	$3,000
Failure to make required measurements or conduct required monitoring	$2,000
Failure to provide station ID	$1,000
Unauthorized pro forma transfer of control	$1,000
Failure to maintain required records	$1,000
Failure to implement rate reduction or refund order	$7,500
Violation of cable program access rules	$7,500
Violation of cable leased-access rules	$7,500
Violation of cable crossownership rules	$7,500
Violation of cable broadcast carriage rules	$7,500
Violation of pole attachment rules	$7,500
Failure to maintain directional pattern within prescribed parameters	$7,000
Violation of main studio rule	$7,000
Violation of broadcast hoax rule	$7,000
AM tower fencing	$7,000
Broadcasting telephone conversations without authorization	$4,000
Violation of enhanced underwriting requirements	$2,000

not like. This use of the media was linked to bombings and murders throughout the country, in 1999 and in the past, including the Oklahoma City federal building bombing and the Columbine High School rampage. The importance of these revelations was emphasized by President Clinton through his choice of the *Waves of Rancor* book for inclusion on his annual reading list.

As the broadcast century came to an end (although technically the new century wouldn't begin until 2001), an NBC News poll asked what people thought were the most important inventions of the 20th century. Broadcasting—radio and television—ranked first. Aviation, the automobile, nuclear power, and computers followed, in that order.

THE CYBER '90S

Chapter TEN

The New Century: The 2000s

Webs and Digits

The first decade of the new century was not only a new millennium for the world but a time of cataclysms and changes in the United States that not only affected the country's social, political, and economic fabric but revolutionized the status and future of all communications, including broadcasting.

New technologies altered the structure, delivery, operations, production, programming, content, and reception of radio and television as we had known them. The traditional radio and television receivers, although having become increasingly portable, saw increasing competition from BlackBerry, iPod, videophones, cell phones, and smartphones, among other devices able to receive audio and video signals or digital signals via the Internet. Increased streaming of programming onto the Internet and, more significantly, the preparation of programming specifically for online distribution, including "Webisodes," challenged the very nature of the broadcast station system. Video on demand (VOD), video compression, retriever software, digital and high-definition reception, and high-quality mobile technology for receiving audio and video were among the developments that created an entirely new playing field for broadcasting and other media by the end of the decade. A key term describing key change is *convergence*, the old media making connections with the new media, not only generically but with specific aspects such as YouTube, Facebook, and Twitter. Although the final changeover from analog to digital television transmission didn't occur until June 2009, early in the decade broadcasters were planning to replace the old signals and, while maintaining their analog signals, many stations began broadcasting in digital as well.

Television programming continued its steady emphasis on reality shows, with a proliferation of such fare increasingly dominating the ratings. By the end of the decade programs such as *American Idol* (a throwback to the 1930s radio and 1950s TV amateur hours) and *Dancing With the Stars* topped the Nielsen charts. The success of some of the earlier reality shows such as *Survivor* and *Who Wants to Marry a Millionaire* spawned virtually every type of survival, deception, victimization, exploitation, and personal embarrassment program one could imagine. Not only did the ratings prompt the spate of reality shows; by and large, they were considerably cheaper to produce than sitcoms and dramas. Some of the "crime and violence"

311

Y2K worries unfounded.

2000

Media mergers still top story as new century unfolds.

DTV STATIONS ON THE AIR
(Licensed or on Official Program Test
Authority) 631 TOTAL
February 25, 2004

STATE	CITY	CALL
AK	FAIRBANKS	KITF-DT
AK	FAIRBANKS	KTVF-DT
AL	BIRMINGHAM	WBIQ-DT
AL	BIRMINGHAM	WIAT-DT
AL	DEMOPOLIS	WIIQ-DT
AL	DOZIER	WDIQ-DT
AL	GADSDEN	WPXH-DT
AL	HUNTSVILLE	WAFF-DT
AL	LOUISVILLE	WGIQ-DT
AL	MOBILE	WEIQ-DT
AL	MOBILE	WPMI-DT
AR	FAYETTEVILLE	KHOG-DT
AR	FORT SMITH	KHBS-DT
AR	JONESBORO	KAIT-DT
AR	LITTLE ROCK	KATV-DT
AR	LITTLE ROCK	KLRT-DT
AR	LITTLE ROCK	KTHV-DT
AR	PINE BLUFF	KASN-DT
AZ	FLAGSTAFF	KTFL-DT
AZ	MESA	KPNX-DT
AZ	PHOENIX	KAET-DT
AZ	PHOENIX	KNXV-DT
AZ	PHOENIX	KPHO-DT
AZ	PHOENIX	KSAZ-DT
AZ	PHOENIX	KTVW-DT
AZ	TOLLESTON	KPPX-DT
AZ	TUCSON	KOLD-DT
AZ	TUCSON	KTTU-DT
AZ	TUCSON	KUAS-DT
CA	BAKERSFILED	KERO-DT
CA	BAKERSFILED	KGET-DT
CA	BAKERSFILED	KUVI-DT
CA	CLOVIS	KGMC-DT
CA	CORONA	KVEA-DT
CA	EUREKA	KVIQ-DT
CA	FRESNO	KAIL-DT
CA	FRESNO	KESN-DT
CA	FRESNO	KGPE-DT
CA	FRESNO	KSEE-DT
CA	HANFORD	KFTV-DT
CA	LONG BEACH	KSCI-DT
CA	LOS ANGELES	KABC-DT
CA	LOS ANGELES	KCAL-DT
CA	LOS ANGELES	KCBS-DT
CA	LOS ANGELES	KCET-DT
CA	LOS ANGELES	KCOP-DT
CA	LOS ANGELES	KLCS-DT
CA	LOS ANGELES	KMEX-DT
CA	LOS ANGELES	KNBC-DT
CA	LOS ANGELES	KTLA-DT
CA	LOS ANGELES	KTTV-DT
CA	MODESTO	KUVS-DT
CA	MONTEREY	KION-DT
CA	OAKLAND	KTVU-DT
CA	PALM SPRINGS	KMIR-DT
CA	PORTERVILLE	KPXF-DT
CA	PORTERVILLE	KTFF-DT
CA	SACRAMENTO	KCRA-DT

FIG 10.1 First page of lengthy directory listing DTV stations in early 2004.

dramas, such as *Law and Order* and its clones, *CSI* and *NCIS*, became staples, and a few high-quality shows such as *The West Wing* and *Boston Legal* reached peaks of critical acclaim and then went off the air. A few medical shows, in particular *ER* and *Gray's Anatomy*, were highly successful, and a tongue-in-cheek satire on suburbia, *Desperate Housewives*, became a hit. Sitcoms such as *Everybody Loves Raymond*, *The King of Queens, Will and Grace*, and an HBO offering, *Sex and the City*, had substantial runs, with the latter part of the decade seeing more sitcoms with serious comment or satire, such as *The Office* and *Two-and-a-Half Men*. *Seinfeld* ended its long run in 1998 and was voted the number-one sitcom of all time in a *TV Guide* poll. Would an older demographic, remembering *I Love Lucy, All in the Family*, and *M*A*S*H*, have agreed?

To many critics, and apparently to many viewers, broadcast fare became more vacuous than stimulating, and more and more viewers turned to the Internet and videos at home for visual fare, with TV networks' and stations' audience numbers consistently dropping. Cable-originated dramas began to outstrip broadcast-originated dramas in prestige and awards, most notably premium channel productions such as *The Sopranos* and *Band of Brothers*. During the decade cable-viewing numbers surpassed broadcast-viewing numbers. "Infotainment" continued to replace information on news programs, including some of the more prestigious newsmagazines such as *60 Minutes, Dateline NBC*, and *20/20*. The ultimate in bottom-line programming—that is, broadcast stations and cable channels devoted entirely to commercial selling—became staples, with revenues of some, such as the QVC shopping network, challenging those of major broadcast networks.

Viewer demographics raised questions about whether younger audiences, especially those of college age, were watching programs with any political or social depth or were content with the "chewing gum for the eyes" of innocuous sitcoms and cartoons. Older demographics, for example, heavily made up audiences for *Boston Legal* and *The West Wing*, whereas younger demographics were attracted to shows such as *South Park* and *The Simpsons*. Inasmuch as the latter shows frequently dealt with similar issues as did the former, does the context and manner of presentation invalidate their impact on the intellectual and emotional growth of their principal viewers?

Program content grew as a divisive issue, especially in relation to perceived indecency. Most of you reading this book remember the infamous "costume malfunction" of Janet Jackson during the 2004 Super Bowl halftime show. It became the hallmark—as innocuous as it was—for congressional complaints and FCC actions. First Amendment supporters were critical of the FCC's crackdown on alleged indecent or profane instances, while many civic and religious groups called for stricter oversight. Fines for violations were increased tenfold. (See the 2007 book, *Dirty Discourse: Sex and Indecency in American Broadcasting*.) Although relatively few complaints reached the FCC about alleged indecency in the context of a sitcom or drama or animated show (for example, *South Park*), concern with the content of shock-jock talk shows increased. An infamous example was Infinity Radio's *Opie and*

LPTV and micro-radio continue their struggle to be seen and heard.

Anthony program's detailed description of two people having heterosexual sex in St. Patrick's Cathedral in New York. Another was rock star Bono's fleeting use of the "F" bomb, at first dismissed by the FCC but then, under pressures emanating from the Janet Jackson incident, reversed and found profane. The FCC's increasing conservatism during the decade reflected the conservatism in government, with expectations of change as a majority Democratic FCC, representing a Democratic White House, replaced a majority Republican FCC in 2009.

Video games grew as sources of video entertainment, with both positive and negative criticism. Some became more violent and bigoted, with the intended victims and "bad guys" represented by specifically designated religious, racial, ethnic, gender, and other groups. Conversely, later in the decade, a few of the new genre of video games were oriented toward social awareness, such as the player acting the role of an immigrant falling afoul of the U.S. immigration system or of a person in a refugee camp in Darfur or Gaza.

In many ways the media both affected and reflected America's social, political, and economic upheavals and transformations. Defining the decade and the benchmark for almost all other events was the September 11, 2001, terrorist bombing of the World Trade Center and the Pentagon. "9/11" was the seminal act of foreign terrorism on U.S. soil; domestic terrorists, members of one of the many armed militia hate groups in the United States, had destroyed an Oklahoma City federal building with a large loss of life the previous decade.

The aftermath of 9/11, especially U.S. government actions in fighting terrorism, attacking the Taliban in Afghanistan, and preemptive incursions in Iraq, created both opportunities and dilemmas for the media. The White House and Congress quickly approved antiterrorist legislation, the USA PATRIOT Act. Inimical to traditional U.S. civil liberties, the PATRIOT Act permitted arrest, search, and seizure without warrant; indefinite incommunicado detention without legal representation or informing the missing persons' families what happened to them; and secret courts martial and possible executions. The media cooperated with the government in conducting secret wiretaps and spying on millions of Americans' private e-mails. Racial profiling resulted in arbitrary arrests of people believed to be Arabic or Muslim, and self-styled vigilantes beat and even murdered many. High government officials approved the torture of prisoners, shocking the world, damaging the United States' moral and ethical reputation internationally, and spurring the growth of anti-American terrorists and suicide bombers globally. Given the media's usual support of their government in a time of fear or an international conflict, the U.S. media, by and large, ignored, covered up, or downplayed the activities noted here. Should the media have been more critical?

In 2003 the United States invaded Iraq on the basis of President Bush's and other high government officials' assurances that Iraq had weapons of mass destruction and was a threat to the United States, and with the implication that Iraq was somehow complicit in the 9/11 attacks. Should the media have made a stronger effort to report to the public that both the U.S. and the U.N. chief weapons inspectors reported to

THE NEW CENTURY 2000S

Thousands of radio stations available on Internet as Web receivers hit market.

Napster does battle with courts and record companies.

the White House that they found no evidence of weapons of mass destruction in Iraq, that Iraq had no relationship to the 9/11 attacks or to its presumed perpetrators, Al Qaeda, and that the CIA reported to the White House weeks before the invasion of Iraq that there was "little or no credible probability" that Iraq would attack the United States? The media ignored or underreported the many protest marches prior to and after the invasion of Iraq by hundreds of thousands of Americans in Washington, D.C., millions through the rest of the country, and multimillions throughout the world. Should the media have informed the public more fully of these protests, similar to the protests that forced an end to the U.S. role in the Vietnam War? These are questions scholars and historians will be probing for decades as a way to better understand the ethical and moral role and responsibility of electronic media.

Fixed on 9/11 and its aftermath, the media only cursorily reported continuing quasi-genocidal actions in a number of areas throughout the world, from Sudan to the Congo to Brazil to Somalia to Palestine, hewing closely to the U.S. government's policies and interests in those areas. In part, media news outreach was hampered by growing economic cutbacks that forced downsizing of staffs at home and in foreign bureaus. Hard in-depth news increasingly took a back seat to features, personalities, and scandals.

The 2000 decade was also a time of greed and fraud, from corporate CEOs looting their companies at the beginning of the decade to the revelation of multibillion-dollar Ponzi scams at the end. Early in the decade the media reported corporate executive pilfering of the funds of some of the United States' leading companies, including media giant WorldCom, absconding with billions of dollars and bankrupting their companies, resulting in the loss of pension funds, jobs, and investments for hundreds of thousands and in turn affecting the economic status of millions. The media reported unsuccessful attempts to obtain documents on secret meetings between high Bush administration officials and some of the corporate looters prior to the revelation of the scandals.

Later in the decade, corporate greed, coupled with incompetence and malfeasance, principally by executives of banking, insurance, and investment companies, created the United States'—and the world's—worst economic disaster since the Great Depression of the 1930s. Unemployment surged, millions of homes were foreclosed, and countless businesses went bankrupt. Key services to communities, including safety, health, and education, were hard hit, while most of the corporate executives responsible for the economic collapse either retired wealthy or continued in their jobs with huge salaries, benefits, and bonuses. Some segments of U.S. society made out considerably better than others, both at the beginning and the end of the decade. Early in the decade 80% of a massive tax reduction went to America's 10% wealthiest people. Near the end of the decade, hundreds of billions in taxpayer money designed to counter the economic recession went primarily to bail out the bankers and other corporate entities and their executives while millions of ordinary citizens lost their jobs and their homes.

One-hundred twenty stations offer DTV signals.

The recurring calamities in the United States' largely unregulated economic system affected broadcasting and other media, too. While consolidation in the media earlier in the decade continued to reduce jobs in the field and eliminate local service and variety in programming, ongoing conglomeration permitted by—and to an extent encouraged by—the Federal Communications Commission, coupled with the economic recession, not only increased job losses later in the decade, it affected programming as well as service in the public interest. Even as the number of audio and visual sources—broadcast, cable, satellite, Internet, and other channels—increased, the consolidation of ownership and the economy resulted in less alternative programming and less diversity of information and ideas. Consolidation extended beyond broadcasting, with the Telecommunications Act of 1996 having opened up the playing field to many more teams; for example, Comcast bought AT&T broadband to become the largest cable multiple system operator (MSO). (Carla Johnston's 2000 book, *Screened Out: How the Media Control Us and What We Can Do About It*, reveals the extent and effects of media mega-monopolies. The 2005 book, *The Quieted Voice: The Rise and Demise of Localism in American Broadcasting*, analyzes how consolidation reduces community service.)

The Internet slowly but inexorably began to complement and then to supplant television and radio (whether distributed through broadcasting, cable, or satellite). Thousands of radio stations began streaming their programs onto the Internet. Digital radio signals reached into homes and automobiles. Radio continued to grow—although by the end of the decade it, too, became a victim of the economy—and was chronicled in *Sounds in the Dark: All-Night Radio in American Life* and *Talking Radio: An Oral History of Radio in the Television Age*.

The increasing control of media by only a few companies also resulted in compliant news media later in the decade, unwilling to challenge legislation designed to prevent a reinstatement of the Fairness Doctrine (see the "1980s" chapter), the only legal provision for providing access for the presentation of alternate or minority viewpoints on radio and television broadcast stations.

Media news operations were frequently criticized as well for their lack of critical coverage—investigative journalism in the Watergate tradition—of two controversial Presidential elections. In 2000 the election hinged on Florida's electoral votes; exit polls showed that the democratic candidate, Al Gore, had won, validating his lead in the national popular vote. However, the official vote showed the Republican candidate, George W. Bush, slightly ahead. With the disenfranchisement of 40,000 African-American voters who likely would have voted strongly for Gore and the invalidation of many ballots where the vote for Gore was not punched completely through, a recount was requested. When it looked like a full recount might swing the advantage to Gore, Bush asked the Supreme Court to stop the recount—which it did, along party lines, thus awarding the Presidency to Bush. The mainstream media fully reported what happened but did not go further to investigate what many continue to claim was a political coup.

Elian Gonzalez creates crisis with Cuba.

Survivor on CBS scores huge ratings and marks programming trend toward reality shows.

Then, in the 2004 election, election night exit polls showed that Democrat John Kerry had won Ohio and the election. The head of the company that made the voting machines used in Ohio, John Diebold, had publicly stated that he would do whatever was necessary to assure Republican George W. Bush's re-election. When the results from the voting machines in Ohio were reported, they had Bush winning the state and the Presidency. The media reported the facts but appeared to do no investigative reporting. Are exit polls misleading and, if so, should they be banned? Do the media have a responsibility to go beyond reporting the facts and seek to determine and inform the public why an event happened, as was done during the Watergate affair? Are the brief and headline nature of electronic media news preventing the in-depth reporting that is necessary for informed public opinion in a democratic society? These were questions asked by many both inside and outside media circles.

FIG 10.2 According to the NAB, local broadcasters give the audience ample political coverage.
Courtesy NAB.

85% Say Local Stations Provided "Right Amount" or "Too Much" Time for Candidates; Most Voters Oppose Mandated Free Airtime Proposals

WASHINGTON, D.C., March 8, 2000 – More than 85 percent of voters polled in five key Super Tuesday primary states yesterday said that local broadcasters had provided the "right amount" or "too much" time covering the primaries. Meanwhile, a majority said they oppose requiring broadcasters to give political candidates free airtime, while only one in three support the idea.

The poll, conducted by Wirthlin Worldwide, surveyed a total of 827 voters apportioned equally between five states – California, Georgia, Missouri, New York and Ohio – holding primaries yesterday. It was commissioned by the Radio and Television News Directors Association (RTNDA) and the National Association of Broadcasters (NAB). The poll's margin of error was plus or minus 3.4 percent.

Q. How do you feel about the amount of time broadcast TV and radio stations spend reporting on political campaigns, debates and the issues? Is it too little time, too much time or about the right time?

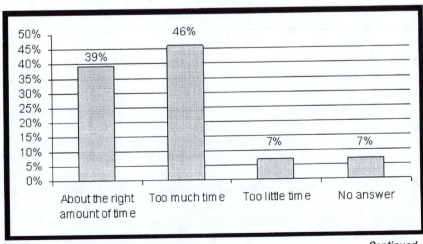

Continued

Antitrust suit seeks breakup of Microsoft.

Prime-time advertising on cable surpasses that on broadcast television.

Q. As you may know, some are proposing that broadcast radio and television stations be required to give free airtime to political candidates to use as they wish. This time would not replace the paid political commercials. In general, do you support or oppose this proposal to give candidates free airtime?

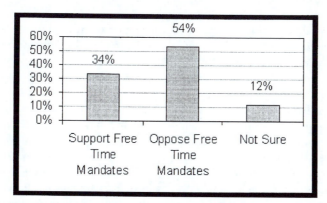

The poll also found that broadcast TV and radio coverage was considered "helpful" to more voters (43 percent) in making their voting decisions than all other sources of information put together:

Q. Thinking about the time you spent in the voting booth today, which ONE of the following was MOST helpful to you in deciding who to vote for?

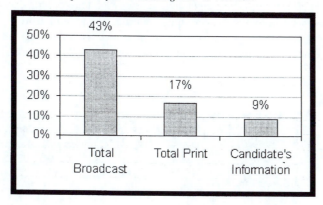

The 2008 Presidential election was another milestone in U.S. politics. For the first time, the Presidential candidate of the Democratic Party would be an African-American or a woman, and for the first time the Vice Presidential candidate of the Republican Party would be a woman. This prompted extensive and intensive media coverage of both the primary and final campaigns. As with its other news operations—this time, for obvious reasons, more intensely—the media concentrated more on the personalities than the policies of the candidates. The power of the media—particularly television—as a critical political factor was manifest. Voters saw on television the Democratic Presidential candidate, Barack Obama, as a confidence-inspiring orator. Conversely, Republican Vice Presidential candidate Sarah Palin appeared uninformed and misinformed in early live interviews and immediately was withdrawn from such media exposure.

Criticism from some quarters continues to take media news to task for its naïve and compliant coverage of the outrageous hike in gasoline prices in the second half of the decade. In reporting the day-to-day rise in the price per barrel of oil and the resulting gas station prices of over $4 per gallon, the media did not report the continuing comparative high prices at the pump when oil costs went down. While motorists and auto sales were suffering, Big Oil continued to set records for profits for any industry, in the tens of billions of dollars. Should the media have investigated Big Oil's profit motive as the reason for high gas prices instead of shifting the blame to the need for more drilling in U.S. protected environmental areas?

Talk radio grew during the decade. While the overwhelming number of radio talk shows were right-wing oriented (for some years there was not a single "liberal" syndicated talk show), toward the end of the decade some liberal commentators reached the airwaves, including a few on cable TV networks. By and large, however, U.S. electronic and print media remained conservative to radical right, and alternative political viewpoints were found mostly on the Internet, through Websites such as Indymedia and FreeSpeechTV and through ever-increasing Web logs, or blogs, posted by ordinary citizens as well as by the famous and powerful. It was not surprising, therefore, that as the decade ended, power brokers were attempting to eliminate "Net neutrality" and give the Internet service providers (ISPs) control over Internet users and content.

FIG 10.3 Web radio receivers make their debut but disappear after Internet radio market flattens. *Courtesy Kerbango.*

Radio and TV offer extensive continuing coverage of flawed Presidential election results for weeks after election.

FCC authorizes 255 low-power radio station licenses.

Music—to the consternation of many radio stations as well as music authors, composers, performers, and publishers—also became an increasingly important part of Internet use. Many students who would be irate if they had written a book or produced a film and received little or no royalties because their work had been pirated and circulated free among prospective audiences or who would promptly sue if any copyright or patent they had registered had been stolen, depriving them of any compensation for their work, had no compunction about pirating copyrighted music downloaded from the Internet, sharing it with or receiving it from friends without paying any fee to the creators and copyright owners. This practice prompted congressional legislation requiring computer and consumer electronics makers to incorporate technology that would prevent downloading music or film that has been copyrighted. Suits by music copyright holders under the Digital Millennium Copyright Act forced hundreds of music pirates to close, a fine for the most prominent Internet pirate, Napster, and prosecution of individual student pirates. Responsible distributors such as Listen, Pressplay, and RealOne Music Pass replaced Napster by paying legal fees for their music and establishing subscription bases for their individual clients. As the decade came to a close, with Internet radio beginning to outstrip terrestrial radio in audience numbers, Internet radio stations joined traditional stations in seeking congressional protection from user fees imposed by music copyright owners.

2000

One prediction of chaos in the new millennium did not happen. A widespread belief was that a Y2K (Year 2000) bug would disrupt and possibly destroy computer communications throughout the world and affect other electronic media as well. Such an apocalypse did not occur on January 1, 2000 (or on January 1, 2001, the technical but less popular start of the new century).

As noted earlier, the big news story of 2000 was the Presidential race, particularly in Florida, because of a confusing paper ballot in some areas of the state, the invalidation of the "hanging-chad" ballots of many older people who had not punched them hard enough, and the suspension of a full recount by the Supreme Court—in effect, the entity designating the new President.

Consolidation saw key mergers in 2000. In 1999 the FCC had approved television duopolies, and the big players lost no time in taking advantage of it. The AOL-Time Warner merger was approved by the FCC and resulted in a $180 billion corporation. CBS-Viacom merged into a $23.8 billion organization. AT&T and Media One's merger cost $69 billion. Radio's Clear Channel bought AMFM and was worth $23.8 billion. News Corp (Rupert Murdoch's Fox conglomerate) bought Chris-Craft, $5.3 billion. Univision, a Spanish-language network, bought USA Networks, $1 billion. On January 1, 2001, *Broadcasting & Cable* magazine summed up the consolidation frenzy: "The big got even bigger."

FIG 10.4 Independent media centers have been established around the globe to provide citizens with noncorporate, nongovernmental perspectives on important issues and trends. We are already into global total interactive communications.

THE NEW CENTURY 2000S

319

Half of U.S. population uses Internet.

Reality TV attracts large audience.

Some of the big media players, however, were not so happy. Broadcast television networks continued to lose viewers. Despite this decrease in viewership, however, all four major networks actually made more money. Total broadcast TV revenue reached a record $33.3 billion, a gain of 17% from the previous year. Broadcast's principal rival, cable, also showed huge monetary gains, up 29% from the year before for a total of $17.4 billion. Cable's increasing fees, however, lured an increasing number of TV homes to switch to satellite; the average hike for cable bills was 5.8%.

FIG 10.5 Audiences for direct broadcast satellite continued to grow in the new millennium. TiVo also debuted to make certain that viewers miss nothing (except commercials). *Courtesy RCA and USSB and the TiVo Store.*

AOL and Time Warner announce merger.

FCC approves AOL and Time Warner merger.

Programming moved in a number of new directions. Ethnic and lifestyle audiences who were not previously fully served were targeted. An all-news Spanish-language radio station began in New York City. Not only more news programs but plots and characters on television shows recognized the growing political and buying power of gay and lesbian audiences. Producers and cable and broadcast distributors continued even greater recognition of the potentials of the Internet and planned to go beyond just streaming programs into cyberspace. Film studios explored video-on-demand services but were concerned about finding ways to prevent a movie version of Napster from pirating their feature films for subsequent pirating through file sharing.

Music programming intensified, aimed at teen and college-age audiences, formats and selections concentrating on the GenY "Gotta-have-it-now" short attention span. Interactive music selection increased on the Internet. Pay per music, which helped artists promote their CDs, was not much competition for free, file-sharing pirated music.

At the end of the year there were 4,685 AM and 5,892 FM commercial and 2,140 noncommercial radio stations on the air. Commercial television stations totaled 721 UHF and 567 VHF, with 250 noncommercial UHF and 125 VHF. Low-power TV (LPTV) stations, often neglected (see the 1999 book, *The Hidden Screen*), continued to outstrip the number of full-power stations, with 1,756 UHF and 610 VHF LPTVs licensed. The two largest cable companies, AT&T and Comcast—which were to merge the following year—had 15 million and 11.7 million subscribers, respectively. Cox was third, with 7.6 million. By the end of the year the FCC had certified 255 eligible applicants nationally for the reinstated low-power radio licenses. Unlike the 10-watt stations abolished 20 years earlier, however, these were for 100-watt power with a radius of about three miles.

2001

The all-consuming event of 2001, the 9/11 terrorist attacks, presented the media with a new test: covering an unexpected attack by an unannounced enemy on targets on U.S. soil. The major networks and stations responded by preempting virtually all other programming for 24-hour coverage of the attacks and their aftermath at the World Trade Center, the Pentagon, and the passenger-aborted hijacked flight that crashed in Pennsylvania. The networks lost between $50 million and $75 million a day in ad revenues. The results of the attacks were graphic, some too graphic for the networks, but CNN and foreign news teams, including those from Canadian stations, showed the horror of victims leaping and falling to their deaths from the highest stories of the World Trade Center. The country later discovered that the enemy was one we had supported and strengthened during the cold war against the Soviet Union. *Broadcasting & Cable*, politically conservative in its editorial policy, stated that "the

FIG 10.6 The CNN Website on 9/11. *Courtesy CNN.*

shock at the intensity of the hatred toward the U.S. may be attributed to underreporting by TV news programs [of world attitudes toward America's economic globalization and foreign policies]."

The media extensively and intensively covered the U.S. attack on Afghanistan, its Taliban government, and Al Qaeda and its leader, Osama Bin Laden. While the destroying of the Afghanistan government and infrastructure appeared to be successful, Al Qaeda and Bin Laden escaped. Having learned how to manage public opinion in the first Gulf War, the Pentagon reinstituted control of journalists' coverage and psychological attitudes by restricting them to "in-bed" assignments with designated Army units. Reports in the U.S. media differed in a number of substantial ways from reports of nonrestricted journalists representing the media of other countries. Reporting from Afghanistan was not easy for any of the electronic media, however, with the weather—sand, dust, windstorms—frequently knocking out and generally corroding video and audio equipment.

On the home front, a new FCC represented the philosophies of the new administration, with an immediate impact on several key areas of broadcasting. Deregulation moved apace. A key area was consolidation. As *Broadcasting & Cable* magazine reported, "Powell's FCC won't impose public-interest conditions on industry acquisitions, mergers, conglomerates." Key mergers included the consummation of the AOL-Time Warner deal. Viacom added cable's BET to its youth- and pop music-oriented holdings such as MTV, VH1, and CMT and its older demographic and ratings-leading network, CBS. Viacom also got FCC approval to own two national TV networks, CBS and UPN. AOL/Time Warner led the big media list, followed by Walt Disney, Vivendi Universal, Viacom, and News Corp. The leading television groups were Fox, Viacom, and Paxson, and the top 25 TV groups owned 44.5% of all U.S. commercial TV stations—up from 41% in 2000 and a huge rise from the 24.6% five years before, in 1996. The top 25 radio groups controlled 24% of all radio stations in the United States and got 57% of radio's total revenues. In a couple of years AOL/Time Warner would change its name to Time Warner, attempting to revive its media rather than its Internet image. Ted Turner, who in 2001 regretted that he had allowed Turner Broadcasting to merge into Time Warner and who was ousted as an officer when the latter merged with AOL, stated that in the near future he believed that there would be only two huge surviving MSOs and only four or five programmers.

Another area the FCC dealt with was indecency. The new strongly conservative attitude in Washington opened the door again for Morality in Media and right-wing ideologues like Jerry Falwell to pressure the FCC with more success than they had had in more recent years. At the same time, the FCC was pressured by broadcasters and by First Amendment advocates to act with moderation. Rapper Eminem's song, "The Real Slim Shady," was generally considered to be in violation of indecency standards. To capitalize on its popularity while avoiding FCC sanctions, stations played a cleaned-up version. The FCC, however, levied fines even for playing the cleaned-up version. A Kaiser Foundation study weighed in on TV drama and sitcoms, stating that two-thirds of all shows have sexual content. The FCC issued guidelines on its enforcement policy regarding indecency, described by its new chair as "a restatement of existing statutory, regulatory and judicial law...establishes a measure of clarity in an inherently subjective area." The policy statement included examples from programs that the FCC considered indecent and from borderline examples that were judged not to be indecent.

Other programming also came under scrutiny, especially by the public. The surgeon general reported that although TV violence might have short-term influence on behavior, it did not have long-term effects. The media went all out in pursuing "infotainment"—for example, covering the disappearance of congressional intern Chandra Levy with full emphasis on her relationship to Representative Gary Condit, reminiscent of the media frenzy in the earlier Monica Lewinsky–President Clinton story. The most-watched program during the summer of 2001—pre-9/11—was Connie Chung's interview with Condit. As counterpoint to what many felt was broadcasting's pandering, a cable channel, Trio, broadcast a 1949 TV presentation of one of America's greatest theatrical productions with the original cast: Arthur Miller's *Death of a Salesman*.

News coverage, even before 9/11, underwent changes. Early morning, pre-breakfast news shows grew in numbers and audiences. The youth audience was targeted by CNN's Headline News, which unveiled a new format, a fast-moving, colorful, multisectioned screen with simultaneous different news items, hypergraphics, and a new slogan, "Real News, Real Fast." Whether it appealed to the computer-savvy generation or not, it wasn't long before its frenzied nature began to turn off at least older viewers, and CNN modified the new approach. While newscasting largely continued the "If it bleeds, it leads" approach, TV backed off from carrying the execution of Timothy McVeigh, who had been convicted of an act of domestic terrorism, the Oklahoma City federal building bombing in 1995.

Spanish-language programming and TV audiences grew, as did television oriented to women, with the Lifetime channel the cable ratings leader and new channels Oxygen and WE moving up. The quality drama *The West Wing*, which made a huge critical splash, sold its syndication rights to cable network Bravo for a record price of $1.2 million per episode. Conversely, some syndicators began to look to cable for their first-run shows. A first for a major TV network, NBC accepted liquor ads. An expected expansion of hard-liquor advertising did not materialize and NBC dropped liquor advertising the following year.

The big programming news was the remarkable success of reality shows such as *Big Brother, Fear Factor, Weakest Link*, and others mentioned at the beginning of this chapter. *Survivor* continued to be milked by CBS, which readied *Survivor 3*. A new game show cable network was aimed at younger audiences. More and more programs were streamed onto the Internet. VH1 put albums on the Internet before their release. A study showed that television viewing was the principal victim of Internet growth. Wide-screen digital TV began to have an impact on the market. Radio music station streaming increased even as the government cracked down on Napster and music piracy.

Prime-time TV ratings continued to fall and for the first time in 10 years prime-time advertising minutes decreased. Networks blamed the Nielsen rating system. In at least one instance the Nielsen system didn't work: Its computers "forgot" to adjust their clocks to daylight savings time and, until the error was remedied, reported inaccurate information. The economic recession—mild compared to the one later in the decade—reached the media and layoffs at the networks pushed an increasing number of broadcasters into the growing ranks of the unemployed.

Satellite services grew, providing additional competition for the beleaguered TV networks. DBS subscriptions were counted for the first time in comparison to cable. DirecTV was third overall, behind AT&T and Time Warner, and Echo Star was eighth. To even the playing field with cable, DBS was required by the courts to carry every local TV channel in the markets it served.

Viacom buys BET.

Average American adult watches four hours of TV daily.

FIG 10.7 Plasma televisions add a new dimension to home viewing. *Courtesy Sony.*

In radio, Rush Limbaugh reflected the success and dominance of right-wing talk shows when he signed radio's richest syndication contract: $250 million for eight years, plus a $35 million signing bonus. (Two years later he would be exposed for illegal drug use. Should that have had any impact on his show or his contract?)

Some sources talked about the reinvention of radio, as satellite stations proposed to offer at least 100 static-free stations with the debut of XM Satellite Radio. The top radio groups in 2001 were Clear Channel, with 1,202 stations in 189 markets and $3.5 billion in revenue; Infinity, with 183 in 41 with $2.3 billion; and Cox a distant third, with 82 in 18 and $455 million in revenue. The National Broadcasting company was 75 years old.

2002

Consolidation! Consolidation! Consolidation! Mergers, acquisitions, and takeovers resulted in fewer and fewer individual owners, larger and larger conglomerates, less and less diversity in programming, and more and more unemployment in the field as the fiscal bottom line became the determinant of media operations and development.

Comcast, following its acquisition of AT&T Broadband, was the largest MSO, with about one-third of all cable subscribers, and generated over $1 billion in ad sales. NBC acquired Telemundo, the Spanish-language network. Expanding Viacom dominated

Cleanup work continues at
Ground Zero.

television, not only through its two networks, CBS and UPN, but notably through cable network holdings, which included Nickelodeon and MTV. Viacom reached one-fourth of all U.S. viewers and a fourth of the highly desired 18–49-year-old audience. Spanish-language television was the fastest-growing advertising medium and prompted the subsequent merger of the two largest players, Telemundo and Univision.

Not everyone, however, was happy with the results of consolidation. Unions representing media employees were unhappy with what they felt were fewer jobs, lower quality, fewer media outlets, less diversity, and higher ad prices. The Writers Guild of America argued that consolidation imperiled creativity. The Association for Local Television was forced to disband after 30 years, stating that most of the organization's members were swallowed up by large conglomerates. The American Federation of Television and Radio Artists (AFTRA) and various record labels decried the giant broadcast groups, alleging that they exerted a form of payola by controlling so many outlets, making it difficult for new and independent artists to get air time and forcing them to go through and pay a small group of promoters. Radio consolidation put two-thirds of all radio revenue into the hands of just 10 radio groups. One of the organizations fighting radio consolidation, the Future of Music Coalition, complained that conglomeration resulted in a "tremendous overlap of songs between supposedly distinct formats" and told the FCC that radio format diversity had become a sham. Even Congress got into the act, blocking a proposed FCC auction of spectrum space that would have allowed a small number of the wealthiest companies to become even bigger.

AOL/Time Warner earned $38.2 billion in revenues; Vivendi Universal, $31 billion; Walt Disney, $25.2 billion, and Viacom, $23.2 billion. The top TV groups in 2002 were Viacom, with 40 TV stations covering 45.4% of all TV homes; Fox, with 34 stations covering 44.7%; Paxson, with 68 stations and 65.9% (many of these were UHF, which were counted as only half, resulting in an FCC figure of 38.1%); and NBC, with 24 stations and 33.7%. In radio, Clear Channels owned 1,238 stations in 190 markets with revenues of $3.2 billion, Viacom 183 in 41 markets and $2 billion in revenues, and Cox 79 in 18 markets and $430 million.

The television network audience numbers continued to fall, and for the first time cable's share of the audience was more than half, with broadcast television getting only 38.4 at one point in 2002, for the first time dropping below 50%. Nevertheless, NBC remained the top money maker among TV and cable nets. QVC, the home shopping network, crept closer, however, as cable's highest income-producing net.

The three-way fight among broadcasting, cable, and satellite intensified. Broadcasting's prime-time ratings continued to suffer in comparison to those of the other two delivery systems. Cable subscriptions slipped after some 20 years of continued growth. Satellite subs, at 18.2 million, were two and a half times more than they'd been just four years earlier.

Putin and Bush sign nuclear treaty.

Milton Berle ("Mr. Television") dies.

FIG 10.8 New audio listening options have drawn users away from traditional radio. *Courtesy Kazaa.*

The aftermath of the 9/11 attacks continued to have an impact on media programming, with the war in Afghanistan leading the news and the public eagerly awaiting fulfillment of the President's promise to capture the instigator of 9/11, Osama Bin Laden. In the meantime, the White House began pushing for a war on Iraq. Some media critics warned of a "wag the dog" scenario. As noted earlier, the mainstream media gave only cursory coverage to the millions of antiwar protesters in the United States and throughout the world, including protests of hundreds of thousands in Washington, D.C., by the Act Now To Stop War and End Racism (A.N.S.W.E.R.) organization. The media appeared to be more interested in covering the sniper killings in the Washington, D.C., area and other "If it bleeds, it leads" stories.

Original cable programming got more public attention, winning Emmy and Golden Globe awards for several of its series, which included HBO's *Sex and the City, Six Feet Under, The Sopranos*, and *Band of Brothers*. Television talk shows, such as those hosted by Rosie O'Donnell and Sally Jessy Raphael, began to go off

DVD sales pass VCR sales.

the air, replaced by the growing number of reality programs. As noted earlier, costs for reality were almost as low as for talk shows and audience participation shows and were garnering higher rating numbers. The networks also began to push prime-time real-life documentaries as a form of reality shows, with *The Osbornes* a prime example.

Indecency continued as a hot topic. Although Opie and Anthony had been fired because of their St. Patrick's Day sex stunt, the FCC initiated an investigation into whether the station's license should be revoked. The St. Patrick's caper set up a louder chorus of concern, including in Congress, about broadcast program content. Cable was not immune from criticism as more and more of its programs added sex and raw language.

Minorities and women were increasing their criticism of broadcasting's "old white boy's club," which was reinvigorated with the continuing demise of affirmative action. African-American broadcasters, for example, called for rewriting all broadcasting ownership regulations as the only way, in a time of increasing consolidation, to open the way for minority ownership. In 2002 women held only 14% of the top executive jobs and 13% of board member positions at the major media companies. Eighty-four percent of the president and CEO positions at the top 120 broadcast and cable channels were filled by men, 16% by women. The National Organization for Women (NOW) accused the six major networks of catering to an "adolescent boy's fantasy world" with what it called "a distorted and often offensive image of women, girls and people of color" in network programming.

Technology made strides in both television and radio. Sirius satellite radio made its debut as a competitor to XM and ended the year with 261,000 subscribers. XM ended the year with 1.36 million subscribers and planned to offer commercial-free music channels in 2004. The FCC mandated digital tuners in all television sets by 2007 as HDTV digital service became available in an increasing number of markets. Some broadcasters were looking at low-power TV as a way of reducing digital transmission costs. With increasing consolidation, increased automation reached into both television and radio control rooms, saving money and increasing profits by reducing personnel.

There was controversy about streaming TV and radio signals onto the Internet. Although broadcasters understood the long-range need to get onto the Internet, some TV executives wanted their signals kept off because they believed that an Internet presence diluted their current advertising base. Radio executives wanted Internet streaming but were concerned that copyright royalty fees were too high. Nielsen ran into a buzz-saw in Boston when stations dropped its service because they objected to the cost and distrusted the accuracy of the new "people meter." It would be a while before the parties came to a new agreement. Though this book does not list all the prominent people in broadcast history who died in a given year, the man known as Mr. Television, Milton Berle, credited with unique contributions to the rapid growth of early TV, died at 93.

Catholic Church sexual-abuse crisis deepens.

MTV reality show
The Osbournes debuts.

FIG 10.9 An index of XM Radio programming.
Courtesy XM Radio.

Theoretically, HDTV has no Relationship with DTV

When digital television was receiving a lot of attention prior to the DTV transition, it was frequently conflated with HDTV, and there is evidence that many consumers wound up purchasing a more expensive HD set when all they wanted was a receiver that would work in a digital environment. There is actually no relationship between the two. Whereas digital is relatively new, HDTV has been around since the late 1960s, when Japan developed MUSE, an 1,125-line picture (even greater resolution than today's HDTV) using analog signals. However, the more lines transmitted, the more bandwidth needed. With analog that simply wasn't realistic, but in a digital era extra signal information can be conveyed using the same spectrum space. But it is not even clear what qualifies as high definition. The National Television Systems Committee 525-line standard had been the norm for well over 60 years. Presently some stations broadcast in 720, others in 1,080, and both are termed high definition. And some employ both, choosing the higher resolution for programming such as live sporting events that augments the experience, and the lower variation for daytime talk or game shows that don't really benefit from enhanced images.

North Korea violates nuclear arms treaty.

Sirius begins digital satellite radio service.

2003

This was another year of vicissitudes. War, a blackout of the Eastern United States, the disintegration of the *Columbia* space shuttle, continued media consolidation and job losses, a failing economy punctuated by continued corporate looting of investors' funds, FCC virtual elimination of ownership caps, and, in two states in particular, Illinois and Massachusetts, final-second dashed hopes for at-long-last World Series bids by the Cubs and the Red Sox.

Despite the opposition of millions in the United States and most of the rest of the world, the U.S. invaded Iraq. After President Bush announced that the war was over, more U.S. military personnel continued to be killed than had been killed during the war. The networks hurried to cover the conflict, but, as in the Gulf War of 1991, found it difficult because of the embedding of journalists within military units. CBS newsman Dan Rather observed that "As journalists, we have to realize there's a very fine line between being embedded and being entombed . . . there is a way to cocoon the journalists and place them in a position so they only report what the top tier of the military wants reported." It became difficult for the media to give the public an accurate picture of what was happening. *Broadcasting & Cable* magazine noted, "It's been hard . . . for the networks to find a focus; all those pieces of war footage from a small army of embeds never makes a whole pie." As in the Vietnam era, those who were critical of the administration's actions were called un-American, and some of the media clamped down on America's tradition of freedom of speech in ways reminiscent of the 1950s McCarthy era. For example, one highly popular singing group, The Dixie Chicks, whose members criticized the administration's war on Iraq, had their songs banned by many stations and were dropped by the Cumulus conglomerate.

Later in the year the media's reportorial freedom was facilitated to enable them to report what the administration proclaimed as a key accomplishment of the war, the capture of Iraq's leader, Saddam Hussein. CBS radio reported it first to the American public. Dan Rather followed about an hour later on CBS television, staying on the air, as one newspaper noted, "an awesome six hours."

Throughout the year media program directors and news divisions gave priority to significant events, sometimes even at the expense of entertainment program advertising revenues. In February it was the loss of the space shuttle *Challenger* as it reentered the earth's atmosphere. In August a huge, extended Northeast blackout precluded any reception that required electricity, although newsrooms had backup generators and continued their coverage. Battery-powered radios played a key role, enabling radio stations to provide information to the public on this largest power blackout in U.S. history. True to its bottom line, however, the media also went overboard with seemingly unending coverage of events such as the California gubernatorial recall and election, giving its headlines to a Hollywood actor without government

Digital Television Promotion Act introduced in Senate.

experience whose publicity and image resulted in his election; to the disappearance and murder of a pregnant housewife; and to the return of a young woman kidnapped and reportedly held hostage by a cult-type figure.

In other programming areas, reality shows continued to dominate. At least two networks began to shuffle around their drama programs to find scheduling slots more conducive to their survival in the competitive waters of reality shows. The reality show *Survivor* was getting $425,000 for a 30-second commercial; two top drama shows, *CSI* and *Raymond*, were getting $400,000 for a half-minute spot. Key live sports events continued to garner the highest ratings and advertising dollars.

Ethnic programming grew. A new African-American cable channel, TV One, was announced as a new competitor to BET. The millions of viewers who watched Spanish-language TV now could watch new programs in the most popular format, the telenovela or soap opera, oriented to their personal experiences. Competitors Telemundo and Univision both launched shows produced in the United States rather than in Latin America or Spain, reflecting their viewers' lives in the North. Their competitiveness became moot later in the year, however, when they announced their intention to merge. Cable channels oriented to programming for women expanded, with Oxygen, We, and SoapNet all showing gains of millions of viewers. But even their successes didn't deter their joining the rush to cloning. WE announced its plans to add three new reality series. Nonstereotyped gay and lesbian characters increased on TV shows. On a popular youth-oriented series, *Buffy the Vampire Slayer*, network TV had arguably its first lesbian sex scene.

The shock-jocks and indecency saga continued. The FCC fined Infinity Broadcasting $375,000 for the 2001 *Opie and Anthony* St. Pat's sex caper and threatened to revoke its licenses for future infractions. The FCC also fined an Infinity radio station in Detroit the maximum amount, $27,500, for one indecency transgression on one station, citing a show in which the host and callers allegedly described explicit sexual techniques and physical assaults on women in an "extremely graphic, lewd and offensive" manner. In a ruling confusing to some, the FCC found that U2 singer Bono's on-air use of the "f" word ("this is really, really fucking brilliant") didn't violate indecency rules and "may be crude and offensive but, in the context presented here, did not describe sexual or excretory organs or activities."

Civil liberties groups such as the ACLU and performers' organizations such as AFTRA objected to the White House, Congress, and FCC policies. Many critics and media professionals attributed the new restrictions to what they believed was a continuing erosion of First Amendment guarantees of freedom of speech, press, and assembly under the George W. Bush administration, including the government's use of the PATRIOT Act and FBI efforts to stifle dissent. The issue of indecency appeared to permeate America's consciousness and media coverage.

The FCC was consistent in its policy of expanding consolidation. It removed more multiple ownership caps, allowing one owner to reach 45% (up from 35%)

2003

MTV reaches 250 million homes worldwide.

Apple iPods offer new audio option.

of the public; routinely waived the cross-ownership newspaper-broadcast station ban; and okayed TV duopolies for smaller markets and triopolies (owning three or more TV stations in a market) in others. A federal court stayed the 45% expansion, and although the Senate voted for a rollback to 35%, the threat of a Presidential veto placed the issue in temporary limbo. Consumer groups, including the long-active Media Access Project, challenged the FCC's new rules and a federal court put the new rules on hold as the FCC filed its own counter-appeal. One of the mergers consummated in 2003 was Rupert Murdoch's (News Corp/Fox TV) acquisition of DirecTV.

In further catering to commercial interests, the FCC banned noncommercial applicants from applying for unreserved radio channels, restricting the noncommercial and public stations to the 20 channels reserved in the 88.1–91.9 FM spectrum. In late 2003 the FCC gave TV stations that had not yet installed DTV/digital just six more months to comply under threat of license revocation. The FCC also angered media companies by raising its regulatory fees for broadcast radio and television, DBS, and cable.

Many programmers who didn't do well continued to blame it on the rating systems. The president of the Cable Television Advertising Bureau, Sean Cunningham, stated that "Nielsen's diary/meter methodology is widely believed to under-report cable viewership by 25% to 50%." The expansion and use of local people meters in a number of top markets (Boston, a holdout, finally agreed to a people meter contract) muted some of the criticism. Many broadcast TV stations and cable systems in particular experienced rating increases. In addition, the local people meters measured demographics to a much greater extent than the passive meters and diaries. DBS continued to gain on cable and broadcasting, adding 1 million subscribers in 2003 for a total of 10.6 million. Amid many broadcasters' cries of gloom and doom, CBS celebrated its 75th anniversary. One note of gloom was the death of the venerable radio and television performer, Bob Hope.

The conservatism of the country's political leaders and media owners appeared to impact programming. MSNBC fired one of the long-time leading liberal talk show hosts, Phil Donohue, and replaced him with radical right-winger Michael Savage to join other MSNBC right-wing personalities Alan Keyes and Pat Buchanan. The national trend was to increasingly conservative talk shows, with the few liberal talk hosts being fired and late 2003 finding not a single liberal talk show with national syndication. John Leland wrote in *The New York Times* that compared to Republicans and conservatives, Democrats and liberals have a "yammer gap." In 2003, however, two of the right-wing's darlings of talk radio were caught with their pants down. Republican Party star commentator Rush Limbaugh had for years excoriated many individuals and groups who didn't agree with him and was particularly harsh through a holier-than-thou approach to lawbreakers such as drug users. Ironically, it was revealed that he had been illegally purchasing and using drugs himself for years. And conservative

Space Shuttle *Columbia* explodes.

Audience for satellite radio grows.

Paul Harvey, in a moment of candid religious bigotry, said on the air that Islam "encourages killing," spurring demands for an apology by civil rights groups. To counter the right-wing dominance of talk media, a new group, Progress Media, announced in late 2003 that it planned to buy stations in major markets for an Air America Network and institute liberal talk shows. Robert Kennedy, Jr., and author and comedian Al Franken were among the first hosts signed, with Franken commenting, in reference to competing with Rush Limbaugh, that "I'm going to try to do [the show] drug free." In early 2004 one liberal talk program, *The Ed Schultz Show*, began syndication by Jones Radio networks in association with Democracy Radio.

Talk radio also experienced a longstanding gender gap, with relatively few women talk show personalities. Few of these shows were syndicated. Of the local shows run by women, almost all were politically conservative.

Public radio received a huge boost in 2003 when the will of Joan Kroc, the widow of the founder of McDonald's restaurants, bequeathed $200 million to National Public Radio (NPR). On the public television side, PBS announced that it will allow 30-second underwriting spots, up from 15 seconds. On an even sadder note, one of its former mainstay performers, Fred Rogers (of *Mr. Rogers' Neighborhood*) died.

Despite advancing technology, consolidation fiscal efficiency, format changes, and economic losses and gains, perhaps one of the most significant comments regarding the state of the media, specifically television, came from Newton Minow, who, as chair of the FCC in 1961, coined the phrase "vast wasteland" in describing TV programming. In an article in the *Federal Communications Bar Journal* in 2003, Minow said that, if anything, the wasteland was now even vaster and that the FCC is to blame because of its laissez-faire attitude toward regulation and consolidation.

FIG 10.10 Radio programs need never be missed with the RadioYourWay recorder. Performing much like TiVo, this device allows listeners to hear programs they cannot listen to in real time or have missed. *Courtesy RadioYourWay.*

2004

The electronic media, with the principal exceptions of C-Span and some public broadcasting stations, appeared to give minimal coverage to the Presidential election primaries. Radio showed its versatility by carrying, in early 2004, the first radio-only debate of Presidential candidates since 1948.

CBS charged $2.3 million for a 30-second spot on the 2004 Super Bowl broadcast. While joining other broadcasters in complaining about government deprivation of some of their First Amendment rights, CBS did an about-face with others' freedom of speech and refused to carry a paid ad from Move On (an ad that called attention to the trillions of dollars of the Bush administration's budget deficit that future generations would have to pay for) during the Super Bowl on the grounds that it didn't wish to air political ads. In what appeared to be hypocrisy, the network did, however, carry a political spot from the Bush White House. CBS refused, too, to carry an ad from People for the Ethical Treatment of Animals (PETA), the animal rights organization.

President Bush declares war in Iraq.

TiVo claims 1 million subscribers.

NPR receives $200 million inheritance.

FIG 10.11 Country format remains hot mid-decade.
Courtesy Arbitron.

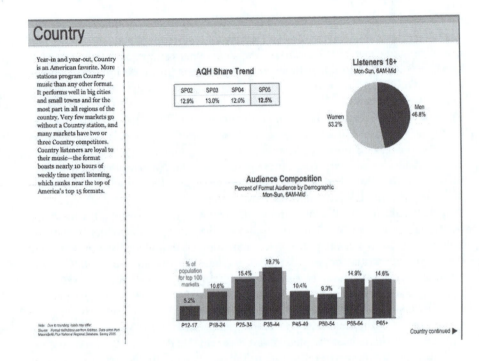

Country

Year-in and year-out, Country is an American favorite. More stations program Country music than any other format. It performs well in big cities and small towns and for the most part in all regions of the country. Very few markets go without a Country station, and many markets have two or three Country competitors. Country listeners are loyal to their music—the format boasts nearly 10 hours of weekly time spent listening, which ranks near the top of America's top 15 formats.

In early 2004 the FCC fined Clear Channel $755,000 for multiple airings of "sexually explicit" material on its *Bubba the Love Sponge* show. Clear Channel fired Bubba the Love Sponge. The incident that sparked the greatest commotion, however, was one that the majority of the American public, in a survey, considered "no big deal": Singer Janet Jackson briefly and partially bared a breast during the half-time entertainment show at the Super Bowl. The "wardrobe malfunction" galvanized conservative groups, members of Congress, the White House, and the FCC, which received hundreds of thousands of complaints. Complaints of alleged indecency on other programs resulted in a sudden spate of fines by the FCC and the removal from the air of several shows and their hosts. The FCC, succumbing to pressure, reversed itself on cases that it had previously ruled were not indecent. Congress was working on legislation that would raise the fine for indecent programming to $500,000 from $17,500 per incident for both the station and the performer. A number of group owners and individual stations cracked down on their shock-jock personalities, some proclaiming a zero-tolerance policy. Clear Channel, for example, removed the *Howard Stern Show* from its stations. Some other owners were not so quick to take action, Zeo Radio president Scott Thomas stating that "new legislation and government involvement will create a much more bland, less compelling radio experience for our country."

United States invades Iraq.

First lesbian sex scene on network TV.

The FCC reversed itself on the Bono F-word ruling and, under increasing public and congressional pressure following the Janet Jackson incident, levied a fine for the fleeting utterance. Is there a way to maintain freedom of speech and at the same time protect young audiences from psychologically harmful material? It is important not to look at the "indecency" controversy as simply a tug of war between Howard Stern and a religious evangelical.

The FCC opened a formal inquiry into violence on television and imposed higher quotas on stations for children's programming.

In 2004 Comcast attempted a hostile takeover of Disney, bidding $66 billion for the company. Rupert Murdoch predicted that in three years—by 2007—there would be only three huge media companies: his own News Corp, Time Warner, and Comcast. Murdoch did indicate that he thought several "very good and well-run" smaller media companies, such as Cox Communications and Echostar, would remain, but he specifically did not mention Disney, Viacom, NBC Universal, or Sony, all major players at the beginning of the new century. While his trend prediction was accurate, the economic disaster in the latter part of the decade precluded, at least temporarily, his anticipated mass consolidation.

As mentioned, in early 2004 one liberal talk program, *The Ed Schultz Show*, began syndication by Jones Radio networks in association with Democracy Radio. However, right-wing talk hosts such as Bill O'Reilly flourished in an increasingly conservative political atmosphere. Not only right-wing shows, as expected, went along with the administration's "terrorist" scare tactics to galvanize public support for its war activities; the media in general did so as well. TV talk shows grew with an increase in younger, more affluent demographics.

Program genres and specific shows that rose to popularity at the beginning of the decade continued their ratings dominance, including *The Apprentice, American Idol, CSI, Survivor, Without a Trace, Friends, Law and Order, Two-and-a-Half Men*, and *Everybody Loves Raymond*. Top advertising came from the auto, pharmaceutical, financial products, and media and telecommunications industries. By 2009, the auto and financial sectors were in shambles and traditional media were fighting to survive. Adult cartoons thrived in prime time. Hispanic television grew in terms of audience, programming, and revenue. Local television and radio broadcast stations were lauded for their on-the-spot coverage of hurricanes Charley and Francis in Florida, staying on the air while cable systems were generally disrupted. In network news programming, Brian Williams assumed the reins of *NBC Nightly News* from retiring longtime anchor Tom Brokaw in December.

Cable viewing was up, broadcast viewing was down, and more and more video was coming to cyberspace. Cable and phone companies were increasingly invading each other's territory, cable companies making more inroads into phone service and phone companies into video services.

The new Nielsen local people meters (LPMs) generated broadcasters' rising anger as they showed lower audience figures for both network and syndicated programs.

2005

Reports of disasters dominated broadcast news in 2005. When Hurricane Katrina devastated New Orleans and nearby areas, broadcast stations in New Orleans were largely destroyed, with station WWL predominantly able to stay on the air. Coverage was principally by satellite. The media did less well in advising the public of the federal government's lag in providing aid and its apparent lack of concern with the continuing plight of the city's residents, primarily those who were poor and black and without personal resources to rescue themselves or their property. Earlier in the year media news devoted more time and effort to a foreign news event than it usually did, reporting on the tsunami disaster in Asia that affected countless communities and hundreds of thousands of lives. Coverage of hurricanes and other natural disasters was a public service that resulted in the loss of advertising revenue for stations and networks.

In the political and war area, the media refrained from investigating or reporting on the alleged manipulation for the invasion of Iraq but instead carried news packages distributed by the White House that promoted President Bush's political and war agendas. While not criticizing this illegal procedure—the federal government, by law, may not operate a domestic broadcast station airing to the public—the FCC did express concern over "prepackaged news" stories and threatened a fine, license revocation, or even imprisonment for not revealing the source or sponsor. While promoting the White House's policies, the media largely ignored the increasing antiwar protests.

In other programming areas, reality shows proliferated, some successfully, others embarrassingly. However, a problem loomed for reality programs, with writers, editors, and producers stating that they wanted representation by the Writers Guild of America. Dramas such as *CSI* and *Law and Order* were highly successful. Other top programs were *Desperate Housewives, American Idol, CSI, Everybody Loves Raymond, Without a Trace,* and *Survivor.* Leading the network ratings, in order, were CBS, ABC, NBC, Fox, UPN, WB, PBS, and Pax. Pay-TV nets, in order, were HBO, Starz, Showtime, and Cinemax. But criticism of Nielsen ratings continued, with a number of small market stations discontinuing the service, questioning its accuracy and high fees. The top media companies in 2005 were Time Warner, Disney, Viacom International, News Corp, and Comcast.

With virtually no mainstream media news, drama, or sitcoms challenging political authority, *The Daily Show* with host Jon Stewart drew young audiences by doing so, often in a comedic or sarcastic vein. *N.Y.P.D. Blue*, groundbreaking in its frank sexuality and realistic language, went off the air after 12 years. However, a new series that turned out to be one of the most effective in TV history to present strong alternative viewpoints on a myriad of real-world issues, be consistently candid in its political criticism, and make people think, David Kelley's *Boston Legal*, made its debut.

FIG 10.12 Reliable network programs continue to attract viewers. *Courtesy NBC.*

Saddam Hussein captured.

Les Tremayne, star of radio dramas, dies.

In terms of content, Congress and the FCC turned up the heat on what they considered indecent programming.

Cable and broadcasting continued their rivalry, with cable viewers once again topping broadcast audiences. They renewed their battle on broadcast-to-cable retransmission payments and on digital must-carry requirements. Both, however, began to prepare for the eventual switchover from analog to digital by using HDTV camcorders.

On the legal front, the federal court again asked the FCC for a rewrite on its ownership rules—the third such request in six years—as consolidation continued to grow. There was increased concern with piracy of copyrighted material through illegal downloads. What eventually would be the biggest concern for broadcasting and cable, however, was in the new media and advancements in technology. Demands for video on demand (VOD) and video online (VOL) presaged what was to come. Convergence—combining two or more previously discrete communication systems—which was virtually dormant after the dot-com crash earlier in the decade, revived. TV stations pushed to reformat their news for the Internet and mobile phone reception. Videos on cell phones heated up. Online programmers now included Cinemax, CNN, CNN International, College Sports TV, E-online, Fox News Channel, GSN (network for games), HBO, TBS, Turner Classic Movies (TCM), Women's' Entertainment (WE), TV Guide, and the Weather Channel.

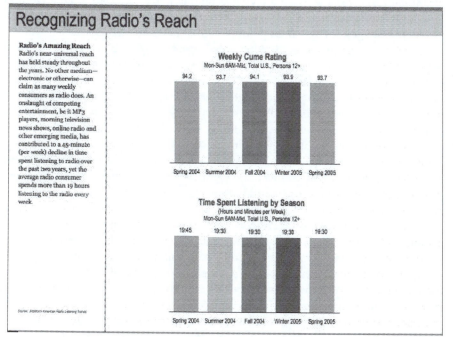

Recognizing Radio's Reach

Radio's Amazing Reach Radio's near-universal reach has held steady throughout the years. No other medium—electronic or otherwise—can claim as many weekly consumers as radio does. An onslaught of competing entertainment, be it MP3 players, morning television news shows, online radio and other emerging media, has contributed to a 45-minute (per week) decline in time spent listening to radio over the past two years, yet the average radio consumer spends more than 19 hours listening to the radio every week.

Source: Arbitron American Radio Listening Trends

Weekly Cume Rating
Mon–Sun 6AM–Mid, Total U.S., Persons 12+

Spring 2004	Summer 2004	Fall 2004	Winter 2005	Spring 2005
94.2	93.7	94.1	93.9	93.7

Time Spent Listening by Season
(Hours and Minutes per Week)
Mon–Sun 6AM–Mid, Total U.S., Persons 12+

Spring 2004	Summer 2004	Fall 2004	Winter 2005	Spring 2005
19:45	19:30	19:30	19:30	19:30

FIG 10.13 Radio still boasts great reach. *Courtesy Arbitron.*

2004

Eddie Fritz, NAB's longtime president who was about to retire, made a farewell address to the 2005 NAB Radio Show in which he lauded localism in radio, noting particularly the medium's coverage of Hurricane Katrina. At the same time, he and NAB supported the FCC's increased deregulation of multiple ownership rules, which would permit increased consolidation and the decrease of localism in radio. (For further discussion of localism, see *The Quieted Voice: The Rise and Demise of Localism in American Broadcasting*.)

2006

The year 2006 continued the gradual and inexorable movement of video and audio to the Internet, with an increasing number of programs from both broadcast and cable streaming to or prepared for online distribution. Nielsen began to extend its research to the Internet. Cable companies added to the growing number of video games online. The big players—companies and programs—continued their domination. The largest income producer was CBS, followed by QVC, ESPN, ABC, NBC, HBO, and Fox. Fox marked its 20th anniversary, its hit programs ranging from *Beverly Hills 90210* to *American Idol* (which was achieving record audiences) plus key sports coverage, confounding critics who predicted it would not succeed. Even while the U.S. economy showed signs of debilitation, U.S. TV grew worldwide, with international distribution and revenue up sharply. Domestically, many stations moved away from syndication and began programming their own shows. One new network, CW, debuted, a merger of UPN and WB, with youth-oriented programming.

Critics' top programs in 2006 were, in drama, *Lost, 24,* and *The Sopranos*; in sitcoms, *The Office, My Name Is Earl*, and *Scrubs*; in reality shows, *American Idol, Amazing Race*, and *Project Runway*. Most popular programs included *Two-and-a-Half Men, Desperate Housewives*, and *Gray's Anatomy. Seinfeld* went into heavy syndication. *The West Wing*, one of the very few shows that dealt with real-world issues and gave an acceptably candid inside view of Washington and White House politics, went off the air after eight seasons. Game and magazine shows rose in the ratings. In preparation for the eventual changeover to digital, more and more shows went into high definition. In other areas relating to new technology, the MTV networks competed with iTunes, Telemundo competed with Univision by pushing online programming, and networks reached out for interactive text messaging to shows and participants. Under increasing criticism from users, Nielsen announced that it was phasing out all paper logs and would use only electronic measurements by 2011.

Congress and the FCC toughened their stances on what they perceived as indecency on the air, *Broadcasting & Cable* magazine describing the FCC's actions as "a full-frontal assault." The Broadcast Indecency Enforcement Act of 2005—enacted in 2006—boosted the maximum fine for indecency to $325,000 (from $32,500) per utterance, up to $3 million per incident. Censorship of political content through outside pressure as well as self-censorship of possibly indecent content was illustrated by the History Channel's canceling of a scheduled documentary entitled *Ottoman Empire: The War Machine*, even after heavy promotion. The program included material on the genocide of more than a million Armenians by the Turks during the 1915–1923 period, an event that Turkey strongly denies.

Media news suffered as budgets were tightened. There were fewer world correspondents and more outsourcing for local news. Coupled with more people getting their news online, this did not bode well for broadcasting or cable. Nonetheless, the traditional media did a good job of covering the actual events of Hurricane Katrina, although, as noted earlier, it did not do much regarding the selective and arguably prejudicial abandonment of many of its victims. A landmark event occurred in network news in September when Katie Couric (formerly of NBC's *Today Show*) became the first solo female to assume the anchor's position of the *CBS Evening News*, replacing the beleaguered Dan Rather. The same month that this change took place saw a number of "specials" marking the five-year anniversary of 9/11. One of the media's "frenzy events" was the revelation of film star Mel Gibson's anti-Semitism when he was arrested for drunken driving, with personalities like Oprah Winfrey, Barbara Walters, and Larry King denouncing him while others like Bill O'Reilly staunchly defended him and sought notoriety interviews.

By and large journalists have long been considered in the forefront of not only bringing information to the public but in revealing the truth, no matter how disturbing. Many have risked their lives to do so, especially in wars. For example, in 2006, 73 journalists had been killed covering the Iraq War, compared to 66 in the Vietnam War, 68 in World War II, and 17 in the Korean War. Nevertheless, by being embedded with the U.S. forces in Iraq and the previous Gulf War, journalists made themselves vulnerable to censorship, with the public getting almost exclusively the administration's political point of view regarding the war. Are there approaches to covering a war, especially an unpopular one, where objective and thorough reporting is possible, the government not unfairly criticized, the lives of the troops not endangered, the media's bottom line not destroyed, and journalists acknowledged for their courage and professionalism?

2007

Convergence continued to affect radio, television, and cable, with increasing online video requiring changes not only in production and delivery systems but in corporate planning for the future as well. Old media were making more connections with the new, including popular venues such as YouTube; Comcast, for example, teamed with Facebook. Broadcasters, increasingly adapting to ever-new technologies such as the growing mobile-TV sector, continued preparation for the transition to digital, with HDTV a predominant subject of discussion at media conferences.

FIG 10.14 *TV Guide* enlarges its cover if not its readership.
Courtesy TV Guide.

2005

| Illegal downloading concerns heat up. | NAB touts localism while promoting multiple ownership and consolidation. | Convergence trend accelerates. |

Following the DTV Transition

The digital transition was the most momentous transformation in television history. Prior innovations, such as color or UHF, never posed a total loss of reception. Homes connected to cable or satellite relied on their suppliers to handle the conversion so that they didn't need to take any additional measures. But the nearly 20% noncable/satellite households and the approximately 40% of connected homes that still used antenna TVs had to either go entirely cable/satellite, purchase a new digital set, or procure, with part of the cost defrayed by government coupons, an external digital tuner. Three months following the changeover and considering the enormity of the endeavor, it has to be considered an overall success. But glitches persist, perhaps the most insidious being with VHF, former prime real estate, often proving ineffective in handling digital without a power boost. But to do so could interfere with other users, prompting a number of broadcasters opting to switch to the previously more spacious UHF only to find that the FCC had sold off chunks of this band. And UHF needs even greater power to match the reach of VHF. All this served to perplex viewers trying to locate their favorite station and choose the correct antenna.

Ratings for even top shows such as *American Idol* and *Desperate Housewives* fell in the 2006–07 season. Station groups that reached the most U.S. homes were Fox (36.6% coverage), CBS (35.7%), ION Media (31.3%), NBC (30.4%), and the Tribune Company (27.5%). The FCC put a cap of 30% on the number of multichannel video subscribers any cable company could have. Comcast was the highest at 27%. The FCC looked into violence on television. Late in the year the FCC issued rules allowing newspaper and broadcast station cross-ownership in the top 20 markets, with waivers available in smaller markets. A court case had overturned a similar FCC action in 2003, prompting one Senator to call the new ruling "unbelievably arrogant," and citizen watchdog groups promised to go to court again. Another Senator stated, "Today the FCC failed to further the important goal of promoting diversity in the media and instead chose to put big corporate interests ahead of the people's interests." A little more than a year later, that Senator, Barack Obama, would be in a position as President to change the composition of the FCC to serve the public interest.

Spanish-language programming boomed with the growth of the U.S. Spanish-speaking population. Paranormal and horror shows began to have an impact on broadcast and cable programming. A new quiz show, *Deal or No Deal*, was a hit. Radio talk show host Don Imus created a huge flap with a racist comment about a Rutgers University women's sports team and was fired—and later rehired. Repeated criticism of television included junk food ads for kids, consolidation impact on localism, and violence in programs.

In November a writers' strike by members of the Writers Guild of America (WGA) against the Alliance of Motion Picture and Television Producers (AMPTP) virtually shut

FIG 10.15 Web radio expands listening options. *Courtesy Live365.*

down scripted shows and the industry in general for months. Reality shows had a field day. The issue revolved around the new media; television writers wanted payment for their work that was sold by producers to secondary markets, specifically the Internet.

The economic recession and the drop in audiences affected the bottom line at all levels. Media stocks, in particular cable stocks, plummeted, and cutbacks put many career media people out of work. One bright spot was the international market for U.S. syndication, which exceeded $7 billion. XM and Sirius announced a merger of their satellite radio companies; the merger was finally approved by the FCC in 2009.

Media news operations were, as usual, vacillating between coverage of serious events and pandering to frivolity. For the former, the media provided good coverage of the massacre at Virginia Tech University. For the latter, the media made even greater celebrities of people such as Hannah Montana, Paris Hilton, Lindsay Lohan, and Britney Spears—being exploited by them and exploiting them and the media audiences. In the critical area of news that impacted the lives and futures of all Americans, the media dropped the ball. There was considerably less coverage of the day-to-day war in Iraq, although some media did report—but failed to investigate further—the increasing evidence of violations of U.S. and international law in respect to the Iraq War, torture being one of the allegations, by high White House and other government officials.

In a 2007 speech, former CBS anchor Dan Rather criticized the current state of journalism, stating that the profession has "lost its guts," reminiscent of *Variety* magazine's description of the media's acquiescence to government policy during the Vietnam War as "no-guts journalism." Rather criticized journalists for their reluctance to question and criticize, if warranted, the politically powerful, and said that journalists have given up their role as watchdogs to become too cozy with people in positions

FIG 10.16 Radio malls dot the urban landscape. *Courtesy CBS Radio.*

Number of inmates in U.S. prisons at all-time high.	Billions spent constructing walls on U.S./Mexico border.	North Korea test-fires missile in defiance of U.N. ban.
FCC boosts maximum fine for indecency.	Media news budgets tighten as revenues decline.	Katie Couric becomes first woman to solo-anchor "CBS Evening News."

FIG 10.17 People go to the online screen in increasing numbers. *Courtesy Marketcharts.com.*

But this "tremendous tool" was beginning to be feared by the rich and powerful, given its ability to organize and galvanize alternative views and even actions that might challenge the controls of the rich and powerful. The issue of Net neutrality—continuing as this is written—came to the fore, with beginning attempts to try to give the ISPs the power to decide who and what content may have online access and whether limits may be placed on free speech and First Amendment rights in regard to the Internet. (The new FCC chair in 2009, Julius Genachowski, stated that the Commission must protect an "Open Internet.")

FIG 10.18 More HD stations enter the airwaves. *Courtesy HD Radio.*

| Bush approves domestic eavesdropping. | | Former President Ford dies. | | Nancy Pelosi becomes first woman Speaker of the House. |

2007

| Ratings for network shows continue to slide. | WGA strike benefits reality shows. | | Cross ownership in top 20 markets allowed by FCC. |

FIG 10.19 The goal is everything in a box.

2008

The writers' strike, intense coverage of the Presidential primaries and election, and the full-blown economic recession accelerated changes on the media playing field. The 100-day writers' strike, from November 5, 2007, to February 12, 2008, spurred the growth of unscripted reality-type shows while delaying the development of new scripted dramas and sitcoms, prompting the seeking of new audiences when production resumed. The recession resulted in less advertising, including a substantial drop from auto companies, previously the largest TV advertiser. Newspapers folded or compacted, with media writers and critics among the most dispensable employees. By playing up the personalities as differentiated from the policies of the candidates, including making an instant star of Republican Vice Presidential candidate Sarah Palin, despite her withdrawal from media contact after early disastrous live interviews, television drew audiences to offset the revenue lost by devoting substantial time throughout the entire year to political speeches, debates, primaries, and conventions. Although the campaigns still relied heavily on TV and radio advertising, use of the Internet grew substantially.

Investigative reporting was a prime casualty of shrinking news budgets. Stations overhauled their newsroom approaches and operations to get Web revenue. Television did provide excellent coverage of the summer Olympics in Beijing, especially host China's remarkably spectacular opening ceremonies and presentations. The chaos on Wall Street also received extensive coverage—concentrating on what, when, who,

FIG 10.20 Portable audience measuring devices enter markets.
Courtesy Arbitron.

THE NEW CENTURY 2000S

Scooter Libby convicted in CIA leak case.	Beleaguered Bush Attorney General Alberto Gonzales resigns.	Economy crumbles under weight of Wall Street corruption.

2008

Issue of "net neutrality" comes to fore.

The Beijing Olympics

FIG 10.21 Most elaborate media coverage of an Olympics.

and where and largely ignoring the why. Despite the recession and firing of many longtime as well as junior personnel, the top 10 U.S. media companies' average yearly pay for their CEOs was over $22 million.

While conservative to far-right political pundits and talk show hosts continued to dominate the airwaves, reflecting the views of the predominant ownership of the media, with Fox the poster-boy channel, alternative views reached people through programs such as *The Daily Show, The Colbert Report, Bill Moyers*, and MSNBC's *Countdown with Keith Olbermann* and its debut of *The Rachel Maddow Show*. The program with the most direct and powerful political and social statements, *Boston Legal*, went off the air. Increasing numbers of people turned to the Internet to obtain alternative views and to present theirs through blogs. Bloggers included prominent and powerful people as well as ordinary Americans, and blogs became a leading source of opinion, information, and discussion among an increasing number of people. Within a couple of years, thanks to the social networking site Twitter, "tweets," virtually recording the moment-to-moment observations, feelings, thoughts, and reactions of the "tweeter," added to the impact of Internet communication. Internet advertising revenues reached record highs, surpassing radio ad revenues.

The Internet was only one of the "new media" systems that affected broadcasting and cable. Interactive cable-Web activities, suggesting future partnerships, spurred cable stocks. The FCC approved use of unlicensed mobile devices in unused TV spectrum space, facilitating more wireless broadband use and giving a further boost to mobile video. Video on demand (VOD) loomed larger. With mandatory switchover to digital from analog due in early 2009, stations had been and continued to prepare with changes in their organization, equipment, staffing, and programming. Sports led the way; many channels already were offering HDTV, with momentum building for three-dimensional (3-D) presentations. Internet radio devices grew in popularity; a Nokia Internet tabletop device was labeled "Home Music Wo-Fo."

Despite the diversion to iPods, satellite, and Internet radio, terrestrial radio audiences grew, even as advertising on terrestrial stations shrank. Some advertisers blamed the latter on consolidation, with so many stations sounding so much alike that they became less relevant to local audiences and concomitantly to local and regional advertisers. Some experts predicted that the future of radio was on the Internet. Eric Rhoads, publisher of *Radio Ink*, stated that the radio industry is using old "radio-like techniques to target online users who want things presented in a new, Internet- and mobile-focused way." He pointed out that listening to radio on a cell phone is different from listening at home or in a car. Both terrestrial and Internet radio were concerned about performance royalties for using copyrighted material, specifically, music. Small stations in particular complained that they might have to fold if they had to pay performance fees. Copyright holders felt, of course, that they were entitled to compensation for their work. A Local Radio Freedom Act was introduced in the House of Representatives, banning any new performance fees or other charge for sound recording used on local radio stations. Internet radio stations sought the same protection.

Four thousandth U.S. death in Iraq.	Same-sex marriages performed in California.	Taliban resurgence in Afghanistan.
TV's coverage of Beijing Olympics lauded.	Programming designed as alternative to conservative pundits increases.	

AT&T and Verizon, the two largest bidding companies, bought two-thirds of all spectrum space auctioned by the FCC early in the year, further decimating localism and diversity and strengthening consolidation. The FCC issued a rule stating that "no qualified person or entity shall be discriminated against on the basis of race, color, religion, national origin or sex in the sale of commercially operated . . . broadcast stations." The order, praised for its surface message, was questioned for its lack of any Affirmative Action provisions facilitating the entry of minorities that could bring diversity into the field. A federal appeals court overturned the FCC's earlier fine for the Janet Jackson Super Bowl incident. The FCC continued to take heat for what appeared to many to be pro-corporate, antipublic interest policies, and the House of Representatives issued a report entitled *Deception and Distrust: The Federal Communications Commission Under [Republican] Chairman Kevin J. Martin*.

Reality and game shows continued in popularity, notably *American Idol, Dancing with the Stars, Survivor, America's Got Talent*, and *Deal or No Deal. 60 Minutes* retained its place in the top 10 ratings. Television's presentation of historian David McCullough's *John Adams* was lauded as a fine drama and an excellent example of a mini-series, despite its many, sometimes flagrant, historical inaccuracies. Do critics have an obligation in reviewing historical dramas to point out the educational harm they do even while praising their production values?

Media Adherence to Official U.S. Policy

There is a mounting evidence to support the contention that American media often hews closely to official government positions. Studies have revealed that this is accomplished through a number of discreet forms, including news frames and emphasis. Emphasis in newspapers is usually where a story is placed, at the very top of the first page for the most important items, while on television it is typically the lead story of the newscast. There is also a subtler mode, the use of descriptive, seemingly compatible nouns. For example, Kobland, et al.[1] compared how *The New York Times*, considered the agenda-setter for the way news is framed, reported on similar civil disturbances protesting repressive governments in an ally, South Korea, and Communist China, at the time considered a hard-line Marxist pariah. The researchers found that in describing events occurring in the nation supported by the United States, protestors were depicted as "rebellious" and "rioters" and the actions of the government portrayed as "restoring the rule of law" or "seizing control from the rebels," whereas in Red China the demonstrators were painted as "pro-democracy" and "freedom loving," and when the regime moved to stifle the unrest, the *Times* reported it as "cracking down" or "crushing" democratic sentiment.

[1]Kobland, C.E., Du, L., and Kwon, J. (1992). Influence of ideology in news reporting: Case study of *New York Times'* coverage of student demonstrations in China and South Korea. *Asian Journal of Communication*, 2, 64–77.

THE NEW CENTURY 2000S

Senate passes economic bailout plan.	Military surge in Iraq reduces casualties.	Barack Obama elected President.

| Bloggers impact traditional news media. | Concern over programming diversity increases. | |

2009

In 2009, the cusp of the next decade (technically, a new decade begins with the "1" year, but popular usage designates the "0" year, as reflected in this book's chapter divisions), presaged what was expected to be a quantum change in broadcasting and newer media in the "teen years" of the 21st century. The economy, continuing technology advances, a changed FCC under a new administration, and, especially, the increasing domination of the Internet already were playing leading roles. Radio was the flashpoint for comparison. Internet advertising surpassed advertising on terrestrial radio. A survey showed that over one-quarter of the U.S. population had listened to Internet radio, still only a beginning inasmuch as the vast majority of Americans still tuned in to terrestrial radio. But terrestrial radio revenues decreased, and in the first

FIG 10.22 Two birds merge.
Courtesy SiriusXM.

| Obama sworn in as 44th U.S. President. | Major U.S. newspapers face bankruptcy. | iPhone acquires more than 10K apps. |

2009

| XM/Sirius Satellite Radios merge. | Digital television switchover takes place after delay. | Radio continues to bleed young music listeners. |

few months alone in 2009, thousands of radio jobs were lost. The first satellite radio device that could receive all Sirius and XM channels made its debut. Car Internet radio was poised to challenge car satellite radio. For the first time, a major market radio station (WWFS-FM, New York) had more listeners to its online stream than to its over-the-air broadcast. New devices included an in-dash auto Internet radio tuner. Radio's hard place in 2009 faced another rock: performance fees. Congress considered two competing resolutions, the Local Radio Freedom Act, which would exempt local stations from fees demanded by copyright holders (Internet radio sites sought inclusion), and the Performance Rights Act, which would permit the negotiation of such fees.

Television's relationship to and with the Internet and the impact of the economy created changes for that medium, too. A report from a conference of the National Association of Television Program Executives (NATPE) noted "the toughest economic environment broadcasters say they have ever seen." Broadcasters reported losses in the billions of dollars, reflected in an up-to-10% decrease in key audience demos. Ironically, the number of TV households grew, approaching 115 million. In a survey, most Americans (56%) said they preferred to get their news from the Internet, 21% from television, and 10% from radio and newspapers, respectively. The WB (Warner Brothers) TV network found new life and new audiences by putting all its programming on TheWB.com. AFTRA and the Screen Actors Guild (SAG) approved new television commercials contracts that, for the first time, included payment for Internet and other new media ads. Amidst all the flux in broadcasting, NAB's head, David Rehr, announced his resignation after only four years in that post.

Because it appeared that several million noncable and nonsatellite homes, despite the years and months of advisories on the air and in newspapers about the changeover from analog to digital TV, had not obtained the necessary adapter equipment, even with a free $40 federal subsidy, the official transformation date was postponed from February to mid-June. FCC chair Kevin Martin stated that this transfer would free TV spectrum for other uses such as wireless broadband. He also defended as one of his accomplishments, with a new FCC chair coming in, not having regulated cable, despite the service's over 70% national penetration. Television looked for creative ways to win back audiences and advertising dollars to prime time. NBC decided to experiment with a comedy talk shows instead of the traditional fare at 10:00 P.M. weekdays; it arranged for Jay Leno to leave his *Tonight Show* to do it. The increase in mobile TV prompted Arbitron to offer a new measurement service for out-of-home TV use.

The one bright spot for broadcasting in 2009 was the resiliency and drawing power of talk shows. Some experts suggested that the income from talk shows saved both AM and FM radio in the economic downturn. The extensive coverage of new President Barack Obama's inauguration was followed up by political "talkers," the volume heavily on the right through key figures such as Rush Limbaugh, Lou Dobbs, Michael Savage, and Sean Hannity and by the relatively very few on the left such as Keith Olbermann and Rachel Maddow. Does the media have an objective center? Would noncontroversial talk shows draw any audiences?

Fighting in Afghanistan intensifies.

Iran presidential election results challenged by massive protests.

New FCC Chair installed.

NAB head resigns after short tenure.

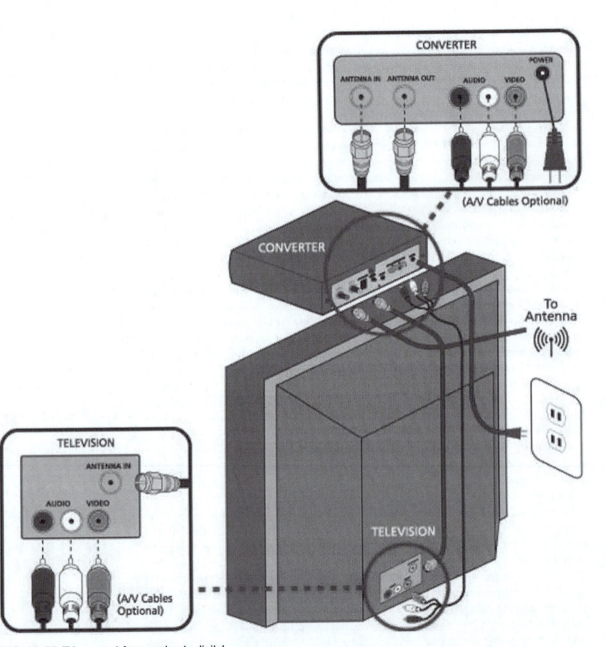

FIG 10.23 TVs convert from analog to digital.

Pop music icon Michael Jackson
dies.

Ethnic unrest in China increases.

Death of Michael Jackson
dominates news.

Looking Back

It may be instructive at this point in our journey to consider where this all began. Undoubtedly looking back makes the past seem more congenial. That was the appeal of the sitcom *Happy Days*, a nostalgic reflection of the 1950s' shallow tranquility, or Woody Allen's *Radio Days*, a wistful reminiscence of the 1940s interlaced with vignettes from radio's Golden Age. And so our rear-view mirror reveals a more innocent era when radio was literally a local "mom and pop" operation; we can compare that to the contemporary landscape that finds broadcasting in the hands of a few media giants with no pretense of localism. Perhaps most disconcerting is that today most Americans receive their television through MSOs, telcos, or satellite providers that also frequently control the content they deliver. They are the ultimate gatekeepers, and their bottom line is the *bottom line* and not operating in the public interest. As this is written, there are ongoing battles between cable networks such as Versus, the NFL Network, and the Tennis Channel and suppliers of these content streams, leaving viewers unsure whether their favorite channels will be available tomorrow. And because of deregulation, the viewers' wants are almost never part of the equation.

The election of an African American as President galvanized the hundreds of organized hate groups in the United States and prompted much increased traffic on the 2000 or so hate Websites originating in this country. Hate crimes, motivated by anti-immigrant prejudice and bigotry toward other groups such as people of color, Jews, and homosexuals, increased, spurred on and tacitly if not openly encouraged, as has happened in the past, by some radio and TV talk show personalities, as well as by the Internet. (The seminal book on the media's role in fomenting hate is *Waves of Rancor: Tuning in the Radical Right*.) FBI reports on hate crimes prompted studies that examined language on shows hosted by Dobbs, Savage, and others on the far right. UCLA Professor Chon Noriega found on these programs "systematic and extensive use of false facts, flawed argumentation, divisive language, and dehumanizing metaphors that are directed toward particular vulnerable groups," characterizing these groups as direct threats "to the listeners' way of life." As happened in earlier years—a most dramatic example was the influence radical-right radio shows had on Timothy McVeigh in his bombing of the Oklahoma City federal building—it appeared that some of the contemporary right-wing talk shows might have influenced the perpetrators of hate crimes in 2009.

Even with a changing of the guard, the FCC continued it zero-tolerance policy toward what it considered to be indecency on the air. A federal appeals court upheld the FCC's ruling that even a single, fleeting word or image can be considered indecent and can merit a fine. President Obama astounded many of his supporters by endorsing congressional legislation that would permanently ban the restoration of the Fairness Doctrine. They had assumed that he would expand free-speech rights for minorities—racial, social, political, religious, ethnic, and others—instead of siding with free-speech rights over the airwaves only for corporate interests and owners. In congressional confirmation hearings on a Democrat (Julius Genachowski) nominated by the President as FCC chair, the candidate was urged to put consumer interests first, as differentiated from priority given to corporate interests under the previous eight years of a Republican-controlled FCC that was under congressional investigation for mismanagement, secrecy, and misuse of data. Will the new FCC do any better? As you read this, you might already have the answer.

FCC totals for licensed broadcast stations in 2009 were:

Radio:		
AM	4,786	
FM	6,427	
FM educational	3,040	
Total		14,253
Television:		
UHF commercial	796	
VHF commercial	582	
UHF educational	252	
VHF educational	129	
Total		1,759
FM translators and boosters	6,120	
UHF translators and boosters	2,476	
VHF translators and boosters	1,513	
Total		10,109
UHF low-power TV	1,763	
VHF low-power TV	535	
Total	2,298	
Low-power FM	859	
Total U.S. licensed broadcast stations		29,832

And Beyond

The next decade? In many ways it is already here, even as this book is written in 2009. In practical terms, you are already experiencing the "teen decade" as you read this book. You should be already ensconced in increased and varied mobile video and audio systems, high-definition 3-D pictures, enhanced out-of-home and in-home video and audio

Top 10 Broadcast TV Programs for the week of June 15, 2009 (Live+SD)

Rank*	Program	Network	Rating**	Viewers***	Chart by Rating
1	NCIS	CBS	7	10.394	
2	MENTALIST, THE-TUESDAY	CBS	6.7	10.118	
3	TWO AND A HALF MEN	CBS	6.5	10.188	
4	CSI	CBS	6.4	9.715	
5	MENTALIST, THE	CBS	6.1	8.969	
6	CSI: MIAMI	CBS	5.6	8.252	
7	60 MINUTES	CBS	5.5	8.305	
8	BIG BANG THEORY, THE	CBS	5.4	8.417	
9	CRIMINAL MINDS	CBS	5.3	8.037	
9	SO YOU THINK CN DANCE-WED	FOX	5.3	8.483	

FIG 10.24 Top-rated TV shows at the end of the decade. *Courtesy Neilsen.*

on demand, more efficient video compression, and highly effective retriever software, among other technological advances. Eric Johnston, president of Pangaea Multimedia Communications Company, notes that producers of broadcast content have already incorporated Internet materials such as Web discussions and e-mail comments into their programs, creating interactive convergence. He states that at the end of the decade:

> on-demand has become mainstream. Internet content is being produced for telephones and high-definition TVs, and TV programming is delivered in high-definition over the Internet. The Internet enables users to download television episodes and full-length films into portable electronic devices to be viewed off-line when the users wish. Video-on-demand, from children's programs to news to TV episodes to movies are available on demand via cable, satellite, Internet and portable devices. 3-D technology is mainstream in theatres and will be a significant option in television programming.

You should be close to convergence, having created a new, dominant model for worldwide communications, an incarnation of the old media, of radio, television, cable, satellite, and audio and video common carrier molded into a new form with the Internet as the base. In part motivated by a debilitating worldwide economy, in part by the increasing power of multinational multimedia corporations, mergers of communication giants, if not stopped by public concern and action, will put the control of all information and entertainment—and concomitantly, control of all political body politics—in the hands of fewer and fewer global "Big Brother" entities.

Will such conglomeration prevent the attainment of humanistic goals possible principally through the media and projected by many citizen groups in many countries? For example, in the United States, Minority Media and Telecommunications Council executive director Howard Honig stated in 2009 that "we hope to witness complete eradication of racial discrimination and its present effects from the nation's most influential and important industries—mass media and telecommunications." What kind of

FIG 10.25 End of decade begs the question, Is everything to emanate from cyberspace?

THE NEW CENTURY 2000S

351

world do you want in the near and far future, and how can you forge that world through the use of the powerful communication technologies that are at your fingertips?

That the Internet is increasingly becoming a focal point for individuals and groups is noted in a study reported in 2009 that the percentage of Americans who spend more time on the Internet than with their families tripled in the preceding few years, reaching 28% and growing. Facebook, MySpace, Twitter, and other online relationship sites were displacing in volume those of the traditional family.

The Internet has provided a new form of worldwide freedom for individuals and groups. Whereas at the end of the first 2000s decade there were tens of thousands of radio and television stations, cable systems, and communications satellites providing worldwide communication, there were literally millions of Internet Websites and sources. In 1989 the fax machine was used to bypass the Chinese government's crackdown on reports from Tiananmen Square in Beijing during the massacre of student political protesters. The government effectively closed down phone and other communication means, but momentarily appeared to forget about faxing, with reports reaching Hong Kong by that means before it, too, was stopped.

As this is written, the Internet has served a similar purpose in reporting Iran's presidential election protests by millions of Iranians. With all foreign journalists and means of communication banned, "twittering" informed the rest of the world through words and pictures of what appeared to be hard-line suppression of the protests. Although such communications are hardly a reliable substitute for reports from professional journalists, they sometimes may be the only reports that escape under a news blackout and suppression of media coverage. The question is, can this freedom of Internet use be preserved? As noted earlier, the issue is Net neutrality.

What will come next is anybody's guess. But, even when it appears that technology has reached its peak, something new certainly will be developed. In 1876 a Western Union memo commented on a new invention by Alexander Graham Bell: "This 'telephone' has too many shortcomings to be seriously considered as a means of communications." In the 1920s David Sarnoff's colleagues responded this way to his recommendation that they invest in the new medium of radio: "The wireless music box has no imaginable commercial value. Who would pay for a message sent to nobody in particular?" Even computers, now the staple necessity of communications, did not have an easy time making it. In 1943 Thomas Watson, president of IBM, said: "I think there is a world market for maybe five computers." And in 1949 *Popular Mechanics* magazine, reflecting the state of the invention at the time, predicted that "computers in the future may weigh no more than 1.5 tons." In 1968 an engineer at the Advanced Computing System Division of IBM was introduced to the microchip and commented, "But what . . . is it good for?" And in 1977, Ken Olson, founder and president of Digital Equipment Corporation, said, "There is no reason anyone would want a computer in their home."

Communications technology will march on, despite the declaration by Charles H. Duell, Commissioner of the U.S. Office of Patents, in 1899 that "everything that can be invented has been invented."

Abramson, A. (2007). *The History of Television, 1942-2000*. Jefferson, NC: McFarland Press.

Aitkin, H. G. J. (1976). *Syntony and Spark*. New York: John Wiley and Sons.

Allen, F. (1954). *Treadmill to Oblivion*. Boston: Little, Brown.

Allen, R. C. (1985). *Speaking of Soap Operas*. Chapel Hill, NC: University of North Carolina Press.

Archer, G. L. (1971). *History of Radio to 1926*. New York: Arno Press.

Baker, W. J. (1971). *A History of the Marconi Company*. New York: St. Martin's Press.

Bannerman, R. L. (1986). *Norman Corwin and Radio: The Golden Years*. Birmingham, AL: University of Alabama Press.

Barlow, W. (1999). *Voice Over: The Making of Black Radio*. Philadelphia: Temple University Press.

Barnouw, E. (1996). *Media Marathon: A Twentieth Century Memoir*. Durham, NC: Duke University Press.

Barnouw, E. (1968). *A Tower in Babel: A History of Broadcasting in the United States to 1933, Vol. 1*. New York: Oxford University Press.

Barnouw, E. (1970). *The Golden Web: A History of Broadcasting in the United States, 1933-1953, Vol. 2*. New York: Oxford University Press.

Barnouw, E. (1991). *The Image Empire: A History of Broadcasting in the United States from 1953, Vol. 3*. New York: Oxford University Press.

Baughman, J. L. (2007). *Same Time, Same Station*. Baltimore, MD: Johns Hopkins University Press.

Benny, M. L., Hilliard, M., & Marcia, B. (1978). *Jack Benny*. New York: Doubleday.

Bergreen, L. (1980). *Look Now, Pay Later: The Rise of Network Broadcasting*. New York: Doubleday.

Berle, M. (1988). *B.S. I Love You: Sixty Funny Years with the Famous and the Infamous*. New York: McGraw-Hill.

Bianchi, W. (2008). *Schools of the Air*. Jefferson, NC: McFarland.

Bilby, K. (1986). *The General: David Sarnoff and the Rise of the Communications Industry*. New York: Harper and Row.

Bliss, E., Jr (1967). *In Search of Edward R. Murrow, 1938-1961*. New York: Alfred A. Knopf.

Bliss, E., Jr (1991). *Now the News: The Story of Broadcast Journalism*. New York: Columbia University Press.

Blue, H. (2002). *Words at War*. Lanhan, MD: Scarecrow Press.

Blum, D. C. (1958). *Pictorial History of TV*. Philadelphia: Chilton.

Buxton, F., & Bill, O. (1972). *The Big Broadcast: 1920-1950*. New York: Viking.

Campbell, R. (1976). *The Golden Years of Broadcasting*. New York: Charles Scribner's Sons.

Cantril, H. (1966). *The Invasion from Mars*. New York: Harper and Row.

Chapple, S., & Garofalo, R. (1977). *Rock n' Roll Is Here to Pay*. Chicago: Nelson-Hall.

Cheney, M. (1983). *Tesla: Man Out of Time*. Englewood Cliffs, NJ: Prentice Hall.

Coe, L. (2006). *Wireless Radio: A History*. Jefferson, NC: McFarland.

Corwin, N. (1994). *Years of the Electric Ear*. Metuchen, NJ: DGA and Scarecrow Press.

Czitrom, D. J. (1982). *Media and the American Mind*. Chapel Hill, NC: University of North Carolina Press.

De Forest, L. (1950). *Father of Radio: The Autobiography of Lee de Forest*. Chicago: Wilcox and Follett.

DeLong, T. A. (1980). *The Mighty Music Box*. Los Angeles: Amber Crest Books.

Doll, B. (1996). *Sparks Out of the Plowed Ground*. West Palm Beach, FL: Streamline Press.

Douglas, S. J. (1987). *Inventing American Broadcasting: 1899-1922*. Baltimore, MD: Johns Hopkins University Press.

Douglas, S. J. (1999). *Listening In: Radio and the American Imagination*. New York: Times Books.

Dreher, C. (1977). *Sarnoff: An American Success*. New York: Quadrangle.

Dunning, J. (1976). *Tune In Yesterday*. Englewood Cliffs, NJ: Prentice Hall.

Edgarten, G. (2009). *The Columbia History of American Television*. New York: Columbia University Press.

Erickson, J. (1974). *Armstrong's Fight for FM Broadcasting*. Birmingham, AL: University of Alabama Press.

Eskanazi, G. (2005). *I Hid It Under the Sheets: Growing Up with Radio*. Columbia, MO: University Press.

Fang, I. E. (1977). *Those Radio Commentators*. Ames, IA: Iowa State University Press.

Fisher, M. (2007). *Something in the Air*. New York: Random House.

Fones-Wolf, E. A. (2006). *Waves of Opposition*. Carbondale, IL: University of Illinois.

Friendly, F. W. (1967). *Due to Circumstances Beyond Our Control*. New York: Random House.

Gitlin, T. (1983). *Inside Prime Time*. New York: Pantheon Books.

Greb, G., & Mike, A. (2003). *Charles Herrold: Inventor of Radio Broadcasting*. Jefferson, NC: MacFarland.

Halper, D. L. (2001). *Invisible Stars: A Social History of Women in American Broadcasting*. Armonk, NY: M.E. Sharpe.

Head, S. W., & Christopher, H. S. (1994). *Broadcasting in America. 7th edition*. Boston: Houghton Mifflin.

Henderson, A. (1988). *On the Air: Pioneers of Radio Broadcasting*. Washington, D.C.: Smithsonian Institute Press.

Hewitt, D. (2002). *Tell Me a Story: Fifty Years on 60 Minutes in Television*. Washington: Public Affairs.

Hilliard, R. L. (1985). *Radio Broadcasting*. White Plains, NY: Longman.

Hilliard, R. L. (1989). *Television Station Operations and Management*. Boston: Focal Press.

Hilliard, R. L. (1991). *The Federal Communications Commission: A Primer*. Boston: Focal Press.

Hilliard, R. L., & Keith, M. (1996). *Global Broadcasting Systems*. Boston: Focal Press.

Hilliard, R. L., & Keith, M. (1999). *Waves of Rancor: Tuning In the Radical Right*. Armonk, NY: M. E. Sharpe.

Hilliard, R. L., & Keith, M. (1999). *The Hidden Screen: Low-Power Television in America*. Armonk, NY: M. E. Sharpe.

Hilliard, R. L., & Keith, M. (2003). *Dirty Discourse: Sex and Indecency in American Radio*. Ames, IA: Iowa State Press.

Hilliard, R. L. (2001). *Media, Education, and America's Counter-culture Revolution*. Westport, CT: Ablex.

Hilmes, M., & Loviglio, J. (1997). *Radio Voices: American Broadcasting, 1922–1952*. Minneapolis: University of Minnesota Press.

Hilmes, M., & Loviglio, J. (2002). *Connections: A Broadcast History Reader*. Belmont, CA: Wadsworth.

Hilmes, M., Loviglio, J., & Jacobs, J. (Eds.). (2008). *The Television History Book*. London: British Film Institute.

Hilmes, M., Loviglio, J., & Jason, L. (Eds.). (2001). *Radio Reader*. New York: Routledge.

Horton, G. (2002). *Radio Goes to War*. Kansas City, MO: Andrews McMeel.

Inglis, A. W. (1990). *Behind the Tube: A History of Broadcasting Technology and Business*. Boston: Focal Press.

Janlowski, G. F., & David, C. F. (1995). *Television Today and Tomorrow*. New York: Oxford University Press.

Johnson, P., & Michael, C. K. (2001). *Queer Airwaves: The Story of Gay and Lesbian Broadcasting*. Armonk, NY: M. E. Sharpe.

Johnston, C. B. (1995). *Winning the Global TV News Game*. Boston: Focal Press.

Johnston, C. B. (2000). *Screened Out: How the Media Control Us and What We Can Do About It*. Armonk, NY: M. E. Sharpe.

Keith, M. C. (1987). *Radio Programming*. Boston: Focal Press.

Keith, M. C. (2009). *The Radio Station, 8th edition*. Boston: Focal Press.

Keith, M. C. (1995). *Signals in the Air: Native Broadcasting in America*. Westport, CT: Praeger Publishing.

Keith, M. C. (2000). *Talking Radio: An Oral History of Radio*. Armonk, NY: M. E. Sharpe.

Keith, M. C. (1997). *Voices in the Purple Haze: Reflections on the Underground Airwaves*. Westport, CT: Praeger Publishing.

Keith, M. C. (2001). *Sounds in the Dark: All-Night Radio in American Life*. Ames, IA: Iowa State University Press.

Keith, M. C. (2008). *Radio Cultures: The Sound Medium in American Life*. New York: Peter Lang.

Keith, M. C., & Watson, M. A. (Ed.). (2009). *Norman Corwin's "One World Flight." The Lost Journal of Radio's Greatest Writer*. New York: Continuum Books.

Kirby, E. M., & Jack, W. H. (1948). *Star Spangled Radio*. Chicago: Ziff-Davis.

Kisseloff, J. (1996). *The Box*. New York: Viking.

Langguth, A. J. (Ed.). (1994). *Norman Corwin's Letters*. New York: Barricade Books.

Lazarsfeld, P. F., & Kendall, P. L. (1948). *Radio Listening in America*. Prentice Hall: Englewood Cliffs, NJ.

Leinwall, S. (1979). *From Spark to Satellite*. New York: Charles Scribner's Sons.

Lenthall, B. (2007). *Radio in America*. Chicago: University of Chicago Press.

Lessing, L. (1969). *Man of High Fidelity: Edwin Howard Armstrong*. New York: Bantam Books.

Levinson, R. (1985). *Stay Tuned*. New York: St. Martin's Press.

In Lewis, P. (Ed.). (1981). *Radio Drama*. New York: Longman.

Lewis, T. (1991). *Empire of the Air: The Man Who Made Radio*. New York: Harper-Collins.

Loviglio, J. (2005). *Radio's Intimate Public*. Minneapolis: University of Minnesota.

MacDonald, J. F. (1979). *Don't Touch That Dial: Radio Programming in American Life, 1920-1960*. Chicago: Nelson-Hall.

MacDonald, J. F. (1990). *One Nation Under Television*. New York: Pantheon Books.

Matelski, M. (1995). *Vatican Radio*. Westport, CT: Praeger Publishing.

McMahon, M. E. (1973). *Vintage Radio: A Pictorial History of Wireless and Radio, 1887-1929*. Palos Verdes Peninsula, CA: Vintage Radio.

McMahon, M. E. (1976). *A Flick of the Switch: 1930-1950*. Vintage Radio: Palos Verdes Peninsula, CA.

Metz, R. (1975). *CBS: Reflections in a Bloodshot Eye*. New York: Playboy Press.

Morrow, B. (1987). *Cousin Brucie*. New York: William Morrow.

Nachman, G. (1998). *Raised on Radio*. New York: Pantheon Books.

Passman, A. (1971). *The Deejays*. New York: Macmillan.

Paley, W. S. (1979). *As It Happened: A Memoir*. New York: Doubleday.

Pierce, D. (2008). *Riding the Ether Express*. Lafayette, LA: Center for Louisiana Studies.

Podber, J. (2007). *The Electronic Front Porch*. Macon, GA: Mercer University Press.

Ramsey, M. (2008). *Making Waves: Radio on the Verge*. iUniverse.

Rhoads, B. E. (1996). *Blast from the Past*. West Palm Beach, FL: Streamline Press.

Richardson, D. (1981). *Puget Sounds*. Seattle, WA: Superior Publishing.

Roman, J. (2008). *From Daytime to Primetime*. Westport, CT: Greenwood Press.

Rudel, A. (2008). *Hello, Everybody! The Dawn of American Radio*. New York: Harcourt.

Sauls, S. J. (2000). *The Culture of American College Radio*. Ames, IA: Iowa State University Press.

Schiffer, M. B. (1991). *The Portable Radio in American Life*. Tucson, AZ: University of Arizona Press.

Settle, I. (1960). *A Pictorial History of Radio*. New York: Bonanza Books.

Shales, T. (1982). *On the Air!*. New York: Summit Books.

Shane, Ed. (2000). *Disconnected America: The Consequence of Mass Media in a Narcissistic World*. Armonk, NY: M. E. Sharpe.

Shane, Ed. (1999). *Selling Electronic Media*. Boston: Focal Press.

Singer, A. J. (2000). *Arthur Godfrey: The Adventures of an American Broadcaster*. Jefferson, NC: McFarland.

Sklar, R. (1984). *Rocking America: How the All-Hits Stations Took Over*. New York: St. Martin's Press.

Slide, A. (1982). *Great Radio Personalities*. New York: Vestal Press.

Slotten, H. R. (2000). *Radio and Television Regulation*. Baltimore: Johns Hopkins University Press.

Squier, S. M. (Ed.). (2003). *Communities of the Air: Radio Century, Radio Culture*. Durham, NC: Duke University Press.

Sterling, C. H., & John, M. K. (2002). *Stay Tuned: A Concise History of American Broadcasting, 3rd edition*. Mahwah, NJ: Lawrence Erlbaum.

Sterling, C. H. (2004). *Museum of Broadcast Communications Radio Encyclopedia*. Chicago: Fitzroy Dearborn.

Sterling, C. H., & Keith, M. C. (2008). *Sounds of Change: The History of FM Broadcasting in America*. Chapel Hill, NC: University of North Carolina Press.

Tebbel, J. (1975). *The Media in America*. New York: Crowell.

Watson, M. A. (1990). *Expanding Vista: American Television in the Kennedy Years*. New York: Oxford University Press.

Wertheim, A. F. (1979). *Radio Comedy*. New York: Oxford University Press.

White, P. W. (1947). *News on the Air*. New York: Harcourt, Brace.

Yoder, A. (2001). *Pirate Radio Stations*. New York: McGraw-Hill.

Note: Page numbers followed by *t* indicates tables; *f* indicates figures; *b* indicates boxes.